The Collected Works of
James M. Buchanan

VOLUME 16
Choice, Contract, and Constitutions

James M. Buchanan,
Citizens for a Sound Economy,
Washington, D.C., November 1986

The Collected Works of

James M. Buchanan

VOLUME 16

*Choice, Contract, and
Constitutions*

LIBERTY FUND

This book is published by Liberty Fund, Inc., a foundation
established to encourage study of the ideal of a society of free
and responsible individuals.

The cuneiform inscription that serves as our logo and as the design
motif for our endpapers is the earliest-known written appearance
of the word "freedom" (*amagi*), or "liberty." It is taken from a clay
document written about 2300 B.C. in the Sumerian city-state of Lagash.

08 20 21 22 23 C 6 5 4 3 2
20 21 22 23 24 P 6 5 4 3 2

Library of Congress Cataloging-in-Publication Data
Buchanan, James M.
Choice, contract, and constitutions / James M. Buchanan.
p.   cm. — (The collected works of James M. Buchanan ; v. 16)
Includes bibliographical references and index.
ISBN 0-86597-243-5 (hc. : alk. paper). — ISBN 0-86597-244-3 (pbk. : alk. paper)
1. Political science—Economic aspects.   2. Economic policy.
3. Social choice.   I. Title.   II. Series : Buchanan, James M. Works.   1999 ; v. 16.
JA77.B83   2001
338.9—dc21   99-41421

LIBERTY FUND, INC.
11301 North Meridian Street
Carmel, Indiana 46032

Contents

4. Constitutional Order

5. Market Order

6. Distributional Issues

7. Fiscal and Monetary Constitutions

8. Reform

Foreword

Constitutional political economy is a theme that runs throughout the Collected Works of James M. Buchanan. As such, it has already been discussed considerably in other volumes, for example, in volumes 1, 3, and 10 of the series, *The Logical Foundations of Constitutional Liberty, The Calculus of Consent,* and *The Reason of Rules,* respectively.[1] For this reason a briefer introduction to this volume of Buchanan's more selective contributions to this topic should be sufficient to pique the reader's interest in exploring more closely this important aspect of Buchanan's work.

Buchanan literally founded the field of constitutional political economy. He insisted that there are two important levels of analysis in economics. Standard economic theory is about how *given* institutions and rules lead to predictable *outcomes* (for example, competitive equilibrium) in the economy. In contrast, constitutional political economy, to Buchanan, concerns the prior problem of how the given rules and institutions themselves are chosen. One might easily think of a sports analogy wherein the rules of play are selected prior to the actual playing of the game. Such choices are in many senses constitutional. They are quasi-permanent and long-lived, they are made by decision makers who may not be able to figure out how their choice of rules will ultimately affect them personally during the play of the game, and they have profound importance in terms of their impact on the subsequent productivity of the economy and society.

Buchanan's insistence on the importance of rules was an important in-

---

1. James M. Buchanan, *The Logical Foundations of Constitutional Liberty,* volume 1 in the series; and Gordon Tullock, *The Calculus of Consent: Logical Foundations of Constitutional Democracy* (Ann Arbor: University of Michigan Press, 1962), volume 3 in the series; Geoffrey Brennan and James M. Buchanan, *The Reason of Rules: Constitutional Political Economy* (Cambridge: Cambridge University Press, 1985), volume 10 in the series.

novation in economics, and, over the past thirty years or so, the analytical and empirical relevance of Buchanan's constitutional perspective has become apparent. The failure of socialism, the postsocialist groping of new nation-states for social and economic orders, the keen interest of modern economists in the impact of institutions on economic growth, and the worldwide movement to devolve power away from central states are just a few examples of the relevance of Buchanan's research program.

A central element in Buchanan's approach to constitutional economics is the emphasis upon agreement as the essence of rule making. Here he draws upon traditions in welfare economics and in contractarian political philosophy. In this approach, agreement among individuals is paramount. There is no external test for what is right or wrong or best or true: It is the agreement of deliberating individuals that counts. These individuals may or may not heed the advice of "experts" with respect to which rule works "best," but ultimately it is their choice that matters and not the opinion of the expert. There is no "truth" to be discovered in this process, only agreement about how to proceed. Moreover, the "agreement" in Buchanan's approach should be broad-based, or Pareto-like, and one of the interesting problems of constitutional economics is how to promote choice processes in which broad-based agreement can be reached.

Buchanan's work in constitutional political economy is but the first step. He has established an intellectual tradition by inducing economists and other scholars to take the constitutional problem seriously. The papers in this and other volumes of his Collected Works suggest the nature of the problem, some ideas and methods by which the problem can be approached, and some of its possible applications, especially in the area of fiscal and monetary rules. Constitutional political economy will clearly be one of Buchanan's legacies, and as this area increasingly attracts young economic and political theorists, the face of modern economics will be changed.

The volume begins in part 1 with several essays that address the definition of constitutional economics. The papers in part 2 expand upon the method of constitutional economics and its links to contractarian traditions in political philosophy. The essays in part 3 address the issue of how individual incentives can be made compatible with the process of constitutional decision making. The papers in parts 4 and 5 address the meaning of constitutional order, as well as how the market process can be interpreted as a type of constitutional order. The papers in part 6 consider how distributional issues can be handled in a constitutional decision-making process. The papers in part 7 apply the constitutional economics paradigm to fiscal and monetary rules. Finally, the papers in part 8 explore the prospects for genuine constitutional reform of democratic institutions.

Buchanan taught us that how we organize a society to produce is just as important as what and how the society produces. In retrospect this seems to have been a simple change of emphasis. But Monday morning quarterbacking pays low wages. It was Buchanan who saw the world through this window and figured out why and how constitutional political economy is so important.

Robert D. Tollison
University of Mississippi
1998

PART ONE

Foundational Issues

Constitutional Economics

The term *Constitutional Economics* (Constitutional Political Economy) was introduced to define and to classify a distinct strand of research inquiry and related policy discourse in the 1970s and beyond. The subject matter is not new or novel, and it may be argued that "constitutional economics" is more closely related to the work of Adam Smith and the classical economists than its modern "non-constitutional" counterpart. Both areas of inquiry involve positive analysis that is ultimately aimed at contributing to the discussion of policy questions. The difference lies in the level of or setting for analysis which, in turn, implies communication with different audiences.

Orthodox economic analysis, whether this be interpreted in Marshallian or Walrasian terms, attempts to explain the choices of economic agents, their interactions one with another, and the results of these interactions, within the existing legal-institutional-constitutional structure of the polity. Normative considerations enter through the efficiency criteria of theoretical welfare economics, and policy options are evaluated in terms of these criteria. The policy analyst, building on the analysis, presents his results, whether explicitly or implicitly, to the political decision-makers, who then make some ultimate determination from among the available set. In this role, the policy analyst, directly, and the theorist, indirectly, are necessarily advising governmental decision-makers, whoever these may be.

By both contrast and comparison, constitutional economic analysis

From *The New Palgrave, A Dictionary of Economics*, vol. 1, ed. John Eatwell, Murray Milgate, and Peter Newman (London: Macmillan, 1987), 585–88. Reprinted by permission of the publisher.

attempts to explain the working properties of alternative sets of legal-institutional-constitutional rules that constrain the choices and activities of economic and political agents, the rules that define the framework within which the ordinary choices of economic and political agents are made. In this sense, Constitutional Economics involves a "higher" level of inquiry than orthodox economics; it must incorporate the results of the latter along with many less sophisticated subdisciplines. Normative considerations enter the analysis in a much more complex manner than through the artificially straightforward efficiency criteria. Alternative sets of rules must be evaluated in some sense analogously to ranking of policy options within a specified institutional structure, but the epistemological content of the "efficiency" criteria becomes more exposed.

The constitutional economist, precisely because the subject matter is the analysis of alternate sets of rules, has nothing to offer by way of policy advice to political agents who act within defined rules. In this sense, Constitutional Economics is not appropriately included within "policy science" at all. At another level, however, the whole exercise is aimed at offering guidance to those who participate in the discussion of constitutional change. In other words, Constitutional Economics offers a potential for normative advice to the member of the continuing constitutional convention, whereas orthodox economics offers a potential for advice to the practising politician. In a real sense, Constitutional Economics examines the *choice of constraints* as opposed to the *choice within constraints,* and as this terminology suggests, the disciplinary attention of economists has almost exclusively been placed on the second of these two problems.

A preliminary illustration of the distinction may be drawn from the economics of monetary policy. The constitutional economist is not directly concerned with determining whether monetary ease or monetary restrictiveness is required for furthering stabilization objectives in a particular setting. On the other hand, he is directly concerned with evaluating the properties of alternative monetary regimes (e.g., rule-directed versus discretionary, fiat versus commodity standards). The ultimate objective of analysis is the choice among the institutions within which political agents act. The predicted behaviour of these agents is incorporated in the analysis of alternative sets of constraints.

I. Constitutional Economics and Classical Political Economy

As suggested, Constitutional Economics is related to classical political economy, and it may be considered to be an important component of a more general revival of the classical emphasis, and particularly as represented in the works of Adam Smith. (The closely related complementary components are discussed briefly in section III.) One obvious aim of the classical political economists was to offer an explanation and an understanding of how markets operate without detailed political direction. In this respect, orthodox neoclassical economics follows directly in the classical tradition. But the basic classical analysis of the working of markets was only a necessary step toward the more comprehensive purpose of the whole exercise, which was that of demonstrating that, precisely because markets function with tolerable efficiency independent of political direction, a powerful normative argument for constitutional structure exists. That is to say, Adam Smith was engaged directly in comparing alternative institutional structures, alternative sets of constraints within which economic agents make choices. In this comparative analysis, he found it essential to model the working properties of a non-politicized economy, which did not exist in reality, as well as the working properties of a highly politicized mercantilist economy, which could be directly observed.

There is no need here to enter the lists on either side of the "ideas have consequences" debate. We know that the economy of Great Britain was effectively de-politicized in the late 18th and early 19th centuries, and from the analysis of Smith and his classical fellow travellers there emerged both positive understanding of economic process and philosophical argument for a particular regime. The normative argument for laissez faire was, perhaps inevitably, intermingled with the positive analysis of interaction within a particular structure of constraints, essentially those that describe the minimal, protective, or night-watchman state. Economics, as a social science, emerged, but in the process attention was diverted from the institutional structure. Even the predicted normative reaction against the overly zealous extension of the laissez faire argument was couched in "market failure" terms, rather than in the Smithian context of institutional comparison. The early socialist critique of market order, both in its Marxist and non-Marxist variants, was almost exclusively negative in that it elaborated putative failures of markets within an unexamined set of legal-political rules while it neglected analysis of the alternative rules that any correction of the alleged failures might require. Only with the debates on socialist calculation in the decades prior to World War II did the issues of comparative structure come to be examined.

It was only in the half-century after these debates that political economy, inclusively defined, returned, in fits and starts, to its classical tradition. Given the legal order of the protective state (the protection of property and the enforcement of contracts), we now know that under some conditions "markets fail" when evaluated against idealized criteria, whether these be "efficiency," "justice," or other abstract norms. We also know that "politics fails" when evaluated by the same criteria. Any positive analysis that purports to be of use in an ultimate normative judgment must reflect an informed comparison of the working properties of alternative sets of rules or constraints. This analysis is the domain of Constitutional Economics.

II. Constitutional Economics and Social Philosophy

Classical political economy emerged from moral philosophy, and its propounders considered their efforts to fall naturally within the limits of philosophical discourse. As a modern embodiment, Constitutional Economics is similarly located, regardless of disciplinary fragmentation. How can persons live together in liberty, peace, and prosperity? This central question of social philosophy requires continuing contributions from many specialists in inquiry, surely including those of the constitutional economists. By their focus directly on the ultimate selection of a set of constraining rules within which ordinary social interaction takes place, constitutional economists remove themselves at least one stage further from the false position of "social engineer" than their counterparts in orthodox economics. Precisely because there is no apparently simple evaluative criterion analogous to "allocative efficiency" at hand, the constitutional economist is less tempted to array alternatives as if an unexamined criterion commands universal assent. The artificial abstraction of "social utility" is likely to be less appealing to those who concentrate on choices among constraints than to those who examine choices within constraints.

If, however, there is no maximand, how can ultimate normative consequence emerge? In this respect, one contribution lies at the level of positive analysis rather than in a too-hasty leap into normative evaluation. Classical political economy contains the important principle of spontaneous coordination, the great discovery of the 18th century. This principle states that within the legal umbrella of the minimal state and given certain conditions the market "works." Even if in the principle's modern embellishment we must add "warts and all," we still have come a long way toward a more comprehensive understanding of the alternatives for social order. To the extent that his efforts expand the public understanding of this principle, in application to all institutional settings, the constitutional economist remains under less apparent compulsion to advance his own privately preferred "solutions" to the ultimate choice among regimes.

III. The New Political Economy

Care should be taken not to claim too much for Constitutional Economics, especially if a narrow definition is used. As noted earlier, this research programme, by designation, emerged in the 1970s to describe efforts at analysing the effects of alternative sets of rules, as opposed to analyses of choices made within existing and unexamined structures. In a more comprehensive overview of developments after World War II, Constitutional Economics takes its place among an intersecting set of several research programmes, all of which have roots in classical political economy. Critical emphases differ as among the separate programmes, but each reflects efforts to move beyond the relatively narrow confines of orthodox neoclassical economics.

In continental Europe, the whole set of subdisciplines is included under the rubric "The New Political Economy." Within this set we can place (1) Public Choice, from which Constitutional Economics emerged; (2) Economics of Property Rights; (3) Law and Economics or Economic Analysis of Law; (4) Political Economy of Regulation; (5) the New Institutional Economics; and (6) the new Economic History. Defined imperialistically, Constitutional Economics would parallel the inclusive term and embrace all of these programmes, since some attention is drawn in each case to the legal-political constraints within which economic and political agents choose. Differences can be identified, however, and it may be useful to summarize some of these here, even if detailed discussion of the other research programmes cannot be attempted.

Public Choice, in its non-constitutional aspects of inquiry, concentrates attention on analyses of alternative political choice structures and on behaviour within those structures. Its focus is on predictive models of political interactions, and is a preliminary but necessary stage in the more general constitutional inquiry. The economics of property rights, law and economics, and the political economy of regulation remain somewhat closer to orthodox economic theory than Constitutional Economics or Public Choice. The standard efficiency norm remains central to these subdisciplines, both as an explanatory benchmark and as a normative ideal. The new institutional economics is directed more toward the interactions within particular institutional forms rather than toward the comprehensive structure of political rules.[1] Some elements of the new economic history closely parallel Constitutional Economics, with, of course, an historical rather than a comparative emphasis.[2]

IV. Presuppositions

Constitutional Economics, along with the related research programmes mentioned above, shares a central methodological presupposition with both its precursor, classical political economy, and its counterpart in modern neoclassical microeconomics. Only individuals choose and act. Collectivities, as such, neither choose nor act, and analysis that proceeds as if they do is not within the accepted scientific canon. Social aggregates are considered only as the results of choices made and actions taken by individuals. The emphasis on explaining non-intended aggregative results of interaction has carried through since the early insights of the Scottish moral philosophers. An aggregative result that is observed but which cannot, somehow, be factored down and

---

1. E. G. Furubotn and R. Richter, eds., "The New Institutional Economics: A Symposium," *Zeitschrift für die gesamte Staatswissenschaft* (1980): 140; B. Frey, "A New View of Economics: Comparative Analysis of Institutions," *Economia delle scelte pubbliche* 1 (1984): 17–28.

2. D. C. North and R. P. Thomas, *The Rise of the Western World: A New Economic History* (Cambridge: Cambridge University Press, 1973).

explained by the choices of individuals stands as a challenge to the scholar rather than as some demonstration of non-individualistic organic unity.

Methodological individualism, as summarized above, is almost universally accepted by economists who work within mainstream, or non-Marxian, traditions. A philosophical complement of this position that assumes a central role in Constitutional Economics is much less widely accepted and is often explicitly rejected. A distinction must be drawn between the methodological individualism that builds on individual choice as the basic unit of analysis and a second presupposition that locates the ultimate sources of value exclusively in individuals.

The first of these presuppositions without the second leaves relatively little scope for the derivation of constitutional structures from individual preferences. There is no conceptual normative bridge between those interests and values that individuals might want to promote and those non-individualistic values that are presumed to serve as ultimate normative criteria. The whole constitutional exercise loses most if not all of its *raison d'être* in such a setting. If the ultimate values which are to be called upon to inform the choices among institutions are non-individualistic, then there is, at best, only an instrumental argument for using individually expressed preferences in the process of discovering those values.

On the other hand, if the second presupposition concerning the location of the ultimate sources of value is accepted, there is no *other* means of deriving a "logic of rules" than that of utilizing individually expressed interests. At base, the second presupposition implies democracy in governance, along with the accompanying precept that this structure of decision-making takes on normative legitimacy only with the prefix "constitutional" appended to it.

V. Wicksell as Precursor

The single most important precursor to Constitutional Economics in its modern variant is Knut Wicksell, who was an individualist in both of the senses discussed above. In his basic work on fiscal theory,[3] Wicksell called

---

3. K. Wicksell, *Finanztheoretische Untersuchungen* (Jena: Gustav Fischer, 1896). Central portions of this work were published in English translation as "A New Principle of Just Taxation," in *Classics in the Theory of Public Finance*, ed. R. A. Musgrave and A. T. Peacock (London: Macmillan, 1959).

attention to the significance of the rules within which choices are made by political agents, and he recognized that efforts at reform must be directed toward changes in the rules for making decisions rather than toward modifying expected results through influence on the behaviour of the actors.

In order to take these steps, Wicksell needed some criterion by which the possible efficacy of a proposed change in rules could be judged. He introduced the now-familiar unanimity or consensus test, which is carried over into Constitutional Economics and also allows the whole research programme to be related closely to the contractarian tradition in political philosophy. The relationship between the Wicksellian and the Paretian criteria is also worthy of note. If only individual evaluations are to count, and if the only source of information about such evaluations is the revealed choice behaviour of individuals themselves, then no change could be assessed to be "efficient" until and unless some means could be worked out so as to bring all persons (and groups) into agreement. If no such scheme can be arranged, the observing political economist remains silent. The Wicksellian contribution allowed the modern economist to bring the comparative analysis of rules or institutions within a methodological framework that utilizes and builds on the efficiency criterion, which, when interpreted as indicated, does not require departure from either of the individualistic presuppositions previously discussed.

VI. *Homo economicus* in Constitutional Choice

Constitutional Economics, as distinct from the complementary research programme on political constitutions that are within the boundaries of law, political science, sociology, and other disciplines, goes beyond the logical presuppositions of individualism to incorporate non-tautological models of individual utility maximization. *Homo economicus* takes a central role in comparative institutional inquiry. Individuals are assumed to seek their own interests, which are defined so as to retain operational content.

Two quite different arguments can be made in support of this postulate in Constitutional Economics. The first is based simply on methodological consistency. To the extent that individuals are modelled as utility maximizers as they participate in market relationships, there would seem to be no basis for postulating a shift in motivation as they behave within non-market constraints. There is at least a strong presumption that individuals do not undergo character transformation when they shift from roles as buyers or sellers in the market-place to roles as voters, taxpayers, beneficiaries, politicians, or bureaucrats in the political process. A more sophisticated reason for postulating consistency in behaviour lies in the usefulness of the model for the whole exercise of institutional comparison. If the purpose is to compare the effects of alternative sets of constraints, some presumption of behavioural consistency over the alternatives is necessary in order to identify those differences in results that are attributable to the differences in constraints.

A second argument for introducing *Homo economicus* in Constitutional Economics is both more complex and more important. It is also the source of confusion because it is necessary to distinguish carefully between the use of *Homo economicus* in predictive social science, specifically in positive Public Choice and in neoclassical economics, and in Constitutional Economics. There is an argument for using the construction in the latter, even if there are demonstrated empirical limits on the explanatory power of the model in the former.

The argument is implicit in the work of the classical economists. It was stated as a methodological principle by both David Hume and J. S. Mill:

> In constraining any system of government, and fixing the several checks and controls of the constitution, each man ought to be supposed a knave, and to have no other end, in all his actions, than private interest.[4]

> The very principle of constitutional government requires it to be assumed that political power will be abused to promote the particular purposes of the holder; not because it is always so, but because such is the natural tendency of things, to guard against which is the special use of free institutions.[5]

The ultimate purpose of analysing alternative sets of rules is to inform the choice among these sets. The predicted operating properties of each alternative must be examined, and these properties will reflect the embodied

---

4. David Hume, "On the Interdependency of Parliament," in *Essays, Moral, Political and Literary* (1741; London: Oxford University Press, 1963).

5. J. S. Mill, "Considerations on Representative Government," in *Essays on Politics and Society,* vol. 19 of *Collected Works of J. S. Mill* (1861; Toronto: University of Toronto Press, 1977).

models of individual behaviour within the defined constraints. Behavioural departures from the presumptive models used in deriving the operating properties will, of course, be expected. But the costs of errors may not be symmetrically distributed around the single best predictive model. The predicted differential loss from behavioural departures from a model that involves "optimistic" motivational assumptions may be much larger than the predicted differential gain if the model is shown to be an accurate predictor. Hence, comparative evaluation of an institution based on an altruistic model of behaviour should take into account the possible non-linearity in the loss function that describes departures from the best estimates. (In legal practice, formal contracts include protections against worst-case behaviour patterns.) In constitutional choice, therefore, there is an argument for incorporating models of individual behaviour that presume more narrowly defined self-interest than any empirical record may warrant.[6]

VII. Applications

Applications of Constitutional Economics, as a research programme, have emerged in several settings. First, consider taxation. Post-Marshallian economic theory, either in its partial or general equilibrium model, was often applied to tax incidence. Analysis was directed toward predicting the effects of an exogenously imposed tax on the private economizing behaviour of persons in their varying capacities as demanders and suppliers of goods and services in the market-place. Building on this base of positive analysis, normative welfare economics allows a ranking among alternative equi-revenue tax instruments in terms of the Paretian standard. In both the positive and normative aspects, neoclassical tax theory embodies the presumption that taxes, as such, are exogenous to the choice process.

The major contribution of modern Public Choice, as a subdiscipline in its own right, has been that of endogenizing political decision-making. In its direct emphasis, public choice theory examines the political decision rules that exist with a view toward making some predictions about just what sort of tax

6. G. Brennan and J. M. Buchanan, *The Reason of Rules: Constitutional Political Economy* (Cambridge: Cambridge University Press, 1985).

institutions or tax instruments will emerge. Constitutional Economics, as an extended research programme that emerges from Public Choice, goes a step further and uses the inputs from both neoclassical economics and public choice theory to analyse how alternative political rules might generate differing tax rules.

The relevant constitutional choice may be that of granting government authority to levy taxes on Tax Base A or Tax Base B. Suppose that under the neoclassical equi-revenue assumption, analysis demonstrates that the taxing of A generates a lower excess burden than the taxing of B. Analysis of the political choice process may demonstrate, however, that government, if given the authority to tax A, will tend to levy a tax that will generate *more* revenue than would be forthcoming under an authority to tax B. The equi-revenue alternatives may not be effective political alternatives under any plausibly acceptable modelling of the behaviour of political agents. Once this simple point is recognized, the normative significance of the neoclassical ranking of tax instruments is reduced. Discussion shifts necessarily to the level of interaction between political decision structures and fiscal institutions.

A second application of Constitutional Economics is found in the post-Keynesian discussion of budgetary policy. The Keynesian advocacy of the use of governmental budgets to accomplish macroeconomic objectives was based on a neglect of the political decision structure. The proclivity of democratic governments to prefer spending over taxing, and hence to bias budgets toward deficit, is readily explained in elementary public choice theory.[7] This essential step in public choice reasoning leads naturally to inquiry into the relationships between the constraints that may be placed on political choice and predicted patterns of budgetary outcomes. Out of this intensely practical, and important, application of Constitutional Economics emerged the intellectual bases for the normative argument that, in the post-Keynesian era when moral constraints on political agents have lost much of their previous effectiveness, formal rules limiting deficit financing may be required to insure responsible fiscal decisions. In the modern setting, such rules would limit spending rates. But it is perhaps worth noting that, in the political en-

---

7. J. M. Buchanan and R. E. Wagner, *Democracy in Deficit: The Political Legacy of Lord Keynes* (New York: Academic Press, 1977).

vironment of Sweden in the 1890s, Wicksell advanced analytically similar proposals for reform in the expectation that if the suggested reforms should be implemented public sector outlay would increase.

The analysis of alternative rules for "the transfer constitution" represents a third application of Constitutional Economics. With the 1971 publication of John Rawls's *A Theory of Justice*,[8] renewed attention came to be placed on principles of distributive justice. Although explicitly pre-constitutional, Rawls's work has a close relationship with the efforts to derive criteria for political and economic rules of social interaction. Economists, as well as other social scientists and social philosophers, have come increasingly to recognize that the untrammelled interplay of interest-group politics is unlikely to further objectives for distributive justice. Analysis of how this politics operates in the making of fiscal transfers suggests that principled adjustments in the post-tax, post-transfer distribution of values are likely to be achieved only if the institutional rules severely restrict the profitability of investment in attempts to subvert the transfer process.

Further applications include the regulatory constitutions, along with the organization of public enterprises. In its inclusive definition, Constitutional Economics becomes the analytical route through which institutional relevance is re-introduced into a sometimes sterile social science. In its less inclusive definition, Constitutional Economics, along with its related and complementary research programmes, restores "political" to "economy," thereby bringing a coherence that was absent during the long hiatus during which "economics" made putative claims to independent status.

8. J. Rawls, *A Theory of Justice* (Cambridge, Mass.: Harvard University Press, 1971).

A Contractarian Perspective on Anarchy

Two-Stage Utopia

I have often described myself as a philosophical anarchist. In my conceptualized ideal society individuals with well-defined and mutually respected rights coexist and cooperate as they desire without formal political structure. My practical society, however, moves one stage down from the ideal and is based on the presumption that individuals could not attain the behavioral standards required for such an anarchy to function acceptably. In general recognition of this frailty in human nature, persons would agree to enact laws, and to provide means of enforcement, in order to achieve the closest approximation to the ideally free society that is possible. At this second level of norms, therefore, I am a constitutionalist and a contractarian: constitutionalist in the sense that I recognize that the rules of order are, and must be, selected at a different level and via a different process than the decisions made within those rules, and contractarian in the sense that I believe that conceptual agreement among individuals provides the only benchmark against which to evaluate observed rules and actions taken within those rules.

This avowedly normative construction enables me to imagine the existence of an ideal social order inhabited by real persons, by men and women that I can potentially observe. In moving from stage one, where the persons are themselves imaginary beings, to stage two, the persons become real, or

From *Freedom in Constitutional Contract: Perspectives of a Political Economist* (College Station: Texas A&M University Press, 1977), 11–24. Reprinted by permission of the publisher.

potentially so, while the rules and institutions of order become imaginary. But I must ask myself why I consider the second stage to be an appropriate subject for analysis and discussion whereas the first stage seems methodologically out of bounds, or at least beyond my interest. Presumably the distinction here must rest on the notion that the basic structure of order, "the law," is itself chosen, is subject to ultimate human control, and may be changed as a result of deliberative human action. By contrast, the fundamental character traits of human beings either cannot be, or should not be, manipulated deliberately. In other terms, attempts to move toward an idealized first-stage order may require some modification of human character, an objective that seems contrary to the individualistic value judgments that I make quite explicit. On the other hand, attempts to move toward a second-stage ideal require only that institutions be modified, an objective that seems morally and ethically acceptable.

As a preliminary step I have called for the adoption of a "constitutional attitude," a willingness to accept the necessity of rules and an acknowledgment that choices among rules for living together must be categorically separated from the choices among alternative courses of action permitted under whatever rules may be chosen. But what happens if I should be forced, however reluctantly, to the presumption that individual human beings, as they exist, are not and may not be capable of taking on such requisite constitutional attitudes? In this case my treatment of an idealized constitutionalist-contractarian social order becomes neither more nor less defensible than the discourse of those who go all the way and treat genuine anarchy as an ideal. Yet somehow I feel that my discussion of idealized social order is more legitimate, more productive, and less escapist than the comparable discussion of the libertarian anarchists, perhaps best exemplified here by Murray Rothbard.[1] I shall return to this proposition below, and I shall attempt an argument in defense.

The Logic of Authority

Before I do return to my proposition, however, I want to examine one possible consequence of abandoning the constitutionalist-contractarian perspective. If

---

1. Murray Rothbard, *For a New Liberty.* See also David Friedman, *The Machinery of Freedom.* I shall not discuss those putative anarchists who fail to see the internal contradiction between anarchy and socialism. The absurdity of such juxtaposition should be apparent without serious argument.

we say that persons are simply incapable of adopting the requisite set of constitutionalist attitudes, which is another way of saying that they are incapable of evaluating their own long-term interests, we are led, almost inexorably, to imposed authority as the only escape from the genuine Hobbesian jungle. Anyone who takes such a position, however, must acknowledge that a "free society," in the meaningful sense of process stability, is not possible. The analysis turns to alternative criteria for authority, both in terms of the basic objectives to be sought and in terms of the efficiency properties of structures designed to accomplish whatever objectives might be chosen. But whose values are to be counted in deriving such criteria? We have, in this setting, already rejected the individualistic base, at least in its universalized sense, from which such criteria might be derived. But if only some persons are to be counted, how do we discriminate? Of necessity, the treatment of the idealized limits to authority must be informed by the explicit or implicit value norms of some subset of the community's membership. In the extreme, the value norms become those of the person who offers the argument, and his alone.

Most discussion of social reform proceeds on precisely this fragile philosophical structure, whether or not the participants are aware of it. When an economist proposes that a particular policy measure be taken—for example, that the ICC be abolished—he is arguing that his own authority, backed presumably by some of the technical analysis of his professional discipline, which had its own implicit or built-in value norms (in economics, Pareto efficiency), is self-justificatory. But since different persons, and groups, possess different norms, there is no observed consensual basis for discriminating between one authority and another. The linkage between the consent of individuals and the policy outcomes is severed even at the purely conceptual level and even if attention is shifted back to basic rules of order.

The implication of all this is that the authority which emerges from such a babel of voices, and from the power struggle that these voices inform and motivate, carries with it no legitimacy, even in some putative sense of this term. The authoritarian paradigm for the emergence and support of the state lacks even so much as the utilitarian claims made for the basic Hobbesian contract between the individual and the sovereign, whoever that might be. There can be no moral legitimacy of government in this paradigm, no grounds for obligation to obey law, no reasons for the mutual respect of individuals' boundaries or rights.

If most persons, including most intellectuals and academicians, view government in this perspective, and more importantly, if those who act on behalf of government view themselves in this manner, both the libertarian anarchist and the constitutionalist-contractarian exert didactic influence in their attempts to expose the absence of moral underpinnings. But does not such activity, in and of itself, reduce to nihilism under the presupposition that universalized individual values are not acceptable bases for moral authority? If individuals are not capable of acting in their own interest in the formulation of social institutions, both the anarchist and the contractarian may be deemed genuinely subversive in their "as if" modeling of society— in their establishment of normative standards for improvement that are empirically nonsupportable. The activity in question weakens the natural subservience to the existing authority, whoever that might be, and may disrupt social order without offering redeeming elements that might be located in some constructive alternative.

Individualistic Norms

These are questions that the libertarian anarchist and the contractarian must ask and somehow answer to their own satisfaction. I pose these questions here in part for their own intrinsic interest and importance but also in part because they place the libertarian anarchist and the constitutionalist-contractarian squarely on the same side of the central debate in political philosophy, the debate that has gone on for several centuries and that promises to go on for several more. Both the libertarian anarchist and the constitutionalist-contractarian work within the individualistic rather than the nonindividualistic framework or setting.[2] I use the term *nonindividualistic* instead of *collectivist* explicitly here because I want to include in this category the transcendent or truth-judgment paradigm of politics, a paradigm that may produce either collectivist or noncollectivist outcomes at a practical level.

I want to argue first that it is normatively legitimate to adopt the indi-

---

2. This is recognized by Plattner when he places John Rawls, an avowed contractarian, and Robert Nozick, almost a libertarian anarchist, in the same category "on the deepest level." Against both, Plattner advances the transcendentalist view of politics as supra-individualistic. See Marc F. Plattner, "The New Political Theory," *The Public Interest* 40 (Summer, 1975): 119–128, notably p. 127.

vidualistic model, regardless of empirical presuppositions, and second that within this model, broadly defined, the constitutionalist-contractarian variant is superior to the libertarian-anarchist variant. It is morally justifiable, and indeed morally necessary, to proceed on the "as if" presumption that individuals, by their membership in the human species, are capable of acting in their own interest, which they alone can ultimately define. Empirical observation of human error, evaluated *ex post,* can never provide a basis for supplanting this "as if" presumption, because there exists no acceptable alternative. If persons are considered to be incapable of defining and furthering their own interests, who is to define such interests and promote them? If God did, in fact, exist as a suprahuman entity, an alternative source of authority might be acknowledged. But failing this, the only conceivable alternative authority must be some selected individual or group of individuals, some man who presumes to be god, or some group that claims godlike qualities. Those who act in such capacities and who make such claims behave immorally in a fundamental sense: they relegate other members of the species to a value status little different from that of animals.

The primary value premise of individualism is the philosophical equality of men as men despite all evidence concerning inequalities in particular characteristics or components. In thinking about men, we are morally obligated to proceed as if they are equals, as if no man counts for more than another. Acceptance of these precepts sharply distinguishes the individualist from the nonindividualist. But we must go one step further to inquire about the implications of these precepts for social order. It is at this point that the libertarian anarchist and the constitutionalist-contractarian part company, but philosophically they have come a long way together, a simple statement but one that is worthy of emphasis.

Anarchy and Contractual Order

The issue that divides the anarchist and the contractarian is "conjecturally empirical." It concerns the conceptually observable structure of social order that would emerge if men could, in fact, start from scratch. Would they choose to live in the idealized anarchy, or would they contractually agree to a set of laws, along with enforcement mechanisms, that would constrain individual and group behavior? This question cannot actually be answered empirically because, of course, societies do not start from scratch. They exist in and through history, and those elements of order that may be observed at any point in time may or may not have emerged contractually.

It is at this point that the constitutionalist-contractarian paradigm is most vulnerable to the criticisms of the anarchist. How are we to distinguish between those elements of social order, those laws and institutions, which can be "explained" or "interpreted" (and by inference "justified") as having emerged, actually or conceptually, on contractual precepts and those which have been imposed noncontractually (and hence, by inference, "illegitimately")? If the contractual paradigm is sufficiently flexible to explain all observable institutions, it remains empty of discriminant content, quite apart from its possible aesthetic appeal.

Careful use of the model can, however, produce a classification that will differentiate between these two sets of potentially observable institutions. For example, the existence of unrestricted political authority in the hands of a political majority could never be brought within contractarian principles. Persons who could not, at a time of contract, predict their own positions would never agree to grant unrestricted political authority to any group, whether it be a duly elected majority of a parliament, a judicial elite, or a military junta. Recognition of this simple point is, of course, the source of the necessary tie-in between the contractarian paradigm and constitutionalism.[3] But what are the constitutional limits here? What actions by governments, within broad constitutional authority, may be thrown out on contractarian precepts?

Arbitrary restrictions or prohibitions on voluntary contractual agreements among persons and groups, in the absence of demonstrable spillover effects on third parties, cannot be parts of any plausible "social contract." For example, minimum-wage legislation and most restrictions on entry into professions, occupations, types of investment, or geographical locations could be rejected, as could all discrimination on racial, ethnic, and religious grounds. This is not to suggest that the appropriate line is easy to draw and that borderline cases requiring judgment are absent. More importantly, however, the classification step alone does not justify the institutions that remain in the

---

3. For an elaboration of the underlying theory, see James M. Buchanan and Gordon Tullock, *The Calculus of Consent: Logical Foundations of Constitutional Democracy.*

potentially allowable set. To conclude that an observed institution may have emerged, conceptually, on generalized contractarian grounds is not at all equivalent to saying that such an institution did, in fact, emerge this way. Many, and perhaps most, of the governmental regulations and restrictions that we observe and that remain within possible contractarian limits, may, in fact, represent arbitrary political impositions which could never have reflected generalized agreement.

Consider a single example, that of the imposition in 1974 of the speed limit of fifty-five miles per hour. Where can we classify this observed restriction on personal liberties in terms of the contractarian paradigm? Because of the acknowledged interdependencies among individual motorists, in terms of safety as well as fuel use, it seems clearly possible that general agreement on the imposition of some speed limit might well have emerged, and fifty-five miles per hour might have been within reasonable boundaries. But whether or not the fifty-five-miles-per-hour limit, as we observe it, in fact would have reflected a widely supported and essentially consensual outcome of some referendum process cannot be determined directly. The observed results could just as well reflect the preferences of members of the governmental bureaucracy who were able to exert sufficient influence on the legislators who established the limit.

Constitutional Contract

If we look too closely at particular policy measures in this way, however, we tend to overlook the necessary differentiation between the constitutional and the postconstitutional stages of political action. Should we think of applying contractarian criteria at the postconstitutional level at all? Or should we confine this procedure to the constitutional level? In reference to the fifty-five-miles-per-hour limit, as long as the legislature acted within its authorized constitutional powers, which are themselves generally acceptable on contractarian grounds, the observed results in any one instance need not be required to meet conceptual contractarian tests.

At this juncture the contractarian position again becomes highly vulnerable to the taunts of the libertarian anarchist. If specific political actions cannot be evaluated per se, but must instead be judged only in terms of their adherence to acceptable constitutional process, the basic paradigm seems lacking in teeth. Improperly applied, it may become an apology for almost any conceivable action by legislative majorities or by bureaucrats acting under the authorization of such majorities, and even strict application finds discrimination to be difficult. This criticism is effective, and the contrasting stance of the uncompromising libertarian anarchist is surely attractive in its superior ability to classify. Since to the anarchist all political action is illegitimate, the set of admissible claims begins and remains empty.

The constitutionalist-contractarian can and must retreat to the procedural stage of evaluation. If his hypotheses suggest that particular political actions, especially over a sequence of isolated events, fail to reflect consensus, he must look again at the constitutional authorizations for such actions. Is it contractually legitimate that Congress and the state legislatures be empowered by the Constitution to impose speed limits? What about the activities of the environmental agencies, acting as directed by Congress? What about the many regulatory agencies? Such questions as these suggest that the constitutionalist-contractarian must devote more time and effort to attempts to derive appropriate constitutional limits, notably with respect to the powers of political bodies to restrict economic liberties. Furthermore, the many interdependencies among the separate political actions, each of which might be plausibly within political limits, must be evaluated. Admittedly, those of us who share the constitutionalist-contractarian approach have been neglectful here. We have not done our homework well, and the research agenda facing us is large, indeed.

Meanwhile, we can, as philosophical fellow travelers, welcome the arguments put forth by the libertarian anarchists in condemning the political suppression of many individual liberties. We can go part of the way on genuine contractarian principles, and we can leave open many other cases that the anarchists can directly condemn. As I have noted elsewhere,[4] the limited-government ideals of the constitutionalist-contractarian may not excite the mind of modern man, and given the demonstrable overextension of political powers, the no-government ideals propounded by the libertarian anarchists may help to tilt the balance toward the individualistic and away from the nonindividualistic pole.

4. See my review of David Friedman's book, *The Machinery of Freedom,* in *Journal of Economic Literature* 12 (September, 1974): 914–15.

I have acknowledged above that the anarchist critique of existing political institutions is probably intellectually more satisfying than that which may be advanced by the contractarian. But where the anarchist critique falters, and where the contractarian paradigm comes on at its strongest, is at the bridge between negative criticism and constructive proposals for change. To the libertarian anarchist, all political action is unjustified. He cannot, therefore, proceed to advocate a politically orchestrated dismantling of existing structure. He has no test save his own values, and he has no means of introducing these values short of revolution. The contractarian, by contrast, has a continuing test which he applies to observed political structure. Do these basic laws and institutions reflect consensus of the citizenry? If they do not, and if his arguments to this effect are convincing, it becomes conceptually possible to secure agreement on modification. The rules of the game may be modified while the game continues to be played as long as we all agree on the changes. But why not eliminate the game?

This question returns us to the initial distinction made between the ideal society of the philosophical anarchist and that of the contractarian. To eliminate all rules and require that play in the social game take place within self-imposed and self-policed ethical and moral standards places too much faith in human nature. Why do we observe rules, along with referees and umpires, in ordinary games? Empirical examination of such voluntary games offers us perhaps the most direct evidence for the central contractarian hypothesis that rules—laws—are generally necessary.

Definition of Individual Rights

I could end this chapter here and remain within the limits of most discussion by economists. Traditionally economists have been content to treat exchange and contract, in all possible complexities, on the assumption that individual participants are well-defined entities capable of making choices among alternatives and in mutual agreement concerning legal titles or rights to things which are subject to exchange. The distribution of basic endowments, human and nonhuman, among persons has been taken as a given for most economic analysis, both positive and normative. The libertarian anarchist has gone further; in order to develop his argument that any and all political structure is illegitimate, he finds it necessary to presume that there are definitive and well-understood "natural boundaries" to individuals' rights. These boundaries on rights are held sacrosanct, subject to no justifiable "crossings" without consent.[5]

The problem of defining individual boundaries, individual rights, or, indeed, the term *individuals* must arise in any discussion of social order that commences with individuals as the basic units. Who is a person? How are rights defined? What is the benchmark or starting point from which voluntary contractual arrangements may be made?

I stated earlier that the primary value premise of individualism is the philosophical equality of men as men. Further, I stated that in thinking about men we are morally obligated to proceed as if they are equals, in that no man counts for more than another. These concepts remain, and must remain, the fundamental normative framework even when we recognize inequalities among persons in reality. The libertarian anarchist accepts this framework, but in a much more restricted application than do others who also fall within the individualistic set. The libertarian anarchist applies the norm of moral equality in holding that each and every man is *equally* entitled to have the natural boundaries of his rights respected, regardless of the fact that, among persons, these boundaries may vary widely.[6] If such natural boundaries exist, the contractarian may also use the individual units defined by such limits as the starting point for the complex contractual arrangements that emerge finally in observed, or conceptually observed, political structures. Within the presupposition that natural boundaries exist, the differences between the constitutionalist-contractarian and the libertarian anarchist reduce to the variant hypotheses concerning the interdependencies among persons, as defined—interdependencies that could be, as noted above, subjected to testing at a conjecturally empirical level.

But do such natural limits or boundaries exist? Once we move beyond the

5. One merit of Robert Nozick's analysis is his explicit discussion of the underlying presumptions of the "natural boundaries" model. See Robert Nozick, *Anarchy, State, and Utopia*.

6. For purposes of discussion here I am including Robert Nozick as being among the libertarian anarchists. Although he defends the emergence of the minimal protective state from anarchy, and specifically refutes the strict anarchist model in this respect, he does provide the most sophisticated argument for the presumption of natural boundaries on individuals' rights, which is the focus of my attention here. See Nozick, *Anarchy, State, and Utopia*.

simple rights of persons in the strictly physical sense, what are the distinguishing characteristics of boundary lines? In all cases where separate individual claims may come into conflict, or potential conflict, what is the natural boundary? Robin Hood and Little John meet squarely in the center of the footbridge. Who has the right of first passage?[7]

Robert Nozick makes a bold attempt to answer such questions by referring to the process of acquisition. In his formulation the legitimacy of the boundary limits among persons depends upon the process through which rights are acquired and not on the absolute or relative size of the bundle that may be in the possession or nominal ownership of a person or group. A person who has acquired assets by voluntary transfer holds these within admissible natural boundary limits. A person who holds assets that have been acquired, by him or by others in the past, by nonvoluntary methods has little claim to include these assets within the natural limits.

What is the ultimate test for the existence of natural boundaries? It must lie in the observed attitudes of individuals themselves. Do we observe persons to act as if there are natural boundaries on the rights of others, beyond those formally defined in legal restrictions? The evidence is not all on one side here. In rejecting the extreme claims of the libertarian anarchists, we should not overlook the important fact that a great deal of social interaction does proceed without formalized rules. For large areas of human intercourse anarchy prevails, and it works. We need no rules for directing pedestrian traffic on busy city sidewalks, no rules for ordinary conversation in groups of up to, say, ten persons, and no rules for behavior in elevators.

In the larger context, however, the evidence seems to indicate that persons do not mutually and simultaneously agree on dividing lines among separate rights. There is surely a contractual logic for at least some of the activity of the state in defining and enforcing the limits on the activities of persons. To accept this fact, however, does not imply that the legally defined rights of individuals, and the distribution of these rights, are arbitrarily determined by the political authorities. If we reject the empirical existence of natural boundaries, however, we return to the initial question. How do we define *individuals* for the purpose of deriving the contractual basis for political authority?

---

7. I use this example in several places to discuss this set of problems in my recent book *The Limits of Liberty: Between Anarchy and Leviathan.*

The Hobbesian Setting

The only alternative seems to be found in the distribution or limits on individuals' spheres of action that would be found in the total absence of formalized rules, that is, in genuine Hobbesian anarchy. There would emerge some "equilibrium" in this setting, some distribution of allowable activities among persons that could be sustained. This distribution would depend on the relative strengths and abilities of persons to acquire and to maintain desirable goods and assets. The "law of the jungle" would be controlling, and no serious effort could be made to attribute moral legitimacy to the relative holdings of persons. But this construction does have the major advantage of allowing us to define, in a conjecturally positive sense, a starting point, an "original position," from which any contractual process might commence.[8] Individuals need not be "natural equals" in this Hobbesian equilibrium, but they would still find it mutually advantageous to enter into contractual agreements that impose limits on their own activities and that set up ideally neutral governmental units to enforce these limits.

The perspective changes dramatically when this essentially Hobbesian vision is substituted for the natural-boundaries or Lockean vision, or when the existence of natural boundaries to the rights of persons that would be generally agreed upon and respected is denied. In the Nozick variant of the Lockean vision, anarchy, the absence of formalized rules—the absence of law along with means of enforcement—offers a highly attractive prospect. By contrast, in the basic Hobbesian vision, or in any paradigm that is derived from it, anarchy is not a state to be desired at all. Life for the individual in genuine anarchy is indeed predicted to be "poore, nasty, brutish, and short." The Hobbesian jungle is something to be avoided and something that people with rational self-interest will seek to avoid through general agreement on law along with requisite enforcement institutions, even if in the extreme the contract may be irreversible and Hobbes's Leviathan may threaten.[9]

---

8. In his much-acclaimed book *A Theory of Justice*, John Rawls attempts to derive principles of justice from conceptual contractual agreement among persons who place themselves in an "original position" behind a "veil of ignorance." Rawls does not, however, fully describe the characteristics of the "original position."

9. The argument of the few preceding paragraphs is developed much more fully in my book *Limits of Liberty*. Also see Gordon Tullock, ed., *Explorations in the Theory of Anarchy*.

Conclusions

We have here a paradox of sorts. The libertarian anarchist and the contractarian share the individualistic value premise. In addition, their diagnoses of current social malaise are likely to be similar in condemning overextended governmental authority. Further, the items on both their agendas for policy reform may be identical over a rather wide range. In their descriptions of the "good society," however, these two sets of political philosophers are likely to differ widely. The constitutionalist-contractarian, who looks to his second-stage set of ideals and who adopts at least some variant of the Hobbesian assumption about human nature, views anarchy, as an institution, with horror. To remove all laws, all institutions of order, in a world peopled by Hobbesian men would produce chaos. The contractarian must hold fast to a normative vision that is not nearly so simplistic as that which is possible either for the libertarian anarchist or for the collectivist. The contractarian seeks "ordered anarchy"; that is, a situation described as one which offers maximal freedom for individuals within a minimal set of formalized rules and constraints on behavior. He takes from classical economics the important idea that the independent actions of many persons can be spontaneously coordinated through marketlike institutions in order to produce mutually desirable outcomes without detailed and direct interference by the state. But he insists, with Adam Smith, that this coordination can be effective only if there are limits to individual actions defined by laws that cannot themselves spontaneously emerge. The contractarian position requires sophisticated discrimination between those areas of potential human activity where law is required and those areas that had best be left alone. Between the libertarian anarchist, who sees no cause for any laws and who trusts to individuals' own respect for each others' reciprocal natural boundaries, and the collectivist-socialist, who sees chaos as the result of any human activities that are not politically controlled, the constitutionalist-contractarian necessarily occupies the middle ground. His ideal world falls "between anarchy and Leviathan," both of which are to be avoided.

The Contractarian Logic of Classical Liberalism

Introduction

In a paper entitled "The Utilitarian Logic of Liberalism," Russell Hardin attempted to derive elements of a liberal social order from utilitarian foundations.[1] I have deliberately borrowed the structure of Hardin's title, emended by my substitution of the word "contractarian" for "utilitarian." Without the "adding-up" possibilities provided by utilitarianism, how can the structural components of social order be related, directly or indirectly, to individualist evaluative norms on a nonprivileged basis? This question, of course, defines the whole contractarian enterprise. My purpose here is the limited one of examining the possibilities of deriving legal-political-constitutional protection for voluntary exchanges from a contractarian starting point that rejects both utilitarianism and any form of natural rights.

The analytical setting incorporates well-defined membership of persons within a polity with each individual presumed to count equally in the ultimate determination of rules. Hence, legitimacy emerges only upon unanimous consent. If agreement is to be brought within the range of the possible

From *Liberty, Property, and the Future of Constitutional Development*, ed. Ellen Frankel Paul and Howard Dickman (Albany: State University of New York Press, 1990), 9–21. Reprinted by permission of the State University of New York Press. Copyright 1990, State University of New York. All rights reserved.

1. See Hardin, "The Utilitarian Logic of Liberalism," *Ethics* 97 (1986): 47–74. There are parallels as well as major differences between Hardin's analysis and my own. The substantive results of my analysis are closer to those reached by John Gray in his more inclusive, and differently directed, paper. See Gray, "Contractarian Method, Private Property, and the Market Economy" (Jesus College, Oxford, 1986, mimeographed).

here, some means of bridging the gap between well-identified individual interests, which will conflict, and the common or general interest, defined by the emergence of agreement, is necessary. The veil of ignorance and/or uncertainty, accompanied by some sense of the quasi-permanency of rules and institutions, offers the only means that seems fully consistent with the contractarian perspective. The question then becomes: behind a sufficiently thick veil of ignorance and/or uncertainty, will the individual in some hypothesized constitutional stage choose to ensure protection for voluntary contractual exchanges? Or, if he chooses to protect some exchanges and not others, where and how will a distinction be made?

Initially, the specific question to be addressed seems straightforward, but closer examination suggests that the basic meaning of "voluntary exchange" must be clarified. What, precisely, is involved in an exchange between two persons?

I. A Simple Example

Consider the simplest possible example in which persons A and B hold initial and fully separable stocks of two potentially exchangeable goods, Apples and Bananas. Prior to entry into a trading relation, A holds a stock of Apples; B holds a stock of Bananas.

It is semantically appropriate, as well as logically useful, to say that A has rights in Apples and B has rights in Bananas prior to entry into exchange. Indeed, without some such legal or mutually respected set of rights, trade, as an institution, would not be possible.[2] But precisely what does having rights in the initial stock of Apples allow A to do? Presumably, these rights allow A to prevent others from consuming, from eating up or otherwise using, the Apples in A's initial endowment without A's consent. Person A is protected in these respects by his rights to the Apples; person B is similarly protected in his rights to the Bananas.

As Armen Alchian emphasized in his early and seminal work on the economics of property, exchange involves a transfer of rights.[3] After a trade, there has been a shift in ownership of at least some of the Apples and some

2. It is possible to derive the initial imputation of such rights from a contractarian logic. On this, see my *The Limits of Liberty,* 1975.

3. See A. Alchian, *Economic Forces at Work,* 1977.

of the Bananas. Note, however, that the initial definition of rights, as such, may (but need not) include entry into potential exchange relationships. As an institution, exchange requires that there be some initial assignment of rights to goods, as indicated, but it also requires a reciprocal granting of "liberties" to enter into the "market" and to make bids and offers. Person A, in our example, holds initial rights to his Apple endowment; he does not hold any initial liberty to offer these in exchange for B's Bananas.

In the strict two-person setting, such a liberty for A will be within the sphere of authority of person B, and he may or may not grant that liberty to person A. Person B may, simply, refuse to deal with person A; B may withhold any liberty of A to enter into a bargaining process, or market. Note that such action on the part of B would not, in any way, transgress on A's rights to the Apples in his initial stock. Person B may, on the other hand, allow A the liberty of entering into the exchange process, while, at the same time, person A may allow B a similar liberty. If this reciprocal granting of liberties to enter exchange takes place, person A will make offers of Apples for Bananas, and person B will make offers of Bananas for Apples. Exchange will take place with a resultant transfer of rights to the units of goods that change hands.[4]

This highly stylized example may seem analytically otiose, since neither person would seem to have any possible interest in withholding the liberty of entering the exchange process from the other—at least so long as we stay within the dimensions of the two-person, two-good model and do not allow noneconomic considerations to enter motivations. I shall demonstrate, however, that the distinction between rights and liberties does become relevant in more complex models, and that the usage of these terms can be helpful in reaching a provisional answer to the basic question posed earlier. I hope to

---

4. The distinction between the rights of ownership and the liberties to enter exchange may seem strained in advanced societies. But, aside from the analytical usefulness for the argument here, the distinction was, presumably, relevant in the "silent trade" settings between tribes that characterized pre-exchange cultures. Such "silent trade" could never have been initiated unless tribes implicitly granted to other tribes the "liberties" of invading territorial rights to the extent of displaying wares along the shorelines. It is possible to think of intertribal relationships in which territorial rights were reciprocally respected but from which no trade could ever have emerged due to the absence of any reciprocal grant of liberties to enter potential exchanges.

show that agreement may be reached on constitutional protection for the reciprocal exchange of liberties to contract that facilitates a voluntary transfer of rights, but that constitutional protection cannot be similarly justified for the exchange of liberties that does not facilitate any transfer of rights, even if this exchange of liberties is itself wholly voluntary on the part of the parties involved.

An alternative formulation, and one that would be more terminologically consistent with Hardin's, would include, with the set of rights to initial endowments, the ability to enter into the contracting process with parties on the other sides of potential exchanges. This formulation would have the semantic advantage of not requiring reference to liberties to enter exchanges, but it has the disadvantage of requiring that some of the rights involved in the exchange process could possibly be made inalienable (nonexchangeable). That which is defined to be a liberty to enter exchange or contract in my preferred terminology becomes that dimension of rights that are made alienable by agreement in the constitutional decision-process under the alternative terminology.

II. Enlarging the Example

Consider now an enlarged, if still highly stylized, example of potential exchange in Apples and Bananas. There are now two persons, A_1 and A_2, both of whom initially have rights to stocks of Apples. There are also, say, ten persons, B_1, B_2, ... B_{10}; each one has initial rights to a stock of Bananas. In this trading community of twelve persons, we assume that, initially, each person has allowed every other person the liberty of entering a market or exchange relationship. Under these conditions, trade will take place as in the two-person model.

In this setting, however, we should note that persons A_1 and A_2 may well find it mutually advantageous to agree, voluntarily, on a reciprocal alienation of some of the liberties to exchange that have been granted to them by the ten persons who have rights to Bananas. Person A_1 might, for example, agree to give up any liberty of entering into a trading relationship with persons B_6 through B_{10} in exchange for A_2's agreement to give up any liberty of entering into a trading relationship with B_1 through B_5. This sort of contract may be mutually advantageous to both A_1 and A_2 because, in this way, each can achieve a monopoly position with respect to a subset of the buyers for Apples. Each of the two can thereby expect to secure a somewhat larger share of the producers-consumers rents in the community than that share anticipated under the competitive adjustment in the absence of the market-sharing contract. The agreement will tend to make A_1 and A_2 better off at the expense of the other ten persons who, because of their larger numbers, are assumed unable to organize a fully effective offsetting market-sharing arrangement.

If we now introduce the contractarian-constitutionalist perspective and place any person behind an appropriately defined veil of ignorance and/or uncertainty, it seems clear that voluntary exchanges like that between the two As just discussed would *not* be provided constitutional protection, unless the value of liberty-to-enter-agreements *as such* is assigned an evaluation over and beyond access to goods that are valued. That is to say, the legal rules chosen behind the veil would not, under standard preference configurations, allow market-sharing agreements to be enforced. Behind the veil, no person could predict his or her status as an A or B. Even in this pure exchange setting, any agreement between persons on the same side of any market will ensure that potential value will not be allowed to come into being. On the other hand, and by contrast, all agreements that result in an exchange of rights to goods and services across both sides of markets will be predicted to be value-enhancing. These latter agreements or contracts will be provided legal enforceability under the agreed-on constitutional structure.

The results here are, of course, familiar. Contracts made in restraint of trade were traditionally unenforceable under the common law. These contracts may involve market shares, as in our simple example, but they may also extend to the setting of prices, along with other characteristics of the terms on which goods and services may be offered on markets. Any such contractual agreement may be interpreted as a mutual exchange of liberties to contract with persons on the other side of markets. In the simple setting here, where we limit analysis to fully partitionable goods and services that involve no spillover or external effects, any voluntary agreement by same-side traders to give up any of the liberties of dealing with other-side traders ensures that value will be destroyed. Goods and services will be prevented from moving to their most highly valued uses, as determined by the evaluations placed on them by the participants in the potential exchange nexus.

III. Politicizing the Example

Let us now assume that voluntary *private* contracts in restraint of exchange are legally nonenforceable within the setting of the same example—the example which includes A_1 and A_2 as sellers of Apples and B_1 through B_{10} as sellers of Bananas, with traders restricted to those trades that directly involve transfers of Apples and Bananas. The legal rules are such that the As cannot make the market-sharing arrangement previously discussed.

Suppose, however, that a majority of the combined twelve-person community imposes a governmental restriction on the exchange. Suppose, specifically, that the sellers of Bananas (or at least seven of them), a clear majority, vote in favor of changing the terms of trade so that the Apple price for Bananas is set well above that price observed under the nonrestricted competitive operation of the simple economy. This legislation will ensure that the ten Banana-sellers secure a larger share for A_1 and A_2. It will also ensure that total value in the economy is reduced. Apples and Bananas will not be distributed, after trade, in such a fashion that will maximize total value in the community.

Behind a veil of ignorance and/or uncertainty as to personal identification, no person would allow the constitution to permit majoritarian political action to restrict exchanges in the manner just described (unless, of course, majoritarianism, *as such,* is positively valued). Such restriction is the political equivalent of private agreements in restraint of trade or exchange. The simple analysis here indicates clearly that the simultaneous enforcement of common-law or statutory prohibitions on private contracts in restraint of trade and of politically orchestrated restrictions on trade is, in principle, contradictory. Emphasis on the essential similarity between private market-sharing contracts and publicly enacted restrictions on exchange calls direct attention to potential flaws in the policy stances of both the extreme libertarians and those who oppose constitutional protection for economic liberties. The libertarian who defends private, cartel-like agreement among contracting parties on the same side of a market, so long as such agreement is voluntary, must have some difficulty arguing against politically orchestrated cartel-like restrictions in particular markets, although the political-legal enforceability of private cartel agreements becomes a critical variable in any such argument. And those who justify majoritarian political interference with free exchanges should find it difficult to defend common-law limits on restraints of trade, as well as anti-trust institutions.

IV. Extensions: Partitionable, Tradeable Goods and Distributional Norms

To this point, the analysis has been limited to very simple exchange models, with almost self-evident results. The contractarian derivation of constitutional protection for the freedom of persons to carry out ordinary exchanges of goods and services is relatively straightforward. But, as the analysis has shown, this protection cannot be extended to freedom of contracts that involve the giving up of liberties to enter the exchange process. These results emerge, however, only in the simple exchange setting that was examined, along with the implied presuppositions that include the partitionability of goods among persons, the moral acceptability of trade in such goods, and the absence of third-party or external effects generated by two-person trades. In this section, I want to retain these presuppositions while examining in some detail the distributional implications of free exchange. I want to concentrate exclusively on the effects on the contractarian calculus that distributional considerations may exert.

We may stay with the Apples-Bananas example to illustrate the conditions that must be present if distributional considerations are to be relevant for the results. If, behind the veil of ignorance and/or uncertainty, a person predicts that those who, before exchange, will be endowed with initial stocks of Bananas will be distributionally worse off than those who will have initial endowments of Apples, there may then arise some argument for asymmetrically enforced prohibitions on restraints on trade, whether privately or publicly introduced. If Banana owners (or producers, if we extend the analysis to a production economy) are systematically predicted to be poor, while Apple owners (or producers) are systematically predicted to be rich, the person behind the veil who is unable to identify his or her own position may consider exchange or terms-of-trade interferences as one means of securing distributional objectives, even in full recognition of the potential loss in total value that any such interference will ensure.

As this example suggests, however, to associate distributional positions with the specific ownership and/or production of specific goods and services seems bizarre. Normally, there would be little or no connection between distributional position and the description of the good that is initially owned or produced. Premarket or pre-exchange endowments may, of course, differ widely, but such differences cannot readily be associated with the terms of trade in particular markets. If this is the case, there would be little or no grounds for trying to relate interferences with markets to ultimate distributional norms. This statement does not, of course, imply anything about the appropriateness (or inappropriateness) or relevance of distributional objectives in a more general constitutional calculus.

There is one market, however, where distributional elements have allegedly been significant in offering putative justification for restraints on voluntary exchange, both restraints that emerge from privately negotiated agreement to give up liberties to exchange and from publicly imposed constraints on individual freedom of contract. I refer here to the market or markets for labor services, where privately agreed restraints on exchange are widely observed to be publicly enforced (e.g., labor union contracts), and, further, where governmentally imposed restraints supplement those that are privately sanctioned. It is necessary to examine with some care the possible contractarian basis for this apparent exception to the generalized principle of classical liberalism. Can restrictions on voluntary labor exchanges be grounded in any way on the rational choices of persons in a constitutional stage of decision?

Consider a setting most highly favorable to the argument for interferences in voluntary exchange. Assume that persons are, at birth, physically separable into two distinct classes, those who must work for others, and those who may fill employer roles. Further assume that all workers are homogeneous, and that each worker is location-specific, and, hence, unable to negotiate exchanges with alternative employers over space. Employees, as a class, being more numerous relative to their opportunities than employers, are predicted to earn substantially less per person than employers.

In this setting, employees or workers are often said to be at a relative bargaining disadvantage, and this allegation has been used as a justification for either privately organized restraints on voluntary labor contracts, through unions, or for compulsory governmental restrictions on the terms of such contracts. But even in this rarefied and highly unreal setting, can such restrictions be derived from a veil of ignorance–uncertainty calculus?

Consider wage negotiations, where the union representing the demands of the workers secures a wage contract that sets payment above that which would emerge in the absence of the union. Fewer workers than before can secure employment at the higher wage. But if we assume that the demand for labor is inelastic (less than one in absolute value) over the relevant range, the total wage bill may be higher. The total payment to workers, as a class, will then increase. But if this institutional change is to be supported on grounds of distributive justice, the increase in the total wage bill is not sufficient. There must also be some means to ensure that, within the class of workers, the gains are more equally shared. As noted, fewer workers will remain employed, but unless those who lose employment by the wage increase are subsidized by those who remain employed at the increased wage, the institutional change will generate undesirable distributive results on almost any criterion of distributive justice. It seems clear that wage setting, as such, without institutional guarantees as to the distribution of benefits from wages above competitive levels, cannot be derived as a consequence of the rational choice calculus of a person behind a veil, even under the most favorable and extreme circumstances postulated here.

If we introduce more realism into the model, and allow for interclass mobility, non-location-specificity, and heterogeneity among both workers and employers, any private or public enforcement of wage levels above those attained in the openly competitive market will tend to impose disproportionately greater harm on those potential workers who are precisely those held to be the most "distributionally deserving" by egalitarians. The generalized conclusion seems inescapable; the principles of classical liberalism that prohibit legally enforceable restraints on voluntary exchange cannot be challenged with a contractarian model of evaluation, even when distributional objectives are fully incorporated into the analysis.

V. Beyond Procedural Norms

To this point, my usage of the contractarian logic of classical liberalism has relied exclusively on procedural criteria for institutional evaluation. The results appear determinate only because many of the substantive issues have been deliberately avoided by the presuppositions of the analysis. I have simply presumed that all persons, whether behind the veil or aware of their place in society, agree on the definitions or classifications of "goods" and "bads."

Further, I have presumed that all "goods" and "bads" are fully partitionable, both in a physical and an evaluative sense. No person is interested in the production or consumption activity of any other person with respect to any identified "good" or "bad."

It is clear that most of the issues involving the putative legitimacy of private or public restraints on voluntary exchanges arise precisely in those settings where these presuppositions do not describe reality. In the terminology of welfare economics, it is the presence of "externality," whether narrowly or broadly defined, that necessarily introduces indeterminism in any attempted normative justification for a regime of generalized constitutional-legal protection for voluntary exchange. The procedural criteria of contractarianism cannot, in themselves, be extended to the substantive issues of definition and classification—at least not directly. I shall examine the limits of these criteria below. But it remains useful to emphasize the force of the contractarian logic, even within these acknowledged limits.

Empirically, persons are observed to agree on definitions of "goods" and "bads" over wide commodity and service groupings, and, further, persons agree that individual or private preferences with respect to the consumption, production, and exchange of many ordinary goods and services are of little concern to those who are not involved in carrying out such activities. Within the domain of social interaction involving the exchange of such ordinary goods and services, the contractarian logic remains unchallengeable, although, of course, defining the limits of such domain remains formidable. Private or public restraints on voluntary exchanges in these ordinary goods and services (bread, clothing, houses, haircuts, consulting) are ruled out by the procedural criteria of contractarianism, along with the empirical observation of agreement on spheres of private action.

There exists another domain of activity within which there remains widespread disagreement concerning the appropriateness of privately motivated exchange activity. There are activities that involve what some persons may define to be tradeable or exchangeable goods and services which other persons do not acknowledge as falling legitimately within the domain of individual choice. Examples abound: alcohol, slavery, sex, drugs, blood, body organs, babies, guns, and so forth. There are still other activities that may involve goods and bads that in some circumstances are deemed exchangeable, but which may in other circumstances generate third-party or spillover effects. Is an individual to be allowed to produce and market a good, the sale and/or purchase of which is predicted to adversely affect others than the direct buyer-consumer?

Can individual liberty to enter into voluntary exchanges of goods and bads that fall into the inclusive domain of externality be derived from the contractarian calculus? If not, is there some characteristic feature of such goods and services that we may identify as offering grounds to justify departure from the general norm of protection for voluntary exchange?

It is useful at this point to recall precisely what the individual is presumed to know when he makes basic constitutional choices behind the veil of ignorance and/or uncertainty. He or she cannot identify which person in the community he or she will be, what role will be occupied, what human and nonhuman endowments will be possessed, or what preferences will be descriptive. On the other hand, the overall or general distribution of these variables among the whole set of persons in the community is presumed to be known, at least within broad limits.

Consider, in particular, the preferences for goods and services, along with the preferences for the activities of others with respect to exchanges of these goods and services. For any one of the potential markets in the domain of externality, the individual behind the veil will predict that there will be a wide range of preference patterns concerning the appropriateness or inappropriateness of entering into unhampered exchange processes. There will be persons whose preferences dictate participation in ordinary exchanges in such markets without regard to the spillover effects on others in the community. There will be others, however, who will find the existence of such exchanges to be either morally outrageous or economically damaging.

Behind the veil, the chooser cannot predict which one of these preferences will describe his or her utility function. Identification remains impossible on this as on other dimensions. The choice of institutions behind the veil must, therefore, represent some judgment as to the relative significance of the varying preference patterns, along with some estimate of the frequency distribution along the spectrum. The constitutional stage chooser must balance off the possible potential gains to those who directly benefit from the exchanges that might take place and the possible potential harms to those who would be damaged by such exchanges. There is no *a priori* judgment that can be advanced in any particular case here, and, hence, no prediction as to the precise definition of the range of goods and services that would have constitutional protection for their voluntary exchanges.

This indeterminacy cannot be avoided. We may suggest, however, that rational choice behavior at the constitutional stage must also include some prediction as to the workings of those institutions that might be constitutionally authorized to intervene in the exchange processes for goods and services falling in the domain of relevant externality. In particular, rational choice here would dictate skepticism with regard to the working of politicized majoritarian intervention with voluntary exchange. As it operates ideally, even if not in practice, majority rule tends to allow majorities with relatively mild preferences to overrule minorities that may feel intensely about alternatives. It seems likely that most of the activities that fall within a relevant externality domain (e.g., smoking) invoke mildly felt meddlesome negative preferences. Hence, simple majorities would presumably choose to prohibit voluntary exchanges in such goods and services.

These considerations suggest that, if restraints on the voluntary exchanges of goods and services are deemed appropriate, these restraints should take the form of adjustments in the legal structure so as to make contracts of exchange nonenforceable. That is to say, the constitutional stage decision should delineate carefully those markets that fall within the domain of relevant externality. There seem to be no grounds for allowing the delineation to be made through the operation of ordinary politics. For example, contracts for perpetual servitude should be constitutionally, rather than legislatively, prohibited; contracts for the exchange of sexual services should or should not be constitutionally permissible, independent of the will of particular legislative majorities. The sale and purchase of alcohol was an appropriate constitutional issue, even if historical experience suggests that the constitutional choice made in the United States was in error. In these cases, as with all tradeable goods and services, there is a *prima facie* argument against overt politicization of restraint on the exchange process.

VI. Contractarianism and Classical Liberalism

There is little that is novel in the preceding analysis. What I have attempted to do is to stay within the contractarian model for evaluation and to examine the possible derivation of constitutional protection of voluntary exchanges between persons or organizations of persons. It seems clear that persons should be allowed, and legally protected, to engage in voluntary exchanges of goods and services that are considered to be appropriate objects for private disposition when such exchanges do not generate significant spillover harms on third parties. This protection cannot be extended to voluntary agreements in restraint of exchanges, at least within any contractarian exercise of justification. For goods and services that are deemed by some persons to be inappropriate for exchanges, or goods and services the exchanges of which are predicted to generate significant spillover damages on third parties, the contractarian model is necessarily indeterminate. No general principle may be laid down for such cases; each market must be treated on its own account, and a constitutional stage decision must weigh the predicted costs and benefits of the alternative institutional arrangements. This choice calculus must incorporate some recognition of the working properties of those institutions of politics that might be expected to operate in the absence of clearly defined constitutional-legal guidelines. The analysis suggests that a strong argument may often be adduced for locating the critical decision at the constitutional stage (rather than at any postconstitutional stage) of politics.

The contractarian logic may be compared and contrasted with the argument from rights that is often employed for a comparable purpose. In a sense, the whole contractarian evaluation commences from a presumption that individuals possess rights in the initial endowments, including talents, assigned to them. Indeed, without some such presumption, we find it difficult to define what an individual is. The contractarian cannot, however, extend the definition of rights to include the particular set of activities allowed to individuals. To take this step would remove from consideration the very issues to be analyzed, and, unless there should be some agreement on what activities are within an individual's rights, the prospects for reasoned argument are necessarily closed off too early.

The contractarian enterprise commences with the rights to initial endowments, but then aims to derive some agreed-on elements of social structure that allow individuals to use these endowments. I have suggested that the individual's rights to the personal and nonpersonal endowments in initial possession do not include the liberty to offer these rights (to goods and services) in exchange to others until and unless others grant such liberties. As I have elaborated at length elsewhere,[5] it is in the interest of every potential trader to extend such liberties of entry to all potential traders on opposing sides of markets. The order of "natural liberty" described by Adam Smith suggests that such maximal extensions of liberty should be constitutionally protected, and that this protection would emerge from agreement behind a veil of ignorance and/or uncertainty. But restraints or restrictions on the trading process through agreements on market shares, price setting, or any other of the generalized terms of trade cannot find support in the contractarian logic.

It is perhaps not surprising that the contractarian exercise yields the essential principles of classical liberalism. These principles may, of course, be justified on general utilitarian as well as contractarian grounds, and, in this application, these two philosophical approaches yield closely similar results. The advantage of the contractarian perspective has always seemed to me to lie in the potential for deriving a logic of institutional structure from the idealized choices of individuals who participate in the structure, as opposed to the equally idealized choice of an external observer who is presumed omniscient.

5. "Towards the Simple Economics of Natural Liberty," *Kyklos* 40 (1, 1987): 3–20.

Constitutional Restrictions on the Power of Government

Introduction

My title is indeed comprehensive, and it should be evident that I cannot, in the space-time of one lecture, do more than offer highly selected comments. Nonetheless, I should defend both my title and my own efforts, here and elsewhere, to call attention to constitutional matters. I use this inclusive term to embody constitutional history, constitutional law, constitutionalism as an approach to political philosophy, and, in particular, constitutional challenges that the United States faces in the 1980s.

I have often suggested that what is now needed is widespread adoption of a genuine "constitutional attitude," a proclivity or tendency to examine issues from a constitutional perspective, as opposed to the pragmatic, short-run, utilitarian perspective that seems to characterize modern academic scholarship as well as day-to-day political discussion and action. As I compare the political discourse of our time, the late twentieth century, with that of the late eighteenth century, when the American Founding Fathers were doing their work, the distinctive difference lies in our century's loss of an earlier "constitutional wisdom."

There are, of course, very good reasons why the American Founders, and especially Madison, Hamilton, and Jay, adopted a constitutional perspective in the 1780s. They were actively engaged in constitution making, and they were trying to articulate the set of ideas that would convince the wider public

The Frank M. Engle Lecture, 1981 (Bryn Mawr, Pa.: The American College, 1981), 1–16. Copyright 1981 by The American College. Reprinted by permission.

that a draft document would work. As we all know, subsequent generations of Americans, including our own, have been beneficiaries of their genius, with respect both to basic design and to their persuasive powers. We still live in the "building" that they constructed for us, and I think that this metaphor is of considerable advantage in thinking about my whole subject matter.

Once constructed and in place, the "building" stood the test of time. It has been added to, changed, twisted out of recognition in some respects, allowed to fall down here and there, deliberately torn down in parts, but perhaps it still remains recognizable as the same "building" that emerged in 1789. These modifications in structure have been allowed to take place, however, almost without conscious attention to the "grand design" of the architects. The changes have been essentially pragmatic responses to particular situations as these arose. It should not be surprising, therefore, that what we now see appears jerry-built and distorted, considerably out of line, strongly tilted, and apparently liable to collapse unless shoring up efforts are commenced, and soon.

Only within the decades of the 1960s and notably the 1970s has there been an emerging awareness that the very bases of our socio-economic-political-legal order are seriously in disarray. For more than a century, and indeed since the debate prior to the Civil War, political leaders, social philosophers, social scientists, constitutional lawyers, and the public generally forgot the simple principles, apparently secure in the false presumption that the American constitutional structure was permanently emplaced and not subject even to potential collapse. I shall discuss the signs of this new awareness later in this lecture, but before I do so, it is necessary to lay out in some detail the fundamental meaning of a *constitution*.

Constitutional and Postconstitutional Choice

I have continued to be surprised that my economist colleagues, all of whom are sophisticated and competent social scientists, seem to have no inkling as to what a "constitution" is, and that they go about their own chores as if the whole subject remains irrelevant and unimportant. I could extend this category beyond economists, to include most modern social scientists, and even to many of those who label themselves as constitutional lawyers. It should not be necessary here to go over what must be very elementary precepts were it not for what I can label only as gross illiteracy on the part of so many who should but do not know them. And perhaps I should stress that it is "knowledge" not "values" or "beliefs" that I refer to here.

WHAT A CONSTITUTION IS

Put in its simplest if possibly confusing terms, "a constitution" is the "higher law." This terminology is helpful because it suggests a two-stage or two-level legal structure. There are "laws" that lay down the rules within which ordinary "laws" are made. The political constitution is the first set of laws here, the higher laws, the basic rules for political order and political decision making. Professor Hayek, in the very title of his three-volume work, distinguishes between the terms "law" and "legislation."[1] These may be translated, in my terms, as "constitutional law" and "ordinary legislation."

On many occasions, and in several places in print, I have used the analogy with games since I think this allows us to present the basic distinction most clearly. Consider a poker game. Participants must initially agree on the set of rules that will define the game to be played. This agreed-on set of rules becomes the constitution of the game. Play takes place within these rules, and this play may be termed *postconstitutional*. As such, it is explicitly constrained by the rules chosen, constrained externally to the actual play itself.

There are two quite distinct stages or levels of choice involved here, and these choices have quite different features. First, there is the choice of the rules themselves, *constitutional choice*. Second, there is the choice among the strategies of play within the rules that define the game. I call this choice of strategy *postconstitutional choice*.

We may think of a single person as he or she tries to establish criteria for evaluating alternatives for choices in these different settings, with the knowledge that he or she is participating in a collective or group-decision process. In constitutional choice, the individual cannot know precisely what his or her own position will be, or precisely how the cards will fall in the poker game analogy. In his or her own self-interest, the person will be led to eval-

1. F. A. Hayek, *Law, Legislation and Liberty,* 3 volumes (Chicago: University of Chicago Press, 1979).

uate alternative rules on something like the "fairness" criterion.[2] For choices made within the constraints of established rules, however, the individual will be able to identify his or her position. He or she will, therefore, aim at maximizing the individual payoffs to be gained, whatever these payoffs might be. Here the appropriate model is one of a maximizing strategy.

CONSTITUTIONAL RULES

Let me now return to the political constitution and apply these basic notions. A political constitution is the set of rules that define the socio-economic-political game that we all must play. These rules define the relative spheres for private and governmental action, and they impose external constraints on the procedures through which political action takes place.

The central confusion in the discussions of politics has been in the failure to recognize that two levels of evaluation and choice exist and that these are quite different from each other, requiring different types of analysis on the part of social scientists. The analysis-evaluation of alternative constitutional rules and arrangements must have as an input some models or predictions as to how choices will be made within or under the alternative sets of rules that might be laid down in the constitution. Modern social scientists have failed to recognize that reform or improvement must have as its direct object change in the rules or constraints within which political decision makers are allowed to operate. They have not been concerned at all with genuine constitutional reform. Instead, modern social scientists have tended to focus on the particulars of policy alternatives or options.

Constitutionalism and Public Choice

These scholars have proceeded as if they are offering advice to some benevolent despot, who is presumed to stand ready and willing to promote "the

---

2. The fairness criterion for evaluating alternative rules has been made familiar to social scientists and social philosophers through the work of John Rawls. See *A Theory of Justice* (Cambridge, Mass.: Harvard University Press, 1971). For a similar evaluative procedure, strictly related to constitutional choice, see James M. Buchanan and Gordon Tullock, *The Calculus of Consent* (Ann Arbor: University of Michigan Press, 1962).

public interest" once it is enlightened as to what such "interest" is by the expertise of those who are doing the advising. Such a procedure is absurd on its face. Government politics—this is not a single-minded decision-making entity. And even if government were such, we surely could not model it to be benevolent. Government as it exists is, of course, an extremely complex interaction process that involves literally thousands of persons, who participate in many different roles and capacities. Out of this process particular outcomes emerge. Of what use is the "advice" of the economist to the effect that this or that policy A is more or less "efficient" than policy B? Persons who participate in political decision making are no different from the rest of us. They respond to the rewards and penalties that the "rules of the game" confront them with, and such persons would indeed be foolish if they took the advice of their economist advisers very seriously.

Public choice analysis

"Public choice"—the new subdiscipline that applies essentially economic methods of analysis to the behavior of persons in political decision-making capacities, involves the study of the whole interaction process. As such, the analysis in public choice is positive rather than normative. It does not advance propositions that politicians, bureaucrats, or voters "should" or "should not" adopt.

Nonetheless, there are important reform implications that emerge from the whole body of public choice analysis, and these implications are those that tie us back into the main theme of this lecture. Public choice analysis, which has as one of its central elements the critical distinction between constitutional and postconstitutional choice, strongly implies that reform or improvement in political outcomes or results is to be sought through possible changes in the rules, in the set of constraints within which political decisions are made, in the *Constitution,* and not in changes in day-to-day policy that temporary politicians may be somehow persuaded to follow.

A somewhat different way of contrasting the constitutional perspective with the standard one taken in most discussions on politics is to note that, with constitutional-institutional reform, there is little or no concern with replacing "bad," "evil," or "incompetent" politicians with others who may be "good," "kind," or "competent." The emphasis in constitutional reform is neither on persuasion nor on selection of "better" persons to act as agents in governing roles. The emphasis stays precisely where it was with the Founding Fathers: on setting up rules or constraints within which politicians must operate, rules that will make it a relatively trivial matter as to the personal characteristics of those who happen to be selected as governors. This emphasis is strictly eighteenth century in spirit, and it is present in Adam Smith's great treatise on economics, *The Wealth of Nations* (1776), as well as in *The Federalist Papers*.

Can Government Be Constrained?

Critics of the constitutional perspective, for three centuries, have made several arguments. Perhaps the most important of these, and surely one that warrants our consideration here, is the charge that constitutions do not and cannot constrain sovereign governments. If this charge is valid, all discussion of constitutional constraints is mere fancy, an illusory and escapist exercise in futility.

Hobbes's view

This position was taken by Thomas Hobbes, who published his book *Leviathan* in 1651. Hobbes argued that persons value the security of life and property so highly that they will assent to the establishment of a sovereign governmental power. They will do so, however, in the full knowledge that, once established, persons can exert no subsequent control over the activity of the sovereign. Government can do as it pleases, once it has attained a position of authority and power. There is no enforcing agent or agency that can require the sovereign to abide by the rules that might be laid down in some conceptual contract, some constitution.

In this Hobbesian perspective, the only constraints on the range and extent of the activities of the sovereign must be self-imposed. Those persons who are in positions of governmental authority may voluntarily choose to restrict their behavior, but they recognize no externally imposed limits in so doing.

I suggest that this rejection of the efficacy of constitutional constraints on government belies the whole tradition that embodies the American political experience. The Founding Fathers did not conceive their own efforts to be illusory; they thought that the framework of rules laid down would, and could, limit the scope of governmental power. And two centuries of history corroborate this hypothesis, despite the record that also exhibits failure, erosion, and explicit violation of constraints that the Founders sought to incorporate into our basic "higher law." I need not list the many aberrations in our constitutional history, aberrations from the basic structure of governance as conceived by our Founders.

I shall assert, however, that even in the 1980s, government is limited by the Constitution, and not by the mere self-impositional behavior of those who act in the name and the authority of government. There are things that government dares not do, even in our era where governmental power seems almost ubiquitous. We may, of course, readily point to areas of activity where government intrusion into our lives and liberties seems unlimited. I shall treat some of these in more detail later, but my primary emphasis at this point is to state categorically that the United States, even in the 1980s, is not "beyond law," beyond some "constitutional limits."

The Electoral Fallacy

Acceptance of the general proposition that government can be constitutionally limited and that in the United States government remains subject to constitutional constraints need not embody the "constitutional attitude" nor reflect the genuine "constitutional wisdom" that seemed characteristic of eighteenth-century political thought. Many modern scholars, along with practicing politicians and members of the public, will acknowledge that basic individual rights, such as those summarized in the first ten amendments, the Bill of Rights, should be and must be accorded constitutional status; that is, such rights should be embodied in the "higher law" of the land and should not be subject to change by temporary majority coalitions in the Congress, acting with the assent of the president.

Such acknowledgment of the constitutional status of basic individual rights may, however, be accompanied by an acceptance of or acquiescence in, and even support for, almost any decision that is reached through constitutionally sanctioned means or processes. So long as individuals possess freedom of speech, press, and assembly; so long as each person has the right to vote; so long as candidates and parties are chosen in free and open elections conducted on agreed-on rules; and so long as agents or representatives are chosen for specifically limited terms of office—if these conditions are guaranteed constitutionally, the results, whatever these might be, are themselves to be treated as "constitutionally legitimate." Or so the standard argument goes to the extent that it is articulated at all.

The whole argument is, I suggest, based on a set of elementary misconceptions or errors. At a fundamental philosophical level, the argument embodies an exclusive evaluation of processes and procedures quite independent of the end-states or results that such procedures may generate. In many of my own writings, I have strongly supported arguments for process evaluation, largely because institutional procedures or rules are the normal objects for choice. However, the choice or selection among different processes or procedures must remain empty unless it is somehow informed by predictions of outcome or end-state patterns that will be generated under alternative rules. To judge a set of procedural rules to be desirable it is necessary to establish at least some proof, within reasonable tolerance, that such rules will "work," that is, will produce end-states that are valued in themselves. To argue that any collective outcome or decision reached by a majority of the community's members (or by some majority of their representatives, themselves elected by simple majorities in defined constituencies) is acceptable merely because it is reached by procedures that are independently evaluated to be desirable is an unwarranted logical step. Procedures themselves must be adjudged in accordance with predicted end-state patterns. Hence, simple majority rule, political equality, and periodic elections—these are to be judged acceptable only if there is independent argument to the effect that such institutions will generate a pattern of end-states that may be judged acceptable independent of procedures.

To put my point in a somewhat different way, I am suggesting that there is nothing sacred in the ordinary institutions of political democracy, nothing that should prevent us from taking a continuing critical look at these institutions to try to understand as best we can just what patterns of results they seem most likely to generate. To assume the opposing stance, to refuse to look at such results, to retain an implicit and blind faith in the efficacy of such institutions—this is to be trapped in what I shall call "the electoral fallacy."

Models of Politics

In order to evaluate alternative political rules and institutions, it is necessary to undertake positive analysis of how they work. It is necessary to model politics and political behavior. Such modeling is much of what "public choice theory" is all about. And what can such modeling tell us? What does it tell us?

Major scientific advances have been made in our understanding of governmental-political processes in the decades since World War II. One of the most shocking proofs, at least to many scholars, was a rediscovery of an earlier demonstration to the effect that simple majority voting does not, on many occasions, result in a stable set of outcomes. A majority may be found that will support almost any choice in a set; there may be no unique majority motion or candidate. Among a set of three options—A, B, and C—a majority may be found to support A over B and B over C, then choose C over A. To expect institutions of majority voting to yield "rational" outcomes was shown to be folly. Political decision rules that incorporate the evaluations of more than one person are inherently unstable, capricious, nonrational.

This proof, associated with the work of Duncan Black and Kenneth Arrow in the early 1950s, shocked those who placed implicit faith in democratic electoral process unbounded by constitutional constraints. But what if actual governments are not so simple as these elementary majority-rule models imply? What if actual politics, as it really works, is not properly modeled as simple majority voting, but instead is best interpreted in terms of the behavior of a monolithic decision maker, a "ruler"? Would not decisions in such cases be consistent, stable, and rational? Would not all problems of cyclical rotation, inconsistency, and nonrationality then disappear? Indeed so, but what arguments are then to be put into the objective or utility function of the decision makers? Unless we somehow can justify a "benevolent despot" presumption here, we find it even more necessary to reexamine the appropriateness of extending constitutional limits beyond the basic protections of rights of speech, press, assembly, and voting. Otherwise, what is to prevent government from taking all that is of economic value for its own purposes?

If models of genuinely democratic politics (one-man, one-vote majority models) are demonstrated to generate nonconsistent patterns of outcomes, and if nondemocratic models (monolithic bureaucracy, dictatorship, one-party states, etc.) dare not embody a benevolence presumption, the argument for some reexamination of constitutional constraints or limits is surely in order. If all politics is flawed, what sort of constitutional constraints can be invented to keep government within tolerable bounds?

The Power to Take and the Power to Tax

I posed the question above: What is to prevent government from taking all that is of economic value from citizens? A preliminary answer to this question is provided in the set of basic rights laid out in the United States Constitution. Government cannot explicitly "take" property without "due process of law," and without appropriate compensation. There are, of course, notable exceptions, and there have been many violations of the taking prohibition that have been allowed to go unchallenged by the courts. Nonetheless, there do exist constitutional limitations on the taking power of government, and these limitations are acknowledged.

But what about the closely related power to tax? If government cannot arbitrarily "take" property from a person, it may accomplish roughly the same purposes by *taxing*. The essential legal difference between "taking" and "taxing" is that, in the latter, there is some acknowledged requirement of uniformity, generality, or nondiscrimination, at least within broad ranges. The difference can perhaps be illustrated by the existing constitutional limits on the government's power to tax in the United States. Neither the federal government, the state government, nor the local government can single out a particular person by name, by clan, by religion, by race, by sex, or by any other arbitrary designation, and levy on that person a particular tax. Such arbitrary treatment would be held unconstitutional. Grounds for differentiation in taxation must be nonarbitrary and must somehow be seen to emerge from reasonable argument. Hence government cannot tax away a substantial part of the economic value earned or owned by a person *unless it also treats like persons similarly.* The proviso for uniformity, generality, or equity is very important for my purposes in this lecture, because, properly understood, it points up a glaring omission in existing constitutional limits on governmental powers to exact economic resources from the citizenry. *There is no existing constitutional limit on the aggregate power of government to tax,* provided only that the uniformity-equity precepts are honored. That is to say, if government treats all persons in comparable situations similarly (say, all persons with incomes over $20,000), then it becomes constitutionally permissible for taxes to be levied confiscatorily. There would be nothing unconstitutional in a coercive tax measure that imposed 100 percent marginal rates on all incomes above some designated figure, say, $25,000 per year, with all incomes below this level totally exempted from taxation.

Before 1913 and the passage of the Sixteenth Amendment no such tax arrangement would have been constitutional, but even then there would have been no barrier against the levy of, say, a 90 percent rate of tax on all incomes. In either case, the point is clear. There are no constitutional constraints on government's power to raise revenues via taxes.

Only in the 1970s did it come to be recognized, grudgingly by some, that the failure to include such absolute limits on the power to tax reflects a rather obvious deficiency in the "law of the land," the United States Constitution, a deficiency that cries out for remedy. It is, of course, easy to understand why the American Founding Fathers did not include any such limit. They could scarcely imagine, two centuries ago, that the central government would come to be the dominant economic force that it has grown to be, and that the rate of growth in government's share in the economy, and hence in real taxes, would increase more than proportionately with the nongovernmental sector.

The Fiscal Challenge of the 1980s

The challenge of the 1980s lies in constitutional reform. Can our society reform itself by imposing fiscal constraints on government's power to tax, and, by inference, on its power to spend monies for governmental purposes, including transfers to those persons and groups who do not pay taxes but who hold rights to the franchise? Alongside such fiscal constraints that may be discussed, there is the accompanying set of issues involving possible constitutional limits on the obtrusive regulatory interferences of modern governmental agencies. But in the remainder of this lecture I shall concentrate attention on fiscal constraints, both because these are easier to analyze and because my own research in the last two years has been largely on the "fiscal constitution," broadly defined.[3]

3. See Geoffrey Brennan and James Buchanan, *The Power to Tax: Analytical Foundations of a Fiscal Constitution* (Cambridge: Cambridge University Press, 1980).

Is constitutional reform possible?

First of all, it is necessary to examine the conceptual possibility of such constitutional reform. Is it idle fancy to think that such fiscal limits might be incorporated in the Constitution? In 1977 many persons might have thought so, but in 1978 California voters did overwhelmingly approve Proposition 13. And further, in 1979 thirty state legislatures did pass resolutions calling on the Congress to authorize a constitutional convention to consider a balanced-budget amendment. Given sufficiently broad citizen-taxpayer support, existing and long-established procedures will allow genuine constitutional changes to be made.

Will the public back it?

Second, however, we come back to the electoral issue discussed above. If it is possible to generate broad-based citizen support for constitutional reform, why is it not possible that the ordinary checks of the democratic electoral process will produce similar results, thereby making resort to constitutional change unnecessary? In other words, if taxpayers-citizens want to turn things around, why won't they throw the big spenders out and replace them with politicians and parties that promise and deliver lower taxes and reduced rates of government growth?

I do not want to deny that some such effect has happened since 1978; politicians, of all persuasion, did get the Jarvis-Gann message. But to depend on electoral feedbacks to reverse the long-continuing trend of public sector expansion would, I think, be a dangerous delusion. In saying this, I am referring to what I consider to be fundamental biases in the taxing and spending process in American politics, biases that insure a continuation of pressures for increased real tax rates, almost independent of just what politicians or parties hold electoral offices. Several of these biases deserve further discussion.

Pressure groups

As our representative democracy works in the context of our legal-constitutional history, prospective beneficiaries of governmental spending programs bring concentrated pressures to bear on elected representatives.

There are no constitutional requirements that benefits from spending programs shall be uniformly or generally distributed; the spending side of the account differs categorically from the taxing side in this important respect. Arbitrary discrimination in providing governmental benefits is constitutionally permissible; hence, the beneficiaries of a program can be sufficiently concentrated to allow for carefully orchestrated efforts. Offsetting these pressure groups, the program costs will tend to be spread out among all taxpayers, no one group of which has much incentive to oppose a particular program. Congressmen respond, quite straightforwardly, to pressures from their constituents, and we should not then be surprised when we see them devote more interest to spending projects in their own districts than to the level of real tax rates imposed on taxpayers throughout the economy.

Once a spending program is established, once it gets across the commencement threshold, the specific beneficiaries become an even more intensive pressure group for maintenance and expansion of rates of outlay. It becomes almost impossible, politically, to cut off program benefits, once these have been commenced, and once recipients come to treat benefits as entitlements.

This basic bias is accentuated by the role of the bureaucracy, which introduces nondemocratic elements in the whole process. Spending programs are often invented by imaginative entrepreneurs in the bureaucracy, who then are led to organize the beneficiary groups and to manipulate the agenda for political action so as to insure program continuation and expansion.

NONTAX SOURCES OF REVENUE

The bias discussed above is inherent in the structure of democratic decision making so long as there is a basic asymmetry between the legal-constitutional norms applied to the taxing and the spending sides of the fiscal account. A quite different bias toward spending emerges from potential governmental access to nontax sources of revenue raising. Even with the decision bias noted above, spending rates would be lower if all programs were required to be tax-financed. Government, however, may have access to both debt issue and money creation as alternative revenue sources. These allow the government to spend without taxing, which is almost the ideal setting for elected politicians. By creating deficits, government is allowed to finance desired programs that provide benefits to potential voters without overt increases in rates of tax.

This bias is important only for governments that have money-creation power; without such power any public debt issued must be borrowed quite like ordinary borrowing. Even for central governments, however, the deficit-spending bias has become important only in the post-Keynesian era, during which Keynesian economics has offered politicians academic-intellectual excuses for pursuing their own interests. Keynesian teachings provided an apologia for deficit creation, producing rapidly increasing public debt accompanied by accelerating inflation generated by use of the printing press.[4] Inflation, in its own turn, increased real rates of taxes on incomes, which, in turn, allowed revenues to be available for increased real rates of governmental outlay. Politicians have been allowed to play out their roles in an ideal setting, to spend without taxing; and, even more surprising in many respects, they have been largely successful in blaming the predictable inflation on the evil machinations of businessmen and labor leaders. The response of the public to the inflation of the 1970s scarcely provides much ground for expecting reforms in this pattern by way of ordinary electoral (i.e., nonconstitutional) channels.

INFLATION EXPECTATIONS

Inflation, like particularized spending programs, cannot readily be "turned off" once inflationary expectations come to be incorporated in contracts. In short-run terms, there is a tradeoff between any reduction in the rate of inflation and economic prosperity. To try to reduce an inflation rate of 15 percent to, say, 10 percent, after the 15 percent rate has come to be expected or anticipated, exerts economic effects that are equivalent to the imposition of a 5 percent deflation on an economy adjusted to monetary stability. Politically it becomes almost impossible for a government to get a continuing inflation under control without major disruption, despite the government's direct role and responsibility in creating the inflation in the first place. There is a bias toward inflationary financing almost independent of the form of

---

4. For an elaboration of this argument, see James M. Buchanan and Richard E. Wagner, *Democracy in Deficit: The Political Legacy of Lord Keynes* (New York: Academic Press, 1977).

government itself, whether this be pure democracy, representative democracy, or dictatorship.

This deficit spending–inflation bias, along with the structural bias discussed earlier, suggests that genuine reform must be sought *constitutionally* rather than *electorally*. That is to say, politicians who find themselves in responsible official positions will almost necessarily find it impossible to impose fiscal constraints, regardless of ideological persuasion. If fiscal constraints on government are to be imposed at all, there must be change in the set of things governments are allowed to do; there must be change in the basic rules, the Constitution.

Procedural and Quantitative Constraints

If we acknowledge that additional fiscal and monetary constraints on government are desired and, further, that these constraints must be implemented constitutionally, we are still confronted with issues concerning specific forms of limits.

MORE THAN A SIMPLE MAJORITY

There are two broad types. The first includes what I have called *procedural* constraints. By these, I refer to possible constitutional changes in the rules for making decisions politically. If simple majority voting rules in legislatures, in Congress, are predicted to generate undesired results on the side of an excessive rate of growth in real tax and spending rates, these rules may be changed so as to require majorities larger than simple majorities for approval of any fiscal measure. Alan Greenspan has proposed that all spending authorizations require two-thirds majorities in each house of Congress. One of the important, and sometimes overlooked, parts of California's Proposition 13 is the requirement that new taxes must have the approval of two-thirds majorities in the state legislature.

LINKAGE OF TAXING AND SPENDING

A somewhat less dramatic procedural change would be one that required more direct linkage between taxing and spending decisions. Legislatures might be required to keep their own accounts in better balance, and to indicate just how revenues sufficient to finance each item of spending are to be raised before the item of spending is approved. This requirement may, but need not, take the form of imposing a balanced-budget constraint, requiring that anticipated tax revenues match anticipated outlays, essentially closing off the debt and money-creation options as revenue-raising devices. The balanced-budget proposal, as a constitutional amendment, was demonstrated in 1979 to have widespread appeal to the public generally. If finally incorporated as an explicit amendment to the United States Constitution, it might do much toward eliminating the proclivity of government toward excessive rates of growth in spending and close up, so to speak, the deficiency on the fiscal constitution noted earlier.[5]

QUANTITATIVE LIMITS ON TAXING AND SPENDING

Additional procedural constraints could be mentioned, but my purpose here is not to list all potential constitutional changes. The general set of procedural constraints should, however, be compared with what I have called *quantitative* constraints, perhaps best exemplified by the proposed constitutional amendment that would relate the rate of growth in federal outlays directly to the rate of growth in national product, an amendment widely discussed in 1979. Variants on this sort of constraint have been introduced in several state constitutions. An additional example of a quantitative constraint is Proposition 13's explicit limit on the rate of tax on real property in California. The quantitative constraints have the advantage of being more specific than the procedural ones, but, like the other side of this same coin, they reduce the flexibility of governmental response to uncertain circumstances somewhat more than procedural requirements.

---

5. Although it is legislative rather than constitutional, the Budget Reform Act of 1974 represents an attempt by Congress to introduce procedural changes in its own fiscal decision processes so as to remove acknowledged biases toward excessive spending. This act does not require budget balance, but, by means of the Budget Resolutions, it does require Congress to consider simultaneously both sides of the budget account. The act's history is too short to allow for much evaluation of its effect. And, of course, its legislative basis means that any Congress could disregard its precepts.

A Fiscal-Monetary Constitution

It should be evident that I could go on to elaborate this discussion of alternative proposals for elements of a fiscal constitution at some length. But this elaboration would hardly be appropriate in the more general discussion of constitutional limits that I have undertaken in this lecture. Let me summarize my previous discussion in a set of statements. I have argued that government can be constitutionally constrained. I have argued that there is a flaw in our existing Constitution that allows for excessive rates of growth in real taxes, real public spending, and in the relative size of the governmental sector. I have argued that observed rates of growth in governmental outlays can be scientifically adjudged to be excessive due to biases in the processes of democratic decision making, as these are legally defined in the United States. Finally, I have argued that there are essentially two separate ways of imposing desired limits to deal with the problem discussed.

I do not, however, want to leave my discussion at such a level of generality. I think that the arguments I have advanced should clearly demonstrate the desirability of changes in our Constitution. This much may be granted, however, without necessary agreement on the specific proposals to be adopted.

In order to end on a positive note, I want to lay out my own set of proposals for constitutional change. Both at the level of academic scholarship and in testimony before committees of federal and state legislatures, I have supported the proposed constitutional amendment that would require the federal government to balance its budget accounts. I have suggested that a four-year phase-in period might be needed to avoid sudden and unanticipated shifts in rates of real taxes and spending. Accompanying this budget-balance amendment, I should also support the adoption of a monetary growth rule. Such a rule would require that the Federal Reserve authorities increase the supply of base money in the economy between 3 and 5 percent annually, with specified penalties for violations of these targets. Note that, with a budget-balance rule in place, there would be much less political pressure on the monetary authorities to exceed defined money-growth targets. The two rules suggested, the fiscal and the monetary, are closely complementary.

The enactment of such constitutional amendments would have major symbolic value, over and beyond the directly constraining effects that are incorporated in them. The enactment of such changes would modify dramatically both domestic and foreign expectations about the future activities of American governments in the third century of our constitutional history. My personally idealized scenario calls for the "constitutional dialogue," which did genuinely commence in the late 1970s, to accelerate in the early 1980s, so much so that the 1980s will become the "decade of constitutional reexamination and reevaluation." The scenario then calls for these efforts to be crowned with success well before we celebrate the bicentennial of the Constitution itself, a celebration that could then take place in confidence and hope.

Contractarian Political Economy
and Constitutional Interpretation

At the American Economic Association meetings in 1974, I presented a paper entitled "A Contractarian Paradigm for Applying Economic Theory."[1] In that paper, along with others,[2] I argued that our subject matter is centrally a "science of exchange" or a "science of contract," and that the exchange paradigm should take precedence over the maximizing paradigm. This shift in the focus of positive inquiry carries normative implications. Conceptions such as aggregate efficiency in the allocation of resources become, at best, examples of functionalist error, along with the more explicitly normative variants of the social welfare function. The contractarian or catallactic approach to economic interaction suggests that systems or subsystems be evaluated in terms of the comparative ease or facility with which voluntary exchanges, contracts, or trades may be arranged between and among members of the community. Normative judgments take the form of statements that array "better" and "worse" *processes* (rules, laws, institutions) within which exchanges are allowed to take place. These judgments are categorically distinct from those that array and evaluate results or outcomes.

This shift in normative political economy has implications for the issues of constitutional interpretation debated by legal scholars and philosophers. These issues involve disputes along several related and intersecting dimen-

From *AEA Papers and Proceedings* 78 (May 1988): 135–39. Reprinted by permission of the publisher.

1. James M. Buchanan, "A Contractarian Perspective for Applying Economic Theory," *American Economic Review Papers and Proceedings* 65 (May 1975): 225–30.

2. See my *What Should Economists Do?* (Indianapolis: Liberty Fund, 1979).

sions: between judicial activism and nonactivism; between judicial deference to legislative authority and judicial independence; between strict constructivism and pragmatism; between original intent and legal environmentalism; between teleological and deontological conceptions of law. My purpose here is to discuss some of these contractarian implications for constitutional interpretation. This is a limited purpose, and I advance no direct and extended argument either on general philosophical issues, or on points of debate in particular legal settings. Any identifiable contribution of the contractarian political economist must emerge from the differentially abstracted order that his perspective imposes on social reality.

Section I covers the familiar distinction between an individualistic and a communitarian starting point. The implication for legal interpretation of constitutional rules is almost self-evident. In Section II, I again go over analysis, developed elsewhere, that extends the catallactic paradigm from the economy to the political order, and, in particular, to the design, selection, and enforcement of constitutional rules.[3] Section III examines the implications for judicial interpretation of the political constitution, and, in particular, the implications for the debate between strict constructivism and pragmatism and between original intent and legal environmentalism. In Section IV, the argument is extended to the contractarian's stance in interpretative confrontation with rules that cannot find a logic in any contractarian ideal.

I. Normative Individualism

The primary question in any contractarian perspective on social order is the definition of the units that potentially engage in exchange. The economists' response here is straightforward; individuals enter into exchange, one with another, either to make direct trades of goods and services, or to create organizations (firms, clubs, states, associations) that, in turn, make such trades on their behalf. If the community exists as an organic entity in some sense prior to and independent of its individual members, and, further, if this community has its own supra-individualistic goals, the exchange perspective clearly breaks down. With whom could the inclusive community, as such, make exchanges?

3. James M. Buchanan and Gordon Tullock, *The Calculus of Consent* (Ann Arbor: University of Michigan Press, 1962).

If, however, the organic or communitarian paradigm is rejected in favor of an individualistic one, implications emerge that embody both methodological and normative content. If individuals, or organizations of individuals, are the units that enter into exchanges, the values or interests of individuals are the only values that matter for the quite simple reason that these are the only values that exist. Such terms as "national goals," "national interest," and "social objectives" are confusing at best. Individuals in a community may, of course, share values in common, and they may agree widely on specific goals or objectives for policy directions to be taken by their political organization. But this very organization, like others, exists only for the purpose of furthering individual values and interests.

This summary of the normative individualist's position is sufficient to suggest the direct implications for constitutional interpretation. The "good society" is that which best furthers the interests of its individual members, as expressed by these members, rather than that society that best furthers some independently defined criterion for the "good." The basic "rules of the game," the law, cannot be conceived as a means through which the community is shifted toward that which judges or intellectuals deem to be good. Any teleological conception of the law, and of the constitution and of the role of the judiciary, is simply out of bounds under any contractarian or exchange conceptualization of social order.

II. Political Exchange

If we adhere strictly to the individualistic benchmark, there can be no fundamental distinction between economics and politics or, more generally, between the economy and the polity. The state, as any other collective organization, is created by individuals, and the state acts on behalf of individuals. Politics, in this individualistic framework, becomes a complex exchange process in which individuals seek to accomplish purposes collectively that they cannot accomplish noncollectively or privately in any tolerably efficient manner. The catallactic perspective on simple exchange of economic goods merges into the contractarian perspective on politics and political order.

But how can ordinary politics as we observe it possibly be modeled as a complex exchange process in which individuals *voluntarily* participate, at least in any sense at all analogous to their participation in markets? Any attempt to extend the exchange perspective to politics seems absurd on its face, since we observe politics to be characterized by conflict rather than cooperation, best modeled as a game that is zero or negative sum. Coercion rather than voluntary participation seems to be the primary relationship embodied in politics. If, however, this coercion-conflict element is elevated to center stage, how can the state ever be legitimized or justified to the individual?

A way out of the apparent paradox is provided if we shift attention from ordinary politics, which is almost necessarily majoritarian, or, more generally, nonconsensual in its operation, to constitutional politics, which may at least approach consensual agreement, at least in its idealization. Individuals may generally agree upon the rules of the game within which ordinary politics takes place, and these agreed-on rules may allow for predicted net gainers and net losers in particularized political choices. The question of legitimacy or justification shifts directly to the rules, to the constitutional structure, which must remain categorically distinct from the operations of ordinary politics, which is constrained by the rules. As noted earlier, the argument does have direct implications for judicial interpretation. The most critical aspect of these implications stems from the categorical separation itself. There is a critically important functional role for judicial review. The "state-as-umpire" function is properly assigned to a branch of the political order that is separated from those branches that operate within the rules. Further, this function is conceptually as well as operationally different from ordinary politics. The judiciary, in its umpire role, must take a truth-judgment approach, an approach that is inappropriate in the workings of ordinary politics. The judiciary must determine whether or not the rules have been violated, whether or not a rule exists, whether or not a rule applies to this or that case. These are truth judgments. It becomes absurd to introduce arguments based on such things as "compromises among interests" or "proper representation of interests" in the whole judicial exercise.

III. Changes in Rules

In an earlier paper,[4] I classified the inclusive political order in terms of three separate functions. The first involves the enforcement of the rules that exist.

4. "Contractarianism and Democracy," in *Liberty, Market and State* (New York: New York University Press, 1986), 240–47.

This embodies the role for judicial review that I have just discussed. The second involves the carrying out of ordinary politics within the rules that exist. This includes taxing, spending, and other activities within the broad rubric summarized as the financing and supply of public goods and services. The third function involves changes in the rules themselves, or constitutional reform. I have argued above that the judiciary, as an independent branch of the political order, properly operates within the first of these three functions. The legislative body, reflecting the interplay of groups' interests, properly operates within the second of these functions. The third function, that of changing the rules, is inappropriate both for the judiciary and for the legislative branch. The rules are changed only through the well-defined procedures for constitutional amendment, procedures that are explicitly more inclusive than ordinary legislation or judicial review. A straightforward implication of the contractarian complex exchange perspective on political order is that the judiciary oversteps its proper limits when it takes on the task of changing the basic rules within which the socioeconomic-legal game is played.

If the judicial function is, and must be, restricted to interpretation of the rules that exist, specific guidelines for judges and courts charged with constitutional interpretation necessarily emerge. Parallel to this restriction on the scope of the judicial role is that placed on the legislative role. The legislature also oversteps its proper limits when it moves beyond existing boundaries and itself makes changes in the constitutional order. From this it follows directly that the judiciary should not be deferential to legislative decisions when these have the effect of modifying the basic rules. In this respect, an activist, rather than a nonactivist, and deferential court is required.

However, because the judicial role is itself limited to interpreting rules that exist, and cannot go beyond this, something akin to strict constructivism seems to be implied here. But the important point to be made is that the court should act as strict constructivist with respect to the constitutional rules that exist in the status quo when the case at issue is confronted. This status quo may, but need not, reflect generally accepted rules that are readily derivative from the original intent of those who designed and emplaced the written documents. The rules reflecting original intent may have been gradually modified by the historical case record to the point where there seems little connection with the rules that describe the status quo.

The indeterminacy in defining the status quo is unsatisfactory to many strict constructivists. How can a court define the rules that exist without direct resort to something like original intent? It is here that the court needs to rely on something akin to the modern economists' notion of rational expectations. Those rules in existence are those that best describe the set of individuals' expectations about the boundaries of political authority when the activities in question were carried out. An analogy from ordinary games may be helpful here. Suppose that the rule book describing the activities that may take place within a game, say, basketball, has remained unchanged for a number of years. But as the game has evolved, within the changing technology and changing skill levels of players, referees have gradually and incrementally modified the effective rules, for example, on walking with the ball. A new referee fulfills his role properly when he tries to enforce the rules that exist; he violates his assigned task when he tries to go back and enforce strictly the rules-as-written in the outdated rule book.

IV. "Bad" Rules

The argument to this point is noncontroversial in the sense that the suggested implications for judicial interpretation of the constitution follow straightforwardly from acceptance of the individualistic-contractarian perspective on political order. A more debatable set of issues arises as we focus attention on the stance of the judge, who fully shares the contractarian perspective, who is faced with the status quo existence of rules that reflect neither original intent nor plausibly justifiable extensions of such intent, and that, further, could never have passed any conceivable contractarian consensus test for legitimacy, even in some conceptual sense. That is to say, there may exist rules which are contained within the expectational set of both citizens and ordinary politicians, that have been imposed nonconsensually. Should the contractarian judge move beyond mere enforcement of the status quo in some attempt to dismantle "bad" law?

Much modern economic regulation (for example, minimum wage laws, rent control laws) presumably fits this category. Should the contractarian constitutionalist deem such laws to be nonconstitutional, despite the fact that prior courts have made judgments to the contrary? My argument suggests that if the prior judicial interpretations have been in place sufficiently long for these interpretations to have formed part of the rational expectations of both the citizenry and the acting political agents, it would not be appropriate for the contractarian judge to seek actively to change the rules. In this respect, my argument places me squarely on the Scalia side of the Scalia-Epstein debate.[5] Retrospectively, the court must defer to the status quo set of rules that exist, which may well embody prior judicial approval for legislation (including judicial legislation) that unconstitutionally shifted the boundaries of the consensual order. To move beyond such deference to the status quo and to assume an activist role in deconstruction, as guided by some ideal, even if this ideal be contractarian, opens up judicial review to precisely those dangers of abuse that Scalia warns against.

On the other hand, my argument suggests that the contractarian judge should be quite jealous in his protection of the existing rules from legislation and judicial intrusion that fails the consensual test. In a prospective or *ex ante* sense, my argument places me on the Epstein side of the debate with Scalia. Deference to legislative authority, per se, cannot be justifiably derived from the three-stage contractarian model of political order outlined.

Scalia argues that the courts should remain passive as legislatures act to constrain economic liberties. Epstein argues that courts should act to protect economic liberties, whether the legislation constraining such liberties has long existed and been upheld by prior court judgments or whether such legislation is recent or newly proposed. Neither Scalia nor Epstein makes the temporal cut that my argument implies. The contractarian position, as I interpret it, requires that the rules that exist, no matter how these might have come into being, be treated as relatively absolute absolutes and enforced by the courts until and unless these rules are changed by defined procedures for change.

My position does depend critically on some ability to define meaningfully just what the set of status quo rules is, an ability that is not centrally important to either Scalia or Epstein. And in this respect I return to the importance of the expectational setting, to which courts should remain highly sensitive. Any legislatively orchestrated change that upsets the legitimately held expec-

---

5. Antonin Scalia, "Economic Affairs as Human Affairs," in James Dorn and Henry Manne, eds., *Economic Liberties and the Judiciary* (Fairfax: George Mason University Press, 1987), 31–37; Richard Epstein, "Judicial Power: Reckoning on Two Kinds of Error," in Dorn and Manne, *Economic Liberties,* 39–46.

tations of citizens should be interpreted as a change in the constitutional structure, and, as such, should be prevented by the courts.

Consider the much discussed taking of property for public purpose. Modern courts have allowed legislatures authority to modify values of privately owned property within very broad public purpose limits. But there do remain limits, and wholly arbitrary intrusion would, presumably, be rejected even by modern courts. My position suggests that courts carefully draw such limits at the set of expectations held in the status quo, as properly measured.

In the three-stage functional classification imposed on political order by the contractarian perspective, the role for the judiciary is clear. The function of the judiciary is protection of that which is, which remains perhaps the most critical function for the maintenance of order and stability. The judicial branch properly serves a stabilizing rather than a reformist or restorationist role. The courts should protect what is rather than try to promote what might be, or try to restore what might have been.

Justification of the Compound Republic

The *Calculus* in Retrospect

Elsewhere I have stated that the public choice perspective combines two distinct elements: the extension of the economist's model of utility-maximizing behavior to political choice and the conceptualization of "politics as exchange."[1] *The Calculus of Consent*[2] was the first book that integrated these two elements into a coherent, logical structure. It will be useful here to compare and contrast the argument developed in the *Calculus* to those that were present in the nascent public choice analysis of the time as well as in the then-conventional wisdom in political science.

The Model of Utility Maximization

Kenneth Arrow published his seminal *Social Choice and Individual Values* in 1951; Duncan Black's *Theory of Committees and Elections* appeared in 1958, following earlier papers published in the late 1940s and early 1950s; and Anthony Downs published *An Economic Theory of Democracy* in 1957.[3] These three writers were all economists, as was Joseph Schumpeter whose *Capital-*

From *Cato Journal* 7 (Fall 1987): 305–12. Reprinted by permission of the publisher.

1. James M. Buchanan, "The Public Choice Perspective," *Economia delle scelte pubbliche* 1 (January 1983): 7–15.

2. James M. Buchanan and Gordon Tullock, *The Calculus of Consent* (Ann Arbor: University of Michigan Press, 1962).

3. Kenneth J. Arrow, *Social Choice and Individual Values* (New York: Wiley, 1951); Duncan Black, *Theory of Committees and Elections* (Cambridge: Cambridge University Press, 1958); Anthony Downs, *An Economic Theory of Democracy* (New York: Harper, 1957).

ism, Socialism, and Democracy contained precursory, if widely neglected, parallels to the inquiries that followed.[4] In each case, analysis was grounded on the economist's model of utility maximization. Indeed, in the Arrow, Black, and later social choice constructions, the individual is viewed as ranking his preferences over alternative social states. Downs's work differs from the social choice strand of inquiry in that he modeled the behavior of political parties analogously to that of profit-seeking firms in a competitive market environment; but ultimately, the construction is also based on the utility-maximizing behavior of office-seeking politicians and interest-seeking voting constituents.

The missing element in these constructions is any justificatory argument for democratic process that embodies individualistic norms for evaluation. Arrow and Black seemed to place stability and consistency in "social choice" above any consideration of the desirability of correspondence between individual values and collective outcomes. Downs seemed to be interested in the predictions of the results of majoritarian political processes independent of overriding the desires of persons in minority preference positions. Arrow dramatically proved that consistent sets of individual orderings need not generate consistent social or collective results under any rule; but he totally neglected any normative reference to the possible coercion of minority preferences or interests in any non-unanimous rule structure.[5]

The Justificatory Basis for Collective Action

These works left us with a dangling question: Why should an individual enter into a collective? The authors of these works presumed, without inquiry, that the individual was locked into membership in a political community and that the range and scope of the collective's activities were beyond the control of the individual and, by inference, beyond the boundaries of analysis amenable to any individualistic calculus. The *Calculus* differed from the precur-

---

4. Joseph Schumpeter, *Capitalism, Socialism, and Democracy* (New York: Harper and Row, 1942).

5. Arrow's emphasis on stability and consistency in *collective* results to the neglect of *individual* interests was the primary target of my own criticism. See James M. Buchanan, "Social Choice, Democracy, and Free Markets," *Journal of Political Economy* 62 (April 1954): 114–23.

sory works in one fundamental respect, namely, it embodied *justificatory* argument. The *Calculus* sought to outline, at least in very general terms, the conditions that must be present for the individual to find it advantageous to enter into a political entity with constitutionally delineated ranges of activity or to acquiesce in membership in a historically existent polity.

The intellectual-analytical vacuum was much more apparent in relation to the early extensions of economic methodology to the political process than it seemed in then-conventional political science inquiry. Precisely because Black, Arrow, and Downs explicitly incorporated individual utility maximization in their analyses, possible differences among persons in preference orderings over political alternatives emerged as a central issue. In a model with identical preferences, the problems addressed by Arrow, Black, and Downs do not directly arise. Once preferences over political choice options are presumed to differ, however, it is but a natural extension to consider the choice among political regimes.

Normative political science in the 1950s offered a dramatically different ideational environment. Influenced in part by Hegelian-inspired idealism, the interest of the individual was treated as being embodied in the state and in politics as process. Even for many of those who could scarcely be classified as falling within the Hegelian tradition, politics was still conceived as a search for truth and goodness, a search from which a uniquely determinate "best" result (for *everyone*) emerges. One important strand of positive political analysis, based largely on the work of Arthur Bentley,[6] focused on conflicts among differing interests but in turn tended to neglect the cooperative elements that are necessary to justify playing the game at all.

If we remain within the presuppositions of methodological individualism, the state or the polity must ultimately be justified in terms of its potential for satisfying individuals' desires, whatever these might be. The state is necessarily an artifact, an instrument that has evolved or is designed for the purpose of meeting individual needs that cannot be readily satisfied under alternative arrangements. In this sense, the great game of politics must be a positive-sum game. If this fact is recognized while also acknowledging the potential for conflict among differing individual interests, the basic exchange model of

6. Arthur Bentley, *The Process of Government* (1908; Bloomington: Principia Press, 1935).

the economist is immediately suggested. In this elementary model, traders enter the interaction process with distributionally conflicting interests but in a setting that offers mutuality of gain from cooperation.

Wicksell's Unanimity Criterion

This second element in the inclusive public choice perspective, that of "politics as exchange," is necessary to make any justificatory argument. In adding this element to the utility-maximizing models for individual choice behavior in politics, Gordon Tullock and I were directly influenced by the great work of Knut Wicksell,[7] the primary precursor of my own efforts in public choice and in political economy generally. Along with a few of his European colleagues, Wicksell sought to extend the range of economic analysis of resource use to the public or governmental sector. He sought a criterion for efficiency in the state or collective use of resources that was comparable to the criterion that had been formally specified for the use of resources in the market sector of the economy. In determining the value of the collective use of a resource, Wicksell adhered to the basic individualistic postulate of market exchange: individuals, who both enjoy the benefits of state-financed services and pay the costs in sacrificed privately supplied goods, are the only legitimate judge of their own well-being. From this individualistic presupposition, there emerged the Wicksellian unanimity criterion—if any proposed public or governmental outlay is valued more highly than the alternative market or private product of the resources, there must exist a tax-sharing scheme that all citizens will agree upon. If there is no tax-sharing scheme that will secure unanimous approval, the proposed outlay fails the test. Note that this basic Wicksellian proposition incorporates the epistemological humility of revealed preference as well as the Pareto criterion for evaluation, both of which emerged as independently developed ideas later.

In proposing a departure from the established majority voting rule in legislative assemblies, Wicksell was suggesting a change in the effective political constitution, the set of constraints within which political choices are made. He shifted the ground for discourse. Rather than discuss the relative efficiency of policy options under an unchanging rules structure, with little or

---

7. Knut Wicksell, *Finanztheoretische Untersuchungen* (Jena: Gustav Fischer, 1896).

no regard given either to what efficiency means or for any prospect for the desired option being chosen, Wicksell sought to open up the structure of decision rules as a variable that might be chosen instrumentally for the purpose of ensuring that collective action meet a meaningfully defined efficiency norm. Wicksell, of course, recognized that the strict requirement for unanimity would offer incentives for strategic behavior to all participants and that some relaxation of this requirement might be necessary for practicable operation. By reducing the requirement to, say, five-sixths of the voting members of the assembly, the incentives for strategic behavior are dramatically reduced and there is insurance against most, if not all, inefficient outlay.

Wicksell, however, did not move beyond the development of criteria for evaluating policy alternatives one at a time. He shifted attention to a change in the decision rules, from simple majority voting toward unanimity, to ensure against collective approval of projects that do not yield benefits equal to or in excess of costs, *on any ordinary project*.[8] Wicksell did not extend his analysis to the operation of specific decision rules over a whole sequence of time periods or separate categories of outlay, which might have allowed for less restrictive criteria for single projects.

Extension of the Wicksellian Criterion to Constitutional Choice

In the *Calculus,* Tullock and I made this extension. We were directly influenced by discussions with our colleague Rutledge Vining at the University of Virginia, who hammered home the argument that political choices are among alternative rules, institutions, and arrangements which generate patterns of results that are at least partly stochastic. We should then evaluate the working of any rule not in terms of its results in a particularized choice situation, but in terms of its results over a whole sequence of separate "plays," separated both intercategorically and intertemporally. Vining's insistence on the relevance of the analogy with the selection of the rules for ordinary games was part of the intellectual environment in Charlottesville, and the

---

8. Wicksell exempted categories of outlay that were considered to be irrevocable commitments, for example, interest on public debt.

shift of the Wicksellian criterion from single projects to rules seemed a "natural" one for us to take.

In the confined Wicksellian choice setting, an individual, behaving nonstrategically, will vote to approve a proposed collective outlay if he anticipates that the benefits he secures will exceed the tax costs. He will oppose all proposals that fail this test. If, however, the individual is placed in a genuine *constitutional* choice setting, where the alternatives are differing decision rules under which a whole sequence of particular proposals will be considered, he will evaluate the predicted working properties of rules over the whole anticipated sequence. If, on balance, the operation of a defined rule is expected to yield net benefits over the sequence, the individual may vote to approve the rule, even if he predicts that he must personally be subjected to loss or damage in some particular "plays" of the political game.

By shifting the applicability of the unanimity or consensus criterion from the level of particular proposals to the level of rules—to constitutional rather than post-constitutional or in-period choices—we were able to allow for the possibility that preferred and agreed-on decision rules might embody sizable departures from the unanimity limit, including simple majority voting in some cases and even less than majority voting in others. The constitutional calculus suggests that both the costs of reaching decisions under different rules and the importance of the decisions are relevant. And because both of these elements vary, the preferred rule will not be uniform over all ranges of potential political action.

The construction seemed to offer justificatory argument for something akin to the complex political structure that James Madison had in mind, much of which finds itself embedded in the constitutional framework approved by the Founding Fathers. There is a justification for the compound republic, for constitutional democracy, that can be grounded in individual utility maximization; but the general argument does not allow the elevation of majority rule to dominating status. This rule, whether in the entire electorate or in the legislative assembly, takes its place alongside other rules, some of which may be more and others less inclusive.

At the constitutional stage of choice among rules, our argument conceptually requires unanimous agreement among all parties. In this sense, we were simply advancing the Wicksell-Pareto criterion one stage upward in the choice-making hierarchy. As we suggested, however, agreement on rules is much more likely to emerge than agreement on policy alternatives within rules, because of the difficulties in identifying precisely the individual's economic interests in the first setting. The rule to be chosen is expected to remain in existence over a whole sequence of time periods and possibly over a wide set of separate in-period choices. How can the individual at the stage of trying to select among rules identify his own narrowly defined self-interest? How can he predict which rule will maximize his own net wealth? He is necessarily forced to choose from behind a dark "veil of uncertainty." In such a situation, utility maximization dictates that generalized criteria, such as fairness, equity, or justice, enter the calculus rather than the more specific arguments, such as net income or wealth.

This construction enabled us analytically to bridge, at least in part, the gap between narrowly defined individual self-interest and an individually generated definition of what could be called the general interest. In this construction, our efforts were quite close to those of John Rawls, which culminated in his seminal book, *A Theory of Justice*.[9] Early papers published in the late 1950s had adumbrated the essential parts of the Rawlsian construction; and while our own construction was independently developed, we were familiar with Rawls's parallel efforts.[10]

Our analysis differed from that of Rawls, however, in the important respect that we made no attempt to generate specific predictions as to what might emerge from the prospective agreement among the contractors who choose rules from behind the veil of uncertainty. Our construction suggested that no single decision rule was likely to be chosen for general applicability over the whole range of political action. We used the construction to eliminate some sets of outcomes rather than to specify those sets that would be selected. By contrast, Rawls was led (we think, misled) to attempt to use the veil-of-ignorance construction to make specific predictions. He suggested that his two principles of justice would uniquely emerge from the preconstitutional stage of contractual agreement.

9. John Rawls, *A Theory of Justice* (Cambridge: Harvard University Press, 1971).
10. We were not familiar at all with the construction of John Harsanyi, which had appeared in the mid-1950s, but with quite a different normative purpose. See John Harsanyi, "Cardinal Welfare, Individualistic Ethics, and Interpersonal Comparisons of Utility," *Journal of Political Economy* 63 (August 1955): 309–21.

The Social Contract Tradition

When constitutional-stage politics is conceptualized as exchange among utility-maximizing individuals, we are obliged to classify ourselves as working within the social contract tradition in political philosophy. Precursors of the *Calculus* are found in the works of the classical social contract theorists rather than in the works of the idealists or the realists. What has been and remains surprising to me has been the reluctance or inability of social scientists, philosophers, and especially economists to understand and appreciate the relationships between the institutions of voluntary exchange, the choice among constitutional rules, and the operations of ordinary politics within such rules. James Madison clearly had such an understanding, which we tried to articulate in modern analytical language a quarter-century ago. There has been some shift toward recovery of the Madisonian wisdom in both public and scholarly attitudes over two and one-half decades. Perhaps the *Calculus* contributed marginally to this change. But both "politics as pure conflict" and "politics as the quest for truth and light" continue as dominant models shaping both public and "scientific" views on collective action.

PART TWO

The Method of Constitutional Economics

A Contractarian Paradigm for Applying Economic Theory

The object for economists' research is "the economy," which is, by definition, a *social organization,* an interaction among separate choosing entities. I return deliberately to this element in our primer, because I think that it has been too often overlooked. By direct implication, the ultimate object of our study is not itself a choosing, maximizing entity. "The economy" does not maximize, and we may substitute "the polity" here without change in my emphasis. No one could quarrel with these simplistic statements. The inference must be, however, that there exists no one person, no single chooser, who maximizes *for* the economy, *for* the polity. To impose a maximizing construction on the models that are designed to be helpful in policy is to insure sterility in results.

Where did economics, as a discipline, take the wrong turn? My own suggestion is that Lionel Robbins marks a turning point.[1] His book defined "the economic problem" as the location of maxima and minima. Almost simultaneously with this, the Edward H. Chamberlin and Joan Robinson books marked a turning inward, so to speak, a shift toward the maximizing problem of a specific decision-making entity.[2] The economics of the firm was born, to be followed by the Hicksian elaboration of the economics of consumer choice.[3] Paul Samuelson put this all together in his *Foundations of Eco-*

From *American Economic Review* 65 (May 1975): 225–30. Reprinted by permission of the publisher.

The author is indebted to Amoz Kats and Gordon Tullock for helpful comments.

1. L. Robbins, *An Essay on the Nature and Significance of Economic Science* (London, 1932).

2. E. H. Chamberlin, *The Theory of Monopolistic Competition* (Cambridge, Mass., 1932); J. Robinson, *Economics of Imperfect Competition* (London, 1933).

3. J. R. Hicks, *Value and Capital* (London, 1939).

nomic Analysis.[4] Importantly, he extended the maximizing construction to welfare economics, extolling the virtues of A. Bergson's social welfare function as the tool through which such extension was made possible.[5] For a quarter of a century, we have witnessed many variations on this theme, with economists hither and yon maximizing objective functions subject to specific constraints.

I should not imply that the maximizing models have held monolithic dominance. The institutional economists, and their successors, have continued their sometimes inarticulate critique of economic theory. Frank Knight, and some of his students, continued to lay stress on the social-organization aspects of the discipline. Game theory, in its solution rather than its strategy search, offered partial redirection of emphasis. More importantly for my purposes, public choice theory emerged as the positive theory of politics, a theory that necessarily treats individual decision takers as participants in a complex interaction that generates political outcomes.

But let me return to mainstream efforts of economists in the years since World War II. I have no quarrel with the elaborations and refinements of the maximizing models for individual and firm behavior, although I have argued that many of these contributions belong, appropriately, to home economics or to business administration rather than to political economy. My strictures are directed exclusively at the extension of this basic maximizing paradigm to social organization where it does not belong. This is the bridge which economists should never have crossed, and which has created major intellectual confusion. "That which emerges" from the trading or exchange process, conceived in its narrowest or its broadest terms, is not the solution to a maximizing problem, despite the presence of scarce resources and the conflict among ends. "That which emerges" is "that which emerges" and that is that.

Return to game theory for analogy. The solution to a game with defined rules is not a maximum, and an external observer of the game would not attempt to seek improvements by operating directly on solutions. He would, instead, look at the prospects for changing the rules, and observed solutions would be information inputs in his evaluation of the game. Solutions are not

4. P. A. Samuelson, *Foundations of Economic Analysis* (Cambridge, Mass., 1947).
5. A. Bergson, "A Reformulation of Certain Aspects of Welfare Economics," *Quarterly Journal of Economics* 52 (1938): 310–34.

directly "chosen" by a welfare function that embodies the preferences of the players, and solutions are not themselves ordered in terms of such a function. In game theory, the attempt to force such a construction would appear (and be) absurd. Yet this seems to me to be precisely what economists try to do within their analogous domain. Game theorists would indeed be surprised if someone should find that solutions could, in fact, be ordered in any manner that was consistent with the values of individual players. And they would not be profoundly shocked, to say the least, if someone should prove that such an ordering could not be made. Yet is this not what most economists experienced when Kenneth Arrow published his famous impossibility theorem in 1951?[6]

My own initial reaction to Arrow's work was, and remains, one of non-surprise.[7] Who would have expected any social process to yield a consistent ordering of results? Only economists who had made the critical methodological error of crossing the bridge from individual to social maximization without having recognized what they were doing would have experienced intellectual-ideological disappointment.

There is no need to limit discussion to Arrow's theorem, although I shall return to this. Economists crossed the bridge from individual to social maximization because they wanted to be able to say something about policy alternatives. They desperately needed some instrument which would allow them to play the social engineer even if they eschewed the explicit intrusion of their own values in the process.[8] With the social welfare function construction, they could then talk as if their policy statements were operationally meaningful, and this ability provided them with a certain inner satisfaction. They have remained unwilling to utilize the Pareto criterion as a mere classification scheme, which Ragnar Frisch had advised them to do,[9] and they have not followed my own suggestion about shifting the application of the

6. K. Arrow, *Social Choice and Individual Values* (New York, 1951).

7. J. M. Buchanan, "Social Choice, Democracy, and Free Markets," *Journal of Political Economy* 62 (1954): 114–23.

8. I am indebted to Charles Plott for suggesting this explanation of the Bergson-Samuelson approach, which is a more sympathetic explanation than the one which I have elsewhere suggested.

9. R. Frisch, "On Welfare Theory and Pareto Regions," *International Economics Papers* 9 (1959), 39–92.

criterion back to the level of institutional choice,[10] where prospects for mutuality of agreement are enhanced.

How would the abandonment of the social maximization paradigm have changed the research thrust of economic theory, especially its potential relevance for social policy? The Pareto criterion classifies all positions into two mutually exclusive sets. Once an initial position is explicitly identified to be "nonoptimal" or "inefficient," we know that there exists at least one means of moving from this position to a position that falls within the optimal or efficient set. The initial position must be dominated, for all persons, by at least one position in the efficient set.

There is no issue here, but what should be the role for the economist who has completed these first steps in applying his expertise? He should neither revert to nihilism nor seek the escapism of social welfare functions. His productivity lies in his ability to search out and to invent social rearrangements which will embody Pareto-superior moves.[11] If an observed position is inefficient, there must be ways of securing agreement on change, agreement which signals mutuality of expected benefits. In the limiting case, compensation schemes can be worked out which will achieve Wicksellian unanimity. Yet how many economists do we observe working out such schemes? How many economists bother with proposed compensations (which must, of course, include structural-institutional rearrangements) to those who will be overtly harmed by the effects of a public or governmental policy shift?[12] Instead of this potentially constructive effort, we find our colleagues continuing to express opposition to tariffs, quotas, minimum wages, price controls, depletion allowances, monopolies, tax loopholes, etc., whether these be existing or proposed. And they continue to stand surprised when the political process, as it operates, pays little or no heed to their advice. As Knut Wicksell noted eighty years ago, economists act as if they are advising a benevolent

10. J. M. Buchanan, "The Relevance of Pareto Optimality," *Journal of Conflict Resolution* 6 (1962): 341–54.

11. This is essentially the suggestion that I made in my paper in 1959. See J. M. Buchanan, "Positive Economics, Welfare Economics, and Political Economy," *Journal of Law and Economics* 2 (1959): 124–38.

12. An exception is W. H. Hutt. In a much neglected small book published in 1943, he proposed that the post-war British economy be swept clear of all market restrictions through the device of compensating all persons and groups who would lose by the change. See W. H. Hutt, *A Plan for Reconstruction* (London, 1943).

despot,[13] in which case their post-Robbins, post-Bergson stance would, of course, be entirely fitting.

There is a place for efficiency in my suggested scheme of things. In this sense, there is little wrong with economic theory per se. Efficiency, as an attribute, is necessarily present when there is a demonstrated absence of possible agreed-on changes. The trading process, broadly conceived, is the means through which the "potentially realizable surplus" is exploited. But there is no uniquely determinate outcome of the trading process, since exchanges must be made and contracts enforced at preequilibrium and, hence, disequilibrium prices. Under the standard assumptions, simple exchange insures that an efficient or optimal position is attained, but this is only one from among a set containing a subinfinity of possible positions. Economists should be satisfied with this result. Within theory itself, search for uniqueness seems to be misguided effort. When the standard assumptions are not descriptive, the simple exchange process will not generate efficient results, and more complex arrangements may be called for. But these arrangements may still be examined in a contractual framework. The specification of these complex contractual arrangements may challenge the skill of the practicing political economist. In facilitating these complex exchanges, which may require the inclusive membership of the whole group, collective-governmental institutions may be necessary. And even though unanimous agreement for change may be conceptually possible, the costs of reaching agreement may be acknowledged to be prohibitively high. This suggests, in turn, that rules or institutions for reaching collective or group decisions may be preselected at some constitutional stage of "trade." It becomes possible in this way to apply the basic contractarian paradigm to the discussion of possible agreement on rules, even if it is anticipated that conflict will emerge at some final stage of application.

Whether the contractarian paradigm is applied at the level of simple exchange, within the constraints of well-defined rules, or at the most basic constitutional level where institutions themselves are the objects upon which agreement must be reached, or at any intermediate level, the emergent results of the trading process are properly summarized as a set of optimal positions, each one of which represents a possible outcome, and no one of

13. K. Wicksell, *Finanztheoretische Untersuchungen* (Jena, 1896).

which dominates any other in the set. This statement is enough to suggest my prejudices toward game-theoretic explorations into mathematics as opposed to the intricacies of complex maximization. The continuing search for solution concepts—the J. von Neumann–O. Morgenstern solution set of imputations,[14] the several cores along with other more sophisticated concepts—seems to me to reflect and in turn to foster an attitude in the theorist that is consistent with, and contributory to, the contractarian approach that I am here suggesting.

The modern efforts to prove that competitive equilibrium exists and lies in the core of an economy are within my own limits for methodological legitimacy. The complementary emphasis here should be placed on the multiplicity of possible equilibria, on the absence of uniqueness. The devices of the Walrasian auctioneer or Edgeworthian perfect recontracting have been required for the proofs here, but I urge those skilled in this particular mathematics to search for theorems that require less stringent assumptions, that incorporate trading at disequilibrium prices.

Now let me return, as promised, to the Arrow impossibility theorem. In his Nobel Prize lecture,[15] Arrow offers a lucid summary of modern economic theory, and he concludes with a discussion of his impossibility theorem. Unfortunately, Arrow does not seem to have gone beyond his initial failure to appreciate the inconsistency between his norms for a social welfare function, or choosing process, and the precepts for a society of free men. In his lecture, Arrow makes it clear that the Bergsonian requirement of "collective rationality" is prior to the set of reasonable conditions that he lays down for his social ordering. Having long ago proved that these conditions cannot be met, Arrow continues to hold that "the philosophical and distributive implications of the paradox of social choice are still not clear." This statement is both surprising and personally disappointing, since it indicates that Arrow has paid no heed to the arguments which I have made, along with many others, against the whole notion of collective rationality.

The so-called paradox may be used as a single and simple illustration of

14. J. von Neumann and O. Morgenstern, *Theory of Games and Economic Behavior* (Princeton, 1944).

15. K. Arrow, "General Economic Equilibrium: Purpose, Analytic Techniques, Collective Choice," *American Economic Review* 64 (June 1974): 253–72.

the profound difference between the maximization paradigm and the contractarian one. There are three voters, A, B, and C, and three alternatives, 1, 2, and 3. The collective choice rule is simple majority voting. Through a series of pairwise comparisons, individual preference orderings may be such that 1 is majority-preferred to 2, and 2 is majority-preferred to 3, while 3 is majority-preferred to 1. This cyclical result is disturbing only to those who seek uniqueness in outcome, who seek to impose the maximization paradigm on a social interaction process where it does not belong. By contrast, to those who accept the contractarian paradigm, who seek only to explain and to understand the behavior of persons who interact, one with another, there is nothing at all disturbing in the paradox. On the assumptions that all side payments have been made, or that institutional constraints are invariant, the tools of economics enable us to classify all three positions, 1, 2, and 3, as falling within the Pareto optimal or efficient set, and no one of these positions dominates the other. If individual preferences produce this set of results, we should be content with this and forego the essentially misleading searches for "philosophical implications" which simply are not there.

In this paper I have restated a position that I have presented in bits and pieces over almost two decades. Knight's favorite quotation from Herbert Spencer says that "only by varied reiteration can alien conceptions be forced on reluctant minds." I hope that I have at least varied the reiteration sufficiently to avoid boredom. I would not presume to think that my own views on methodology would convince more than a minority of my professional colleagues, and I am under no illusions as to the continued dominance of the maximization paradigm in modern economics. Nonetheless, I think that progress has been made during the last twenty years. Game theory, after a series of disappointing attempts to work out optimal strategies for players, has shifted toward a more comprehensive, and more appropriate, consideration of solution concepts. Public choice has emerged as a subdiscipline in its own right, and one that is currently thriving, both within economics and in political science. But intellectual developments have perhaps been overshadowed in effect by the march of events. As persons, both from the streets and the ivory towers, observe modern governmental failures, they can scarcely fail to be turned off by those constructions which require beneficent wisdom on the part of political man. And they can hardly place much credence in the economist consultant whose policy guidelines apply only within institutions that embody such wisdom. Something is amiss, and economists are necessarily being forced to take stock of the social productivity of their efforts. When, as, and if they do so, they will, I think, come increasingly to share what I have called the contractarian paradigm.

As I have argued elsewhere,[16] economics comes closer to being a "science of contract" than a "science of choice." And with this, the "scientist," as political economist, must assume a different role. The maximizer must be replaced by the arbitrator, the outsider who tries to work out compromises among conflicting claims. The Edgeworth-Bowley box becomes the first diagram in our elementary textbooks; the indifference curve–budget line construction is relegated to subsidiary treatment. Eugen v. Böhm-Bawerk's horse traders are the basic examples, not the housewife who shops for groceries in the supermarket. Game theory, in its most comprehensive sense, becomes the basic mathematics for the professional, and solutions to n-person games replace the nth order conditions for maxima and minima. The unifying principle becomes *gains-from-trade*, not maximization. These principles merge, of course, at the level of the individual chooser's calculus, but they become quite distinct when attention shifts to the social interaction that we call "the economy."

16. J. M. Buchanan, "What Should Economists Do?" *Southern Economics Journal* 30 (January 1964): 213–22; "Is Economics the Science of Choice?" in *Roads to Freedom: Essays in Honour of Friedrich A. von Hayek,* ed. E. Streissler, G. Haberler, F. A. Lutz, and F. Machlup (London, 1969), 47–64.

Boundaries on Social Contract

Introduction

The central question examined in this paper may be stated at the outset. What are the boundaries or limits on changes in the distribution or assignment of rights among persons in a society that may be "explained" on grounds of continuing social contract? I do not provide more than a few suggestions toward a set of answers. I should argue, nonetheless, that the question is of vital importance in the 1970s. We witness everywhere what must be described as an erosion in the rights of individuals, rights that were previously acknowledged. As social scientists, we are under some obligation to "explain" what is happening, and we must keep in mind that simplest of principles; diagnosis precedes prescription for cure.

The Social Function of Social Contract

A contract theory of the State is relatively easy to derive on the basis of plausibly acceptable assumptions about individual evaluations, and careful use of this theory can yield major explanatory results. To an extent, at least, a "science" exists for the purpose of providing psychologically satisfying explana-

From *Reason Papers* 2 (Fall 1975): 15–28. Reprinted by permission of the publisher.

The central arguments of this paper were initially presented in a seminar on anarchy at Blacksburg, Virginia, in the Spring of 1972. This earlier presentation, under the title "Before Public Choice," appears in the volume of essays *Explorations in the Theory of Anarchy*, edited by Gordon Tullock (Center for Study of Public Choice, Virginia Polytechnic Institute and State University, Blacksburg, Virginia, 1973).

The general position expressed in this paper is developed more fully in my book *The Limits of Liberty: Between Anarchy and Leviathan* (Chicago: University of Chicago Press, 1975).

tions of what men can commonly observe around them. Presumably, we "feel better" when we possess some explanatory framework or model that allows us to classify and interpret disparate sense perceptions. This imposition of order on the universe is a "good" in the strict economic sense of this term; men will invest money, time, and effort in acquiring it. The contract theory of the State, in all of its manifestations, can be defended on such grounds. It is important for sociopolitical order and tranquility that ordinary men explain to themselves the working of governmental process in models that conceptually take their bases in cooperative rather than in noncooperative behavior. Admittedly and unabashedly, the contract theory serves, in this sense, a rationalization purpose or objective. We need a "logic of law," a "calculus of consent," a "logic of collective action," to use the titles of three books that embody modern-day contract theory foundations.[1]

Can the contract theory of the State serve other objectives, whether these be normative or positive in character? Can institutions which find no conceivable logical derivation in contract among cooperating parties be condemned on other than strictly personal grounds? Can alleged improvements in social arrangements be evaluated on anything other than contractarian precepts, or, to lapse into economists' jargon, on anything other than Paretian criteria? But, even here, are these criteria any more legitimate than any others?

In earlier works, I have tended to ignore or at least to slight these fundamental questions. I have been content to work out, at varying levels of sophistication, the contractarian bases for governmental action, either that which we can commonly observe or that which might be suggested as reforms. To me, this effort seemed relevant and significant. "Political economy" or "public choice"—these seemed to be labels assignable to work that required little or no methodological justification. It was only when I tried to outline a summary treatment of my whole approach to sociopolitical structure that I was stopped short. I came to realize that the very basis of the contractarian position must be examined more thoroughly.

---

1. See Gordon Tullock, *The Logic of Law* (New York: Basic Books, 1970); James M. Buchanan and Gordon Tullock, *The Calculus of Consent* (Ann Arbor: University of Michigan Press, 1962); Mancur Olson, *The Logic of Collective Action* (Cambridge: Harvard University Press, 1965).

We know that, factually and historically, the "social contract" is mythological, at least in many of its particulars. Individuals did not come together in some original position and mutually agree on the rules of social intercourse. And even had they done so at some time in history, their decisions could hardly be considered to be contractually binding on all of us who have come behind. We cannot start anew. We can either accept the political universe, or we can try to change it. The question reduces to one of determining the criteria for change.

When and if we fully recognize that the contract is a myth designed in part to rationalize existing institutional structures of society, can we simultaneously use the contractual derivations to develop criteria for evaluating changes or modifications in these structures? I have previously answered this question affirmatively, but without proper argument. The intellectual quality as well as the passionate conviction of those who answer the question negatively suggest that more careful consideration is required.

How can we derive a criterion for determining whether or not a change in law, or, if you will, a change in the assignment of rights, is or is not justified? To most social scientists, the only answer is solipsist. Change becomes desirable if "I like it," even though many prefer to dress this up in fanciful "social welfare function" or "public interest" semantics. To me, this seems to be pure escapism; it represents retreat into empty arguments about personal values which spells the end of rational discourse. Perhaps some of our colleagues do possess God-like qualities, or at least they think they do, but until and unless their godliness is accepted, we are left with no basis for discourse. My purpose is to see how far we can rationally discuss criteria for social change on the presumption that no man's values are better than any other man's.

Wicksellian Contract, Constitutionalism, and Rawlsian Justice

Is *agreement* the only test? Is the Wicksellian-contractarian-Paretian answer the only legitimate one here? If so, are we willing to accept its corollaries? Its full implications? Are we willing to forestall all social change that does not command unanimous or quasi-unanimous consent?

Provisionally, let us say that we do so. We can move a step beyond, while at the same time rationalizing much of what we see, by resorting to "constitutionalism," the science of rules. We can say that particular proposals for social change need not command universal assent provided only that such assent holds for the legal structure within which particular proposals are enacted or chosen. This seems to advance the argument; we seem to be part of the way out of the dilemma. But note that this provides us with no means at all for evaluating particular proposals as "good" or "bad." We can generate many outcomes or results under nonunanimity rules. This explains my initial response to the Arrow impossibility theorem, and to the subsequent discussion. My response was, and is, one of nonsurprise at the alleged inconsistency in a social decision process that embodies in itself no criteria for consistency. This also explains my unwillingness to be trapped, save on rare and regretted occasions, into positions of commitment on particular measures of policy on the familiar efficiency grounds. We can offer no policy advice on particular legislative proposals. As political economists, we examine public choices; we can make institutional predictions. We can analyze alternative political-social-economic structures.

But what about constitutional change itself? Can we say nothing, or must we say that, at this level, the contractarian (Wicksellian, Paretian) norm must apply? Once again, observation hardly supports us here. Changes are made, changes that would be acknowledged to be genuinely "constitutional," without anything remotely approaching unanimous consent. Must we reject all such changes out of hand, or can we begin to adduce criteria on some other basis?

Resort to the choice of rules for ordinary parlor games may seem to offer assistance. Influenced greatly by the emphasis on such choices by Rutledge Vining, I once considered this to be the key to genuinely innovative application of the contractarian criteria. If we could, somehow, think of individual participants in a setting of complete uncertainty about their own positions over subsequent rounds of play, we might think of their reaching genuine agreement on a set of rules. The idea of a "fair game" does have real meaning, and this idea can be transferred to sociopolitical institutions. But how far can we go with this? We may, in this process, begin to rationalize certain institutions that cannot readily be brought within the standard Wicksellian framework. But can we do more? Can we, as John Rawls seems to want to do in his *A Theory of Justice*,[2] "think ourselves" into a position of original con-

2. John Rawls, *A Theory of Justice* (Cambridge: Harvard University Press, 1971).

tract and then idealize our thought processes into norms that "should" be imposed as criteria for institutional change? Note that this is, to me, quite different from saying that we derive a possible rationalization. To rationalize, to explain, is not to propose, and Rawls seems to miss this quite critical distinction. It is one thing to say that, conceptually, men in some genuinely constitutional stage of deliberation, operating behind the veil of ignorance, might have agreed to rules something akin to those that we actually observe, but it is quite another thing to say that men, in the here and now, should be forced to abide by specific rules that we imagine by transporting ourselves into some mental-moral equivalent of an original contract setting where men are genuine "moral equals."

Unless we do so, however, we must always accept whatever structure of rules that exists and seek constitutional changes only through agreement, through consensus. It is this inability to say anything about rules changes, this inability to play God, this inability to raise himself above the masses, that the social philosopher cannot abide. He has an ingrained prejudice against the *status quo*, however this may be defined, understandably so, since his very role, as he interprets it, is one that finds itself only in social reform. (Perhaps this role conception reflects the moral inversion that Michael Polanyi and Craig Roberts note; the shift of moral precepts away from personal behavior aimed at personal salvation and toward moral evaluation of institutions.)

Hobbes and the Natural Distribution

Just what are men saying when they propose nonagreed changes in the basic structure of rights? Are they saying anything more than "this is what I want and since I think the State has the power to impose it, I support the State as the agency to enforce the change"? We may be able to get some handles on this very messy subject by going back to Hobbes. We need to examine the initial leap out of the Hobbesian jungle. How can agreement emerge? And what are the problems of enforcement?

We may represent the reaction equilibrium in the Hobbesian jungle at the origin in the diagrammatics of Figure 1. If we measure "B's law-abiding behavior" on the ordinate, and "A's law-abiding behavior" on the abscissa, it is evident that neither man secures advantage from "lawful" behavior individually and independent of the other man's behavior. (Think of "law-abiding" here as "not stealing.") Note that the situation here is quite different from the

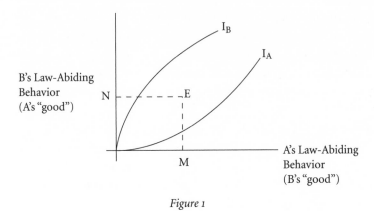

B's Law-Abiding Behavior (A's "good")

A's Law-Abiding Behavior (B's "good")

Figure 1

usual public-goods model in which at least some of the "good" will tend to be produced by one or all of the common or joint consumers even under wholly independent adjustment. With law-abiding as the "good," however, the individual cannot, through his own behavior, produce so as to increase his own utility. He can do nothing other than provide a "pure" external economy; all benefits accrue to the other parties. Hence, the independent adjustment position involves a corner solution at the origin in our two-person diagram. But gains-from-trade clearly exist in this Hobbesian jungle, despite the absence of unilateral action.

It is easy enough to depict the Pareto region that bounds potential positions of mutual gains by drawing the appropriate indifference contours through the origin as is done in Figure 1. These contours indicate the internal or subjective rates of tradeoff as between *own* and *other* law-abiding. It seems plausible to suggest that the standard convexity properties would apply. The analysis remains largely empty, however, until we know something, or at least postulate something, about the descriptive characteristics of the initial position itself. And the important and relevant point in this respect is that individuals *are not equal*, or at least need not be equal, in such a setting, either in their relative abilities or in their final command over consumables.[3] To assume sym-

3. The formal properties of the "natural distribution" that will emerge under anarchy have been described by Winston Bush in his paper "Income Distribution in Anarchy" (Virginia Polytechnic Institute and State University, Center for Study of Public Choice Research Paper No. 808231-17, March 1972).

metry among persons here amounts to converting a desired normative state, that of equality among men, into a fallacious positive proposition. (This is, of course, a pervasive error, and one that is not made only by social philosophers. It has had significant and pernicious effects on judicial thinking in the twentieth century.) If we drop the equality or symmetry assumption, however, we can say something about the relative values or tradeoffs as between the relative "haves" and "have-nots" in the Hobbesian or natural adjustment equilibrium. For illustrative purposes here, think of the "natural distribution" in our two-person model as characterized by A's enjoyment of ten units of "good," and B's enjoyment of only two units. Both persons expend effort, a "bad" in generating and in maintaining this natural distribution. It is this effort that can be reduced or eliminated through trade, through agreement on laws or rules of respect for property. In this way, both parties can secure more "goods." The post-trade equilibrium must reflect improvement for both parties over the natural distribution or pretrade outcome. There are prospects for Pareto-efficient or Pareto-superior moves from the initial no-rights position to any one of many possible post-trade or positive-rights distributions.

Let us suppose that agreement is reached; each person agrees to an assignment of property rights, and, furthermore, each person agrees to respect such rights as are assigned. Let us suppose, for illustration, that the net distribution of "goods" under the assignment is fifteen units for A and seven units for B. Hence, there is a symmetrical sharing of the total gains-from-trade secured from the assignment of rights. Even under such symmetrical sharing, however, note that the relative position of B has improved more than the relative position of A. In our example, A's income increases by one-half, but B's income increases more than twofold. This suggests that the person who fares relatively worse in the natural distribution may well stand to gain relatively more from an initial assignment of rights than the person who fares relatively better in the pretrade state of the world.

The Dilemma in Maintaining Contract

Agreement is attained; both parties enjoy more utility than before. But again the prisoners' dilemma setting must be emphasized. Each of the two persons can anticipate gains by successful unilateral default on the agreement. In Figure 1, if E depicts the position of agreement, A can always gain by a shift to N if this can be accomplished; similarly, B can gain by a shift to M. There may, however, be an asymmetry present in prospective gains from unilateral default for the person who remains relatively less favored in the natural distribution. In one sense, the "vein of ore" that he can mine by departing from the rules through criminal activity is richer than the similar vein would be for the other party. The productivity of criminal effort is likely to be higher for the man who can steal from his rich neighbor than for the man who has only poor neighbors.

This may be illustrated in the matrix of Figure 2, where the initial pretrade or natural distribution is shown in Cell IV, and the post-trade or positive rights distribution is shown in Cell I. Note that, as depicted, the man who is relatively "poor" in the natural equilibrium, person B in the example, stands to gain relatively more by departing unilaterally from Cell I than person A. Person B could, by such a move, increase his quantity of "goods" from seven to twelve, whereas person A could increase his only from fifteen to seventeen. This example suggests that the relatively "rich" person will necessarily be more interested in policing the activities of the "poor" man, as such, than vice versa. This is, of course, widely accepted. But the construction and analysis here can be employed for a more complex and difficult issue that has not been treated adequately.

Dynamics and the Atrophy of Rights

Assume that agreement has been attained; both parties abide by the law; both enjoy the benefits. Time passes. The "rich" man becomes lazy and lethargic. The "poor" man increases his strength. This modifies the natural distribution. Let us say that the natural distribution changes to 6:6. The "rich" man now has an overwhelmingly more significant interest in the maintenance of the legal *status quo* than the "poor" man, who is no longer "poor" in natural ability terms. The initial symmetry in the sharing of gains as between the no-trade and the trade position no longer holds. With the new natural distribution, the "rich" man secures almost all of the net gains.

The example must be made more specific. Assume that the situation is analogous to the one examined by Winston Bush. The initial problem is how manna which drops from Heaven is to be divided among the two persons.

		B: Abides by "Law"	B: Observes no "Law"
A	Abides by "Law"	I 15,7	II 6,12
A	Observes no "Law"	III 17,3	IV 10,2

Figure 2

The initial natural distribution is in the ratio 10:2 as noted. Recognizing this, along with their own abilities, A and B agree that by assigning rights, they can attain a 15:7 ratio, as noted. Time passes, and B increases in relative strength, but the "goods" are still shared in the 15:7 ratio. The initial set of property rights agreed to on the foundations of the initial natural distribution no longer reflects or mirrors the existing natural distribution. Under these changed conditions, a lapse back into the natural equilibrium will harm B relatively little whereas A will be severely damaged. The "poor" man now has relatively little interest in adherence to law. If this trend continues, and the natural distribution changes further in the direction indicated, the "poor" man may find himself able to secure even net advantages from a lapse back into the Hobbesian jungle.

The model may be described in something like the terms of modern game theory. If the initial natural distribution remains unaltered, the agreed-on assignment of rights possesses qualities like the core in an *n*-person game. It is to the advantage of no coalition to depart from this assignment or imputation if the remaining members of the group are willing to enforce or to block the imputation. No coalition can do better on its own, or in this model, in the natural distribution, than it does in the assignment. These core-like properties of the assigned distribution under law may, however, begin to lose dominance features as the potential natural distribution shifts around "underneath" the existing structure of rights, so to speak. The foundations of the existing rights structure may be said to have shifted in the process.

This analysis opens up interesting new implications for net redistribution of wealth and for changes in property rights over time. Observed changes in claims to wealth take place without apparent consent. These may be interpreted simply as the use of the enforcement power of the State by certain coalitions of persons to break the contract. They are overtly shifting from a Cell I into a Cell II or Cell III outcome in the diagram of Figure 2. It is not, of course, difficult to explain why these coalitions arise. It will always be in the interest of a person, or a group of persons, to depart from the agreed-on assignment of claims or rights, provided that he or they can do so unilaterally and without offsetting reactive behavior on the part of the remaining members of the social group. The quasi-equilibrium in Cell I is inherently unstable. The equilibrium does qualify as a position on the core of the game, but we must keep in mind that the core analytics presumes the immediate formation of blocking coalitions. In order fully to explain observed departures from *status quo* we must also explain the behavior of the absence of the potential blocking coalitions. Why do the remaining members of the community fail to enforce the initial assignment of rights?

Enforcement Breakdown

The analysis here suggests that if there has been a sufficiently large shift in the underlying natural distribution, the powers of enforcing adherence on the prospective violators of contract may not exist, or, if they exist, these powers may be demonstrably weakened. In our numerical example, B fares almost as well under the new natural distribution as he does in the continuing assignment of legal rights. Hence, A has lost almost all of his blocking power; he can scarcely influence B by threats to plunge the community into Hobbesian anarchy, even if A himself should be willing to do so. And it should also be recognized that "willingness" to enforce the contract (the structure of legal rules, the existing set of claims to property) is as important as the objective ability to do so. Even if A should be physically able to force B to return to the *status quo ante* after some attempted departure, he may be unwilling to suffer the personal loss that might be required to make his threat of enforcement credible.[4] The law-abiding members of the community may

---

4. For a more extensive discussion of these points, see my paper "The Samaritan's Dilemma," in Edmund Phelps (ed.), *Altruism, Morality and Economic Theory* (New York: Russell Sage Foundation, 1975), 71–86.

find themselves in a genuine dilemma. They may simply be unable to block the unilateral violation of the social contract.

In this perspective, normative arguments based on "justice" in distribution may signal acquiescence in modification in the existing structure of claims. Just as the idea of contract, itself, has been used to rationalize existing structure, the idea of "justice" may be used to rationalize coerced departures from contract. In the process those who advance such arguments and those who are convinced may both "feel better" while their claims are whittled away. This does, I think, explain much attitudinal behavior toward redistribution policy by specific social groups. Gordon Tullock has, in part, explained the prevailing attitudes of many academicians and intellectuals.[5] The explanation developed here applies more directly to the redistributionist attitudes of the scions of the rich, e.g., the Rockefellers and Kennedys. Joseph Kennedy was less redistributive than his sons; John D. Rockefeller was less redistributive than his grandsons. We do not need to call on the psychologists since our model provides an explanation in the concept of a changing natural distribution. The scions of the wealthy are far less secure in their roles of custodians of wealth than were their forebears. They realize perhaps that their own natural talents simply do not match up, even remotely, to the share of national wealth that they now command. Their apparent passions for the poor may be nothing more than surface reflections of attempts to attain temporary security.

The analysis also suggests that there is a major behavioral difference fostered between the intergenerational transmission of nonhuman and human capital. Within limits, there is an important linkage between human capital and capacity to survive in a natural or Hobbesian environment. There seems to be no such linkage between nonhuman capital and survival in the jungle. From this it follows that the man who possesses human capital is likely to be far less concerned about the "injustice" of his own position, less concerned about temporizing measures designed to shore up apparent leaks in the social system than his counterpart who possesses nonhuman capital. If we postulate that the actual income-asset distribution departs significantly from the proportionate distribution in the underlying and existing natural equilibrium, the system of claims must be acknowledged to be notoriously unstable.

5. See Gordon Tullock, "The Charity of the Uncharitable," *Western Economic Journal,* 9 (December 1971), 379–91.

The idle rich, possessed of nonhuman capital, will tend to form coalitions with the poor that are designed primarily to ward off retreat toward the Hobbesian jungle. This coalition can take the form of the rich acquiescing in and providing defense for overt criminal activity on the part of the poor, or the more explicit form of political exploitation of the "silent majority," the constituency that possesses largely human rather than nonhuman capital.

This description has some empirical content in 1976. But what can the exploited groups do about it? Can the middle classes form a coalition with the rich, especially when the latter are themselves so insecure? Or can they form, instead, another coalition with the poor, accepting a promise of strict adherence to law in exchange for goodies provided by the explicit confiscation of the nonhuman capital of the rich? (Politically, this would take the form of confiscatory inheritance taxation.) The mythology of the American dream probably precludes this route from being taken. The self-made, the *nouveau riche,* seek to provide their children with fortunes that the latter will accept only with guilt.

All of this suggests that a law-abiding imputation becomes increasingly difficult to sustain as its structure departs from what participants conceive to be the natural or Bush-Hobbes imputation, defined in some proportionate sense. If the observed imputation, or set of bounded imputations that are possible under existing legal-constitutional rules, seems to bear no relationship at all to the natural imputation that men accept, breakdown in legal standards is predictable.

We Start from an Ambiguous "Here"

Where does this leave us in trying to discuss criteria for "improvement" in rules, in assignments of rights, the initial question that was posed in this paper? I have argued that the contractarian or Paretian norm is relevant on the simple principle that "we start from here." But "here," the *status quo,* is the existing set of legal institutions and rules. Hence, how can we possibly distinguish genuine contractual changes in "law" from those which take place under the motivations discussed above? Can we really say which changes are defensible "exchanges" from an existing *status quo* position? This is what I was trying to answer, without full success, in my paper in response to Warren

J. Samuels' discussion of the *Miller et al. v. Schoene* case.[6] There I tried to argue that, to the extent that existing rights are held to be subject to continuous redefinition by the State, no one has an incentive to organize and to initiate trades or agreements. This amounts to saying that once the body politic begins to get overly concerned about the distribution of the pie under existing property-rights assignments and legal rules, once we begin to think either about the personal gains from law-breaking, privately or publicly, or about the disparities between existing imputations and those estimated to be forthcoming under some idealized anarchy, we are necessarily precluding and forestalling the achievement of potential structural changes that might increase the size of the pie for *all*. Too much concern for "justice" acts to insure that "growth" will not take place, and for reasons much more basic than the familiar economic incentives arguments.

In this respect, the early 1970s seemed a century, not a mere decade, away from the early 1960s when, if you recall, the rage was all for growth, and the newfound concern about distribution had not yet been invented. At issue here, of course, is the whole conception of the State, or of collective action. I am far less sanguine than I once was concerning the possible acceptance of a reasonably well-defined constitutional-legal framework. If put to it, could any of us accurately describe the real or effective constitution of the United States in 1976? Can we explain much of what we see in terms of continuing change in this effective constitution while we continue to pay lip service to nominal constitutional forms?[7]

The basic structure of property rights is now threatened more seriously than at any period in the two-century history of the United States. In the paper "The Samaritan's Dilemma," noted above, I advanced the hypothesis that we have witnessed a general loss of strategic courage, brought on in part by economic affluence. As I think more about all this, however, I realize that there is more to it. We may be witnessing the disintegration of our effective constitutional rights, regardless of the prattle about "the constitution" as

6. See Warren J. Samuels, "Interrelations between Legal and Economic Processes," *Journal of Law and Economics,* 14 (October 1971), 435–50; and my "Politics, Property and the Law," *Journal of Law and Economics,* 15 (October 1972), 439–52.

7. William Niskanen offers this as an explanation for public-sector growth. See his "The Pathology of Politics," in R. Selden (ed.), *Capitalism and Freedom: Problems and Prospects* (Charlottesville: University Press of Virginia, 1975), 20–35.

seen by our judicial tyrants from their own visions of the entrails of their sacrificial beasts. I do not know what might be done about all this, even by those who recognize what is happening. We seem to be left with the question posed at the outset. How do rights re-emerge and come to command respect? How do "laws" emerge that carry with them general respect for their "legitimacy"?

Constitutional Design
and Construction
An Economic Approach

I shall present a very general summary—and it must be a summary neces-sarily—of my own thinking about what we might broadly call "The Eco-nomic Theory of Political Constitutions," at least the way I think about it, and which will involve a statement of my own approach to many of these types of constitutional problems. In a sense, it will also involve my own dis-cussion of what should be the proper role of the economist in public policy, and in that sense it will be a critique of the methodological position that is taken by many modern economists.

Perhaps I should say that the primary influence on my own thinking was the great Swedish economist Knut Wicksell, whom I should perhaps rank as the top economist that we have ever had in the world, in his vision of many aspects of economic order and, in particular, the role of the economist.

In his first work, which was his dissertation on Public Finance, Wicksell adopted what I should call a constitutional approach. He warned his fellow economists throughout the world—and his book, after all, was written in 1896, more than eight decades ago—against proceeding under the assump-tion that their task was simply to give advice to some benevolent authority. He suggested in particular, that they should look at the functioning of insti-tutions, rather than laying down value statements in a normative way, this or

From *Economia* 3 (May 1979): 293–314. Reprinted by permission of the publisher.

Transcript of a lecture by Professor James Buchanan, given in November 1978 at the Faculty of Economics, New University of Lisbon. The text has been edited by Professor António S. P. Barbosa and revised by the author.

that tax, this or that spending program, no matter how reasonable the arguments were.

He sought to introduce efficiency into tax and spending outcomes, by changing the institutions of the political order, by proposing constitutional changes, by proposing, for example, that when a political body brought up some proposal to spend public funds, a decision on behalf of how those funds are going to be raised should in fact be required at the same time that the spending bill was enacted. To guarantee efficiency in the public sector as opposed to efficiency in the private sector, he proposed something approaching a unanimous vote in a legislative assembly. But he recognized that this would be tremendously costly and he recognized possible departures from this extreme position. On the other hand, however, those positions can serve as benchmarks against which proposals are made. But the important part of the Wicksellian lesson, so to speak, was the concentration on the institutions of social order and on reforming these institutions as opposed to simply going out and looking at what would be ideal and discussing the ideal type of policy without recognition of the institutions of the social order. That is what I essentially call a constitutional approach.

Gordon Tullock and I published a book in 1962 which we called *The Calculus of Consent*. It turned out that this was quite a popular title; all we tried to do in that book was to look at the whole structure of political decision-making rules from the point of view of the economist, and to make the assumption that individuals were in fact maximizing utility. What kind of rules would they want to impose on themselves politically? We examined various decision-making rules. The device that we employed in that book is one that is now much more widely known than it was at that time. If you just say, "Well, people are put together in a group and are going to try to decide on rules." If you look at that, you have a sort of zero-sum type game going on, persons with clearly identified interests fighting with each other, struggling with each other through political conflict. How do you in fact get away from that conflict? How do you get individuals to take a role that is outside that struggle vis-à-vis each other?

The device that we used at that time was one in which we said that if people are uncertain about the role they would play under the operation of these rules, then they can be led to agree on a set of rules that would be fair or desirable, no matter what their position is. If you talk about long range reforms or changes, if you talk about long range quasi-permanent political institutions, such that you really do not know what your own role will be under these constitutions, then you will be led to be much more flexible in your own attitude towards particularized reform proposals.

I use a very simple analogy of an ordinary card game. Suppose you are going to play cards with six people. The first thing you must do is, of course, to agree on a set of rules by which you are going to play. But how do you choose those rules, how do you agree on those rules? Obviously you do not know how the cards are going to fall through the play of the game during that session, so you are led to choose those rules on the basis of some kind of a notion of fairness, i.e., no matter how the cards fall, you hope the outcome is reasonably fair. And so you move in that direction to get at some of these constitutional approaches in analysing various rules.

As I have said, that approach or attitude which you can call a constitutional or contractarian attitude has now become much more popular than it was twenty years ago. In particular it has been popularized in social philosophy by a book that has caused a great deal of attention in the United States in this decade, namely John Rawls' *Theory of Justice,* in which he tries to derive basic principles of justice with precisely that kind of device. He advances the notion that people will be led to agree on basic principles of justice in the social order, by getting themselves behind what he calls "the veil of ignorance." That is, by essentially not knowing in what role or position they are going to be in a social order, they select a set of rules which he calls fair rules. And fairness is defined not because there is something intrinsically fair about a particular rule, but rather because those are the rules upon which people might be led to agree. The book had a tremendous impact on the thinking of social philosophers in the United States. We are getting now, in America, for the first time in almost a century, a whole wave of interest in social philosophy. That particular book had a big impact on economists, political scientists, social philosophers, lawyers, etc. But Rawls essentially used the same device that Tullock and I used in *The Calculus of Consent* in evaluating political rules. I am not claiming that we invented it. Rawls had written some pieces in the 50's with this approach and other people, including Harsanyi and others, had used precisely the same approach, but the point is that it does give us a way of looking at the rules of the game as opposed to sitting out there and trying to judge something independent of where we are.

Now, let me shift a little bit and talk about the interest in basic constitutional questions. It seems to me that there is going on in my country, and certainly in Great Britain and in much of the rest of Europe, a great deal of constitutional questioning now, discussion about constitutions. Of course, you are having your own discussion here. I have been in Spain for four or five days, and there is also a lot of discussion about your constitution. I was in Great Britain at a conference in April and Lord Robbins told me that for the first time in his lifetime there is now a very active discussion in Britain about constitutional reforms, about possibilities of reforming the constitution. In Great Britain for the first time they are beginning to question the absolute supremacy of Parliament. The British Constitution as you know is an unwritten constitution, essentially, and Parliament can do whatever it pleases. The British are beginning to question that, and to talk about the possibility of reforming that constitution.

In the United States, we are beginning to see that the set of rules that our Founding Fathers developed two hundred years ago, which seemed to work tolerably well for us for a long time, have not been able to control the governmental processes. In particular, we have had built-in in the American Constitution a good deal of protection to individuals' personal rights. I think it worked fairly well on that score, but we have not been able to control the size and growth of the public sector and the growth of the bureaucracy. We have had a gradual increase in the share of our national product that is used by government. There is now in the United States a tremendous upsurge of pressure on the part of the electorate to put constitutional control on the total share that government can take away from people in taxation.

All of you have read about the famous referendum in California, in June 1978, Proposition 13, through which by more than 2 to 1, the voting population in California approved an amendment to the State Constitution, that will cut back taxes on property by more than one-half. In the elections of this month, some six other states put in comparable types of restrictions and there is now very active discussion about something at the federal governmental level that would be comparable to that.

There is discussion now of this basic constitutional question. And not only by ordinary political scientists, but by economists and everyone else. And essentially this fits in very closely with the type of work that I have been doing for a long, long time.

What we were in a sense doing is rediscovering a wisdom that was present in the eighteenth and early nineteenth centuries but has essentially been lost since that time, that is, the problem of controlling the governmental sector as well as the private sector through constitutional rules. For a century, we went through a period in which we had implicit faith somehow that as long as our political institutions were "democratic" in the sense that politicians were elected and we had representative assemblies, nothing more was needed.

I am not familiar with the Portuguese situation but it is something perhaps that you should be aware of as you think about some of these constitutional questions. In other words, you might need more than electoral guarantees. As I say, in this discussion, I think that what will come out is my own position about the role that an economist might play in terms of an analysis of political rules and how we might think about political reform.

It seems to me that discussion must proceed at several levels. We must first of all analyse in a strictly scientific way, how different political rules or institutions work. Obviously we need to know how different institutions work, before we can say anything about what is good or bad about the institutions. Very basic positive analysis must precede any sort of normative evaluation of alternative institutions. And so this area that I have been associated with, this general area called "public choice," is essentially that. It is essentially a positive scientific analysis of the workings of alternative political decisions rules. This is a subdivision, if you want to call it that, between economics and politics that is really coming to its own, only in the last twenty years, rather surprisingly if you think about it, with the work on the positive theory of how majority voting rules actually work, or how does a two-house legislature versus a one-house legislature work, or how does the veto power work, or how does a bureaucracy operate. We have all sorts of subdevelopments in this area, which is strictly positive scientific analysis of political institutions. Now, with that scientific analysis of political institutions you can begin to make some evaluations of alternative rules and talk about choosing alternative political rules. And I now go back to what I said earlier about Wicksell's approach.

You begin to make reforms and you try to get things improved by improving the institutional structure. In a sense, all my own work has been within this area of institutional economics, if you want to call it that, which was a sort of an outmoded type of emphasis earlier on. It is institutional economics versus formal theories of economics. Economics in particular within the last thirty or forty years, it seems to me, has in fact got itself into a situation where it is of no value because what it amounts to is applied mathematics.

I am talking now about microeconomics rather than macroeconomics. Most people who work in microeconomics essentially talk about maximizing functions subject to certain constraints. However, it makes no sense at all to generalize from the level of utility maximizing individuals to a social order. It makes no sense at all to apply the same sort of logic to the level of a group that you apply to the individual. It is perfectly all right to talk about, and it helps us in understanding, the choice behaviour of an individual when we say "let us set something up here, that we call a utility or preference function, and let us examine how the individual would behave in maximizing that utility subject to his income constraint and other constraints that he might have." That is elementary first-course economics. That is fine. But the big and illegitimate jump is to transfer that logic over to the social group because the group maximizes nothing. It is completely illegitimate to apply that logic to a social group whether it be a club, state, subdivision, region, city, or whatever you have. Because there you have the separate individual units interacting with each other under a set of institutional rules and what emerges as outcomes depends on the structure of those institutional rules. It is a completely false application to try to impose on that structure this sort of maximizing or organic view of things unless of course you take the view—and people do, of course, but I categorically reject it—that there is some transcendental entity that is "the people" or "the state" or something like that, independent of the people in it. I have never understood the attractiveness of that position but, as you know, throughout history certain people have taken that view. If, however, you do not take that view and take instead the Kantian view that what matters are the individual units in any group, individual people, then any group is essentially a group of interacting persons and the outcomes that emerge depend on the rules through which people are allowed to interact with each other.

If you are going to improve the net results by improving rules, improvement as measured by the evaluations of the individuals themselves and by nothing else, nothing external to the group, the mathematics of maximization simply do not apply. We do not really know what is in the social or group preference function. There is no such thing as a social welfare function. We are not maximizing social welfare. We are trying to adopt, if we can, rules, procedures, institutions, that can further whatever it is we want to achieve. We do not know what we want to achieve. We have no idea of what we want to achieve. It is an uncertain and complex world, and we do not know in advance how the game is going to proceed. But we want somehow to choose a set of rules that will allow us to accomplish whatever our objectives might be as they emerge in the process. Orthodox economics just has no way of getting at this, unless they go back and take this Wicksellian type of approach, i.e., look at the way different institutions work.

I am not necessarily talking about this as a descriptive approach. We can have a good deal more, I think, than we have had of descriptive institutional analysis. We need actually to get out there in the real world and look at how institutions work. We need comparative institutional analysis, more of economic history, history of institutions. We need much more international institutional comparisons. We also need more of what I would call conceptual analysis, positive scientific analysis, at the level of models. We need to try to model the behaviour of different institutions. We did try to model the behaviour of the bureaucracy, for example, to model the behaviour of an individual bureaucrat holding a position in a governmental hierarchy in a particular department, charged with doing a certain function. We need to model his behaviour, to make some predictions about what he is likely to do, what are the rewards and punishments that he faces as he tries to do this or do that.

We need to discard this sort of outmoded view of bureaucracy that was developed by Max Weber, for example, in which the bureaucrat was a sort of faceless individual who simply carries out policy made by the politicians. Bureaucrats have their own power. We need to know how much that power is. What are the limits of what they can do? How can they convert public funds to their own purposes, for example? How can they in fact maximize their own utility? This is what we mean by the economic approach to bureaucracy.

In the United States, this approach is very close to another type of work that is going on, which is sometimes called the economics of property rights. That is, we look at the particular rights that an individual has in particular positions. What can he do with what he has? We can make some predictions about what the outcomes are likely to be. You need to do all that and then you need to look at how we might reform these rules and change the institutions in such a way that we can expect to secure outcomes that would be more favourable to everyone. And again, I come back to my critique of orthodox economics here. The orthodox economist essentially does not have much way to respond. He has the wrong mathematics, if you want to call it that. I am not criticizing mathematics at all. I am criticizing the maximization paradigm, not the mathematics. The game theoretic paradigm, a very complex mathematics as you know, is perfectly appropriate. It is perfectly appropriate to the interaction of individual players, of individual units under different constraining rules, as opposed to somehow imposing a maximization paradigm or maximization model on a social order *as if* the people had a block or a unit existence and somebody is writing out the social welfare function and maximizing it.

As my remarks have perhaps indicated here, I think the only productive way we can proceed is the Wicksellian way, that is, talking about how we might have better rules, how we might improve the rules, how we might improve the basic structure of the basic constitution. In the United States, as I say, and it is the only country I am familiar with, we are discussing very actively now how we might impose some restrictions on the power of the state to take away money from us, private people, as taxes. We are trying to impose some tax limits. We are trying to rewrite the tax constitution.

As a matter of fact, I am writing a book now with a colleague of mine on what we call the tax constitution. Once you start looking at those problems that way, you come out with a completely different set of results from what you get if you look at taxation in an orthodox way. You look at taxation in the orthodox way on the assumption that the government out there is going to do good and nothing but good. But you never question what the government is going to do. You are just giving advice to that government. Then you start looking from the other point of view. You look at people in government as essentially just like everybody else. This is not a critique of people in government at all; it is just the presumption that people in government are just like the rest of us. That's all. They are likely trying to maximize their own utility, given the role that they are playing, given the institutional structure. And their own utility function does include their own income, wealth, assets, purposes, their own whatever it is that satisfies them.

Looking at it that way, you recognize the simple point that anybody in government is likely to want his agency to increase in size. You thus get a built-in growth of the government budget, and you have to put some constraints on it. So you start talking about how would we organize the tax constitutions in such a way that we might start putting some constraints on the size of government. And you come out with a completely different view towards what would be, for example, the best tax system. It is not something that is out of the skies best; it is rather what would work best given the way people are, and given what the economist can say about the behaviour of people. And I think the economist can say a great deal about the behaviour of people.

Again I go back to the point that we have lost a lot of wisdom and we are just gradually regaining that wisdom. From the eighteenth to early nineteenth century, we know a lot about the behaviour of people. It is not that everybody is somehow narrow, self seeking, always out to grab his own interest and trying to increase his own income share. But if we are talking about organizing institutions, that is the best presumption we can make.

I have been reading a very interesting book, a debate between James Mill and Mccaulay that took place in the eighteen-twenties, one hundred fifty years ago. And their view of the institutional process is much different from what you find anywhere today. So in a sense I am calling for a kind of return to the thinking of that period, in thinking about institutional rules. In this sense, and I am not at all sure that this might not apply in your country or in Europe generally, I am optimistic.

I think the level of sophistication among economists and among scholars generally who discuss this sort of question has improved over the last twenty years. I think it is very difficult now to find economists who would come out and base their policy recommendations on the idea that governments are going to work perfectly. We are gaining a realistic attitude, at least in America, on the part of the academic economist, political scientist, sociologist, lawyers, and others, on how the government is likely to work, where twenty years ago this was a completely unrealistic attitude. But we are in a paradox of sorts in the sense that always modern problems arise, and we do not know where to turn. We are not recovering, if we ever had any sort of positive belief or faith in the efficacy of the market process. So we are not turning things back to the market, but we do not trust the government either. We have a very sceptical view of how institutions and our government still grow with a sort of built-in dynamic. But the fact that we are beginning to translate some of this scepticism into a new constitutional dialogue is, it seems to me, a quite hopeful sign, at least in my country.

I have just done nothing more here than to give you a very general summary of my own approach to the methodology that I think economists ought to get into if they are going to talk about policy with some notion about the need for looking at political institutions if they want to reform those institutions. I suggested the adoption of what I might call an institutional-constitutional perspective on things. I tried to sketch that out a little bit for you in very general terms, relating it very generally to some of the work that I have done and I am doing.

The Use and Abuse of Contract

In this chapter I propose to examine the limits of the basic contractarian paradigm in helping us to understand and to suggest meaningful improvements in the social order that we observe. I shall defend the contractarian position against modern critics who have mounted attacks from at least two sides of an imaginary spectrum. Social contract theory is pilloried because it is seen as legitimizing everything about the modern state that seems objectionable, while at the same time but from quite different quarters the theory is castigated because it appears to offer a not-too-subtle defense for the ruling classes in the status quo.[1] Each of these criticisms is, within its advocate's interpretation, valid. Both are misdirected when the contractarian paradigm is appropriately articulated.

There are limits to both the explanatory-evaluative potential of contractarianism and its ability to satisfy the normative yearnings for a better world. In part, my aim here is to deflate the excessive claims for social contract theory that have been advanced, directly or indirectly, by some of the theory's critics while upholding the claims that may be properly defended. I shall proceed by first discussing in some detail the explanatory-evaluative use of contractarianism. Following this, I shall discuss the implications for social policy action that may emerge. I shall try to show that it is in the social policy im-

From *Freedom in Constitutional Contract: Perspectives of a Political Economist* (College Station: Texas A&M University Press, 1977), 135–47. Copyright 1977 James M. Buchanan. Reprinted by permission of the Texas A&M University Press.

1. The first criticism is one of the central themes of the late Alexander Bickel's much-acclaimed book *The Morality of Consent.* Bickel holds up his preferred Whig approach in contrast to his caricature of the contractarian position. The second criticism is advanced perhaps most clearly by Warren Samuels in "The Myths of Liberty and the Realities of the Corporate State: A Review Article," *Journal of Economic Issues* 10 (December, 1976): 923–42.

plications that the most serious distortions of the social contractarian's position may be identified. By defending against the first set of critics, however, my argument may seem to lend support to those who condemn the contractarian limits on normative grounds. The relationship between social contract theory and the alleged defense of the status quo must be squarely faced.

The Economist as Contractarian

Let me commence with my economist's habits, which can be turned to good account here. Economists look at the world and try, or should try, to explain as much of it as they can. They are specialists in exchange; they know, or should know, how the various institutions of exchange work.[2] When they observe a social interaction, they interpret the results in exchange terms, as possibly emergent from voluntary actions. To the extent that results can be fitted into the exchange pattern, economists can infer that *all* parties secure gains, as these gains are measured in terms of the participants' preferences and not those of the observer.

This explanatory task of the economist is, of course, drastically simplified when the exchange process, in itself, may be directly observed. When one person is seen to transfer goods voluntarily to another while the second person is seen to reciprocate with a return transfer, there is relatively little ambiguity in classifying the results as *efficient* and the process as *efficiency-increasing*, terms that necessarily carry with them evaluative meaning. This explanatory-evaluative task for the economist may be extended from the simplest to the most complex institutional structures.

The economist is allowed to say that "markets fail," or, to use the terminology introduced above, to say that an exchange process is not "efficiency-increasing" and the results not "efficient," when he is able to identify, conceptually or in actuality, nonvoluntary changes in personal endowments of goods and services. For example, the welfare economist raises questions when an exchange between A and B inflicts apparent damage on C, who is not a

---

2. This specialization in the institutions of exchange is the domain of the economist; he is not appropriately defined as a specialist in applied maximization, despite much evidence to the contrary in modern economists' practice. For the methodological defense of my position here, see my paper "What Should Economists Do?" *Southern Economic Journal* 30 (January, 1964): 213–22.

party to the contract between A and B. He is also likely to evaluate negatively the results of an exchange between E and F when he observes that G and H have apparently been prevented from entering the potential exchange as either alternative buyers or alternative sellers.

In this familiar explanatory-evaluative role the economist is remaining within the *contractarian paradigm,* although this term is rarely applied in this context. Before shifting discussion from the economist to the social scientist generally, however, it is useful to clarify the economist's evaluative task. What lies beyond diagnostic evaluation? Suppose that a feature in the environment is defined to be "inefficient." From this it follows that a shift toward "efficiency" should be socially desirable. But it is precisely at this point that many economists become inconsistent with their own contractarian model. They fail to keep within the bounds of voluntary exchange. To say that a situation is "inefficient" is to say indirectly that there must exist means to move toward "efficiency" by voluntary agreement. It is not to say that all moves toward "efficiency" in results are independently desirable, including those moves which might have to be imposed against the desires of participants. Any economist worth his salt can diagnose a tariff as generating inefficient results in terms of the standard criteria; he *cannot* use this diagnosis as the basis for recommending that the tariff simply be repealed.

The observing economist can suggest ways and means through which improvements may be made by agreement among all parties, and the test of his hypothesis lies only in agreement itself.[3] In the tariff example, agreement may require that those owners and workers in industries previously protected be compensated, that their existing entitlements be "purchased" by those in the community who stand to secure net benefits by the removal of the tariff barrier. If the tariff does, indeed, generate inefficient results, the gains will be more than sufficient to compensate those who are harmed.

In terms of the economist's standard criteria, observed inefficiency may or may not be consistent with agreed-on constitutional rules. Some inefficiency must be predicted to emerge from the sequential operation of any

---

3. This basic normative position for the economist was discussed in some detail in my paper "Positive Economics, Welfare Economics, and Political Economy," *Journal of Law and Economics* 2 (October, 1959): 124–38; the paper was reprinted in my *Fiscal Theory and Political Economy,* 105–24.

less-than-unanimity decision rules, and the costs of securing unanimity may exceed those reflected by such economic inefficiency. To an extent, at least, some economic restrictions such as tariffs may fall within this category. On the other hand, the economic inefficiencies observed may exceed those limits imposed by the costs of less-than-unanimity decision rules, reflecting in this case a situation that could not have emerged from the agreement among informed participants at the constitutional stage.[4]

It is the latter situation that places in clear relief the most difficult question that the contract theorist confronts. Suppose that an entitlement in the status quo is acknowledged to be demonstrably contrary to that pattern of entitlements that might have emerged from voluntary contract, from agreement among parties at some stage of constitutional negotiations. Is this entitlement to be respected in the sense that its holder (or owner) is to be considered as a necessarily willing participant in any change? Is the status quo distribution to be respected as the starting point or basis from which contracts may be renegotiated for the purpose of implementing change? In my view we must answer these questions affirmatively, not because the entitlements deserve "respect" in some normatively evaluative sense, but because there exists no alternative means of deriving acceptable judgments about change.

Can Prescription Follow Diagnosis?

Implicit in several of the modern criticisms there is what might be called a pseudocontractarian position involving a quite different stance. This position suggests that something akin to a contractarian logic is to be applied in evaluating the existing pattern of entitlements, but that there exists no contractual constraint on imposing changes in the status quo. It is precisely this use of hypothetical contract as the basis for nonvoluntary impositions of changes in political-legal structure that Bickel so sharply criticizes. In this interpretation the whole contractarian argument becomes little more than

---

4. The economist can readily diagnose cases of inefficiency in the first sense noted. He faces a much more difficult task in trying to determine whether or not the "economic constitution," which includes the costs of decision making as well as the costs of the results, is or is not "efficient."

rhetoric for construction of the observer's own version of a "social welfare function."[5]

The normative constraints within which the contractarian must operate seemingly become much more severe when we shift away from the familiar economic examples—tariffs and restrictions on entry into trades and professions—toward examples of political and legal entitlements. I shall introduce only one example that has been recently important in American constitutional law, the issue of apportionment of legislatures. Using the notion of social contract in its evaluative role, can an observed disproportion in representation among districts be rejected out of hand? That is, would a legislative assembly containing members from rural districts smaller in population than those represented by urban members necessarily be inconsistent with contractarian precepts? Could such a structure have emerged from a constitutional agreement in which potential residence was unknown? The answers here depend on the predicted working properties of alternative structures of representation. If predictions were made to the effect that rural citizens tend to be more stable in some meaningful sense than their urbanized counterparts, the apparent divergencies in political power may be rationalized, even on strict contractarian grounds.

By comparison, however, consider a situation in which legislative districts vary widely in population, but in which such variations exhibit no relationship to meaningful criteria for stability or anything else, and in which the observed pattern seems clearly to have been produced from explicit discriminatory motives. In this case the observer can reject the status quo apportionment on contractarian principles. But from this it does not follow that reapportionment is thereby justified in the absence of consensus or agreement. Just as in the more familiar economic examples, the shift from diagnostic evaluation to action independent of agreement involves a leap beyond contractarian limits. Diagnoses based on hypothetical contract can be useful in making initial evaluations of existing institutions, evaluations that can become inputs in attaining consensus upon suggestions or proposals for change. But hypothetical contract provides no justification for the imposi-

---

5. This is the interpretation, or misinterpretation, that Sidney Alexander placed on Rawls's work in "Social Evaluations through Notional Choice," *Quarterly Journal of Economics* 88 (November, 1974): 615.

tion of change nonvoluntarily. In this respect hypothetical contract has no advantage over the more familiar transcendental norms—economic efficiency, natural law, reason, truth, God's will, and so on. The contractarian construction used in evaluative diagnosis finds its advantage only when attempts are made to reach agreement on change.

But why should persons who possess advantages in the distribution of entitlements in the status quo ever agree on any change? Why should voters in the small-number districts ever agree to proposals for equitable reapportionment? Once again we may refer to the tariff example for comparison. We suggested above that for the latter, compensations might be required to secure the agreement of those owners and workers who have been protected behind an existing tariff barrier. Legal-political institutions that may be judged to be "inefficient" on contractarian principles are different from economic institutions only because they seem more difficult to analyze in value-equivalent terms. In principle there is no difference between suggesting that those protected by an existing "inefficient" tariff be compensated in order to secure their agreement on some change in trade policy, and suggesting that those who have been assigned more political power by historical gerrymandering of legislative seats be compensated in order to secure their agreement on some change toward a more "efficient" and equitable apportionment.

I am not suggesting that the compensations required to secure the approval of presently advantaged groups on changes from "inefficient" to "efficient" institutional arrangements will be easy to work out, whether the institutions be economic or political. I am suggesting that in the absence of general agreement or consensus the contractarian has no more license to impose his preferred changes than has any other "reformer." This restriction implies that the contractarian who genuinely seeks improvement on his own terms must necessarily enter the sometimes grubby world of debate, discussion, compromise, bargains, long-range deals, logrolling, package arrangements, and side payments. This apparently pedestrian effort, which may fail even in what may appear to be potentially the most promising opportunities for improvement, is necessarily less appealing aesthetically than the manipulation of imposed idealist solutions with or without the power to impose them on the community.

Because I write as an economist and because I use economists' terminology, it is necessary that I clarify the meaning of *compensation* in the discussion, lest my argument be seriously misinterpreted. The compensation pay-ment required to secure agreement is measured only by the result itself, only by the observed agreement on the part of those who, for any reason, initially stand in opposition to proposals for changes that might emerge from a con-tractarian diagnosis. Consider the apportionment example once again. If soundly based contractarian argument succeeds in convincing holders of dif-ferentially greater political power in the status quo that the existing situation is unjust, they may possibly agree to a constitutional change even in apparent contradiction with their own economic interest. In this context the con-vincing argument itself is the compensation; it meets the test of achieving agreement. It is precisely in this sense that basic contractarian argument on principles of justice, exemplified by the work of John Rawls, may be highly productive. To the extent that argument, debate, and discussion can generate consensus on change, on reform, the need to resort to more overt means of compensation is reduced or eliminated. But regardless of means, the aim of compensation is to secure agreement and in so doing to further the pros-pects for achieving genuinely voluntary reform.[6]

If the normative use of the contractarian paradigm is restricted as I have suggested, the second major criticism becomes applicable. If contractarian evaluation is not to be employed for the derivation of standards that may be imposed on all participants in the social order, changes from the status quo secure normative approval only to the extent that they emerge from volun-tary action. That is to say, normatively sanctioned movements must them-selves be "contractual" in the broadest meaning of this term. (The contrac-tual elements may, of course, be applied at several levels of institutional structure.) This restriction suggests to some critics that the whole contrac-tarian argument necessarily lends support to the relative distribution of en-titlements in the existing status quo.

6. I can place my argument here more directly in a Rawlsian context. We may interpret *A Theory of Justice* as an essay in persuasion, as an attempt to convince readers that they should agree on, and by implication implement, Rawls's "principles of justice" where these principles are not met by existing institutions. It would be, in my view, a misinter-pretation to suggest that Rawls's effort was aimed at offering a putative normative basis for the imposition of his "principles" by whoever might possess the power to modify ex-isting institutions, independent of agreement.

Contract and the Status Quo

I have suggested that the first argument against the contractarian approach is misdirected and that it is aimed at a "pseudocontractarianism" which cannot be defended. The second argument is more critical, since it is directed against the limited applicability of contractarian precepts that I have attempted to defend above. Bickel has attacked pseudocontractarianism because it justifies too much; Samuels has attacked "Wicksellian" contractarianism because it justifies too little. The status quo distribution of entitlements must be the starting point for the limited application of the normative contractarianism that I have outlined above. It is superficially plausible to suggest that this position must be an implicit defense of the status quo.

There are several effective counterarguments that may be made. First of all, it is essential to distinguish between *external* and *internal* evaluation and action. The contractarian rejects the role of external observer, the omniscient being who stands outside the network of personal interaction that a social community represents and whose values are not directly related to those of the participants, save as the latter may enter into the observer's own utility or preference function. The contractarian who remains himself a participant, and who acknowledges such a role, cannot simply "jump outside himself" and take on the trappings of a god. For the person who chooses to act in such a capacity, everything is possible, and he may approve or reject any given structure of holdings at will. Discussions among would-be gods are likely to be uninteresting to the contractarian who seeks to improve the world in which he lives.

Even if the possibility of external evaluation is rejected, however, and even if the observer acknowledges that he is among the observed in a complex social order, there seems nothing to prevent the observer from assigning his own private and personal value weights on alternative distributions of rights or entitlements among all participants.[7] And in such an evaluation process, the particular distribution existent in the status quo may be ranked well below many preferred alternatives. It is the operational usefulness instead of the intellectual possibility of such an evaluation that must be called into question here. The participant-observer may deplore the imputation of en-

---

7. For purposes of simplifying the argument at this point, we may assume that the evaluation is not based on contractarian criteria, as earlier discussed.

titlements that exists, but this reaction amounts to little more than ranting unless and until it begins to inform those who have power to modify the existing order. If the participant-observer does possess such power, he will presumably exercise it; he will impose involuntary changes in the positions of those who have no power to prevent them. We could, however, scarcely refer to a status quo distribution of rights or entitlements in any equilibrium sense until all such moves have been completed. That is, meaningful description of a status quo distribution of rights among members of a community must presume that all unilaterally motivated changes that are within the powers of the persons concerned to implement have been made. We may then ask: What is the meaning and purpose of a *cri de coeur* in such a setting, a protest that is centered on the notion, passionately held, that something other than the status quo would be "better"?

Such protests may, of course, be explicitly "revolutionary," in the sense that their purpose is to incite people to form new coalitions that may exploit the coercive power implicit in joint action to impose the changes desired. To a large extent, normative discussion of social policy falls within this category. Most reform advocates consider themselves to be engaged in a persuasion effort which, if successful, will produce a coalition that will command sufficient political power to enforce its will. And the reform advocates of this stripe express no moral inhibitions about imposing their preferred outcomes on all of their fellows, independent of expressed agreement or consent. In part, this demonstrated willingness to impose nonvoluntary changes on the existing pattern of entitlements in social order finds its own moral support in some "truth judgment" conception of politics generally. To the extent that the existence of "truth" in politics is accepted, the intellectual problem is one of discovery and definition. Once "truth" is found, there is no moral argument to be raised against its implementation. Consent is meaningless in this context. Opposition can be variously characterized as stemming from ignorance, folly, or the exercise of selfish interest. In any case, the views of those who actively oppose the truth-carrying zealots are not treated as worthy of respect. And any requirement to compromise with such views arises only because the reformists might otherwise lack the power to impose "truth" unilaterally.[8]

---

8. See my review of *Rational Decision*, Nomos Ser. No. 7, ed. Carl J. Friedrich, in *The Annals* 359 (May, 1965): 189–90.

The contractarian acknowledges from the outset that he holds no such universal keys to social wisdom. There is no "truth" in politics that is at all akin to that in science. Politics is beyond truth; it is concerned with a process of social interaction involving individuals. Once the participants are defined by the entitlements they claim in the existing order, each person's attitudes count for as much as any other person's.

At some personal level the contractarian may, along with his fellow non-contractarian observer-participant, deplore elements of apparent "injustice" in an existing distribution of entitlements. But he is morally prevented from imposing changes in this distribution, even should he, or a political coalition armed with his advice, possess the power to do so. Who is to say that A's claims should be reduced so that B's claims might be increased? The contractarian cannot assume the moral arrogance that would enable him to answer such questions. And more importantly, he denies the legitimacy of any such arrogance on the part of any person or group of persons in the community.

Indirectly, however, this position may seem to provide moral sanction for the distribution of entitlements, *any* distribution, that may come to exist in the historically determined status quo. If no one is allowed to say that A's claims should be increased at the expense of B's, then are we not saying that both A's claims and B's claims, as they now exist, are somehow "just," or, at the least, "legitimate"? As I have suggested earlier, the contractarian must acknowledge the status quo as the starting point or basis for any agreement upon change. Does such an acknowledgment of existential reality amount to an entitlement theory of justice? Surely the contractarian need not go further than, or even nearly so far as, Robert Nozick in attributing "justice" to the status quo distribution.[9] Using his own version of hypothetical contract, the observer may identify and classify existing institutions as "unjust." But this identification and classification process can be appropriately used only to provide inputs in a discussion that might lead to agreement upon change. To classify an institution as "unjust" does not allow the observer to make a major moral leap beyond this classification and say that such an institution should be eliminated or reformed in the absence of consent.[10]

9. Robert Nozick, *Anarchy, State, and Utopia*.
10. In this context "justice" may be likened to "truth" in scientific inquiry. A scientist may advance an argument to the effect that a proposition is "true." His argument is en-

It should be evident that the contractarian paradigm is more natural to the economist than to his fellow social scientists and philosophers, and it is not surprising that modern contractarian discourse has been conducted within a logical, analytical structure that is like that employed by economists. Contractarian precepts can be conceived as ultimately productive of genuine social reforms as long as application is limited to economic institutions. "Inefficiency" seems to be more readily identified through the analysis of welfare economics, and both the direction and the quantitative dimensions of the compromises that might be worked out seem capable of estimation. It is not nearly so easy to see the advantages of a contractarian approach to social reform of legal and political institutions. "Efficiency" in the operation of such institutions seems to lose the more precise meaning that is present when evaluating the performance of economic institutions.

The difference in precision is more apparent than real. Even in the simplest economic examples a position is defined to be "efficient" or "optimal" when gains from trade have been fully exhausted. There is no objectively identifiable "efficient" allocation apart from the observations of traders' unwillingness to engage in further exchanges. Economic institutions lend themselves to contractarian evaluation no better than do political institutions. But economists, who are specialists in exchange, do possess some comparative advantage both in understanding the contractarian logic and in appreciating its potential for application to social reality. Another way of stating this is to say that economists tend to concentrate their attention on a particular form of social interaction, on situations in which participants have divergent interests that are partially in conflict, but in which there exist potential gains to all. In the terminology of game theory, the emphasis is on positive-sum settings.

To the extent that real-world institutional reform can embody mutual gains, only the social contract theorist is intellectually and emotionally

---

tered into the scientific discourse, which may succeed in establishing a consensus among his fellow scientists. But the "truth" of the proposition emerges only in this agreement and not from some original objective reality. The scientist who originally advances the proposition has no grounds for imposing his hypothesis about its "truth" on his fellow scientists independent of the process of discussion leading to agreement. This is what Frank Knight meant when he stated that social scientists and social philosophers should adopt the morals instead of the methods of the physical scientists.

equipped to provide the initial critical groundwork for some ultimate organization of consensus. The noncontractarian tends to be too impatient. He will rarely seek out the consensus paths toward reform, even if such paths exist. And his apparatus does not allow him to make either a moral or an empirical distinction between positive-sum and zero- or even negative-sum prospects. On the other hand, the social contract theorist must acknowledge his own inability to say much about alternatives that fall within the range of pure conflict, the regime of zero-sum social games. If "exchange," conceived here in its broadest possible meaning of cooperation and agreement, is not possible, all solutions are equal. The transcendentalist, of any one of several variants, may be able to discuss purely distributional shifts more adequately than the contractarian if only because his thought patterns force him to treat all social and political changes within a pure conflict paradigm.

A Public Philosophy

In conclusion, I want to stress the importance of contractarianism as a part of a public philosophy. Even if the processes through which political and institutional changes are made do not require generalized consent or agreement among all persons and groups in the community; even if majority coalitions in legislative assemblies are observed to be decisive on many issues; even if the sometimes arbitrary dictates of the executive agencies and the judiciary can modify the distribution of entitlements within wide limits, the public attitudes toward these decision-making institutions are critically important. On the one hand, these institutionalized departures from contractual processes at the postconstitutional level can be viewed as embodying the continuing struggle of opposing interests, each one of which seeks to capture the arms and agencies of the state to promote and to further its own private ends, be these "noble" or "selfish." On the other hand, these institutional forms of postconstitutional decision making can be viewed as second-best alternatives to more inclusive decision rules made necessary by the presence of political transactions costs, but still reflecting consensus at the constitutional level. In the latter view, the results are still evaluated by the degree of consensus produced instead of the "victory" of one group over others.

In the latter contractarian view, the state in all its forms is interpreted as a necessary part of a complex exchange process that generates mutuality of gain. In the former view, the state becomes a mechanism or means through which some groups in the community secure "profits" at the expense of other groups. Social philosophers should recognize that their own conceptions of the state can have critically important effects on the attitudes of the citizenry.

PART THREE

Incentives and Constitutional Choice

Constitutional Choice, Rational Ignorance and the Limits of Reason

Viktor J. Vanberg and James M. Buchanan

1. Introduction

Elementary to any study of constitutional choice is the distinction between *constitutional* and *sub-constitutional choice* and the corresponding distinction between *constitutional* and *sub-constitutional preferences*. Constitutional choices are choices *among* alternative rules (constraints); sub-constitutional choices are among alternative strategies available *within* rules (constraints). A chooser's constitutional preferences reflect trade-offs among alternative rules that might be chosen. Sub-constitutional preferences reflect trade-offs among alternative courses of action or end-objects which are available for choice within a defined set of rules.

For sub-constitutional choices the prevailing rules or constraints are "relatively absolute absolutes"[1] in the sense that for these choices the rules are taken as parameters that define or limit the set of options. The rules are only "relative absolutes," however, since they can, themselves, be changed at the categorically separate constitutional level of decision. Constitutional choices may, of course, themselves be constrained by "higher" rules, relative to which they must be considered "sub-constitutional." Wherever one deals with a multilayered system of rules (i.e., systems that include rules for choosing rules) the

From *Jahrbuch für Neue Politische Ökonomie* 10 Band (1991): 61–78. Reprinted by permission of the publisher.

1. James M. Buchanan, "The Relatively Absolute Absolutes," in *Essays on the Political Economy* (Honolulu: University of Hawai'i Press, 1988), 32–46.

distinction between constitutional and sub-constitutional choices may be applied to any two adjoining levels of choice within a hierarchy.

In an earlier paper we have discussed some of the implications that result from the fact that constitutional preferences, like any other preferences, can be assumed to embody two conceptually separable components, an *interest-component* and a *theory-component*.[2] This distinction suggests that a person's preferences over alternative rules, among which he can exercise choice, reflect a combination of both his *theories* about the working properties of these rules (that is, his expectations concerning the overall pattern of outcomes that alternative rules will produce) and his *interests* in the expected outcome patterns.[3] For an example, a person may oppose the imposition of a highway speed limit because it is predicted to be unenforceable (a theory-component) or because he or she enjoys driving at high speeds (an interest-component). Because these two components underlie preferences over alternative rules, disagreement in constitutional choice may result from differences in theories as well as from differences in interests.

Neo-contractarian approaches to the issue of constitutional choice largely concentrate on divergences in interests as a source of disagreement with a view toward modification in the constitutional choice setting so as to reconcile such divergences.[4] A principal remedy for interest-based obstacles to constitutional agreement involves the introduction of some means of insuring persons' inability reliably to foresee their future *particularized* interests, as these may be affected by different rules, thereby inducing persons to make constitutional choices on some assessment of the *general* working properties of alternative rules, and divorced from particularized interests. The Buchanan-Tullock *veil of uncertainty* and the Rawlsian *veil of ignorance*

---

2. Viktor Vanberg and James M. Buchanan, "Interests and Theories in Constitutional Choice," *Journal of Theoretical Politics* 1 (January 1989): 49–62.

3. "A person's constitutional theories are about matters of fact. They are his predictions (embodying assumptions and beliefs) about what the factual outcomes of alternative rules will be. These predictions may, of course, be arranged in a true or false, correct or incorrect scalar. His constitutional interests, on the other hand, are his own, subjective *evaluations* of expected outcomes, evaluations to which attributes like true or false, correct or incorrect cannot be meaningfully applied" (ibid., 52).

4. John Rawls, *A Theory of Justice* (Cambridge: Harvard University Press, 1971); James M. Buchanan and Gordon Tullock, *The Calculus of Consent: Logical Foundations of Constitutional Democracy* (Ann Arbor: University of Michigan Press, 1962).

are, in this sense, assumed to render persons uncertain or ignorant about their particularized interests, while not inhibiting their capability accurately to anticipate the general effects of potential alternative rules. Indeed, in Rawls' construction the participants in constitutional choice are assumed to be fully informed about the general working properties of potential alternative constitutions.[5]

In this paper our focus is quite different. Instead of considering the interest-component as the principal source of problems in constitutional choice while taking the theory-component as unproblematic, we shall explore the reverse assumption. We shall consider the interest-component as unproblematic and concentrate on issues that arise when the participants in constitutional choice are assumed to be less than fully informed about the general effects of rules and to hold potentially conflicting constitutional *theories*. We shall, in other words, exclusively concentrate on the *knowledge-problem* rather than the interest-problem in constitutional choice. We shall, for the purposes of this paper, assume that there is no conflict in constitutional interests among those for whom and/or by whom a constitutional choice is to be made, so that the only issue is to find or select the rules that best serve the commonly shared constitutional interests. (To remain with a road traffic example, all road users agree on the objective which is to minimize commuting time over a network; they share this common interest. Disagreement may, however, arise concerning what set of rules will be most likely to achieve such a result.) This assumption of shared interests and divergent theories is, of course, just as artificial as its obverse. In reality both the interest-problem and the knowledge-problem coexist in an intertwined fashion. It is nevertheless useful for analytical purposes conceptually to separate the two and to consider their respective effects in isolation.

The remainder of this paper is organized as follows: Section 2 discusses some general characteristics of the knowledge-problem in constitutional

---

5. ". . . I assume that the parties are situated behind a veil of ignorance. They do not know how the various alternatives will affect their own particular case. . . . It is taken for granted, however, that they know the general facts about human society. They understand political affairs and the principles of economic theory; they know the basis of social organization and the laws of human psychology. Indeed, the parties are presumed to know whatever general facts affect the choice of the principles of justice" (Rawls, *A Theory of Justice*, 136f.).

choice and draws attention to the differences between two distinct aspects, (1) *rational ignorance* and (2) the *limits of reason*. Section 3 elaborates on the first of these two aspects, and Section 4 considers the role of experts as a potential remedy. Section 5 discusses the "limits of reason" problem and the role that constitutional competition can play in this context. Section 6 argues that persons who are aware of and anticipate the knowledge-problem in constitutional choice should have a predictable interest in adopting a meta-constitution that allows for and encourages explorative constitutional competition. Section 7 concludes the paper with some reflections on constitutional choice as a creative process.

2. The Knowledge-Problem in Constitutional Choice

While potential interest-based conflict in constitutional choice is alleviated as the choosers' uncertainty/ignorance of their prospective particularized interests increases, potential knowledge-based disagreement obviously requires the opposite cure. So far as the interest dimension is concerned, the prospects for reaching constitutional agreement are enhanced by whatever tends to increase uncertainty, that is, to thicken the veil. By contrast, potential knowledge-grounded disagreement is alleviated as the participants are made more aware of the prospective general working properties of rules. Or, in terms of the veil metaphor, the knowledge-problem is alleviated by whatever tends to make the veil that covers the general properties of rules more transparent.

There are two elements of constitutional epistemology to be distinguished here. One concerns the prospects of securing agreement in constitutional theories among persons who are empowered to choose. When we assume that the participants in a constitutional choice setting share the same constitutional interests, the source of disagreement in expressed constitutional preferences can be a matter only of conflicting theories. If, in addition, we should also assume that all participants are perfectly informed about the general working properties of the rules under consideration, agreement would necessarily emerge on what—relative to their common interests—the best rules are. Shared "perfect knowledge" is, in this sense, obviously a sufficient condition for resolving epistemological sources of constitutional conflict. Agreement may, however, emerge without "perfect knowledge." Less than perfectly knowledgeable choosers may agree on mistaken theories. This presents the second element to be considered. Rational participants who are aware of their imperfect constitutional knowledge will not only be concerned about constitutional agreement per se; they will also wish to insure that agreement emerges on those rules that will, in fact, best serve their commonly shared interests. And the prospects for identifying and adopting good or efficient rules, i.e., rules that serve their interests best, are enhanced by whatever improves their mutually shared information and knowledge about the general working properties of rules.

For the knowledge-problem in constitutional choice, the notion of *constitutional discourse* is, in some sense, the analogue to the notion of the veil as it is used in the Rawls-Buchanan-Tullock contractarian perspectives. The veil notion can be seen as a summary label for factors that, by increasing uncertainty, tend to alleviate potential conflicts in constitutional interests. By contrast, the notion of discourse can be interpreted as a summary label for factors that tend to alleviate the knowledge-problem by eliminating disagreement in constitutional theories and, at the same time, improving the quality of these theories.[6] In this interpretation, "discourse" includes everything that advances the acquisition, communication and processing of general constitutional information and knowledge. The issue examined in this paper can be rephrased as that of the role of discourse in constitutional choice.

As we shall discuss more carefully in the following sections, the role of discourse in constitutional choice is subject to two kinds of limitations. It is subject to what may be called *motivational limitations,* i.e., limitations in the willingness of the members of the constitutional constituency to incur the costs that participating in constitutional discourse involves. And it is subject to *cognitive limitations,* i.e., limitations in the constitutional constituency's cognitive capacity to discern and anticipate reliably the general operating properties of alternative rules. In what follows, the issue of the motivational limitations will be discussed under the rubric of *rational ignorance,* the issue

---

6. The relation between a *discourse* and a *contractarian* perspective on constitutional agreement is discussed in more detail in Vanberg and Buchanan, "Interests and Theories in Constitutional Choice."

of the cognitive limitations under the rubric of *the limits of reason*. As will become apparent, the remedies for the problems that are associated with these two limitations are in part the same.

3. Constitutional Choice and Rational Ignorance

One of the most familiar principles in Public Choice is the rational ignorance hypothesis,[7] which states that in large electoral constituencies it is privately rational for a single voter to remain ignorant about the alternatives of collective choice because of the negligible influence of his or her own vote on the outcome. Obviously, the argument applies *a fortiori* where, as we assume here, there are no conflicts of interest. If the participants in a constitutional choice setting have the same constitutional interests, an improvement in the quality of the rules that are adopted is a pure public good. Consequently, so far as any such improvement is concerned, any individual expenditure on constitutional information/knowledge is a contribution to a pure public good which rational actors cannot be expected to make. Therefore, under the assumptions made here, we should expect the members of the constitutional constituency to remain rationally ignorant and potentially to adopt inferior rules.

It is useful to recall the original, precise meaning of the rational ignorance hypothesis. The specific, and limited, claim is that in a large constituency (with a secret ballot),[8] the impact of a single vote on the outcome is insignificant; therefore, the prospects of an individual's improving the outcome by casting a single better informed vote do not provide significant incentives for a voter to incur the costs of becoming better informed, even if these costs are quite small. Note that the "rationality of ignorance" is claimed only with reference to the ultimate impact of a vote on the outcome of the col-

7. Peter Aranson, "Rational Ignorance in Politics, Economics and Law," *Journal des Economistes et des Etudes Humaines* 1 (Winter 1989/1990): 25–42.

8. Though normally not explicitly mentioned, a secret ballot has to be presumed because with public vote-casting—and apart from such issues as "preference falsification" (Timur Kuran, "Sparks and Prairie Fires: A Theory of Unanticipated Political Revolution," *Public Choice* 61, no. 1 [April 1989]: 41–74)—the actual impact of a vote on the outcome would be dependent on certain contingent facts such as, e.g., the public standing of a voter. The crucial characteristic of a secret ballot, namely that the impact on the outcome of any and every vote is $1/n$, does not hold per se for an open ballot.

lective choice. Wherever informational investments are potentially relevant for other activities with other prospective payoffs, it is the size of these payoffs which determines whether—and to what extent—it is rational to remain ignorant.

For the issue of constitutional choice, the rational ignorance hypothesis does not support the unqualified conclusion that rational actors in a large constituency will remain constitutionally ignorant. Instead, whether or not it is rational to invest in constitutional information/knowledge will depend on one's involvement in other activities—other than casting votes—through which such investments may promise to pay off. And it would seem obvious that the broader category of activities which fall under the rubric of "constitutional discourse" includes some that are likely to provide incentives for some such investment. The examples that we shall consider are: Private or public engagement in discourse on constitutional issues, and prospects of securing and retaining public office or acting as a political entrepreneur.

The same argument that explains why a rational actor—in the absence of selective incentives—cannot be expected to contribute to a public good, can also explain why those who are part of the group of potential beneficiaries can be expected to have an interest in *others* contributing. The external benefits that contributing behavior produces, while not providing incentives for one's own contribution, create an interest in the behavior of others. And such interest, again, is likely to generate a normative expectation that others *should* contribute, an expectation that may find its behavioral expression in ways that provide selective incentives for others actually to contribute. Public goods situations are, in this sense, prone to generate mutually reinforced normative expectations which originate from an interest in the behavior of *others,* but are mirrored in expectations such that everybody in the respective constituency confronts such a normatively impregnated environment. Applied to the problem under consideration: Rational individuals, in a constitutional constituency with the characteristics assumed here, can be expected to have an interest in others making investments in constitutional knowledge, and such interest is likely to generate a mutually reinforced and expressed normative expectation that, as a good citizen, one *should* make an effort to be informed. To the extent that, because of such shared expectations, being perceived as a "good citizen" is instrumental in getting access to valued goods, a rational actor will find it in his interest to make some investment in constitutional information/knowledge.[9] In this sense, an "ethic of constitutional citizenship" may find its roots in rational self-interest.[10]

Intertwined with, but distinguishable from, the "public goods–normative expectations" nexus is a person's interest in being respected as an informed and sought after participant in conversations, an interest that to some extent provides incentives for investments in constitutional knowledge. A similar argument can also be made for persons who seek or hold offices for which constitutional expertise is a qualifying attribute, as well as for persons who seek the potential rewards that political entrepreneurship promises. The general conclusion from the preceding arguments is that the rational ignorance hypothesis has to be qualified as one goes beyond its original limited claim concerning voting behavior in large constituencies. There are numerous other activities for which investment in constitutional knowledge promises payoffs and which, therefore, make constitutional ignorance less "rational" than the exclusive focus on voting behavior suggests.

Although, as we have argued above, various incentives may make at least some investment in constitutional information/knowledge rational, such incentives are unlikely to sustain an overall level of expertise that would fully meet the ultimate *constitutional preferences* of individuals. That is to say that, if persons could choose among constituencies with varying levels of constitutional expertise, other things equal, they can be expected to prefer one with a higher level of constitutional knowledge or wisdom than that which will be sustained by the incentives noted. There would, in other terms, be a constel-

9. A more complete version of this argument could be construed along the lines of David Gauthier's argument on the rationality of adopting a *moral disposition:* To be perceived as a moral person makes a person a desirable partner for cooperative activities and, thus, provides access to cooperative gains that otherwise could not be obtained. To the extent that the prospects for effective, cost-saving mimicry are limited, actually to possess a moral disposition can be a necessary prerequisite for getting access to such cooperative gains, hence the rationality of morality (David Gauthier, *Morals by Agreement* [Oxford: Clarendon Press, 1986]; Viktor Vanberg and James M. Buchanan, "Rational Choice and Moral Order," in *From Political Economy to Economics . . . and Back?* ed. J. H. Nichols and J. H. Wright [San Francisco: ICS Press, 1990]). For the present argument, the respective logic would be that, where effective mimicry is not feasible, actually doing the things that define a "good citizen" may be the precondition to obtain access to the rewards that result from being perceived as such.

10. James M. Buchanan, "The Ethics of Constitutional Order," in *The Economics and the Ethics of Constitutional Order* (Ann Arbor: University of Michigan Press, 1991), 7.

lation where their separate individualized choices to invest in constitutional knowledge would not generate the state of affairs that would ultimately be preferred—a constellation that is characteristic of any kind of the generalized *social dilemma*. The question then arises concerning what, if any, reforms might be suggested.

Individuals in a constitutional constituency who anticipate the presence of rational ignorance, even if qualified in the above sense, can be assumed to share an interest in incorporating provisions in their constitution which promise to cure or alleviate this problem. Such provisions may be designed either to provide additional incentives for investments in constitutional knowledge or to decrease the costs of providing such knowledge. And they may be designed simply to circumvent the problem. The first of the three options would include, for instance, adopting constitutional constraints which make some kind of constitutional training mandatory—such as a requirement that everyone participate in certain programs for constitutional education. Such schemes, even if they would be effective in their intended purpose, are, however, likely to be perceived as undesirable in other respects. Provisions for lowering the costs of providing constitutional knowledge would include the use of specialized experts, a device that will be discussed in the next section. And, finally, provisions for circumventing the rational ignorance problem might include the use of —what we will call—*constitutional competition* (to be discussed in Sections 6 and 7).

4. Rational Ignorance and Constitutional Experts

Any socioeconomic arrangement of even moderate complexity has to provide for the possibility that individuals can benefit from knowledge that they do not themselves possess privately. This point is central to Hayek's argument concerning the "use of knowledge in society" and his inference concerning the superior characteristics of markets as "utilizers of dispersed knowledge."[11] The division of labor across markets allows participants in the exchange nexus to benefit from contributions of highly specialized experts without any necessity to acquire for themselves even a small fraction of the total expert knowl-

11. Friedrich A. Hayek, "The Use of Knowledge in Society," in *Individualism and Economic Order* (Chicago: University of Chicago Press, 1948), 77–91.

edge utilized. Most of us drive cars, use computers or telefax without knowing much about their basic technology. Possession of such knowledge is not prerequisite to the enjoyment of the benefits of these technological achievements. Could any comparable role for experts be feasible in the realm of constitutional construction?

The notion that "experts" should be entrusted with governmental-constitutional authority has, of course, a long tradition, ranging at least from Plato's "philosopher king" to the communist fiction of the "enlightened avant-garde." The objections to such notions are also well known. They have mainly to do with the implied tendency to legitimize the role of a self-appointed elite which remains beyond the control of those who are subject to government. It is obvious that the authoritarian-totalitarian version of the "constitutional expert" model does not qualify in any meaningful sense as an analogue to the above-mentioned role of experts in markets. Relevant analogues can be identified, however, by considering what role rational actors, anticipating the problem of rational ignorance, would be willing to assign to *constitutional experts.*

One scheme might be some analogue to the model of political competition that is embodied in the ordinary constitutional structure of representative democracy. In terms of this model, individuals in a constitutional constituency would select from a set of competing experts those whom they consider most competent. If, as we assume here, there exist no conflicts of constitutional interest in the constituency, the selection problem reduces to that of assessing the relative competence of those who would claim to be experts. And, to the extent that a comparably reliable choice among competent experts is less costly—requires less investment in constitutional knowledge—than the raw choice among constitutional alternatives themselves, rational individuals will have a reason to choose the lower-cost procedure.[12] The putative experts' motivation for acquiring constitutional competence derives from the prospects of securing the advantages attached to the office, given the constraints that the competitive setting imposes.

12. In an earlier article on the role of experts in constitutional choice (James M. Buchanan and Viktor Vanberg, "A Theory of Leadership and Deference in Constitutional Construction," *Public Choice* 61, no. 2 [April 1989]: 15–28), we have discussed this aspect as well as related issues, though with a focus that is somewhat different from our present inquiry.

Closer comparison suggests that there are significant differences between the two above-mentioned roles for experts in markets and in representative democracy. For the latter, the rational ignorance problem reasserts itself again because, in a large constituency, a single person's vote is unlikely to decide which among a competing set of experts will be chosen. Hence, the effect on the electoral outcome itself cannot be considered an important source of incentives for acquiring knowledge which would make for a better informed vote. To be sure, in the sense discussed above, there may be other reasons (other than the electoral outcome) for investing in constitutional information/knowledge. And, to the extent that a reliable choice among experts involves less information-costs, the discrepancy between actually acquired and ideally required knowledge may be less for the choice among experts than for the raw choice among constitutional alternatives. However, the essential difference from the market-expert model remains, a difference the significance of which becomes apparent when one imagines, for instance, how a system might work when a choice among motor cars is delegated to an automotive "expert" to be chosen in some electoral process.

There are two respects here in which the choice procedures would be different. There is, on the one side, the difference between individual and collective choice and, on the other side, the difference between a choice among the experts themselves and a choice among their products. The two differences have important motivational and informational implications. The ordinary consumer choice in the automobile market is an individual choice among the products of competing expert-producers. That it is an individual choice implies that there is no requirement, though it may conceivably be the factual outcome, that everybody in the relevant community purchase the same model. And it implies, in particular, that the benefits as well as the costs of choice are fully sensed by the individual. The cost of an uninformed choice is the increased probability of ending up with an inferior product. The situation would be dramatically different if the choice among models should be made collectively, i.e., if the community as a collective would decide by vote which model to choose. In this case there would not only be one model; more importantly, for a single voter the benefits/costs of an informed/uninformed vote are, in a large constituency, as negligible as the likelihood that a single vote will be decisive. The incentives for investing in the relevant kind of knowledge are dramatically reduced.

As for the difference between choosing among experts and choosing among their products, ordinary consumer choice in the automobile market falls into the latter category and, as such, does not require any assessment of the producer's competence in any direct sense. For an informed choice no more is required than a comparative assessment of relevant working properties of the expert-products, an assessment for which relevant information is much more readily available, and that can be done reliably with little knowledge of the technical expertise that actually lies behind production. On the other hand, if consumers, instead of directly choosing among cars, would have to choose from competing automobile-producers, with the one chosen then, for some specified period, to be authorized as exclusive supplier, the informational requirement for an intelligent choice would be significantly higher, and the performance of the industry would probably be quite different.

The analysis suggests that the electoral choice among constitutional experts is likely to exhibit significantly less responsiveness to constituents'/consumers' interests than the market choice among expert-products, for two reasons: Because it operates through collective rather than individual choice, and because it requires a choice among the experts themselves rather than their products. The question that, upon such diagnosis, suggests itself is, of course, whether, for the realm of constitutional choice, a procedure may be conceivable that incorporates more of the working properties of the market model, i.e., that allows for a greater role of *individual choice among constitutions* instead of *collective choice among constitutional experts*.

There is, in fact, something like a "constitutional analogue" to the ordinary market-role of experts. Any entrepreneur who organizes cooperative arrangements of whatever sort is, in a real sense, also a constitutional entrepreneur, even if the legal fixation of a set of predefined contractual-legal forms (like partnership, joint stock company, etc.) has narrowed down the range for potential variation. In setting up and managing an ongoing cooperative arrangement, an entrepreneur, in effect, establishes and maintains a constitutional order among all those who take part in the joint venture, whether as investors or as contributors of labor, skills and know-how. These other participants are typically in a position to choose individually and separately among alternative constitutional-organizational arrangements—as stockholders to invest in company A rather than B; as employees to contract with firm C rather than D—and they will typically base their decision on their assessment of what are to them relevant working properties of alternative cooperative arrangements, i.e., of the expert-product, rather than on an assessment of the entrepreneur's-expert's competence per se. And the entrepreneur's prospects for success or failure will depend on his ability to produce a constitutional-organizational order with working properties which, in an environment of competing alternative options, are sufficiently attractive to those whose cooperation has to be secured. Similar arguments apply to other kinds of social-organizational arrangements, like clubs or associations, that are voluntarily formed in a competitive environment.

If a comparable role for individual choice among existing alternative constitutional arrangements could be realized at the level of polities, this would have obviously significant implications. As one moves from collective choice among alternative constitutions to collective choice among constitutional experts to, finally, individual choice among alternative constitutional arrangements, not only are the informational requirements for an intelligent choice dramatically reduced, the individual's incentives for making an informed choice significantly increase. While it may be very difficult to predict reliably the working properties of alternative constitutional rules, and also difficult to assess the true competence of constitutional experts, individuals will have much less difficulty in assessing the relevant working properties of actually operating constitutional systems. And, as they individually and separately choose their own "constitutional environment," they also have much more reason to make an informed choice, compared to their participation in a collective choice among constitutional rules or among constitutional experts.

5. Constitutional Choice and the Limits of Reason

So far, our discussion on the knowledge problem in constitutional choice has been confined to those aspects that can be viewed as a consequence of the "rational ignorance problem." The previous line of argument could remain unchanged if we should assume that "perfect constitutional knowledge" is, in principle, available and that the only problem is to provide appropriate incentives for "experts" to acquire it. The problem takes on a wholly new dimension, however, once we recognize that such perfect knowledge is not available and that there are no perfectly knowledgeable experts who would be able rationally to design a perfect constitutional system. The claim to such knowledge is part of the mind-set that Friedrich A. Hayek has criticized as *constructivist rationalism.*

Hayek's critique is, in fact, directed against two distinguishable, though interrelated, versions of the "pretense of knowledge" that he sees in constructivist rationalism. The two versions correspond to two dimensions of the "knowledge problem" which we may distinguish as "horizontal" or "cross-sectional" on the one side, and "inter-temporal" on the other (p. 179).[13] The first, or "horizontal," problem is the principal issue in Hayek's critique of the notion of central planning. He argues there that it is impossible for any planner or planning agency to know, and to make use of, the particular knowledge about locational and temporal contingencies that exists fragmented and dispersed among the individual contemporaries in society. And, as mentioned above, he concludes that such dispersed knowledge can best be utilized in markets where individuals are free, within the constraints of general rules of conduct, to make their own choices and to trade freely with each other.

Of particular importance in the present context is, however, not the first, but the second, the "inter-temporal" dimension of the knowledge problem. While the first explains, in Hayek's account, why we have to rely largely on general *rules,* rather than commands, in order to coordinate our efforts efficiently, the "inter-temporal" dimension concerns the issue of how we can know what *good rules* are. What Hayek criticizes as "pretense of knowledge" in this regard is the claim that we can rationally design, based on abstract reasoning, an appropriate framework of rules, a desirable institutional order. Such claim ignores, he argues, that our cognitive limitations simply prevent us from having reliable a priori knowledge of how imagined alternative rules work out in practice, and from being able to determine by ex ante reasoning which system of rules will generate the most desirable socioeconomic order.

If we liken, as Hayek suggests, rules to "tools,"[14] in the sense that they serve to solve recurrent problems, and, accordingly, view social rules as "tools"

---

13. Viktor Vanberg, "Hayek as Constitutional Political Economist," *Wirtschaftspolitische Blätter* 36 (1989): 170–82.

14. Viktor Vanberg, "Innovation, Cultural Evolution and Economic Growth" (Center for Study of Public Choice, George Mason University, 1990, mimeographed), 5 ff.

for solving recurrent social interaction problems, then the "limits of reason" argument can be restated as saying that, on pure rational grounds and through logical deduction, we cannot discern ex ante what the best "tools" are. We are unable to do so because we simply do not possess as explicit knowledge the accumulated experience that underlies the system of rules and institutions we live in. And we are unable to do so for two more reasons: Because our knowledge changes over time, and we cannot know today what we will know in the future, and second, because our problems—or our perception of them—change as well, and we cannot know today what our future problems will be. Our search for *good rules* has, therefore, to be guided by the kind of experience that accumulates in an ongoing, open-ended process of trial and error.

It is in this sense that Hayek emphasizes the necessity for us to rely, in matters of constitutional choice, on the experiences that have been made by previous generations and have become incorporated in time-tested traditions. And it is in this context that he introduces the notion of cultural evolution as a spontaneous process of "winnowing and sifting" that supposedly selects for efficient rules, a notion that is subject to criticism.[15] Yet, even if one rejects a Hayekian acquiescence to cultural evolution as poor guidance in constitutional matters,[16] it has to be acknowledged that in our efforts at deliberate constitutional construction we cannot but operate on the basis of *conjectural* and *hypothetical* knowledge, and that we can never predict with certainty how potential constitutional alternatives will work out under ever-changing circumstances. Looked at from this perspective, competition among constitutional experts and competition among alternative constitutional arrangements are of importance not only for the motivational and informational reasons discussed earlier. They are also important in their role as a "discovery procedure" for finding desirable constitutional arrangements.[17] That is, they are important because of their *dynamic* role, as *constitutional exploration*,

---

15. Viktor Vanberg, "Spontaneous Market Order and Social Rules," *Economics and Philosophy* 2, no. 1 (April 1986): 75–100.

16. James M. Buchanan, "Cultural Evolution and Institutional Reform," in *Liberty, Market and State* (New York: New York University Press, 1985), 75–86.

17. Friedrich A. Hayek, "Competition as a Discovery Procedure," in *New Studies in Philosophy, Politics, Economics and the History of Ideas* (Chicago: University of Chicago Press, 1978), 179–90.

for the inventing of and experimenting with new solutions to constitutional problems.

With regard to the issue of *constitutional exploration* it is useful to remember the previously discussed differences between an electoral competition among constitutional experts and the market-type competition among alternative constitutional arrangements. In the constitutional realm, as elsewhere, it is not the fact of competition per se that is of interest, since all human social activities take place under *some kind* of competition. The critical issue is *what kind* of constitutional competition can be expected to operate in a desirable way, where "desirable" is to be defined in terms of some normative criterion, by which the performance of a constitutional order is to be judged. If responsiveness to constituents' wants and interests is what we deem desirable, it should be obvious that—where feasible—a market-type constitutional competition is superior to electoral competition.

As for the feasibility of market-type constitutional competition, there is, to be sure, a critical difference between constitutional arrangements at the level of polities and the kind of voluntary organizational-constitutional arrangements that we described in the introductory paragraph to this section, a difference that limits the feasibility of individual constitutional choice at the polity-level. Polities typically have a "territorial base," and membership in political communities is, therefore, essentially defined in residential territorial terms, such that a change in membership affiliation typically requires a corresponding change in residency.[18] To the extent that such residential implications increase the individuals' costs of separately choosing among alternative constitutional arrangements, their responsiveness to constituents' wants will tend to be reduced or, in Albert O. Hirschman's terms, to be more dependent on the exercise of "voice."[19] The interest of rational constituents in securing responsiveness to their constitutional interests should, therefore, suggest that the "cost of exit" itself becomes of concern for constitutional

18. We ignore here the complexities that are introduced by the possibility of a dissociation of citizenship and residency, because it has no relevant implication for the central concern of our argument.

19. Albert O. Hirschman, *Exit, Voice, and Loyalty: Responses to Decline in Firms, Organizations, and States* (Cambridge: Harvard University Press, 1970), and "Exit, Voice and the State," in *Essays in Trespassing: From Economics to Politics and Beyond* (Cambridge: Cambridge University Press), 246–65.

considerations. Securing low-cost options for individuals to choose separately among alternative constitutional regimes may not only provide a remedy for the problems with "rational ignorance" and the "limits of reason." It may also alleviate problems that result from differences and conflicts in constitutional interests by allowing for constitutional diversity and the "sorting out" of divergent constitutional preferences.

6. A Meta-constitution for an Open Society

Rational actors who are aware of the fallibility of their efforts in constitutional construction, who know that they cannot know in advance what the best solution to their constitutional problems is—nor, as a matter of fact, what they will perceive as constitutional problems in the future—can be expected to have an interest in providing for the possibility of *constitutional learning*, for the possibility of correcting and further developing their constitutional arrangements in the light of new experience.[20] The "experimenting" that such learning requires is, to be sure, that which takes place in a competitive environment where individuals can compare, and act upon, the performance characteristics of alternative constitutional provisions. It cannot be expected to result from the global and sequential reorientations that have been characteristic of the way in which the centralist socialist "experiments" of this century have been carried out.

It is in this context that the Hayekian notion of cultural evolution can be usefully reintroduced in a modified sense. The essential problem with Hayek's use of this notion is his failure to specify the conditions under which a process of rule-evolution can be expected to select for rules that are "desirable," if we take the wants and interests of those who are to live under these rules as the relevant measuring rod.[21] Hayek is certainly right in his emphasis on the lim-

---

20. "If the future is unknowable, not only will individuals make mistakes . . . but such mistakes will be expected . . . (I)ndividuals will wish to 'build in' to any system of social arrangements provisions for the correction of previous error (as revealed by the divergencies between the expected and the actual outcome of plans)" (Jack Wiseman, "Principles of Political Economy—an Outline Proposal, Illustrated by Application to Fiscal Federalism," *Constitutional Political Economy* 1, no. 1 [Winter 1990]: 101–24).

21. In fact, despite the normative individualism of classical liberalism that is at the foundation of Hayek's system of thought, in his discussion on "cultural evolution" Hayek

its of rational constitutional design and on the need for us to rely on experience which emerges from the trials and errors of a competitive evolutionary process. Yet, as our earlier remarks on "kinds of competition" imply, not just any competitive evolutionary process can be expected to select in favor of rules that are "desirable" in the above sense. Rather, whether this will be the case or not will critically depend on the terms of evolutionary competition, specifically on the role that the constituents' interests and desires play in the selection process. Conditions conducive to such a role cannot be presumed spontaneously to prevail but are likely to require deliberate constructive effort.

The above arguments can be translated into the conjecture that rational actors who are aware of the fallibility of their constitutional constructions, and who, therefore, want deliberately to employ the explorative potential of an evolutionary competitive process, should have an interest in adopting a *meta-constitution* which is designed to secure favorable conditions for a constitutional competition that is responsive to constituents' interests.[22] A fundamental principle informing such a meta-constitution would be to favor provisions which tend to reduce the costs of individual choices among constitutional alternatives.

An obvious minimal requirement, in this regard, would be the removal and avoidance of deliberately imposed exit-barriers as they have been— and, at some places, still are—a common practice of totalitarian regimes.[23]

---

is not at all unambiguous about the normative standard, if any, against which he judges the forces of cultural evolution to work "beneficially."

22. This amounts to what one may call *organized constitutional evolution,* a combination of deliberate design and evolutionary learning: The design of a framework of meta-rules within which efforts in constitutional construction are subject to a kind of evolutionary competition that promises to select in favor of rules which serve the interests of the respective constituencies.

23. This is not to imply that *any* deliberate exit-barrier is necessarily to be considered illegitimate. The members of a constituency may agree to impose on themselves certain exit-costs, as a commitment, in order to allow for the realization of benefits which otherwise would be unattainable. Yet, in their "calculus of advantage" the benefits to be gained would have to be weighed against the undesirable consequences of inhibiting individual "mobility."

An interesting issue, though one that we cannot discuss in the present context, is the role of *entry-* as opposed to *exit-barriers.* Though both create obstacles to individual choice among alternative constitutional arrangements, they are clearly different, both in

And the general provision by which the "natural" costs of individual choice among alternative constitutional arrangements can be reduced is *decentralization* in two principal forms, for which the concepts of *federalism*[24] and *consociationalism*[25] seem to be appropriate labels. Under the rubric of federalism we subsume all provisions for *territorial decentralization*, i.e., provisions which are informed by the principle of allocating political tasks in such a way that, wherever feasible and reasonable, preference is given to local sub-units over more inclusive polities. The concept of consociationalism includes all provision for *nonterritorial decentralization*, i.e., provisions which are based on the principle that political tasks should be allocated in such a way that, wherever feasible and reasonable, preference should be given to nonterritorial units over territorially based polities. The principle of federalism or territorial decentralization is exemplified by measures that transfer political authority from more encompassing to smaller polities. The principle of consociationalism is exemplified by measures that transfer authority from territorially based polities to organizations in which membership is dissociated from the residential-territorial dimension.

The appropriate level for effective agreements on a *meta-constitution*, in the sense of the above discussion, will, to some extent, be the level of international accords. International agreements—in particular concerning the free movement of persons, resources and ideas—can serve as commitments of nation-states that constrain their ability to interfere with their constituents' freedom of "constitutional choice."[26] But there may also be other con-

---

their factual implications and with regard to the kind of arguments that might be advanced in their support.

24. Vincent Ostrom, "Constitutional Considerations with Particular Reference to Federal Systems," in *Guidance, Control and Evaluation in the Public Sector*, ed. F. X. Kaufmann et al. (New York: Walter de Gruyter, 1986), 111–25; Wiseman, "Principles of Political Economy."

25. Daniel J. Elazar, ed., "Federalism and Consociationalism: A Symposium," *Publius: The Journal of Federalism* 15, no. 2 (1985).

26. Such commitments could be made effective, without the need to create some specialized enforcement agency, e.g., by specifying rights for individual constituents that they can claim at domestic courts. A free trade agreement, for instance, could give any individual a legal claim against his government if the latter legislates any measures that amount to protectionist privileges for particular industries. On this issue, see Jan Tumlir, "International Economic Order and Democratic Constitutionalism," *ORDO* 34 (1983): 71–83; Peter Moser,

ceivable forms in which relevant meta-constitutional provisions could be laid down. To investigate the nature and workability of such provisions is a worthy research program in constitutional political economy.

7. Constitutional Choice as a Creative Process

The recent discussions in the natural sciences, on the evolutionary self-organization paradigm that is associated with the names of Ilya Prigogine and others,[27] have reminded us of the understanding of human social inter-relations embodied in the work of David Hume, Adam Smith and others among the group that we usually refer to as the Scottish Moral Philosophers, and from which economics emerged as an independent discipline. These pre-Darwinian thinkers offered a theory of social order and human history that is evolutionary in the sense of emphasizing the open-endedness of a process in which the complex interactions of human efforts produce an order without being directed toward any predetermined end. Looked at from this perspective, our efforts in constitutional construction would be totally misunderstood if they should be seen as steps in a process that might over time approximate to a "perfect" constitutional-institutional order. The notion of the "perfectibility of society" may, in this regard, be just as misleading as the misplaced notion of the "perfectibility of man."[28] There is no uniquely perfect constitutional order "out there," waiting to be revealed and discovered through our trials and errors, no "optimal solution" toward which we might gradually approximate. If there is no "predetermined future" waiting for us, if, instead, we create our future by our choices, then the problems for which constitutional remedies may be needed are also a creation of our choices, and so are the solutions that our imagination may bring forth. The gigantic and, retrospectively, absurd "socialist experiment" that has so tragically shaped this century is a case in point, in that it provides ample dem-

---

The Political Economy of the GATT (Grüsch, Switzerland: Verlag Rüegger, 1990); Viktor Vanberg, "A Constitutional Political Economy Perspective at International Trade" (Center for Study of Public Choice, George Mason University, 1990, mimeographed).

27. On the nature of this paradigm and its relevance for economics, see James M. Buchanan and Viktor Vanberg, "The Market as a Creative Process" (Center for Study of Public Choice, George Mason University, 1990, mimeographed).

28. John Passmore, The Perfectibility of Man (London: Duckworth, 1970).

onstration for problems created by erroneous constitutional analysis and misguided constitutional construction.

For rational actors who are aware of the fallibility of their constitutional efforts and who recognize their embeddedness in an open-ended evolutionary process which is, in part, molded by their own choices, the fundamental problem of constitutional choice can be stated in the following question: How can we maintain a desirable constitutional order amongst ourselves, given that—at every and any point in the continuing process—we cannot know what will be known, invented and created tomorrow, we do not know what potential problems-solutions may be available to us, nor can we know what problems we will face—or what we will perceive as problems—tomorrow. The only reasonable answer to this question can be that such rational actors would have an interest in providing for the possibility of continuous learning, for adaptability to changing and unforeseen problem-scenarios. Or, in other terms, they should have an interest in, what we have called above, a meta-constitution for an open society.

How Can Constitutions Be Designed So That Politicians Who Seek to Serve "Public Interest" Can Survive and Prosper?

Distributional politics in modern democracy involves the exploitation of minorities by majorities, and as persons rotate membership, all parties in the "game" lose. This result emerges only because *differences* in treatment are permissible. If the principle of *generality* (analogous to that present in an idealized version of the rule of law) could, somehow, be introduced into politics, mutual exploitation could be avoided. The analysis offers support for such policies as (1) flat-rate taxes, (2) equal per head transfers or demogrants and (3) uniform regulation of all industries.

In a short paper, "Public Choice after Socialism,"[1] I argued that the structure of modern democratic politics is such that the "players," the participants in the distributional game among competing constituency agents, are effectively forced to behave as if they are exclusively motivated by narrowly defined or differential special interests. Political players who might seek to fur-

From *Constitutional Political Economy* 4 (Winter 1993): 1–6. Reprinted by permission of the publisher, Kluwer Academic Publishers.

The argument here was initially presented as a Liberty Fund Conference talk in July 1992 under the title "Political Ethics as a Criterion for Constitutional Design." I am indebted to my colleagues Viktor Vanberg and, especially, Hartmut Kliemt for helpful comments on an earlier draft.

1. J. M. Buchanan, "Public Choice after Socialism," *Public Choice* 77 (1993): 67–74.

ther some conception of an all-encompassing general, or public, interest cannot survive. They tend to be eliminated from the political game in the evolution-like selection process.

In this note, I want to extend this argument further by asking the question: How could the structure (constitution) of modern politics be changed so that it would allow players who might try to further a more encompassing interest to survive and prosper? Or, in other terms, how could the constitutional framework be reformed so that players who advance generalized interests are rewarded rather than punished? As indicated in the other paper, the response is clear. The distributional elements in the inclusive political game must be eliminated, or at least very substantially reduced. But I want here, to the extent possible, to go beyond this generalized statement, even if the argument remains highly abstract.

I want first to ask, and to answer, the basic question: Why does the game of distributional politics guarantee that players (legislators as agents for constituencies) adopt strategies that reflect the promotion of narrowly defined differential interests rather than the interests of the all-encompassing membership of the polity?

Let me introduce the familiar two-person, two-strategy symmetrical matrix construction with the ordinal payoffs shown in figure 1. The interaction is assumed to occur in a state of nature, with each person having available only the two private or independent courses of action indicated. The outcome in Cell IV emerges from the separate and independent actions of players A and B, each of whom chooses to defect (d) due to the row or column dominance in the structure of payoffs. Each of the two players succeeds in avoiding the role of sucker; each player avoids being exploited by the other, while recognizing that a higher payoff might be secured through mutual co-

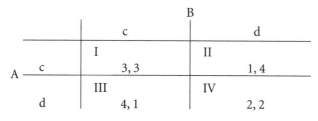

Figure 1. Classic PD

operation. But so long as no explicit means of coordination is available, a single player cannot, independently, achieve the cooperative outcome (c, c).[2]

Collectivization of the activities described in the interaction may be recognized to be one means of securing the larger payoffs. The collective choice set includes the four possible outcomes: (c, c), (c, d), (d, c) and (d, d). And, while the mutually desirable outcome (c, c) may be attained through collective action, an individual, independently, cannot protect against an exploitative result, (c, d) or (d, c), as is the case under autarky. Unless collective choice operates under an effective rule of unanimity, the individual must be vulnerable to potential exploitation.[3]

Consider a polity with many members, but with only two sets of orderings, such that any person can be represented by one or the other of the orderings shown ordinally in figure 1.[4] Collective action is assumed to be majoritarian, but no individual knows whether an effective majority coalition will be made up of persons with the A or B orderings. The outcome of the collective choice process will lie in either Cell II or Cell III, the off-diagonals in the matrix. Collective action is taken over a whole sequence of periods, and if we make the heroic assumption that membership is symmetrical among all participants, with each person holding equal prospects for membership in the majority and minority coalitions, the results will be "as if" the Cell IV payoffs are received, provided we make the assumption that distributional gains and losses are symmetrical in utilities. All persons will be dissatisfied with the distributional politics that they observe, and in which they are required to participate. Further, there may be a general recognition that any attempted escape from such politics by the emergence of a new ethics will be unlikely to succeed.

The direction of constitutional reform is obvious, even if we rule out the implementation of an effective unanimity rule. If, somehow, the off-diagonal solutions are simply made impossible to achieve by the introduction of some

2. My interest here is not in the prospect for cooperative strategies that might emerge in an iterated game between two players in the state of nature setting. My interest lies exclusively with the implications of the basic structure for large number interaction.

3. J. M. Buchanan and G. Tullock, *The Calculus of Consent* (Ann Arbor: University of Michigan Press, 1962).

4. The players may be identical in preferences, in which case the different ordering of outcomes simply reflects different distributional effects.

rule or norm that prevents participants from acting or being acted upon *differently,* one from the other, the off-diagonal attractors are eliminated and the players operate with the reduced matrix of figure 2. In this setting, each player, as a member of a political coalition, knows that any choice of an action or strategy must involve the *same* treatment of all players (constituencies). Differing treatments are not within the possible, given the constitutional constraints on the attainable set of possible outcomes.

The issues here are not, of course, nearly so simple as the analysis makes them appear. On the other hand, the directions for reform suggested by the extremely reduced abstract models should never be overlooked.

What the simple construction fails to suggest is that there may be many options that fall within the generalized ordinal solution in Cell I, and that there may be differential distributional consequences of these options. That is to say, the elimination of the off-diagonals may be less efficacious than the simple construction indicates. On the other hand, the normative thrust of the argument seems clear enough. To the extent that the political equivalents to the off-diagonal solutions to collective actions may be eliminated, the chances for the survival of encompassing interest as a political motive force are enhanced. The whole set of issues subsumed under the rent-seeking label can be viewed from this perspective as being generated by the potential for differential treatment. As such differential treatment—the availability of the off-diagonals—is reduced, so is the inducement to rent-seeking behavior.

Note that, in figure 2, with the off-diagonals eliminated, the motivation for the actors (or their agents) need not reflect self- or own interest at all. Individual A may, instead, choose to further the interest of B, and/or vice versa, without in any way modifying the result. Or, if we treat the payoffs as cardinal utility indicators, the substitution of some aggregative magnitude for individual differential interest as the effective objective for strategy choice leaves the result unchanged.

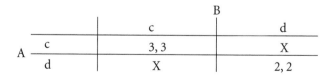

Figure 2. Diagonal choices

As indicated, however, even if we limit political action to the choice among options that affect all parties *generally,* there may be widely differing evaluations placed on the options that qualify under this rubric. And these differing evaluations may be in part distributionally motivated. Consider a proposal to enact a general law requiring scrubbers on smokestacks in order to improve air quality. The law is general because it applies equally to all smoke generating plants, regardless of location or type of product. But the congressional district that contains relatively more of these plants will be adversely affected, relative to other districts, by the general law. It will be harder for the agent representing such a district to evaluate such a proposed law in terms of some consideration of the encompassing general interest than for the agent whose district contains relatively fewer such plants. But, also, note that it will indeed be much easier, even for the agent who represents the district with relatively more smoke generating plants, to act in accordance with an interpretation of the encompassing interest in this setting than it would be in one in which the proposal is one that allows for particularized territorial or product-category exemptions from the scrubbers-on-smokestacks requirement. Any move toward generality in treatment embodied in political action opens up the prospect for the consideration of the more general interest and thereby shifts the focus from distributional politics.

Without making any attempt to be comprehensive, I shall simply present below a two-column classification of familiar political proposals, or features of proposals, with the distinction made in accordance with the generality criterion. To the extent that the center of gravity in democratic politics can be shifted leftward in the table, the potential efficacy of leadership exercised on behalf of some version of the all-encompassing interest of all members of the polity is increased.

There is nothing new or novel in the normative argument advanced here. Indeed, the argument is at least as old as Sir Henry Maine's reference to liberal progress as moving "from status to contract." One of the basic flaws of the welfare state as it has burgeoned in this century has been its implicit failure to understand the dependence of effective democracy upon the equality of persons and groups before the law, *and in politics.* As and to the extent that politics has come to be seen as the instrument for distributing the gains from collectivization *differentially,* the voices of those political leaders who would espouse the public or general interest are overwhelmed. Public choice theory

Table 1. Examples

Toward Generality	Toward Particularity
Law	
—equality in treatment of all persons	—special treatment for any group for any reason
Taxation	
—broad based taxes —uniform rates of tax —absence of exemption —inclusion of all persons in a tax structure	—exclusion of voters from tax rolls —shelters, exemptions, exclusions, special treatment of sources and uses of tax base —differential rates of tax, as among persons, forms of organization, professions, locations, products or other classificatory bases
Expenditures	
—collective consumption goods, with benefits coincident with whole territory of polity —fiscal federalism, or subsidiarity, financing by political authority coincident in inclusivity with program benefits —demogrants as transfer payments	—local public goods centrally defined
Regulation of Industry	
—environmental controls over whole economy —uniform tariffs on all imports —uniform subsidy for all industry	—differential control, by territory, by industry, by product etc. —differential tariff or quota protection product by product —differential subsidization by product, territory or other base

models the behavior of those politicians who survive and prosper; public choice theory does not induce those politicians who might seek to do otherwise to behave sinfully or selfishly.

If a more wholesome ethics is to be introduced into the observed behavior of our politicians, and especially our legislators, it will be necessary to remake the constitutional structure. Distributional politics is viable and tends to become dominant to the extent that differential treatment is constitutionally permissible. Each and every step toward replacing differential treatment with equal treatment, or generality, must measure progress toward achievement of the general interest.

Interests and Theories in Constitutional Choice

Viktor Vanberg and James M. Buchanan

Abstract: The paper contrasts two interpretations of the role of *agreement* in politics, a *social contract notion* and a *dialogue notion*. It is argued that the two notions can be viewed as complementing each other if one explicitly separates two components in human choice that in rational choice theory are often inseparably blended in the concept of *preferences*—an *interest-component* and a *theory-component*. It is suggested that the contractarian agreement notion primarily focusses on the interest-component; the dialogue notion on the theory-component in constitutional choice.

I. Introduction: Agreement and Legitimacy in Constitutional Choice

The notion that agreement among all parties concerned is the fundamental principle by which the legitimacy of a community's basic constitutional order is assured seems to be widely shared across a broad range of otherwise quite different intellectual traditions. Upon closer examination it becomes apparent, however, that the notion of agreement takes on somewhat different meanings in different contexts and that, accordingly, there exist systematically different interpretations as to what *kind of agreement* actually carries with it legitimizing force. In this regard various dimensions are potentially

From *Journal of Theoretical Politics* 1 (January 1989): 49–62. Copyright 1989 by Sage Publications. Reprinted by permission of Sage Publications Ltd.

We are indebted to Elinor Ostrom for helpful comments on an earlier draft.

relevant along which "agreement" may be qualified, concerning, for instance, the conditions under which agreement is achieved, the process by which it is achieved, or the way in which it is "revealed" (e.g., verbal agreement vs. implicit agreement, original agreement vs. ongoing agreement, etc.).

The present paper focusses on the relation between the *social contract notion* and the *dialogue notion* of agreement, the former being represented by authors like J. Rawls, D. Gauthier, or J. M. Buchanan, the latter by authors like J. Habermas, B. Ackerman, and J. S. Fishkin. Our purpose is less in reconstructing the "genuine meaning" that the two notions carry in the specific contexts in which they have been put by the various authors than in advancing a (re)interpretation that allows us to integrate social contract and dialogue into a more fruitful approach to the analysis of constitutional choice processes than either one of the two perspectives provides on its own. More specifically, we want to argue that the two notions—or, at least, certain of their crucial elements—can be viewed as naturally complementing each other if one explicitly separates, what we call, the "interest-component" from the "theory-component" in human choice, two components that in rational choice theory are often inseparably blended in the concept of *preferences*. We suggest that the contractarian-agreement notion is primarily directed towards the interest-component while the dialogue notion can be most fruitfully seen as being concerned with the theory-component.

The paper is organized as follows: Section II deals with the distinction between the two components of choice, the interest-component and the theory-component, a distinction that we argue to be of particular importance for the study of constitutional choice. Section III focusses on the interest-component and its relation to a contractarian-constitutional perspective, in particular to the "veil of uncertainty" and related theoretical concepts. Section IV concentrates on the theory-component in constitutional choice. The Habermas notion of an "ideal speech situation" and related concepts are (re)interpreted as pertaining to the cognitive dimension of constitutional choice. Some conclusions are drawn in section V.

II. Interests and Theories in Constitutional Choice

The economist's standard interpretation of choice behavior is in terms of *preferences* and *constraints*. Preferences are considered to be reflected in a utility function over which a rational actor maximizes, subject to whatever constraints he faces. As commonly *understood,* the concept of preferences is purely about *subjective values.* It refers to an actor's evaluations of potential objects of choice. As it is commonly *used,* however, the concept typically has more than just an evaluative dimension. It is typically used in a way that blends *evaluative* and *cognitive components,* or, in other terms, that blends a person's *evaluations* of—or *interest* in—potential outcomes of choice and his *theories* about the world, in particular his theories about what these outcomes are likely to be.[1]

For many purposes it may be convenient to use the notion of preferences in a way that does not explicitly separate the genuinely evaluative components from the cognitive components. For some analytical purposes it may be useful, however, systematically to separate interests and theories as distinct elements in the choice process. How a person chooses among potential alternatives is not only a matter of "what he wants" but also of "what he believes," and for some kinds of choices an actor's beliefs or theories may play a most crucial role. We suggest that the second element is particularly important for constitutional choices, that is, for choices among rules.[2] It follows that constitutional analysis can profit from explicitly distinguishing between the evaluative and the cognitive dimension of constitutional choice.

The notion of *consumer* or *household production,* as notably advanced by

1. For instance, an actor's preference for, say, European-built over American-built cars does not simply reflect certain values or interests that he may harbour. It is heavily impregnated with factual predictions—or "theories"—about the consequences that are likely to result from buying a European rather than an American car, predictions that can turn out to be right or wrong, in contrast to the *genuinely evaluative components* of his "preference" that cannot be properly subjected to a true/false judgement. (Incidentally, *advertising* may be viewed from this perspective as affecting persons' *theories* about relevant characteristics of goods, rather than affecting their values or interests.) T. Page draws a distinction between "preference (utility)" and "belief (probability)" that in some respects parallels our distinction between interests and theories (Talbot Page, "Pivot Mechanisms in Probability Revelation" [California Institute of Technology, 1987, mimeographed]).

2. Although stated in different terms, the relatively greater importance of the theory-component in constitutional as opposed to ordinary political choice was noted earlier in Buchanan's "Politics and Science" (in James M. Buchanan, *Freedom in Constitutional Contract* [College Station: Texas A&M University Press, 1977], 50–77, esp. 72 ff.).

G. S. Becker,[3] provides a useful framework for stating somewhat more systematically the evaluative/cognitive distinction that is central to our argument. In the context of the consumer production theory, the universe of potential objects of choice is divided into two subsets: On the one side, there are the "*ultimate* objects of desire" (food, shelter, sex, etc.) with regard to which all men have the same invariant preferences, simply because of their common human nature. And, on the other side, there are those objects of *choice* that are potential inputs into the production of the ultimate objects of desire rather than being desired in and by themselves. The demand for these "instrumental" goods is a *derived demand*, derived from the demand for ultimate goods to the production of which they are expected to contribute. These "non-ultimate" goods become the object of most choices that are empirically relevant for the purpose of social theory.

Independent of Becker's own specific interpretation, the usefulness of his conception for our purposes lies in the suggestion that people's *preferences* for "ordinary" objects of choice—like diet softdrinks, books, or karate cruises—are typically *derived* preferences, preferences that are an amalgam of preferences for more fundamental goods (like health, beauty, entertainment, social esteem, etc.) and theories about how these "ordinary" objects of choice contribute to the production of the more fundamental goods. To the extent that potential objects of choice are instrumental to the production of more fundamental goods, theories about their respective conduciveness in this regard play obviously a crucial part in a person's choice.

There is, one may say, an interest-component and a theory-component in almost any choice, from the choice among ice-cream flavours to the choice of a mate, though, of course, the relative importance of the two components may dramatically vary over different categories. For many ordinary market choices the theory-component will play a minimal role, while others may be heavily theory-laden. On the constitutional level, it should be obvious that people's *theories* about the working properties of alternative rules and rule-systems, and not just their interests in expected outcomes, are of crucial relevance to their choice behaviour.

Constitutional choices are concerned with the choice of rules for a com-

---

3. Gary S. Becker, *The Economic Approach to Human Behavior* (Chicago and London: University of Chicago Press, 1976), 131 ff.

munity or group. By their very nature the rules that are to be chosen are *public* in the sense that they define the terms under which actions and transactions within the respective community may be carried out. That is, they constrain everybody in the relevant community, though not necessarily everybody in the same way. In addition to their "publicness," constitutional choices are clearly of an instrumental nature. Rules are typically not objects valued in themselves. Rules are valued because of the pattern of outcomes that they are expected to produce.[4] We may use the term *constitutional preferences* to refer to a person's preferences over alternative rules or sets of rules, preferences that may be revealed in voting choices or in other ways. A person's constitutional preferences concern the ordering of rules that might be implemented in his community, or, stated differently, they describe the evaluation of the constitutional environment.

As noted earlier, constitutional preferences can be analytically decomposed into two components: *constitutional theories* and *constitutional interests*. A person's constitutional theories are about matters of fact. They are his predictions (embodying assumptions and beliefs) about what the factual outcomes of alternative rules will be. These predictions may, of course, be arranged in a true or false, correct or incorrect scalar. His constitutional interests, on the other hand, are his own subjective *evaluations* of expected outcomes, evaluations to which attributes like true or false, correct or incorrect cannot be meaningfully applied. The cognitive and the evaluative components of a person's constitutional preferences are critically different in this regard, and because of this difference one should expect that the question of how *constitutional agreement* may be reached raises different issues with regard to "constitutional interests" as opposed to "constitutional theories."

III. Constitutional Interests and Choice "Behind the Veil"

The contractarian agreement notion focusses central attention on the interest-component in constitutional choice. Social contract theories typically concern

---

4. As F. A. Hayek states: "The rules of conduct . . . are multi-purpose instruments developed as adaptations to certain *kinds* of environment because they help to deal with certain *kinds* of situations" (*Law, Legislation and Liberty*, vol. 2 [London: Routledge & Kegan Paul, 1976], 4).

themselves with the issue of how agreement on rules can be achieved among persons with potentially conflicting constitutional interests.

One characteristic way of how a social contract theory may approach this issue is paradigmatically exemplified by John Rawls' *A Theory of Justice*.[5] In Rawls' construction the prospect of agreement is secured by defining certain "ideal" conditions under which constitutional choices are hypothetically made. The choosers are assumed to be placed behind a "veil of ignorance" that makes it impossible for them to know anything *specific* about how they will be personally affected by alternative rules. Ignorant about their prospective specific interests in particular outcomes, they are induced to judge rules "impartially." Potential conflict in constitutional interests is not eliminated, but the veil of ignorance transforms potential *inter*personal conflicts into *intra*personal ones. In the context of our paper it is important to mention a second essential feature of the Rawlsian construction. While the persons behind the veil are assumed to be totally ignorant about their prospective *specific* interests in particular rules, they are, at the same time, assumed to be perfectly knowledgeable about the working properties of alternative rules. In our terminology, their constitutional theories are supposed to be perfect and non-controversial. Informational problems with regard to the general workings of rules do not exist.

A standard objection against the Rawlsian type of contractarianism is that the conceptual reconstruction of some hypothetical agreement under ideal conditions carried little normative and explanatory significance with regard to actual constitutional choices that are made in a world where people are neither totally ignorant about their identifiable constitutional interests nor perfectly knowledgeable as far as their constitutional theories are concerned. The remainder of this paper is in part about how the social contract notion may be employed in the analysis of constitutional choices that occur under such more realistic conditions.

In parts of what has become known as the "rent-seeking literature" in economics[6] there is a certain tendency to suggest that conflicts of interest are no less characteristic for choices among rules than for choices within rules

5. John Rawls, *A Theory of Justice* (Cambridge, Mass.: Harvard University Press, 1971).
6. See, e.g., James M. Buchanan, Robert D. Tollison, and Gordon Tullock, eds., *Toward a Theory of the Rent-Seeking Society* (College Station: Texas A&M University Press, 1980).

and that, therefore, the idea of some genuine constitutional agreement is a mere illusion when placed in a real world context. People with identifiable specific constitutional interests will, it is argued, attempt to achieve implementation of rules that promise to be differentially advantageous to them, and their distributionally motivated struggle for "biased" rules will inhibit any mutually beneficial constitutional reform. Though rules may be conceivable that would allow for a "better game," rules that would make everybody in the respective community better off, from this kind of rent-seeking perspective, people's concern for their identifiable and conflicting constitutional interests prevents them from actually realizing the potential gains from constitutional cooperation.

The rent-seeking skepticism is correct in its diagnosis that identifiability of particular constitutional interests in real world settings makes agreement on rules more difficult to achieve. But it may be overly pessimistic to jump to the conclusion that, under real world conditions, genuine constitutional agreement is impossible. To draw such a conclusion as this is to deny the possibility that rational persons recognize the "rent-seeking trap" and engage in concerted effort to escape. A more optimistic and, maybe, even more realistic approach should investigate the conditions under which, and the potential means by which, constitutional agreement may be facilitated in real, non-hypothetical choice situations.[7]

It is, of course, true that in real world settings people are typically not totally ignorant about their particular constitutional interests. But they are not perfectly certain about these interests either. In constitutional matters people typically find themselves behind a *veil of uncertainty* that prevents them from accurately anticipating the particular ways in which they will be affected by the prospective workings of alternative rules. The veil of uncertainty can be more or less transparent, or, in other terms, its "thickness" may vary, dependent on certain characteristics of the actual choice situation. As the veil's "thickness" increases so will the prospect of achieving agreement.

The degree to which persons are uncertain about their particular, iden-

---

7. Such a "more optimistic" approach is informed by an assumption similar to that articulated by D. Gauthier: "As rational persons understand the structure of their interaction, they recognize a place for mutual constraint, and so far a moral dimension in their affairs. . . . Agreed mutual constraint is the rational response to these structures" (*Morals by Agreement* [Oxford: Oxford University Press, 1985], 9).

tifiable constitutional interests is not a determined and unalterable constraint. The variables that affect the veil's thickness can, to some extent, be manipulated, and rational actors may take deliberate measures designed to put themselves behind a thicker veil, thereby enhancing the prospects of realizing potential gains from constitutional agreement. Most important for these purposes is probably the fact that the degree of uncertainty is, in part, a function of the sort of rules that are under consideration. The essential dimensions here are the *generality* and the *durability* of rules.[8] The more general rules are and the longer the period over which they are expected to be in effect, the less certain people can be about the particular ways in which alternative rules will affect them.[9] They will, therefore, be induced to adopt a more impartial perspective, and, consequently, they will be more likely to reach agreement.[10]

It is not only through the veil of uncertainty that fairness may be induced and agreement facilitated in constitutional choice. An additional and independent factor—independent from the uncertainty factor, but working in the same direction—is the *concern for stability*. The purpose of entering a constitutional agreement is the prospect of realizing gains that can be derived from operating under the respective constitutional constraints. The possibility of realizing such gains is not just a matter of securing some *initial* agreement; it is also a matter of continuing acquiescence in an ongoing cooperative arrangement. *Stability* refers to the viability of a constitutional arrangement over time. Rational actors can be expected to take considerations of stability into account when engaging in constitutional choice. And to the extent that *fairness* and *stability* of constitutional arrangements are interrelated, the concern for stability will induce a concern for fairness. It will do

8. On this issue, see Geoffrey Brennan and James M. Buchanan, *The Reason of Rules: Constitutional Political Economy* (Cambridge: Cambridge University Press, 1985), 28 ff.

9. James M. Buchanan, "The Constitution of Economic Policy," *American Economic Review* 77 (1987): 243–50, esp. 248.

10. The potential for rational actors deliberately to increase uncertainty in order to facilitate agreement is vividly described in the following quotation from F. A. Hayek: "That it is thus ignorance of the future outcome which makes possible agreement on rules . . . is recognized by the practice in many instances of deliberately making the outcome predictable in order to make agreement on the procedure possible: whenever we agree on drawing lots we deliberately substitute equal chances for the different parties for the certainty as to which of them will benefit from the outcome" (*Law, Legislation and Liberty*, 4).

so, as mentioned before, in addition to and independent of the veil of uncertainty. The latter works by moderating the differences among identifiable constitutional interests. The concern for stability induces a preference for more impartial rules even in persons who may be perfectly aware of the particular effects that alternative rules will have on them. It is not the uncertainty about one's own particular position, but the anticipation that a constitutional arrangement is unlikely to be stable if it is designed only to serve one's own particular interests that will induce impartiality.

With regard to the potential relation between *stability* and *fairness* it is important to distinguish between two aspects of the stability problem that are not always sufficiently separated in discussions on the issue, namely, the *compliance problem* and the *renegotiation problem*.[11] In order for a constitutional arrangement to be stable over time it has to command a sufficient level of compliance and a sufficient level of ongoing agreement. Both—defection and pressure to renegotiate the terms of the arrangement—will undermine the prospect of realizing the very benefits that motivate the constitutional agreement in the first place. Rational actors will, therefore, have a reason, at the constitutional stage, to be concerned about both problems and to incorporate appropriate precautions into their constitutional agreements. What is relevant for our purpose is that their constitutional concerns about compliance and renegotiation do not relate to the fairness issue in the same way.

Though there may be some indirect relation between fairness of rules and compliance with rules, the latter is certainly not a direct function of the former. That is, the fact that rules are perceived as fair by the relevant group of persons does not, *per se,* guarantee a willingness to comply with those rules.[12]

11. A very informative discussion on this issue is provided in Edward F. McClennen, "Justice and the Problem of Stability" (National Humanities Center, 1987, mimeographed). On the distinction that is of relevance here McClennen states: "[A] consensus on a principle of justice will be unstable not only if those who come to agree on it subsequently are prone to unilaterally defect from the agreement, but also if they are disposed to press for the rejection of that principle and the adoption of some other, i.e., to press for a renegotiation of the social contract" (6 f).

12. To be sure, there may be—as Elinor Ostrom suggested to us (in a comment on an earlier draft): "an empirical relationship between the perceived fairness of a rule and the cost of enforcing compliance." That such a relationship exists appears intuitively appealing and, as Elinor Ostrom indicated, her recent research on the "commons problem" provides indirect evidence for such a relationship.

The compliance problem results from the fact that there are potential gains from defecting. Whether such gains exist or not is not, *per se*, dependent on the fairness properties. And to the extent that such gains exist, a compliance problem is present even with perfectly fair rules.[13]

There is a much more direct relation between the fairness issue and renegotiation. And it is with regard to renegotiation rather than with regard to compliance that the concern for stability can be expected to induce a concern for fairness.[14] A constitutional agreement that favours particular interests may be achievable under "suitable" conditions, but such agreement can be expected to be less robust with regard to potential changes in circumstances than fair arrangements.[15]

Finally, we should note that stability, in both the compliance and the renegotiation aspects, is necessarily a more important consideration in constitutional choice than in non-constitutional or post-constitutional choice. By their very nature rules imply quasi-permanency; they are expected to remain in force over more than one period of time during which ordinary political choices are to be made within such rules as exist. This basic characteristic of rules ensures that the present value (at the time of choice among rules) of predicted non-compliance or of agitation for renegotiation is substantially higher for long-term than for short-term rules. Hence, as increased durabil-

13. David Gauthier's theory in *Morals by Agreement* seems to be partly based on the assumption that there is some direct link between fairness and compliance. See, e.g., David Gauthier, "Morality, Rational Choice, and Semantic Representation: A Reply to My Critics" (University of Pittsburgh, 1987, mimeographed): "Stability plays a key role in linking rational choice to contractarian morality. Aware of the benefits to be gained from constraining principles, rational persons will seek principles that invite stable compliance. . . . An agreement affording equally favourable terms to all thus invites, as no other can, stable compliance" (22). On this issue see also Viktor Vanberg and James M. Buchanan, "Rational Choice and Moral Order" (Center for Study of Public Choice, 1987, mimeographed).

14. Douglas D. Heckathorn and Steven M. Maser discuss the different, though related, issue of how the concern for fairness may affect the constitutional bargaining process and the prospects of reaching agreement ("Bargaining and Constitutional Contracts," *American Journal of Political Science* 31 [1987]: 142–67, esp. 153 ff.).

15. John Rawls discusses this issue in terms of the contrast between "acceptance as a mere *modus vivendi* and *overlapping consensus*," the former being less robust since "its stability is contingent on circumstances remaining such as not to upset the fortunate convergence of interests" ("On Achieving Consensus under Pluralism" [1987, mimeographed], 7).

ity may be deliberately invoked to thicken the veil, and to facilitate agreement, the concern for stability, in the process of reaching agreement, increases *pari passu*.

IV. Dialogue and Reason in Constitutional Choice

The contractarian notion and the dialogue notion of agreement both imply a *procedural* criterion—as opposed to an outcome criterion—of legitimacy. From both perspectives the legitimacy of basic constitutional principles is judged not against some predefined "ideal system" but in terms of the process from which these principles emerge. The normative focus is on the characteristics of the process of constitutional choice, not on characteristics of choice-outcomes as such. Furthermore, in both perspectives a "good" or "proper" process is defined as one that assures *fairness* or *impartiality* in the rules that emerge.[16]

The difference between the two constructions lies in their somewhat different understanding of the procedural characteristics that are to assure fairness. And it lies in their somewhat different interpretation of fairness itself. To the contractarian notion, the individuals' interests are the "basic inputs" into the constitutional process. The choice process is supposed properly to reflect these interests, whatever they may be. It is not considered a process in which these interests themselves are judged or rated in any way. *Fairness* is considered a matter of the *constraints* under which constitutional choices are made, not as a matter of the "quality" of interests that enter into such choices. In particular, it is the *voluntariness* of choice that, from a contractarian perspective, constitutes the essential prerequisite of fairness. Fairness and voluntariness of agreement are, in a sense, the same. Fairness is not defined independent of that upon which persons voluntarily agree. In other words, agreement is strictly viewed in a *social contract* dimension as defining what is mutually acceptable to voluntarily choosing persons.[17]

16. See, e.g., James S. Fishkin, *Beyond Subjective Morality* (New Haven and London: Yale University Press, 1984), 24 f., 95 ff.; Gauthier, *Morality*, 31 f.; Jürgen Habermas, *Moralbewusstsein und kommunikatives Handeln* (Frankfurt: Suhrkamp, 1983), 75 ff.

17. It should be noted that our stylized characterization of the contractarian conception is supposed to focus on what we consider its essential difference from the dialogue

By contrast, within the dialogue or discourse theory framework the notions of agreement and fairness tend to carry a characteristically more "objectivist" or *cognitive* meaning in the sense of implying more than just the notion of intersecting or coinciding individual interests. Within this framework, constitutional agreement is not simply—as in the contractarian context—a matter of *compromise* among separate individual interests. Individuals' interests are not simply viewed as the basic inputs that the process of constitutional agreement is supposed properly to reflect. These interests are themselves to be evaluated and possibly transformed in the process of constitutional discourse. Whether this idea is stated in terms of a distinction between "brute motivations" and "refined motivations"[18]—where the former are to be transformed into the latter through "purging of bias and indoctrination"; or whether it is invoked through the notion of an "impartial *evaluation* of the interests of all who are concerned" ("die unparteiliche *Beurteilung* der Interessen aller Betroffenen"):[19] What is implied is a critical shift towards a "truth-judgement" interpretation of constitutional agreement. Stated differently, *agreement* is viewed as a *discovery* process, a process by which persons do not simply reach a compromise but "discover" what—in some objective sense—*is* fair or just.

Within the contractarian framework, agreement carries normative significance in and by itself. Agreed-on principles are considered legitimate simply because they are the ones that command agreement, not because agreement is indicative of some other "quality" that distinguishes these principles.[20] Observed agreement may be normatively qualified in terms of its *voluntariness,* i.e., in terms of the constraints under which the parties involved express their agreement. But, in its contractarian sense, it cannot be meaningfully qualified in terms of a standard that goes beyond agreement itself. The claim to such qualification is, however, apparently inherent in the dialogue construc-

---

construction. It is not necessarily intended to be descriptive of all variants of contractarianism.

18. James S. Fishkin, "Bargaining, Justice and Justification: Towards Reconstruction" (1987, mimeographed), 16 f.

19. Habermas, *Moralbewusstsein,* 78.

20. Jules L. Coleman's distinction between an "epistemic" and a "criterial, semantic" interpretation of agreement parallels the distinction that we want to stress here ("Market Contractarianism and the Unanimity Rule," *Social Philosophy & Policy* 2 [1985]: 69–114, esp. 106).

tion. According to Habermas,[21] valid or legitimate norms are not simply those on which persons under specified conditions happen to agree, it is those norms that *deserve* to be intersubjectively acknowledged because they embody some interest that is *recognizably* common to all persons concerned. And whether they deserve such recognition has to be examined in practical discourse. Constitutional agreement that emerges from ethical discourse has legitimizing force not simply because it is "agreement," but because it indicates that the agreed-on rules deserve to be classified as "equally good for everybody involved."[22]

To be sure, Habermas's style of reasoning typically leaves considerable room for interpretation, and one might argue that some of his statements can well be read in a way that is much less in contrast to a contractarian conception than our interpretation suggests. But Habermas himself explicitly notes the critical difference between his discourse notion and a *compromise notion* of agreement, emphasizing the *cognitive claims* of his own construction.[23] He characterizes his discourse construction as being critically dependent on the assumption that claims concerning the validity of norms carry a cognitive meaning and can be treated like truth-judgements.[24] And he strongly rejects the "skeptical premise that the validity of norms cannot be interpreted analogously to the validity of truth-judgements" ("die skeptische Grundannahme, dass sich die Sollgeltung von Normen nicht in Analogie zur Wahrheitsgeltung von Propositionen verstehen laesst").[25]

21. Habermas, *Moralbewusstsein*, 73–84.

22. Ibid., 18: "In einem solchen Prozess wird *einer dem anderen Gruende* dafuer nennen, warum er wollem kann, dass eine Handlungsweise sozial verbindlich gemacht wird. . . . Und einen solchen Prozess nennen wir eben den praktischen Diskurs. Eine Norm, die auf diesem Wege in Kraft gesetzt wird, kann 'gerechtfertigt' heissen, weil durch den argumentativ erzielten Beschluss angezeigt wird, dass sie das Praedikat 'gleichermassen gut fuer jeden der Betroffenen' verdient."

23. Ibid., 81 ff., in particular pp. 82 f.: "Im praktischen Diskurs versuchen sich die Beteiligten ueber ein gemeinsames Interesse klar zu werden, beim Aushandeln eines Kompromisses versuchen sie, einen Ausgleich zwischen partikularen, einander widerstreitenden Interessen herbeizufuehren."

24. Ibid., 78: "Eine Diskursethik steht und faellt also mit den beiden Annahmen, dass (a) normative Geltungsansprueche einen kognitiven Sinn haben und *wie* Wahrheitsansprueche behandelt werden koennen, und dass (b) die Begruendung von Normen und Geboten die Durchfuehrung eines realen Diskurses verlangt." See also ibid., 131 f.

25. Ibid., 78.

As described, the contractarian and the dialogue interpretation of constitutional agreement appear to represent alternative and opposing views: *Agreement as compromise* versus *agreement as truth-judgement*. And, as intended by their authors, some of the conceptions advanced on the two sides may indeed by diametrically opposed. As mentioned earlier, however, our interest here is not in authenticity of interpretation. Instead, our interest is in exploring the potential for fruitful integration. And such potential clearly exists if the two constructions are interpreted in the context of the distinction between *constitutional interests* and *constitutional theories* as analytically separable components in constitutional preference and constitutional choice.

As stated in Buchanan's earlier discussion on the relation between "Politics and Science,"[26] constitutional choice involves both individuals' genuine *evaluations* of alternative rules as well as their *predictions* about the working properties of such rules. Observed constitutional *disagreement* may reflect disagreement in either one or both of these components. And the process of reaching agreement can, conceptually, be discussed in different terms dependent on which one of the two components is concerned. To the extent that disagreement over rules reflects genuine differences in *interests,* reaching constitutional agreement is clearly a matter of compromise, of finding terms that are acceptable to everybody, and definitely not a matter of "discovering the truth." To the extent, however, that disagreement is a matter of differences in constitutional *theories,* the process of reaching agreement clearly is about "truth-judgements" and it can be properly compared to scientific discourse, to controversy over alternative theories in science.[27]

---

26. Buchanan, *Freedom in Constitutional Contract.*

27. To quote from Buchanan's earlier treatment: "The appropriate location for genuine constitutional choice seems to be somewhere between the limits imposed by the choice among scientific explanations on the one hand and the choice among alternative publicly supplied goods on the other. There may be differences in individual evaluations of alternative rules—differences that may, in one sense, reflect basic value orderings. To this extent agreement will not be produced by open discussion. Something more than evaluation is involved in many cases, however. Individual differences may be based, to a large extent, on differing predictions about the working properties of the alternative rules under consideration. Within these limits meaningful discussion and analysis can take place, and the careful assessment of alternative models can closely resemble scientific process of the standard sort" (*Freedom in Constitutional Contract,* 72).

Though interest-components and theory-components are *conceptually separable* inputs into constitutional preferences, there is, of course, no practical way of strictly separating them in actual constitutional choice. We simply cannot know with any degree of certainty whether, or to what extent, observed disagreement reflects "merely" differences in constitutional theories, or whether they are based on genuinely different evaluations. In this sense, acknowledgement of the legitimate role of potentially conflicting individual evaluations in constitutional choice clearly excludes an interpretation that assigns, as Habermas does, a truth-judgement function to the constitutional process as such. Failure to reach agreement in actual constitutional discourse may, but need not necessarily, reflect disagreement in theories. Even with perfect agreement in the theoretical dimension, potential for disagreement in evaluations may persist. And respect for such potential disagreement commands that the limits of "discourse" and the ultimate role and the need for *compromise* in constitutional matters be recognized.[28]

However, within the limits specified above, there is an obvious "role for reason," for science-like discourse in constitutional choice. Compared to ordinary market-choice, there seems to be a dramatic shift in relevance from the interest-component to the theory-component when choices among alternative rules are concerned.[29] Persons' preferences over alternative rules or

28. To quote from Buchanan's earlier discussion: "If politics at the constitutional level involves a process of discovery and exploration analogous to that of science, must we assume that there is a unique explanation, a unique set of rules which defines the element of good society and which, once discovered, will come to be generally accepted by informed and intellectually honest men? . . . To some omniscient being . . . who can view man's interactions one with another solely in terms of his own evaluative criteria, the answer may be in the affirmative. But to man himself the existence of such singularity in solution seems highly dubious. Values would seem to differ, and perhaps even widely, even among enlightened men, and different men will tend to value different rules. My ideal 'good society' need not be identical with yours in general or in its particulars even if we fully agree on the working properties of the alternative rules under discussion" (ibid., 75).

29. The difference between ordinary market choices and constitutional choices in terms of the dramatically greater role of theoretical components in the latter is discussed in Karen I. Vaughn, "Can There Be a Constitutional Political Economy?" (George Mason University, 1984, mimeographed), 10 ff.; see also Viktor Vanberg, "Individual Choice and Constitutional Constraints: The Normative Element in Classical and Contractarian Lib-

systems of rules do not simply reflect "basic values," they are largely a product of their constitutional theories, and, therefore, may be changed through information that impacts on their theories. To the extent that persons' revealed constitutional preferences are informed by their predictions of the working properties of the rules that are under consideration, constitutional agreement can be facilitated by a process that systematically encourages critical examination and discussion of alternative theoretical constructions, separate from and independent of any procedural devices that aim at facilitating agreement in the interest dimension.

V. Conclusion

The dialogue or discourse notion can be fruitfully interpreted as drawing attention to the importance of the informational dimension in constitutional choice, even though its advocates might not agree to such limited interpretation. Rational actors to whom *efficiency* as well as *fairness* are relevant attributes of a constitutional contract have reasons to be concerned not only about the interest-dimension but also about the theory-dimension in constitutional choice. Both concerns have certain implications for the kinds of "procedural constraints" that can be expected to facilitate actual agreement, implications that need not be in perfect accordance.

So far as the *interest-dimension* is concerned, agreement is facilitated by whatever increases persons' uncertainty about the *particular* effects that alternative rules can be expected to have on them. In the interest of facilitating agreement, rational actors may, therefore, deliberately choose to increase uncertainty, to "thicken the veil." So far as the *theory-dimension* is concerned, prospects of agreement on desirable rules are enhanced not by creating uncertainty but, on the contrary, by raising the level of mutually shared information on the general working properties of alternative rules.

---

eralism," *Analyse & Kritik* 8 (1986): 113–49, esp. 141 ff. It should be noted that our attention in the present context is exclusively on the relevance of the theory-component. We deliberately ignore here the familiar problem of "rational ignorance" that is commonly stressed in comparisons between market choices and voting choices, i.e., the problem that the incentives to be "well informed" are dramatically lower in the voting than in the market context, because of the systematically different expectations concerning the impact of one's own choice on oneself.

The fact that the public discourse on rules—as political debates in general—is typically carried out by *reasoning arguments* but can be supposed to be motivated by *interests,* is sometimes taken as evidence that the political rhetoric is mere camouflage, concealing real interests. And there is a tendency—e.g., in parts of the rent-seeking literature—to conclude from this that it is ultimately only interests and the power behind interests that count in the political process, while arguments and reason lack any power "of their own." Such interpretation disregards the relevance of the genuine *theoretical* component in all political and, *a fortiori,* in all constitutional preferences. And it ignores that winning support for one's own visions and theories is an important part of the political process. The very fact that political discourse is carried out in terms of reasoning argument rather than simple declaration of interests, by itself imposes certain constraints on how one may seek support for one's own proposals.

To the extent that persons share a *common* subset of non-conflicting interests that can be met instrumentally through constitutional rules, the argument over alternative rules reduces to argument over *theories.* If the interests that may be met through constraining rules cannot be factored down into a commonly shared set, while, at the same time, the rules must be public in the sense of imposing constraints on *all* members of the community, divergent *interests* must, somehow, be reconciled. At this level, the function of discussion, dialogue, reason, cannot be to generate agreement on the "correctness" of alternative theories. Cooperation can replace conflict only if the differing interests, held with varying intensities by persons, can be traded-off or compromised, actually or symbolically, in a *social contract.*

Student Revolts,
Academic Liberalism, and
Constitutional Attitudes

Should the student have a share in controlling university policy and structure equal to or comparable with that exercised by the salaried administrator or tenured professor? The case to be made for the student's side of this currently relevant issue deserves more careful consideration than it is often accorded. The student finds himself participating in a game described by rules that he had no part in making. The institutional order of the university, its traditional procedures, regulations, and methods: these are imposed upon him. The student can, and does, with conviction claim a "right" to an increased participatory role in reshaping and modifying this institutional structure to meet what he considers to be his own ideals.[1]

From *Social Research* 35 (Winter 1968): 666–80. Reprinted by permission of the publisher.

Author's Note—When the Editor invited a contribution to this Symposium, my response was that I did not classify myself as "conservative," but that I was prepared to submit a paper in defense of methodological individualism in social science. After two abortive attempts, I abandoned this effort. In the place of general methodology, I now discuss a currently relevant issue of social policy, the students' revolts of the late 1960's, in a more general commentary on social structure. An "approach" to social issues is developed, one that is methodologically and philosophically individualistic, and which also incorporates a vision of social structure along with an implied role for social science. I am indebted to Craig Roberts and Gordon Tullock for helpful comments.

1. To avoid misunderstanding, I should point out that the discussion in this paper largely applies to a model in which the university is conceived as a collectivity. The fact that many persons do conceive the university in this image makes the discussion relevant for some of the issues now faced. More importantly for my purposes, the larger problems

The sheltered academician's probable response has become familiar. The student is to be tutored, not welcomed as a participant in a genuinely democratic community. He is, at best, a relatively short-term resident of a long-lived institution which has developed its own set of traditions and practices, and embodies its own wisdom. To allow the student, who is uninformed, uneducated, and immature, to exercise a voice in the governance of the university represents manifest absurdity.

This response fails to convince the revolutionary-minded student, despite its too-obvious reasonableness in the eyes of the established authorities. Intuitively and inarticulately, the student senses the contradiction in the position of his elders, a contradiction that they themselves often ignore. The senior academician, proudly liberal in his value standards, argues persuasively for the preservation of simple constitutional order and attitude in the narrow world of his own affairs. At the same time, this liberal academician refuses to face the apparent fact that he and his own kind have been instrumental in undermining constitutional order and attitude in the society at large. The student revolutionary sees through the sham; he properly understands that if modern liberal attitudes toward sociopolitical processes are turned inward to the university setting, the existing structure of the university must be dramatically reformed. The revolutionary refuses to allow his academic adversary to wallow in his inconsistency. In effect, the revolution-

---

of social order that I want to discuss in this paper can be treated only in this university-as-collectivity model.

The use of this model does not, however, preclude the discussion of an alternative model, nor does my discussion imply the rejection of the relevance of such an alternative. Insofar as the student faces effective educational alternatives in the form of many institutions competing for his custom, the appropriate analogy becomes the firm selling its services in the open market. In this model of analysis, the university-as-firm is directly controlled by the student "consumers" (or by their parents). There is no scope for collective decision-making in any autonomous sense, and the student who objects to particular rules descriptive of one institution simply selects another one more to his liking. If, in fact, universities and colleges should be financed exclusively or primarily by tuition payments (which might be but need not be publicly granted to students), the university-as-firm model would be more appropriate than the university-as-collectivity model used in this paper. The latter model increases in relevance as the relative share of tuition payments in university financing is reduced. On some of the effects of this change, and especially as related to the zero-tuition argument in California, see A. A. Alchian, "The Economic and Social Impact of Free Tuition," *New Individualist Review* 5 (Winter, 1968), 42–52.

ary says: "Join us in the streets (as indeed some Columbia academicians did in 1968) or extend the constitutional defense of the university's order to the larger problems of society." The academic liberal who then joins the demonstrations may be misguided, but he can claim some consistency in his behavior patterns. His colleague who cries loudest for the restoration of order in the university community while condoning the disregard for constitutional order expressed by the Warren Court may be intelligent, but if he is so, his behavior reveals hypocrisy.

The day is past when the Southern scapegoat allowed the academic liberal to make his own private and careful distinction between "just" and "unjust" rules of order. The local statutes that were violated by the restaurant sit-ins of the early 1960's were "Southern" laws, of course, and properly and universally condemned as "unjust." The university regulations that were violated by the campus sleep-ins of 1968 were reasonable and "just." Something has simply gone wrong, someone has the wrong signals. But how is Martin Luther King's moral decision to be distinguished from Mario Savio's or Mark Rudd's? If individual consciences are to be the arbiters in such matters, why are some individuals more respected than others? The simply pretentious arrogance of those who think that all men must agree on "truth" as defined by their own provincial standards has now been finally exposed. The intolerance that has masqueraded as social purpose becomes itself intolerable when the purpose is defined by those whose standards differ. The academic liberal seems hoisted by his own petard. Is he reduced to arguments strangely akin to those advanced by the "racist," "hate-mongering" states' righters of the 1950's?

If the academic liberal is forced to think by all this, the students' revolts will serve a major social function. If critical intelligence can begin to replace intolerance among intellectuals, perhaps restoration of effective social order can be expected in due time. Optimism would be misplaced for any short-term perspective, because there are major time lags between ideas and realization. We currently reap the whirlwind of past intellectuals' follies. But, at the least, if thinking now begins, a new spirit of critical inquiry may provide some hope for emergence from chaos, provided we can survive the interim without succumbing to the increasingly relevant fascist temptation. Perhaps, and I emphasize the perhaps here, the excesses of student demands will make the excesses of totalitarian democracy unnecessary. In miniature we may see the future, and there may still be time to change it. If this be the course of events, praise be to the student revolutionaries. If the intellectuals refuse to see and to make the proper inferences about their own behavior, our society will get the order that it deserves.

Any optimism must be tempered, however. The academic liberal is the least sensitive of men. It will be difficult for him to make the required transference of ideas; he will only with struggle take those ideas that seem obvious to him in his private university setting into his thought patterns about the world at large. He will cling to his defenses of the established rules, regulations, and authorities of his university because these, to him, are "true," or "right," not because they were adopted by orderly institutional procedure. He will cry "good riddance" to those traditions of legal order that the Warren Court has overthrown even when this court has assumed a nonjudicial role. He does so because such traditions were "wrong." To this academic liberal, the student revolutionary is unfortunately blind to the subtle distinctions between established rules that are "right" and those that are "wrong"; between "truth" and "untruth" in judgments on social policy. It simply does not occur to my straw man to raise the question: If the student revolutionary fails to see "truth" in his judgments about the university, is it not possible that the modern social revolutionaries might have failed to see "truth" in their more general judgments about social order? Once he raises such a question, the academic liberal is on the road to wisdom. (As Professor Frank Knight noted, Socrates had to die, not because he recognized how little he knew, but because he also recognized how little others knew.)

If doubts begin to stir about the private vision of "truth" possessed by the academic liberal, he may take the next and most vital step, which is that of questioning the existence of "truth" itself in matters of social policy. Is it possible that reasonable and equally well-informed men might disagree finally on particular configurations of the "good society"? Is it possible that the despised and dismissed bigots may have been deserving of more consideration? Once he starts to ask such questions, the academic liberal may recognize that his "truth-judgment" approach to politics and to social issues generally is fundamentally illiberal and intolerant. "Truth," in the final analysis, is tested by *agreement*. And if men disagree, there is no "truth." Acknowledgment of this prompts an attitude of respect for and tolerance of the views of others, for dissenters, whoever these might be. But this attitude comes close to being the precise opposite of that espoused by the academic liberal in his nonuniversity role, the attitude imitated by the student revolutionary when he repudiates the equal freedom of others to hold views of their own. The point is that the arrogance and intolerance concerning the equal freedoms of others displayed so aggressively by the student revolutionary are simply miniaturization in extreme of characteristics that the postwar academic liberal has exhibited. The student may be censured; but he may be censured not because his behavior is unorthodox. If we are to be successful in persuading the student revolutionary to respect the views of others who might disagree with him, to behave with tolerance toward those whose commitments differ from his own, and, finally, to accept the notion that "truth" is measured only in agreement, we must put the modern liberal thought patterns to the same test and demand the same changes. Repression of student rebellion will not suffice. The call for law and order, for respect for established authority, for adherence to rules—all this is empty rhetoric until and unless it is supported by critically intelligent argument by men who themselves command respect. The argument is itself hypocritical if advanced by the academic liberal who disdains the views of others about the constitutional structure of society. Ambivalence in advocacy is rarely convincing.

In what respects has the modern or academic liberal's attitude been blameworthy? My attack must be supported, but I face difficulties because of the very generality of the attitude that I criticize. In sum, the view has been one that holds that society, the sociopolitical structure, can be remade at will to serve the explicit objectives dictated by the apparent "truths" of the 1950's and 1960's. To me, this represents a terrible perversion of the constitutional attitude initially adopted by the Founding Fathers and held throughout the first century and one-half of our history. At some stage liberal thought became confused and underwent major transformation. The attainment of specifically defined objectives or goals for the collectivity was allowed to take precedence, in some rank order sense, over the traditional and classically liberal emphasis on the construction and maintenance of a social order within which individuals and groups with divergent goals could live in an atmosphere of mutual respect and cooperation. Once this transformation had taken place, it became necessary to distinguish categorically between the classical and the modern liberal. In continental Europe this confusion has not emerged. A continental "liberal" remains classical; the academic liberal of America becomes honestly "socialist" in European terminology. Only in the United States has the confusion been manifest, so much so that some clear definitional distinction seems to be required. Many variants have been proposed; none has been widely accepted. On an earlier occasion, I suggested the labels, "left-liberal" and "right-liberal." The word "libertarian" is perhaps more commonly used than any other to refer to the classical position. I shall not, however, discuss here the details of labels. In this paper, I shall refer to the classically liberal, right-liberal, or libertarian position as one embodying a "constitutional attitude," and to a person who holds this position as a "constitutionalist." I use these terms here, not in particular advocacy of their adoption in all applications, but because they best convey the characteristic features upon which my discussion and emphasis are concentrated.

One further point should be made to avoid terminological confusion. I do not equate "constitutional" and "conservative." The genuine conservative may support the existing social and political constitution because it exists and has been long established. But the obverse need not hold: the genuine "constitutionalist" need not be conservative. He may seek radical reforms in social structure. He differs from the academic liberal, not in his radicalism, and not in his willingness to propose change, but in his objectives for change. The constitutionalist seeks to reform the social structure by modifying the general rules of order, and by doing so in a process that preserves orderly measures for making further changes that are now unpredictable but which may be desired in the future. He places "preserving the means for change" high on his scale of valuation relative to "securing the specific objectives of change." He values "process" relative to "social priorities." By contrast, the academic liberal concentrates his attention, expediently and pragmatically, on specific short-run objectives that he desires the collectivity to achieve. He seeks the "good" directly, and he tends to be relatively unconcerned about the process through which it is sought. To secure the ends, he stands willing, if needs be, to subvert or even to destroy the prospects for orderly change in an unknown future.

Once again these differences are summarized in the intolerance exhibited by the modern liberal. Why should we not seek the "good" and the "true," and why not do so directly? Since all men who are not bigots must agree with us, why should we really bother about constitutional process in the making of social reforms? Are not the reforms themselves the relevant and important things? What is wrong with the attitude of the Warren Court when it simply declares to be "constitutional" that which it conceives to be the "good" and "true"? The modern liberal raises such questions only to answer them in his sneers at those who think otherwise. He seldom asks: What happens when disagreement arises, disagreement among those who cannot be readily separated into the right-thinkers on the one hand and the bigots on the other?

In a very fundamental sense, therefore, the constitutionalist views society differently from the academic liberal. The constitutional attitude emerges from a vision of social structure in which individuals and groups hold widely differing objectives of attainment. Collective organization and control are properly directed to prevent conflicts among individuals and groups when privately sought objectives produce clashes and toward the exploitation of joint-production possibilities for commonly shared goods and services. Beyond these limits, the "good society" of the constitutionalist embodies the Jeffersonian ideal of "least government." To such a person, the modern clichés about the loss of "national purpose" seem meaningless; he considers absurd the attempts to define "national goals." And he should have seen the essentially opposing attitude incorporated in Kennedy's famous call: "Ask not what your country can do for you—ask what you can do for your country."

In sharp contraposition, the liberal vision of social order, well summarized in the Kennedy statement, is one of an organic entity in which individuals exist largely to serve the ends of the collectivity. In communist theology as well as practice, this vision is explicitly described and implemented. In the creed of the modern American liberal the collectivism is not so evident, but it remains as the only consistent interpretation of a vision that seems often blurred and, of late, somewhat shopworn.

The student revolutionary, the advocate of the "New Left," adopts a curiously mixed pattern of attitudes. Explicitly and categorically, he rejects the implied collectivism of the academic liberal. He recognizes that the nation-state is a dead god, that individuals do not, and should not be thought to, exist to serve the collectivity in the large. In this individualism, which has its base in philosophical anarchism, the student revolutionary finds common ground with the genuine constitutionalist. His behavioral slogan that each man does "his own thing" becomes immediately congenial to that person who holds the constitutional attitude. On the other hand, the revolutionary too often brings with him the intolerance of academic liberalism, and sometimes in extreme forms. His remains a "truth-judgment" approach, or, what is even worse in the modern context, a "commitment" approach which often refuses to allow time for even rudimentary doubt. In all this, the revolutionary fails to see that the two sides of his ideology are mutually inconsistent. Each man's freedom to do his own thing—this implies the principle of equal freedom upon which constitutional order is based. One man's thing differs from another's, and this, in turn, implies that no man can act out of his own commitment so as to prevent others from acting.

Let us consider the dialogue, first, between the student revolutionary and the academic liberal, and, secondly, between both of these and the constitutionalist who stands on the sidelines. In the first of such confrontations, as I have already suggested, the academic liberal appeals to values. He says that the revolutionary is "wrong," that he is blind to the "truth." The student's response is that such notions do depend on values, and, since he rejects the values of middle-aged, middle-class America, there is no basis for discussion. The dialogue is ended before it has begun. The constitutionalist, who observes the frustration in the adversaries, has a contribution to make in commencing genuine dialogue in which all can participate. He says to both the student revolutionary and the academic liberal: "Your values differ one from the other and from my own perhaps, and 'wrongness' or 'rightness' in behavior, 'truth' or 'untruth' in judgments, depend on what values one holds. But both of you, and I, should be interested in developing and in maintaining an institutional structure within which all of us, and others, can exercise the freedom to differ in basic values and to behave differently in accord with those values. I criticize the student revolutionary not because he is 'wrong,' but because his behavior tends often to deny similar behavior on the part of others. Is it not possible for us to discuss rules under which individuals and groups with widely divergent value standards can go about doing their own things in harmony and mutual respect?" Perhaps both the student revolutionary and the academic liberal are too intolerant to enter into such an invitation to discussion, but, at the least, the constitutionalist has offered a prospect for dialogue.

I do not wish, in this paper, to present the student-university confrontation as a precise miniaturization of the individual-collectivity confrontation even if the university-as-collectivity model is accepted. But there seem to be sufficient parallels to make some further discussion of the analogy useful. Consider the university as a community, as a social order. The student revolutionary rejects what he considers to be the misguided objectives and goals of the university. He seeks to change these, and, in his clamor for reform, he seeks to substitute demands of his own invention for those in being. The objectives, the goals and purposes of the university as these exist, seem to have been defined by old-fashioned, outdated authorities, with little relevance to modern reality. The constitutionalist observes and suggests a new vision of the university which provides the base for mutual coordination. He denies the existence of collective goals, objectives, or purposes, specifically and as such. His vision is of the "community of scholars," with each man and each group in this community exercising the freedom to carry out his own or its own objectives as privately conceived, with the university, as such, described by a set of rules designed primarily if not exclusively to insure against conflicts among individuals and groups within the community and to promote mutual respect among them.

If the collectivity does more than this, and if agreement does not spontaneously and mysteriously emerge, the will of the strongest must be imposed on all. Authoritarian definitions of objectives and coercion aimed at implementing these objectives must follow. Authoritarianism is the only effective alternative to constitutional order, whether the social interaction be characteristic of a university, a local community, or nation. When this simple truth is fully recognized, all parties must acknowledge and accept limitations on their own power to implement their desires, in exchange for constitutional protections against having the will of others imposed on them in turn. But even when a genuinely constitutional structure is in being, some decisions must still be made collectively and for application to all members of the community.

Again let us use the university as our example, while continuing to acknowledge some of the larger implications of the argument. In some constitutionalist ideal we may think of the "community of scholars" characterized by an interaction system that allows some spontaneous order to emerge from the private behavior of individuals and voluntary sub-groupings with little or no centralized decision-making. Properly designed, the university might come reasonably close to such an ideal. Within practical limits, however, there would remain functions to be performed by the collectivity as an entity, decisions to be made that would, once made, be applicable to all members. This amounts to saying that, even if the modern university should be stripped of many of its artificially derived powers of control over the free-search processes of its members, there will remain a set of decisions that can be made only for the whole entity. Who shall be admitted to membership? How shall members participate in decision-making? What procedures shall be used to allocate scarce budgetary resources? How shall such decisions be made and by whom?

It is here that we return once more to the question posed in the first sentence of this paper. Shall the student, as a member of the university, be granted a share in decision-making, and, if so, should this be an equal or comparable share with that granted the salaried administrator or tenured faculty member? Concentrating on this question in its university setting is especially helpful because answers that seem clear in this focus are not so readily transferable to the larger world of political democracy. The liberal's standard response has already been noted: the student's voice should be listened to with respect, but he is uninformed, uneducated, and immature, and, most importantly, he is a short-term resident of a long-lived institution. One-man-one-vote, as a decision-making principle, is not applicable to include students in the university's democratic processes. Some members are more equal than others in this community.

If this one-man-one-vote principle is *denied* elementary validity in the university setting, however, should it be *granted* elementary validity in political order generally? Again the student revolutionary who demands his share of power senses the contradiction in the academic liberal's position. How can the liberal applaud the reapportionment decisions of the Supreme Court, based on an extremely naive interpretation of the one-man-one-vote principle of democratic process, while denying to the student the relevance of the same principle in university constitutional procedure? The short-term membership of the student should be equally relevant with the short-term citizenship of the Arlington bureaucrat who temporarily resides in Virginia. Yet the Court held that Virginia's argument based on the short-term residence of the bureaucrat was wholly inappropriate in allocating legislative seats, again with the near-universal applause of academic liberals.

Once again the liberal must face up to issues that he has for too long been allowed to evade. Is he the majoritarian democrat that he seems, or does he support apparent democratic process only so long as his own objectives promise to be advanced? Does the liberal's adherence to the one-man-one-vote principle last only so long as predicted practical implementation of this principle achieves specific short-run collective results? Is he democrat first and collectivist second, or the other way around? I submit that his values are reversed. The modern academic liberal is, first and foremost, collectivist, in that he seeks direct and expedient implementation of policy objectives which he thinks to be possible only through the exercise of centralized governmental powers. He remains relatively uninterested in the processes through which decisions are made, and he is willing to limit his support for democratic procedures if need be. He will be the first to applaud the subversion of orderly constitutional process, as indeed he has so amply demonstrated in the 1950's and the 1960's. No better example could be provided than the liberal's chameleon-like behavior with respect to presidential powers in the 1960's. He called, loudly, for an expansion of these during the Kennedy reign; he reversed his position dramatically within a few months after Johnson took office. He calls now for an abolition of the electoral college; he would applaud this college if its workings had prevented the election of Richard Nixon in 1968. The modern liberal will be the first to abandon the one-man-one-vote crusade when he senses that majorities inimical to his own interests are likely to emerge with force.

By my references to what I have called the "academic liberal," perhaps I have been whipping a horse already dead, despite his occupancy of seats of power in many university communities. How does the constitutionalist respond to the students' demand for a share in university decision-making? First of all, and to repeat, the constitutional attitude requires a drastic reduction in the number and scope of centralized decisions that are made. The constitutionalist's first response for many issues is that collective decisions should not be made at all, in the sense of searching for outcomes that are to be applied to all members of the community. His vision is that of the "free university," within limits, and in this he again finds much that is common ground with the potential student revolutionary. In this respect, the constitutionalist may willingly acquiesce in major dismantling of the existing power structure of the modern university, provided only that one power structure is not simply replaced by another. But how does the constitutionalist respond to student demands to share decision-making power for those decisions that all agree must be taken collectively? On balance, the constitutionalist is likely to be democratic in a much more meaningful sense than his liberal counterpart. He is democratic, however, only because he sees greater evils emergent from alternative decision systems. While the constitutionalist may hold fast to the Jeffersonian principle of political equality, he recognizes the "as if" nature of the assumptions that must be made in framing constitutions. He is likely, therefore, to agree to assign the student a share in decision-making while trying to insure that the decisions that are made are minimized. Perhaps more importantly, the constitutionalist sees little merit in majority rule, *per se,* and he may well consider that the constitution of the university should lay down varying rules for varying sorts of issues. By definition, once the truth-judgment approach is dropped, majority rule implies coercion of minority interests, and the constitutionalist desires to minimize coercion.

As I have noted on several occasions, and as would have been obvious even without my notice, I have employed this discussion of the students' revolt within the university community as a vehicle for commentary that has much wider applicability. The university is not a miniature of society at large, but the comparisons are relevant within proper limits. In conclusion, however, I shall shift explicitly from the student-university confrontation and discuss briefly the central issue that seems to be presented in all this. I could rephrase the initial question without reference either to the student or the university. Should the uninformed and uneducated eighteen- or twenty-one-year-old voter be granted a share in the control over the structure of political society that is equal to that of any other man? Should the illiterate, even if he is mature, be allowed the franchise? These are questions that are now too seldom raised. Can a viable society exist when voters are allowed to decide questions that they cannot remotely understand? Can man be allowed to ask questions that he cannot answer? This is the dilemma that has been posed in progressively serious form since the Enlightenment.

Only in the constitutional attitude is a partially satisfactory answer to be found. If men can learn to live with one another in a social structure where coercion is minimized, in which collective action is rigidly restricted within constitutional limits, political equality and universal suffrage can be constructive features of a free and participatory democracy. If, on the other hand, constitutional process is subverted, if collective action is unbounded, the way is open for the political demagogue to appeal to the lowest common denominator among the rabble. There is no other than the authoritarian way. We have, I think, seen ominous signals in recent years. I am not personally optimistic. It now seems likely that we must undergo the painful and tortuous process of trying, and perhaps belatedly, to learn again what the Founding Fathers knew only too well. As a people, we have forgotten the simple principles of governing in a free society. The urgent question of our time is: Can we relearn these simple principles before destruction makes them irrelevant?

A Theory of Leadership and Deference in Constitutional Construction

James M. Buchanan and Viktor Vanberg

1. Introduction

How do we explain the behavior of James Madison in 1787, along with the behavior of those who followed his intellectual leadership? More generally, we address two questions. First, can models of rational choice be extended to cover the behavior of persons who are observed to invest scarce resources, particularly time and intellectual energy, in becoming more fully informed about constitutional alternatives? Secondly, can such models of rational choice be extended further to apply to the behavior of persons who are observed to defer to the opinions of those who do choose to become more fully informed?

Our response to the two questions takes the form of developing what we shall call a theory of *rational deference*, a term that we have selected deliberately to suggest parallels with the theory of rational ignorance, which has been introduced in application to individual choice behavior in voting by Anthony Downs and Gordon Tullock.[1]

Our theory of rational deference must, however, embody a second or ad-

From *Public Choice* 61 (April 1989): 15–27. Reprinted by permission of the publisher, Kluwer Academic Publishers.

Paper prepared for panel "Constitutional Choice II" at the Public Choice Society Meetings 1988, 18–20 March, San Francisco, California.

1. A. Downs, *An Economic Theory of Democracy* (New York: Harper, 1957); G. Tullock, *Towards a Mathematics of Politics* (Ann Arbor: University of Michigan Press, 1967).

ditional behavioral dimension that analogy with the theory of rational ignorance does not suggest. As our second question indicates, we may explain why rational choice behavior on the part of individual participants dictates deference to those persons who do invest resources in becoming informed about constitutional alternatives. But we must then also address the first question. We must explain why some members of the collective group make such investments. This dimension is not paralleled in the theory of rational ignorance, and, indeed, straightforward extension of the familiar theory of voting choice would suggest that no such investment would be made. A comprehensive model of rational choice must explain both why some participants defer to others whom they observe to be relatively better informed and why some others choose to become informed in the first place.

Our inquiry is narrowly circumscribed and limited to a highly stylized model. Our model is that of a constitutional convention, with a relatively large number of participants, charged with choosing among alternative sets of *general* rules for the political-legal-economic order. In such setting, the individual is led to deliberate on his *constitutional preferences,* i.e., he is led to array potential constitutional alternatives according to their relative desirability. By the nature of the choice setting, as defined, issues of possible conflicts between individual interests in the *in-period, within-rule* choice context do not arise. In particular, the issue of potential discrepancy between persons' in-period *compliance* or *action* interests and their *constitutional interests* does not arise.[2] The only issue that the constitutional convention model focuses on is that of individuals' preferences over alternative rules for the political-legal-economic order under which they expect to live, and of the kind of behavior that they can be expected to exhibit in the collective choice process by which such rules are adopted.

The particular aspect under which this issue will concern us here is related to the fact that an individual's *constitutional preferences* can be viewed as embodying an *interest component* and a *theory component.*[3] A person's ranking

2. For an expanded treatment of the second of these issues, see V. Vanberg and J. Buchanan, "Rational Choice and Moral Order," *Analyse & Kritik* 10 (December 1988): 138–60.

3. For a more detailed discussion of this distinction, see V. Vanberg and J. Buchanan, "Interests and Theories in Constitutional Choice," *Journal of Theoretical Politics* 1, no. 1 (January 1989): 49–62.

of alternative rules is informed, first, by his *interests* in the patterns of outcomes that may result from different rules, and, second, by his factual expectations or his *theories* about the kinds of outcomes that will result from alternative rules. Potential disagreement in constitutional preferences among participants in a constitutional convention may result from both these sources, from conflicting interests in outcome-patterns, from disagreement in theories, or from both.

The central concern of the *contractarian* approach to the issue of constitutional choice has been with those characteristics of the constitutional choice setting that tend to eliminate potential conflict in constitutional *interests,* or, more specifically, that tend to translate potential *inter*personal conflicts of interests into *intra*personal ones. The Buchanan-Tullock (1962) *veil of uncertainty* construction as well as the Rawlsian (1971) *veil of ignorance* construction both serve the purpose of presupposing a choice context in which interpersonal conflicts in constitutional interests are largely or, in the Rawlsian construction, even perfectly eliminated. If, under such conditions, constitutional agreement is considered unproblematic, an underlying assumption is, of course, that major obstacles do not result from conflicting constitutional *theories,* i.e., from individuals' different expectations concerning the factual working properties of alternative rules. In fact, in Rawls' construction, such disagreement over theories is excluded by the assumption that each participant is fully informed about the *general* effects of the alternatives.

The concern of our present paper is the reverse one of inquiring into the "information side" of the constitutional choice issue. We explicitly do *not* assume that the participants in the constitutional convention are perfectly informed about the general working properties of potential alternative rules, but rather, that they have to invest resources, i.e., to incur costs, in order to become better informed about what the relevant alternatives are and what outcomes they are likely to produce. Specifically, we want to inquire into the reasons why, as can be observed in real world constitutional choice settings, some persons are willing to make such investments while others choose to remain uninformed and to defer to the constitutional expertise of others.

In order to isolate the informational dimension in constitutional choice, we presuppose a choice context in which, due to some sufficiently thick veil of uncertainty, conflicts in constitutional *interests* are absent. That is, by presupposition, an individual cannot identify, in advance, what rules or set of rules will maximize the furtherance of his own interests, or the interests of the group that he represents. Under such assumptions, the process of reaching constitutional agreement is not a matter of reconciling potentially conflicting interests but of identifying the set of rules that best serves the participants' commonly shared constitutional interests.

Where participants to a constitutional convention are divided by conflicting interests, the concern for their identifiable interests does, one might be inclined to argue, provide an incentive for individuals to become knowledgeable about constitutional alternatives. The before-mentioned "theory of rational ignorance," however, has pointed to the reasons why, for large electorates, such reasoning may be flawed. The smaller the probability that his own vote will be decisive and the larger the subgroup of those voters with whom he shares common constitutional interests, the less incentives a person has to incur costs in order to become a better informed voter. Quite obviously, the logic of the rational ignorance argument applies *a fortiori* if, as in the context of our present analysis, we presuppose the absence of conflicting interests. Under such conditions, constitutional knowledge cannot be employed as a means for protecting or furthering one's differentially identifiable interests. Unable to identify potential differential interests, individuals are induced to favor *fair* rules, and they can expect others to be similarly motivated. Given that, in this sense, the issue of fairness is taken care of, the remaining issue for which *constitutional knowledge* would seem to be a relevant concern is that of overall "quality" of rules, quality in terms of some commonly shared standard for the desirability of patterns of outcomes.[4]

The quality or productivity of rules in the defined sense obviously is a genuine public good to the inclusive group of participants in the constitutional convention. Consequently the question arises: Why will any participant, in such a stylized (large-number) setting, supply the genuine "public good" that is presumably involved in becoming informed about the relevant alternatives? Strictly applied, rational choice on the part of partici-

---

4. Our implicit assumption here is, of course, that " fairness" and "quality" are attributes of rules that, in some sense, may vary independent of each other: Rules may be *fair* in the sense of their effects on the distribution of benefits and costs among participants, and at the same time may be *poor* in generating only an inferior level of "welfare." That is to say, for a desirable social order to be generated, it is not only the fairness of rules that is of relevance but their "overall quality" or "productivity" as well.

pants would seem to dictate relatively little investment in the acquisition of information. And, if all participants act in this fashion, we could predict that the constitutional choices that emerge will exhibit properties of instability, cyclicity, and erratic swings, all of which might be associated with the dominance of expressive voting, as opposed to rationally based interest voting.[5] Or will it be rational for some subset of the participants to make the investment in analysis of the working properties of constitutional alternatives and for other participants to defer to the opinions of those who do make such investment?

2. Rational Deference

Recall that, by presupposition here, the participant who is to vote in the constitutional convention is assumed to be ignorant in two distinct ways. Each participant, both among those who are passive and among those who might be active in information acquisition, remains, by presupposition, ignorant or uncertain in the Rawlsian sense. Each and every participant remains unable to identify his own interest in relation to the working of the choice alternatives in periods after the constitutional choice has been made by the group. This sort of Rawlsian constitutional ignorance may facilitate agreement because it offers a motivation for participants to make choices in terms of generalizable rather than particularized criteria. But the participant also remains ignorant as to the generalized working properties of the alternatives for choice. As mentioned before, this second sort of ignorance is not present in the stylized Rawlsian setting, where each participant is presumed fully informed as to the general patterns of effects of the alternatives. In our setting, not only does the individual participant fail to know what set of rules will further his interests; he also does not know what sort of rules will maximize the achievement of the generalizable criterion that may be used.

We postulate that the second sort of ignorance can, however, be eliminated by a sufficient investment of resources in the acquisition of knowledge. In this section, we do not examine the choice behavior of the person who

---

5. For a treatment of the relevance of expressive voting in large-number electorates, see G. Brennan and J. Buchanan, "Voter Choice: Evaluating Political Alternatives," *American Behavioral Scientist* 29 (November/December 1984): 185–201.

might consider such investment. We want instead to concentrate attention on the participant who chooses not to make such an investment, who chooses to remain ignorant of general effects of potential constitutional alternatives. We shall, in Section 3, examine the choice behavior of the participant who chooses to make the investment required to become informed about the general working properties of the alternatives. For now, we simply presume that some persons in the group, some participants, are observed to make such investment. We want to concentrate on the choice behavior of the person who remains outside this informed set, this constitutional illiterate who yet retains a voting power equal to any other member of the constituent assembly or convention.

Such a participant now faces a choice setting that is quite different from that which is faced when all participants are equally ignorant. He now is presented with predictions as to the working properties of the alternatives as these are advanced by those who claim to have become informed. The "experts" offer their opinions, and the constitutional illiterate can choose among the experts, the intellectual leaders, rather than make some raw choice among the alternatives, as such. That is to say, the uninformed participant may rationally *defer* to the opinion of someone who has gained his respect.

In order for deference to the opinion of some selected informed participant to be rational for the participant who remains uninformed, the choice among those informed persons to whom one might offer deference must be less costly in some sense than the raw choice among constitutional alternatives themselves. If the uninformed participant must himself become informed in order to choose rationally among the informed, then there is nothing to be gained by the additional step. The problem is the familiar one of choosing one's doctor. To choose one's doctor rationally may, in the limiting case, require the acquisition of sufficient information as to make the seeking of the doctor's advice totally unnecessary. By both observation and presumption, the investment required to choose among doctors rationally must be less than that which would be required to make the advice of doctors redundant. Doctors who offer their services exhibit certain readily accessible signs of badges of merit (diplomas, licenses, certificates). Further, both through word and deed, and both directly and indirectly observable, doctors present a "sample" that allows a plausibly acceptable generalization to nonobserved and nonobservable areas of potential competence. The individual considers it fully rational to defer to the opinion and advice of the doctor whom he selects from among those offering their services.

The analogy with an uninformed individual's choices among constitutional alternatives seems appropriate here. Precepts of rationality need not imply that the individual actually "vote" expressively on the basis of emotional prejudice, on some lottery-like hunches, or cursorily on the basis of the minimal knowledge that is possessed. The uninformed participant, who acknowledges his own informational-knowledge status, may rationally defer to a "constitutional doctor," whom he deems to be well informed and more competent to array the alternatives. He may choose to become a follower of an intellectual "leader," who earns the deference by his own differential investment in the acquisition of knowledge, an investment that may be exhibited directly or indirectly, in ways and means fully analogous to those of the physician. In transferring his direct influence on the collectively selected outcome to someone considered to be more informed, the uninformed participant is rationally protecting his own interests, to the extent that these are known in the constitutional choice setting.

Note that rational deference to the authority of the well-informed "leader" that is chosen is not fully analogous to the delegation of decision-making authority to a selected agent. In the principal-agent relationship, the central issue is one of controlling the agent that is selected so as to insure that he does, indeed, carry out the preferences of the principal. By comparison, in the deference-to-authority relationship, the problem is not one of keeping the agent under control; the problem is, instead, that of selecting an authority whose superior knowledge allows for an ultimate choice that will more accurately promote the participant's own interests.

3. Rational Leadership

The model of rational deference that has been outlined in the previous section is mainly a variation of the standard theory of rational ignorance. Like the latter, it emphasizes that voters in large-number settings have little incentive to invest in the acquisition of information, and it simply adds to the argument that deference to some "authority" may be a lower cost substitute for such investments.

When the theory of rational ignorance is taken as a "reference model," it should be kept in mind that its logic strictly applies only if "casting a better informed vote" is considered the exclusive benefit from being more knowledgeable about the issues at stake. It is only under this assumption that the expected payoffs from informational investments can be said systematically to decrease as the size of the electorate increases, and to be negligibly small in large-number settings. To the extent that there may be other expected payoffs from informational investments—other than the improved "quality" of one's own vote—the theory of rational ignorance has to be reconsidered, in the sense that it becomes an empirical question again whether or not such investments are "rational," measured against whatever benefits knowledgeability may generate. This consideration may be relevant for the calculus of an "ordinary" voter to whom such knowledgeability is a potential asset, e.g., in everyday conversation. It is, however, particularly relevant as we approach the issue of how a model of "leadership" may be constructed in the idealized setting for constitutional choice.

By presumption here, it is possible for an individual to remove the non-Rawlsian type of ignorance through an investment of time and intellectual energy. The potential leader can interpret the historical records; he can conduct comparative institutional analysis; he can simply spend time reflecting on the relevant alternatives; he can imaginatively construct and manipulate models; he can simulate patterns of behavior under varying constraints and varying assumptions about motivations. Finally, he can live through experiences in real time. Deference to elders is one of the traditional conventions.[6] Our concern is not, however, with the last-mentioned means of acquiring wisdom or knowledge. Our concern is with the acquisition of knowledge or information that becomes possible through explicitly allocated investment of resources.

Why should any participant undertake such investment? To the extent that only the effects on his voting behavior are considered, such investment would seem beyond the boundaries of a rational calculus. Under the assumptions of our stylized constitutional convention model, there is no source of differential profit from informed voting because of the participant's uncertainty about his particularized post-constitutional interests. Further, despite the fact that he

---

6. In cultures where communication media are not developed, the veneration of elders seems readily explainable.

can, by presumption, make informed choices concerning the choice alternatives, he cannot, through his individual vote, exert more than a small influence on the outcome that will emerge from the collective choice process.

It is only as we consider other expected benefits from informational investments, benefits that go beyond the negligible potential payoffs from "improved" individual voting behavior, that such investments may be explained
in rational choice terms. As we include some other expected benefits from
"constitutional knowledgeability" as relevant arguments in utility functions
for at least some of the participants in our stylized constitutional convention,
we may plausibly explain the investment decisions of those who hope to assume roles as intellectual leaders. Such other benefits may, for instance, be
identified by looking at the demand side of "deference." As noted in Section
2, some individuals may supply deference to those whom they consider to be
more informed. But, at the same time, those who purport to be relatively
better informed "demand" deference in the sense that they place a positive
value on having others influenced by their opinions and findings. For such
persons, the potentiality that others may be intellectual followers is positively
valued—either in and by itself or instrumentally, e.g. (but by no means
only), because of the directly instrumental effect exerted through enhanced
power to determine the ultimate collective result.[7]

The model here may be formalized.[8] The individual, i, has two arguments
in his utility function, X, a composite bundle of all "goods" of the standard
sort, and D, which we describe as deference offered by other persons in the
relevant collective group. Hence,

$$U_i = U_i(X,D) \tag{1}$$

where preferences over these two arguments are assumed to exhibit the normal properties.

---

7. The ability to influence others is always of this instrumental value to any participant
because, probabilistically, any additional voting power increases control over the outcome
of collective choice. For a formal analysis of this aspect of the issue in a standard voting
model, see J. M. Buchanan and D. Lee, "Vote Buying in a Stylized Setting," *Public Choice*
49, no. 1 (1986): 3–16.

8. The analysis of this section is related to that developed by our colleague David Levy
in his draft paper "Fame and the Supply of Heroics" (Center for Study of Public Choice,
George Mason University, 1987).

The individual also confronts a production function that describes the rates at which X may be traded for D and vice versa.

$$F_i = F_i(X,D) \tag{2}$$

By allocating time and other resources away from the "production" of X, the individual can "produce," or anticipates that he can produce, D. To attain individual equilibrium, when utility is maximized the individual must select X and D such that the following familiar condition is satisfied:

$$\frac{U_{ix}}{U_{id}} = \frac{F_{ix}}{F_{id}} \tag{3}$$

where the second term in the subscript denotes the derivative of the utility and production functions with respect to the arguments designated. Non-algebraically, utility is maximized when the marginal rate of substitution between X and D in the individual's utility function is brought into equality with the marginal trade-off that he confronts in production.

This formal construction is, of course, empty of explanatory content. We need to go further and specify the process through which some persons, but not all, will be led to make the necessary investment of resources in information acquisition, and, further, to examine the process that limits both the amount of investment and the number of those who will seek to fill the roles as intellectual leaders, as demanders of deference.

Interestingly perhaps, and despite the inherent plausibility of assuming inequalities among participants, we need not postulate initial differences among participants, either in utility functions or in production possibilities.[9] That is to say, there need be no differences in preferences for deference relative to other goods, nor need there be differences in the opportunity costs of producing deference relative to other goods. Note that deference cannot be "privately demanded and supplied" within the economy of a single individual. That is to say, the deference relationship exists only in interaction among persons; it cannot exist in a Crusoe setting.

The person who remains uninformed offers deference to another person; the person who receives deference does so from another person. Note, how-

---

9. The emphasis here is on *initial.* An investment in information acquisition, once it is made, is likely to impact on the investor's human capital and, hence, to affect his future production possibilities.

ever, that the simple exchange conceptualization does not apply readily to this interaction. The person who remains uninformed does not supply deference to another "at a price"; he does not "sell his vote" directly for some privately excludable quantity of a numeraire or other partitionable good or service. He supplies deference, through following the leadership of another, only in some sort of indirect exchange for the general knowledge of the alternatives that is made available to him, and to all others, as a nonexcludable "public good." The person who undertakes the investment in acquiring knowledge does not use stocks of the goods in X, or his capacity to produce such goods, to "purchase" deference directly from others. Instead, he uses these stocks or these capacities to produce nonexcludable public goods, namely information about the constitutional alternatives, in anticipation that, indirectly, he will secure the deference of others as he makes these public goods available to others.[10]

We do not require initial differentiation among persons in preferences or in opportunity costs because of the inherent extreme or polar-case publicness of that which is produced as a means of earning deference. Both of the qualities that define polar publicness are present here. Once the knowledge about constitutional alternatives is generated and made available to one person, it can, without additional cost, be made available to all persons in the relevant group.[11] Nonrivalry in "consumption" of this "good" is complete. Also, once made available to one person, others cannot be excluded from utilization of the same "good."

4. Industry Equilibrium

Let us now examine the process through which the "industry" of information-knowledge acquisition attains equilibrium. Suppose that, in some initial time

10. Obvious indirect benefits can be secured in any setting where the constitutional expert may instrumentally use such deference of others in order to further a professional political career. And, conversely, the competition among candidates in such settings may impose constraints that encourage production of "constitutional knowledge." In other terms, the production of the public good "constitutional knowledge" may be in part a by-product of persons' efforts to advance their political career chances.

11. There may, of course, be costs involved in the process of transmitting whatever constitutional knowledge is generated to other persons in the group.

period, all persons in the stylized constitutional convention are equally ignorant and uninformed. Suppose, now, that by chance, by error, or by some
other device, one participant makes a *minimal* resource investment in acquiring information and knowledge. He immediately becomes the seer; others defer to his demonstrated superior knowledge and others seek and act on
his advice about the selection of constitutional alternatives. This person, in
effect, becomes the law-giver for the community. As he achieves this status,
he is observed to enjoy the positively valued deference offered to him by others, as valued either instrumentally or in and by itself.

This situation is clearly not one that describes an industry equilibrium.
The supplier of knowledge is using up only a minimal quantity of the composite good, X, while securing a large quantity of deference, D. He is shifted
to a level of utility well above that attained by his fellows, all of whom are
here postulated to be his equals in all respects. Others will be attracted to
enter the knowledge acquisition and promulgation industry. Competition
will take the form of differentiation by way of additional investment in
knowledge, which may be observed both directly and indirectly. The initial
entrant will respond to the threat of his competitors by himself investing
more resources in acquiring knowledge about the alternatives.

In equilibrium, the expected utility of any person will be equal as between
"employment" in the knowledge industry and "employment" exclusively in
the production of X. Several interesting aspects of this equilibrium are worthy of attention. First of all, note that the enjoyment of X, the composite
bundle of ordinary goods and services, must be higher for those outside the
knowledge industry than for those who enter the industry. The members of
the latter group must sacrifice some potential consumption-enjoyment of X
in order to secure the knowledge-information that is expected, indirectly, to
allow for the enjoyment of deference. If "incomes" are measured exclusively
in X, then incomes of those in the knowledge industry must, in equilibrium,
remain below those of persons outside the industry.

Secondly, note that it is expected utility that is relevant in motivating both
entry into the industry and the level of investment by those who do enter.
Because of the polar publicness of that which is supplied by those within the
industry, there need be no equalization of attained levels of utility between
employment in and outside the industry by those who actually enter the industry. Deference may actually be offered to, and hence enjoyed by, only a

few of those who supply knowledge (in the limit only one). The successful among those offering leadership in this sense will achieve utility levels superior to that which might have been attained by remaining outside the industry, while those who are unsuccessful will actually achieve utility levels below those that might have been attained by outside employment.

A related feature suggests that, in terms of the orthodox efficiency norm, there may be resource wastage in industry equilibrium. There may be excessive investment in the acquisition of knowledge that is closely akin to the rent-seeking wastage involved when artificial scarcities are introduced. The potential for waste occurs here, not due to artificial restrictions, but due to the peculiar characteristics of the investment required to secure knowledge and information. The hours spent in acquiring knowledge by separate individuals, all of whom are expecting to become leaders, do not generate public goods of an additive nature, at least to the extent that is present in the orthodox case. While it might have been fully rational for some member of the Philadelphia convention, in the expected utility sense, to seek to oust James Madison from his position as intellectual leader, to do so would have required that this person invest time and resources in reviewing constitutional histories that duplicated that already undertaken by Madison. In some community-wide sense, such resource investment must be deemed wasteful.[12]

How many persons will enter the knowledge-information industry and how much investment will be made? The answer to both of these questions will depend on the value placed on D and on the costs, in terms of X, of acquiring the knowledge that, in turn, produces D. If persons, generally, place little or no value on becoming and being leaders of opinion, we should expect relatively little investment in the acquisition of knowledge in our highly restricted model. Similarly, even if deference should be valued highly, if the costs of securing deference through the acquisition of knowledge are very high, little investment might be predicted to emerge. These costs can be high for two separate reasons. The acquisition of the relevant knowledge may

---

12. Note that the possible excessive investment in our model does not stem from the same source as that which is central in Earl Thompson's model of competitive supply of *excludable* public goods. See E. Thompson, "The Perfectly Competitive Production of Collective Goods," *Review of Economics and Statistics* 50, no. 1 (February 1968): 1–12.

itself require high investment, both in terms of some threshold of achievement and in terms of continued resource outlay. In addition, even when knowledge is acquired, deference may not be forthcoming if the climate of interaction is such that the respect and trust of uninformed participants are difficult to capture.

The converse of these conclusions also follows. If deference is highly valued and if it can be produced at relatively low costs, we should expect a high level of investment, and, possibly, a high level of resource wastage in the sense discussed above.

5. Posthumous Deference

The restrictiveness of our basic model should be emphasized. To this point we have worked within the constraining assumptions that all participants are equal both in preferences and in relevant productive capacities and that the deference that is valued is *contemporaneous*. That is, the "good" that enters in utility functions as a positively valued argument is measured by the observed patterns of deference offered by persons who exist in the same time period. We have not considered an argument that reflects what we may call posthumous deference, or, more descriptively, fame.[13]

This argument may, nonetheless, be important in explaining why persons invest resources in the acquisition and promulgation of knowledge. Over and beyond, and even quite distinct from, any expected influence on the ideas of contemporaries, individuals may seek to influence those that "live after them," and they may voluntarily make investments to this purpose. It becomes terminologically incongruous to use "expected utility" with reference to this "good," which perhaps calls the whole notion of the expected utility language into question. It is, however, evident that persons do place value on posthumous deference, and we could readily adjust our formal model to include the additional argument. We could, also, extend the statement of the conditions of industry equilibrium to account for this additional element.

13. See Levy, "Fame and the Supply of Heroics"; also see D. Adair, *Fame and the Founding Fathers* (New York: Norton, 1974).

If we consider only the behavior of those who make investments in knowledge, any inclusion of valuation for posthumous deference would tend to increase the level of investment, as compared with that which would be observed in the presence of only contemporaneous deference. If, however, we also include the behavior of those uninformed persons who might offer deference, a somewhat different result follows. To the extent that persons, in periods long past, have been successful in "purchasing" posthumous deference, their influences remain. And persons in the here and now may prefer to give deference to the ideas of those who lived in earlier periods than directly to those who offer their current services as potential intellectual or opinion leaders. To the extent that this residue of past influence remains, to the extent that James Madison, rather than some contemporary scholar, informs and shapes the attitudes of the commoner today, there is *less* rational incentive for the potential investment in knowledge today. Those who seek to influence and to lead current participants must compete for deference, not only with their contemporaries who have entered the knowledge industry, but also with all of those persons who, in past periods, have made such investments and whose ideas have been embodied in documents that are transferable through time. In a community characterized by stability through time, and especially a community with a written historical record, this influence seems likely to dominate the first one noted above. There is, in such community, presumably less investment in knowledge than there would be in the total absence of posthumous deference.

6. The Community of Unequals

As suggested, we have worked within a highly restricted and stylized model. If we drop the restrictive assumption that persons are equal in preferences and/or relevant productive capacities, then it becomes much easier, and more plausible, to develop a general model of rational deference. If we do nothing more than postulate that, by either preferences or capacities, there are "natural" followers and "natural" leaders, the two patterns of behavior discussed above fall even more readily within rationality precepts. Further, if, among those who might possess the capacities to command deference through some investment in knowledge acquisition, there are discernible differences in the opportunity costs of making the relevant trade-off between X and D, we can explain the pattern of entry into the industry that acquires and disseminates knowledge and information.

As we indicated at the outset, our inquiry is narrowly focused. We have sought to use a rational choice model or models to explain the motivation for genuine constitutional evaluation and possibly for constitutional reform. Our exercise has been one of "extending the limits" of rational choice models. In so doing, we have not intended to convey the impression that rational choice models offer the only explanatory tools that are possible. We do not claim to have offered *the* explanation for either the behavior of James Madison or that of those persons who deferred to him in constitutional construction. We have, we think, offered *an* explanation of this behavior that utilizes the familiar tools of social science.

Individual Rights, Emergent Social States, and Behavioral Feasibility

All men . . . are endowed . . . with certain unalienable rights.

—Thomas Jefferson (1776)

Abstract: Individuals retain control over at least some minimal dimensions of personal behavior. If this is acknowledged, social states are not, and cannot be, objects of choice. Social states emerge from the interdependent choices made by acting individuals and groups. Individuals may ordinally rank social states, but the objects for collective choice must be assignments of rights or rules. Failure to appreciate the distinction here leads to misguided efforts to attain positions that may be imagined but that are beyond the limits of behavioral feasibility.

1. Introduction

In my early criticism of Arrow's analysis of the relationship between "social choice and individual values," I advanced two quite separate arguments.[1] First, I questioned the whole normative framework that attributes positive

From *Rationality and Society* 7 (April 1995): 141–50. Copyright 1995 by Sage Publications, Inc. Reprinted by permission of Sage Publications, Inc.

Author's Note: I am indebted to my colleagues Hartmut Kliemt and Viktor Vanberg for helpful comments.

1. James M. Buchanan, "Social Choice, Democracy, and Free Markets," *Journal of Political Economy* 62 (1954): 114–23; Kenneth J. Arrow, *Social Choice and Individual Values* (New York: John Wiley, 1951).

value to consistency in a "social" ordering of alternatives. I challenged the basic presumption that any social decision rule should be evaluated in terms of its ability to generate an ordering of alternatives that exhibited a set of desirable features. Second, I criticized Arrow's interpretation of "the market" as a social decision rule. I emphasized the emergent as opposed to the chosen properties of the allocative-distributive outcomes produced by market interaction. Market outcomes emerge from the separated but interdependent choice behavior of many actors, and, as emergent rather than explicitly chosen *social states,* these outcomes are not within the feasible choice set of either separate participants or the collectivity of individuals in the organized community.

Four decades later, and after extended analyses in social choice, game theory, public choice, property rights, constitutional economics, the new institutional economics, and other related research programs, I now recognize that my second argument should have been extended to incorporate the first, that I accepted the social choice paradigm all too readily as being applicable to the nonmarket spheres of interaction among individuals. I should have recognized that the very notion of social choice is an analytical mirage, and that "choice" can never be applicable to a selection among social states. Instead, choices are necessarily restricted to selection among alternatives that may be arrayed along a set of dimensions of activity that can never be fully determinate of a social state, even in some conceptual sense.

I have been led into my current state of thinking on these matters by a reconsideration of Amartya Sen's theorem on the difficulties in reconciling liberalism and Pareto optimality.[2] In the discussion of this theorem, Sen, along with his critics, and especially Peter Bernholz,[3] introduced the questions that involve "rights" to choose. These questions, in turn, raise others that are concerned with definitions of rights and with careful specification of the alternatives over which rights to choose may be exercised.

My basic proposition is that, in any social setting, individuals have rights,

---

2. Amartya K. Sen, "The Impossibility of a Paretian Liberal," *Journal of Political Economy* 78 (1970): 152–57, and "Liberty, Unanimity, and Rights," *Economica* 43 (1976): 217–46.

3. Peter Bernholz, "Is a Paretian Liberal Really Impossible?" *Public Choice* 19 (1974): 97–107, and "A General Constitutional Possibility Theorem," *Public Choice* 51 (1986): 249–65.

by which I mean that individuals retain personal control over actions along at least some minimal set of dimensions of behavioral adjustment. Once this elementary proposition is accepted as a positive description of social reality, the logical fallacy involved in any analyses of choices among social states stands clearly exposed. Social choice, in any meaningful sense, must be behaviorally multidimensional, and to proceed analytically as if it is unidimensional may have, and has had, serious consequences for the reform of institutional-organizational-constitutional structures.

2. The Pure Slavery Model: Illegitimate Abstraction

Consider a setting in which one biologically defined person is master, and all other persons are slaves. If slaves have no behavioral discretion at all, they must act along every conceivable behavioral dimension precisely as the master dictates, even to the extent that their actions remain unresponsive to punishments or rewards. Behavior along each and every dimension is directly dictated by the master, and slaves have available no response. It is difficult even to imagine such a model, which would rule out any and all incentives for the master to offer either rewards for preferred behavior or punishment for undesired behavior by the slave. In this setting, the slave must be analogous to a mechanical device, say, a clock, without even the response potential of a living being, say, a dog. The model may, nonetheless, be useful as a benchmark for the analysis.

In such an extreme model, a slave has nothing that allows a bargain with the master, either direct or indirect. There is no basis for any contractual agreement, explicit or implicit, that might lead to the emergence of a position that would be mutually advantageous both to the slave and to the master, and that might provide the first step in a chain of contractual agreements that would ultimately generate the emergence of a legal order in which more than the single actor retains control over at least some set of behavioral dimensions.

If, however, we relax the extremely confining assumptions of this model and allow slaves, from the outset, to retain internal, personal control over at least one dimension of response behavior that is of interest to the master, we have the basis for potential exchanges in the form of agreement on mutually advantageous behavioral adjustments. Consider a two-person, master-slave relationship in which the master dictates every other activity of the slave (hours of work, type of work, consumption pattern, leisure activity, etc.),[4] but in which the slave retains ultimate control over the intensity of effort exerted in work. Behavior along this single dimension of activity remains within the choice set of the slave, a de facto element in existence as a human being. Note that this right, defined here as the minimal sphere of residual individual control, need not be inalienable in one strict definitional sense. The slave may voluntarily relinquish such control over behavior, but the exercise of the control cannot be assumed or taken over by the master without the sacrifice of some valued "good."

In this setting, there may exist potential gains from trade between the master and the slave, but this potential may or may not be realized. The issue of prospects for exploiting the mutual gains of exchange is not my central concern. My emphasis is on a quite different point, to the effect that the outcome of the social interaction, the social state, to be observed, whether trade takes place, depends on the separate choice behavior of *both* the master and the slave. The master cannot, on his or her own account, choose the social state; neither can the slave. And, more important for my purpose, there is no collective or social choice of that outcome that emerges, whether the potential gains from trade are or are not realized. Two behavioral dimensions are necessarily involved in generating the emergence of the interactive result.[5]

I introduce this highly restricted model for the express purpose of demonstrating that a social state cannot be chosen, whether by a single person with authority or by a group of persons who might try to make collective decisions through some rule. Nonrestricted choice of a social state would require the n-person analogue to the first master-slave model discussed above. The person or group charged with authority or right to choose must be able to select from among all states that are possible to define or imagine, consistent only with natural or physical constraints. It follows that no other person, or group, could be allowed simultaneously to choose and to act along any behavioral dimension.

---

4. Robert Nozick, *Anarchy, State, and Utopia* (New York: Basic Books, 1974), 290–91.

5. This feature of interaction is not in any way dependent on nonstrategic behavior. Either one or both parties may attempt to secure strategic advantage by failing to reveal true preferences. Such behavior does not, however, remove the emergent property of the outcome finally reached.

These restrictive conditions seem so absurd that, even as an abstract exercise, analysts do not really mean what they say when they refer to choices among social states, or to social states as objects for choice, whether individual or collective.[6] Even in the most authoritarian of settings, and quite independent of any constitutional limits, rights of choice can be assigned only over some subset of the components of the vector that conceptually defines the whole of a social state. And it is the intersection of this subset with other subsets that defines the social state that ultimately emerges. That is to say, there must be some simultaneous exercise of rights to choose by separate units, each of which selects among the alternatives that are described to fall along the dimensions over which the assigned rights apply.[7]

3. Imagination, Preference Ordering, and Choice

That which may be chosen or selected in some social choice process is an assignment of rights, separately, to participants in interaction, or, in alternative terminology, a set of rules that specify the separated domains for the exercise of choice, and action, by the participants. Given any assignment, the simultaneous exercise of choice by the participants will generate an emergent social state or, more generally, a predicted pattern of possible states. The suggested emendation in construction here may seem straightforward enough, and little more than semantic confusion may seem present when social states are treated analytically as the direct objects for social choice. I suggest, however, that there are more profound implications worthy of consideration. If social choices are made only among alternative assignments of rights, which,

6. Arrow is quite specific. He states: "The objects of choice are social states. The most precise definition of a social state would be a complete description of the amount of each type of commodity in the hands of each individual, the amount of each productive resource invested in each type of productive activity, and the amounts of various types of collective activity" (*Social Choice and Individual Values*, 17). Sen is more succinct: "each social state being a complete description of society, including every individual's position in it" ("The Impossibility of a Paretian Liberal," 152).

7. This statement summarizes my initial criticism of Sen's proof of the theorem that demonstrates the possible contradiction between liberalism and the Pareto criterion. If the objects for choice are, indeed, social states, as defined, it becomes logically impossible that more than one person could be assigned rights to choose. See Sen, "The Impossibility of a Paretian Liberal" and "Liberty, Unanimity, and Rights."

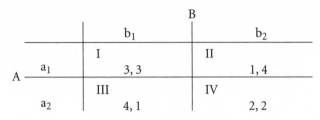

Figure 1. The classical PD

in turn, are exercised by actors who behave in accordance with precepts of rationality, the domain of possible social states is severely restricted. Many social states may be imagined, and ordinally ranked, by participants in social interaction, but may never emerge under any assignment of rights consistent with behavioral reality.

The argument may be illustrated by the familiar two-person, two-strategy PD matrix (Figure 1) with ordinal payoffs. The equilibrium in Cell IV is necessarily the emergent outcome if the players act independently.[8] My point here is that this independent-adjustment outcome (Cell IV) and the Pareto-superior outcome (Cell I), which may result from a voluntary exchange of rights between the players, are the only outcomes (social states) consistent with precepts of rational choice behavior. The social states represented in Cells II and III can, of course, be imagined and ordinally ranked by the participants. But these outcomes cannot emerge from an interaction that allows for the exercise of the separate rights for the participants to choose and to act along the dimensions indicated, which include the rights to exchange such rights in a voluntary transaction. The outcomes in Cells II and III are beyond the boundaries of behavioral feasibility, although, by presumption, these outcomes may be within the limits imposed by purely physical or natural constraints.

The difference between the set of social states that may be imagined and ordinally ranked and the smaller set that may emerge from the choice behavior of rational actors under any assignment of rights tends to be overlooked, especially when the analysis of social interaction is mathematicized. In the simple matrix illustration here, the solution in Cell II or III might, it would

8. For a careful refutation of all arguments to the contrary, see Ken Binmore, *Game Theory and the Social Contract,* vol. 1, *Playing Fair* (Cambridge: MIT Press, 1994).

seem, be within the realm of behavioral feasibility, if control over both players' behavior is assigned to either one or the other player. If B is appointed dictator, the Cell II outcome will be chosen. And, conversely, Cell III is the preferred outcome for A and will be chosen if he or she is dictator.[9] But generalization of this result to all dimensions of adjustment clearly violates the condition previously discussed, that which requires some minimal rights allowed to each participant. Person B, as dictator, can select his or her most preferred outcome from those that may be imagined only if no response at all is available to Person A. We are back in the stylized model of pure slavery, which is, as I have suggested, illegitimate, even as an abstraction.

A real-world example is available that suggests that the analytical ambiguity identified above has exerted tremendous effects on human societies. I refer to the organizational-institutional-constitutional revolutions that were motivated, at least in part, by the Marxian normative precept: From each according to ability, to each according to need. It is possible, of course, to imagine a social state in which each member of a community creates or produces economic value at some idealized optimal level consistent with physical capacities and survival and in which each member, in a wholly divorced relationship, withdraws for his or her own consumption or use such economic value as dictated by some ideally objectified criteria of need. It is not, however, possible to predict that any such social state would emerge from an assignment of rights (or set of rules) that reflects a recognition of the minimal control over production-consumption activity that cannot be extracted by any authority. Production without consumption: This is a socialist idyll, not a social state subject to choice.[10]

4. That Which Is Valued Is Not That Which Is Chosen

There is nothing in the alternative approach to social choice that I am advancing here that requires a jettisoning of the conventional teleology of normative welfare economics. People may be presumed to place ultimate value

9. See Bernholz, "A General Constitutional Possibility Theorem," for a discussion of rights assignments as means to general social states.

10. James M. Buchanan, "Production without Consumption: The Impossible Idyll of Socialism," working paper, Center for Study of Public Choice, George Mason University, Fairfax, Va., 1992.

on the characteristics of social states that may, first, be imagined, and, second, be arrayed in some order of preference. There need be no deontological intrusion that introduces any evaluation of processes or rules, per se. The approach here implies only that that which is valued cannot, itself, be directly chosen in any meaningfully defined process, whether this be private (individual) or collective. Individuals participate in the choices among assignments of rights, among rules that, in turn, generate social states as participants rationally choose among alternatives within the structure of rights so chosen. Assignments of rights may be valued only as they are predicted to allow for the emergence of valued outcomes. It becomes an empty exercise to evaluate rules independent of the outcomes that are predicted to emerge under their operation. It should be equally empty to evaluate imagined social states without consideration of the structure of rights, or rules, that may be expected to generate them. Unfortunately, however, romantic dreaming remains a part of our psychological reality.

The problem is that there is no obvious and at the same time general means through which the set of behaviorally feasible outcomes may be separated from the set of imagined but not behaviorally feasible states, a separation that is accomplished only by careful analyses of the predicted working properties of the alternative assignments of rights, assignments that are the objects of social choice. At the possible expense of some redundancy, let me elaborate. My claim is that, subject only to natural or physical constraints, there exist social states that can be imagined by people but that cannot be brought into existence as emergent outcomes under any possible assignment of rights. But what is there that serves to restrict the domain of all imaginable states?

It is necessary to impose conditions on individual preference orderings that are more restricted than those present in the rationality postulates of orthodox social choice theory, post-Arrow. Refer, once again, to the simplified PD matrix in Figure 1, with the four cells taken to represent the set of imagined social states. As noted earlier, the participants can ordinally rank these outcomes. If the payoffs are as shown, however, the outcomes in Cells II and III are not behaviorally feasible under individual exercise of rights because, by inserting the payoffs, we have defined "goods" and "bads" for each of the two players in the interaction. Any shift rightward along the horizontal dimension is a good for B and a bad for A; any shift downward along the vertical dimension is a good for A and a bad for B. Once the definition of goods and bads is made, the postulates for rational choice on the part of the actors require patterns of behavior that will preclude the emergence of a subset of the imagined social states.[11]

The analysis prompts the inquiry: Why have conventional social choice theorists failed to introduce behavioral feasibility constraints on the domain of ordinally ranked social states? Implicitly, through their failure to impose such constraints, these theorists have worked exclusively within a pure slavery model, the model that I have suggested is illegitimate, even as an abstraction. By this I mean that behavioral constraints can be ignored only if the actors in social interaction are presumed to be unable to respond along any dimension of adjustment, in which case, of course, the assignment of rights to choose among social states is equivalent to choosing directly among such states.

If the whole research program is taken literally to refer to choices among social states, it must be adjudged an empty vessel. Rescue from this totally negative assessment might be effected by an initial acknowledgment that social states, as literally defined, cannot be chosen, regardless of process, and that the proper subject of inquiry is choice among alternatives that meet the criteria for technologically determined publicness in the strict Samuelson sense,[12] with all other components in the comprehensive vector acknowledged to be determined by the separated behavior of all people as they exercise their assigned rights along the many dimensions of adjustment. Note that the stylized definition of *publicness* applies criteria to the good so classified that are equivalent to those that characterize the pure slavery model above. No distributional adjustments with respect to such a good can be allowed to occur, and if all relationships of complementarity and substitutability between such a good and others (that can be subject to adjustment

11. The necessary definition-classification of goods and bads allows for a resolution of the old debate between Gary Becker and Israel Kirzner on the necessary motivational assumptions required for predictions in economic theory. See Gary Becker, "Irrational Behavior and Economic Theory," *Journal of Political Economy* 70 (1962): 1–13, and "A Reply to Kirzner," *Journal of Political Economy* 71 (1963): 82–83; and Israel Kirzner, "Rational Action and Economic Theory," *Journal of Political Economy* 70 (1962): 380–85, and "Rejoinder," *Journal of Political Economy* 71 (1963): 84–85.

12. Paul A. Samuelson, "The Pure Theory of Government Expenditures," *Review of Economics and Statistics* 36 (1954): 387–89.

through independent behavior) can be adjudged insignificant and relegated to a pound of ceteris paribus, analysis can proceed as if choice is unidimensional. The choice of a public good becomes, in this setting, analytically analogous to the choice of a social state, and all of the problems involved in aggregating individual preference orderings remain central to the inquiry. Unless, however, (a) the conditions for publicness in the technological sense are satisfied and (b) the individual adjustments along all other dimensions of activity are, in fact, unimportant, the restriction of analysis to the presumed single dimension for choice may suggest the illusory attainment of positions beyond any frontier of behavioral feasibility.[13] Unfortunately, failure to meet these requirements need not exert an inhibiting effect on the domain over which actual choices are exercised. Political choice may, in particular, be made on the bases of romantic projections of results that cannot be generated by behavioral reality. And the feedback loops between disappointed expectations and change in the evaluations of rights assignments and rules structures do not work with either the speed or the directness that would characterize counterparts in physical reality.

5. Conclusion

This article contains several themes that initially may not seem closely related, but that are all required to develop the integrated argument. A central proposition is that spheres of behavioral adjustment exist that are beyond control. These naturally uncontrolled spheres amount to the same thing as artificially or legally guaranteed rights. In this sense it seems acceptable to

---

13. In several recent papers, both completed and in process, I have suggested that structural features of the assignments of rights, or of rules, may embody artificially imposed restrictions on the domain of emergent outcomes, restrictions that correspond to publicness requirements. See James M. Buchanan, "Production without Consumption: The Impossible Idyll of Socialism," working paper, Center for Study of Public Choice, George Mason University, Fairfax, Va., 1992; "How Can Constitutions Be Designed So That Politicians Who Seek to Serve 'Public Interest' Can Survive?" *Constitutional Political Economy* 4 (1993): 1–6; "Foundational Concerns: A Criticism of Public Choice Theory," working paper, Center for Study of Public Choice, George Mason University, Fairfax, Va., 1993; "Markets, Politics, and the Rule of Law," working paper, Center for Study of Public Choice, George Mason University, Fairfax, Va., 1993.

refer to both indiscriminately as rights. Acceptance of this starting point implies that the observed outcomes of all social interaction processes, that is, all social states, must always be understood to be emergent from the separate choices made by behaving units, each one of which chooses the most preferred option available from alternatives along the dimensions of adjustment assigned. This result forces a recognition of the elementary fact that the objects of social choice are alternative assignments of rights, or alternative rules structures, rather than alternative social states, although individuals' evaluations of such assignments or structures may depend solely on ultimate evaluations of predicted patterns of emergent outcomes.[14]

This shift of emphasis away from the choices among social states, which has been the subject of inquiry in formal social choice theory, has far-reaching implications. The set of imagined social states consistent only with physical constraints is much more extensive than the set of social states that may be predicted to emerge from the operation of rights assignments based on the recognition that individuals have residual freedom of choice, no matter how minimal the set of allowable responses may be. This recognition of some nonreducible domain for individual exercise of choice, along with the postulate of rationality, defines a behavioral feasibility frontier that cannot be violated.

Science fiction is a familiar literary genre based largely if not entirely on that which might be imagined when the laws of physical nature are superceded. There are few examples of economic science fiction based on what might happen if and when our science's laws are violated. Much of the human misery of our century might have been avoided by an expanded understanding of the distinction between that which is behaviorally possible and that which is not.

14. The emphasis that the necessary objects for social choices are sets of rules has long been central to the work of my former colleague Rutledge Vining (*On Appraising the Performance of an Economic System* [Cambridge and New York: Cambridge University Press, 1984]).

PART FOUR

Constitutional Order

Contractarianism and Democracy

I. Introduction

If politics is to be interpreted in any justificatory or legitimizing sense without the introduction of supra-individual value norms, it must be modelled as a process within which individuals, with separate and potentially differing interests and values, interact for the purpose of securing individually valued benefits of cooperative effort. If this presupposition about the nature of politics is accepted, the ultimate model of politics is *contractarian*. There is simply no feasible alternative.

This presupposition does not, however, directly yield implications about the structure of political arrangements and hence about "democracy" in the everyday usage of this term. We must acknowledge that in terms of ordinary language usage, "non-democratic" political institutions may be analytically derived from fully consistent contractarian premises.

Hobbes offers, of course, the classic example. Finding themselves in the war of each against all, persons contract with the sovereign; they give up natural liberty for the order and security that the sovereign promises. Decisions taken by the sovereign subsequent to this initial contract are not "democratic," in any meaningful sense of the term. While useful in setting the stage for discussion here, however, the Hobbesian contractual metaphor need not be extended to Hobbes' own gloomy predictions concerning the prospects

From *Liberty, Market and State: Political Economy in the 1980s* (Brighton, England: Wheatsheaf Books, 1986), 240–47. Copyright 1986 by James M. Buchanan. First published in Great Britain in 1986 by Wheatsheaf Books Ltd, Brighton, Sussex. Reprinted by permission of Pearson Education Limited.

Material in this chapter was initially presented at a Liberty Fund Conference on "Individual Liberty and Democratic Order" in Crystal City, Virginia, in June 1984.

for limiting the power of the sovereign. The Hobbesian metaphor suggests, nonetheless, that so long as the sovereign remains within the agreed and assigned limits of the initial contract, so long as the role remains the maintenance and enforcement of internal order, "democratic" attributes of the sovereign's decision-making would be out of place and, indeed, would be counter-productive.

The principle here may be placed in a more general setting, and it warrants some discussion because failure to understand the principle has been, and continues to be, the source of widespread confusion. In the most inclusive definitional sense, "politics" embodies all activities within institutions that are co-extensive with membership in the collectivity, the organized polity. Politics includes, therefore, the whole structure of legal institutions, the law, as well as political institutions defined in the ordinary sense. It is essential, however, that three quite different stages or levels of collective action be distinguished one from another.

First, there are those activities that involve the enforcement of the law that exists. This classification includes the legitimate activities of the Hobbesian sovereign, those that are included in what I have called the "protective state," which Nozick has called the "minimal state," and which some nineteenth-century philosophers called the "night-watchman state." In the familiar game analogy, the role here is that of the umpire or referee, who is appointed to enforce the rules, to police the playing of the game.

Second, there are those activities that involve collective action within the limits of the law that exists. I have referred to this set of activities as belonging to the "productive state." Hayek refers to "legislation" as distinct from "law." In terms familiar to economists, this set of activities involves the financing, supply, and provision of "public goods and services," those goods and services that may not be supplied efficiently by the activities of individuals and private groups acting within the existing legal rules.

Third, there are those activities that involve changes in the law itself, changes in the set of legal rules that exist. In American usage, this set can perhaps best be described as "constitutional law," although Hayek uses the general term "law" in this context. In the game analogy, the activities here are those that involve changes in the rules of the game that has been and is being played.

In the chaotic intellectual and political setting of the mid-1980s we can observe that the three sets of activities are confusedly intermingled. Those agents whose proper role should be confined to the first set feel no compunction whatever (and are encouraged to feel none by their scholastic mentors) in acting within the third set. Modern legal-judicial practice places us all in an ongoing game where the umpires themselves continually change the rules and, indeed, openly proclaim this to be their annointed social role. Those representative agents, legislators, whose role properly falls within the second set of activities, do not themselves consciously acknowledge the existence of limits. Modern politicians are encouraged to legitimize any and all extensions of legislative activity so long as "democratic" procedures prevail. Hence, both judicial and legislative agents invade the territory that the third category describes, and both groups do so under cloaks of claimed legitimacy. It is difficult to imagine a deeper and more widespread confusion than that which now exists, not only among the citizenry but, tragically, among those who might and do exert disproportionate influence on opinion.

We must recognize the intellectual confusion for what it is, and we must studiously avoid the temptation to apply contractarian derivations prematurely to observed institutions that have been warped out of all fit with their proper roles. The derivations must first be applied to meaningful categories. Therefore, within the three-part classification of politics outlined, I shall proceed to examine possible contractarian bases for democratic decision rules, if indeed such bases exist.

II. The Enforcement of Law

I have already suggested, in earlier reference to Hobbes, that there is no obvious role for "democratic" decision-making procedures in the state's role as law enforcer. In its activities as umpire, the state, through its agents, determines when the existing rules are violated and punishes those who are the violators, again within the rules. In such activity, truth-judgements are involved. Was the law violated or was it not violated? Varying institutional arrangements may be evaluated in terms of comparative efficacy. The appointed expert judge and the multi-person jury may be alternative means of generating desired patterns of results.

To introduce "democratic" decision procedures, with *all* members of the polity equally weighted (*ex ante*) in collective choices, in the determination of law violations would be quasi-contradictory to the very meaning of law. To allow a designated plurality, or majority, of all citizens to decide whether a single citizen or a group has or has not broken the law would almost directly imply that "law" does not exist independently. Such an institutional arrangement would indeed allow for tyrannization by the designated plurality or majority.

It seems evident that these arrangements could never emerge from any contractual agreement that persons enter voluntarily. The first normative principle that emerges from the contractarian perspective is that any agreed delegation of authority to the state or its agents be *limited by law.* I shall not in this chapter go through the derivation of this precept. I note only that the principle emerges directly without the necessity of assuming risk averseness in the standard sense.

III. Collective Action within the Law

The law, inclusively defined, may include a range for collective or state action, a range that is not in itself independent of the rules for reaching decisions within the range that is allowed. There may be goods and services that can only be or can most effectively be provided under the auspices of the collectivity as a unit. There may be "public goods" in the modern economists' meaning of this term, and decisions as to how such goods are to be provided may be assigned to the state. The question at issue here involves the possible role for democratic procedures in the making of such decisions. Will individual contractors necessarily adopt majority rule for those political choices that may be confronted within allowable ranges of state action?

The direct answer to this question is clearly negative. Majority rule may well emerge from contractual agreement entered into by all citizens. But it does so only as one among a set of plausibly acceptable decision rules, any one or all of which might be chosen with equal validity. The removal of the sacrosanct status accorded to majority rule was one of the main purposes of Buchanan and Tullock's *The Calculus of Consent* (1962). As the analysis there demonstrated, the rule that emerges from contractual agreement reflects the results of cost-benefit calculations on the part of the contractors. Because differing sorts of potential collective actions embody differing predicted cost and benefit patterns, there may be scope for the co-existence of several collective decision rules. For many decisions, simple majority voting, both in the selection of political representatives and in the operation of legislative assemblies, may well offer the most effective instruments. For other choices, however, which may be predicted to embody potentially more important consequences in costs and benefits, qualified majorities may be required for positive collective action. For still other ranges of state activities, authority may well be delegated to single agents or agencies.

Majority rule, as a uniquely legitimate principle for the making of political decisions, cannot be derived from the contractarian perspective as such. The perspective is not so empty as it seems, however. It would be difficult, indeed, to derive normatively a delegation of wide-ranging decision-making authority to an hereditary monarchy or to a family-defined aristocracy from any contractual process in which all members of the polity participate. Much the same could be said concerning delegation to a self-perpetuating, essentially cooptive, ruling elite. Delegation to a selected oligarchy that is regularly rotated through some guaranteed electoral process might possibly emerge in a contract, although the limits within which such an oligarchy might operate would tend to be more tightly drawn than those under more inclusive decision structures.

A critical element in any contractarian perspective, regardless of where the criteria are applied, is *political equality,* and especially in the *ex ante* sense. In an idealized contractual setting, the individual is modelled as making a choice among alternative decision rules without knowing how the operation of particular rules will impact on his own personal interests or values. In the Rawlsian limit, the person does not know who he will be in the settings where the chosen rule is to be operative. In the somewhat less rarified Buchanan-Tullock idealization, the person may himself be identified, but there is such uncertainty about the effects of rules on separate individual positions that particular interests cannot be related to particular rules. In either case, the contractual process will tend to exclude from consideration decision rules that explicitly deny some persons or groups *ex ante* access to political process. In the Rawlsian logic, the contractor, not knowing whether he will find himself red, white, green, or black, is unlikely to agree on any rule that does not assign equal weights, *ex ante,* to persons from all groups. In the Buchanan-Tullock logic, the red, white, green, or black person will not agree to assign choices over policies in set X to a rule that fails to incorporate *ex ante* equal weighting, since he cannot know how choices within the set will impact on his own well-being.

Majority rule satisfies the criterion of *ex ante* political equality provided that the voting franchise is co-extensive with membership in the polity. As previously noted, however, other alternatives also meet this criterion. With all decision rules other than unanimity, however, *ex post* political equality is violated. The interests and values of those whose choices dominate the outcome are ultimately accorded more weight than those whose choices are ignored. If A is selected by a majority vote of 60 per cent, those in the coalition who supported A secure more than those in the 40 per cent minority who supported B.

If, however, *ex ante* equality is ensured through the open franchise, and if political decisions are effectively decentralized over both issues and time, *ex post* differential weights on particular outcomes may be no cause for concern. Over a whole pattern or sequence of political choices (plays in the ongoing game), the ensured *ex ante* equality may map into some proximate *ex post* equality of weights.

IV. Changes in Law

Discussion in the preceding section summarizes the argument developed in *The Calculus of Consent,* from almost a quarter-century's hindsight and with an attempted focus on the question addressed in this chapter. Now, as then, democracy defined as *ex ante* political equality can be contractually derived, whereas democracy, defined as majority rule, passes muster only under a restricted set of circumstances and is in no sense uniquely related to contractual agreement. As we move to the constitutional stage, where the relevant set of choices are those relating to changes in the law, in the rules that constrain both private and public activity, there is *no* place for majority rule or, indeed, for any rule short of unanimity.

It is at this stage, and only at this stage, that the ultimate contract takes place, either in conceptualization or in actuality. It is here that the basic exchange or cooperative paradigm for politics takes on dramatically different implications from those generated by the truth-judgement or the zero-sum paradigm. If politics in the large, defined to encompass the whole structure of governance, is modelled as the cooperative effort of *individuals* to further or advance *their own* interests and values, which only they, as individuals, know, it is evident that *all* persons must be brought into agreement.

The simple analogy with market exchange illustrates the point. It would seem obvious that both parties to an exchange of apples and oranges must agree on the terms of trade if the reallocation of endowments generated by trade is to qualify as value enhancing for both parties. An enforced "exchange," whether by a third party or by only one of the two traders, cannot satisfy the individualistic value-enhancing criterion.

The complex exchange that describes a change in the constitution (in the rules) is not different in this fundamental respect from a simple exchange between two traders. A change in the rules (the law) that is applicable to all members of the polity can be judged as value enhancing only on the expressed agreement among all participants. There is no contractually derivable justification or legitimization for basic structural rules of governance that cannot meet the restricted consensus test. Any justification or legitimization of rules changes that fails the unanimity test must call upon noncontractarian criteria of evaluation, which must be *non-individualistic* in origin or, at least, non-individualistic in any universalizable sense.

V. From the Abstract to the Real

As noted, the analysis to this point is developed with reference to the highly abstract three-stage classification of politics. In this setting, the relationships between contractarianism and democracy can be presented in relatively straightforward fashion. The observed world of politics, however, embodies a confused and confusing mixture of the three stages, with law enforcement, legislation, and law-making undertaken by almost all political agents. Despite the confusion, attempts are made to assign meaningful descriptive attributes such as "democratic" or "non-democratic" to political arrangements as they are rather than to the idealized models which do not, have not, and possibly could not exist. In this intensely practical realm of discourse, the relationships cannot be nearly so sharply traced.

Nonetheless, we can isolate and identify critical attributes of observed political process that must be present if any contractarian legitimization is to be advanced. The most important requirement is that law exist, in a meaningful sense of the term. That is to say, both the private and the public activities of individuals must be limited by *constitutional constraints.* State or collective power to operate without limits, *regardless of the particular decision rule,* could never find contractarian justification. I have referred elsewhere to the "electoral fallacy," which has been the source of major misunderstanding, the notion that, so long as "democratic" decision rules are guaranteed, anything goes. Even here, however, there would have to be constitutional prohibitions against changing such rules.

Within the constitutionally or legally authorized exercise of governmental or state power, political arrangements must be characterized by political equality of all those who are included in the polity's membership, at least in some ultimate *ex ante* sense. This requirement need not, as noted earlier, guarantee that all persons carry equal weight in a defined collective choice. Nor does the requirement guarantee against overt coercion of some persons or groups by the collectivity. What is required here is that all persons possess equal access to political influence over a whole pattern or sequence of collective choices. In practical terms, this means that the franchise be open to all, that political agents be rotated on some regular basis, and that gross bundling of separate collective choices be avoided.

Finally, there must exist an observed and honoured distinction between collective actions carried out within the allowed constitutional constraints, within the law, and collective or group actions that involve changes in the law itself. A polity in which neither practising politicians nor political-legal scholars distinguish between legislation and law cannot be justified on contractarian grounds. If the distinction here is made, and widely acknowledged, the effective decision rule for changing the basic law must be observed to be more inclusive than the rule for making collective decisions within the law. The abstract contractarian logic need not be pushed to its extreme here, which would require that constitutional changes be reached only through unanimous agreement.

To summarize, a political-legal order can broadly be classified as "contractarian" if the following attributes are observed to be present:

1. Both private and public agents are constrained in their activity by the law, by operative constitutional limits.
2. Within the law, all members of the polity have equal access to decision-

making structures, and all have equal weights in the determination of collective decisions in the appropriately defined *ex ante* sense.

3. There is a recognized distinction between collective action within the law and action taken to change the law, with the decision rule for the latter being necessarily more inclusive than the former.

VI. Limited and Unlimited Contractarian Application

Note that the criteria for classification listed above do *not* include reference to the history of how existing rules might have emerged. To say that a political-legal order that satisfies the listed criteria qualifies as "contractarian" is to say something about the *operation* of that order. And there is moral-ethical content in such a statement. But confusion has emerged through a failure to recognize the severely limited scope of such contractarian justification. To say that, given the rules that exist (which must include the distribution of endowments among persons who operate, privately and collectively, within the rules), an observed political-legal order, in its operation, may be conceptually "explained-interpreted-justified-legitimized" by a contractarian-exchange model of interaction, is to say nothing whatsoever about the moral-ethical aspects of the distribution of the nominally claimed endowments of persons in some conceptualized "pre-operative" stage of politics.

A simple analogy with market exchange may again be helpful here. Suppose that there are two potential traders, each one of whom has an endowment of apples and oranges. Mr A has, before trade, ninety-three apples and forty-three oranges. Mr B has, before trade, two apples and four oranges. After trade, Mr A has ninety apples and forty-four oranges; Mr B has five apples and three oranges. The limits of the ethical-moral justification of free and non-fraudulent exchange are contained in the argument that *both* parties *gain* in the trading operation. There is no implication that the distribution of endowments, either before or after trade, is justified or made legitimate by the prospects for trade or by its reality.

To extend the contractarian criteria beyond the limited application to the operation of existing political-legal rules, to derive the implied contractarian features of the structure itself, is the task that John Rawls set for himself. There is no call for my own judgement here concerning an evaluation of his success or failure. In my own efforts, I have, perhaps not always consistently, been content with the more limited application. But my sympathy with and affinity for Rawls' effort has been, I hope, evident. At base, we share, along with fellow contractarians of all stripes, an unwillingness normatively to evaluate politics with non-individualistic standards or positively to interpret politics exclusively as the clash of conflicting interests.

Democracy within
Constitutional Limits

It is not easy for Western political economists either to understand post-revolutionary developments in the former socialist countries or to proffer meaningful normative advice. The histories of these societies must evolve spontaneously, even if necessity dictates a dramatic compression of the time-scale, at least in any comparative sense. At best, political economists who are external to the process can isolate and identify features of Western institutions that may be worth noting, and especially in a precautionary fashion, by those who may find themselves in positions to make critical choices during the institution-building phases of transition.

In this chapter, I shall draw largely upon my own country, the United States, as a source for identifying elements of current political structure that reflect departures from the normative standards that were both expressed in our founding documents and embodied in our political history for a significantly long period. It is not an exaggeration to say that we have now, in the United States, lost our constitutional way. We have lost our generalized understanding of the relationship between the two normative objectives: political equality among citizens, summarized under the rubric democracy, and the liberty or independence of each citizen from the coercion of the state—an objective that was presumably to be achieved by constitutional constraints on governmental authority. The American structure as initially imagined, and to a surprising extent realized over long periods of our history, was accurately

From *Post-Socialist Political Economy: Selected Essays* (Cheltenham, U.K.: Edward Elgar, 1997), 182–89. Reprinted by permission of the publisher, Edward Elgar Publishing, Limited.

described as a *constitutional democracy*. And I emphasize that both words are important, with *constitutional* taking precedence over *democracy*, if, indeed, any such ordering is desired. Unfortunately, it is the constitutional understanding that has been largely lost from public consciousness, with consequences for all to see.

Citizens in the former socialist countries live now in the post-revolutionary moment during which there may exist opportunities to design and construct elements of political-economic orders that, once emplaced, will prove difficult to reform. The urge towards democratization is surely easy to understand, and the association between nondemocratic political structures and the suppression of individual liberties leads perhaps naturally to a neglect of the potential democratic danger to individual autonomy. The institutionalization of democratic procedures of governance may produce consequences desired by no one unless these procedures are limited by constitutional boundaries.

In the second section of this chapter, I shall discuss the relationships between political democracy and the market economy, both of which are nominally listed as objectives for post-revolutionary institutional reforms in the countries that were previously organized on socialist principles. In the third section, I shall summarize briefly the distinction between constitutional politics and ordinary politics, and I shall discuss the relevance of this distinction for the viability of a market economy and, indirectly, for a liberal society. In the fourth section, I shall sketch out the operation of a politics within rules, and, in the fifth section, I follow this sketch by outlining specific implications for areas of policy. The final section presents a general statement of position.

Democracy and the Market

Reformers in the countries that were classified as socialist prior to the revolutions of 1989–91 are as one in their stated twin objectives: (1) political reorganization towards introducing democracy and (2) economic reorganization towards introducing a market economy. (China, whose authoritarian leaders crushed its incipient revolution, is identified by its difference here. China seeks to shift towards economic organization based in part on market principles while putting down pressures towards democratization of its political structure.) As regards the reform leaders in the societies of Eastern and Central Europe and the republics of the former Soviet Union, it is, I think, appropriate to ask whether or not the relationships between political democracy and a market economy are well understood.

It is, of course, easy to understand why the historical experiences under the totalitarian rule of the Communist Party have generated urges towards democratic reform in politics and economic reform towards markets. Individuals seek to be able to exercise political voice, to sense that they, individually, can at least share in the decisions that shape their own lives. At the same time, and for different reasons, individuals simply observe the economic failure of attempted command-control institutions to produce economic value. The system did not deliver the goods, as measured by the size, quality and content of the bundle ultimately desired, and furthermore the bundle was not growing larger over time.

But do the political reformers, both those who have attained positions of authority and those who might aspire to authority under fledgling democratic procedures, understand that the necessary conditions for the effective functioning of a market economy require that the range and scope of democratic authority be limited? At one level of discourse, there seems to be near universal acknowledgement that private or several ownership of productive resources must be substituted for collective or state ownership-control. But the secure ownership that is required for viability of an economy implies protection of holdings against political takings, including takings that may be orchestrated through the auspices of democratic politics. Almost by definition, a market economy both requires and itself facilitates a restricted range for the operation of government, independent of whether or not the actions of government are subject to the indirect controls of democratic politics. Indeed, I would suggest that this political function of the market economy is, in some evaluative sense, more important than the economic function, as measured by the size of the bundle of valued goods generated.

Properly understood, therefore, the revolutions were, and are, directed towards the devolution or decentralization of political authority, or depoliticization, which only a market organization of the economy makes possible, and, further, only within which genuinely democratic processes of decision can attain some semblance of meaning. The organizational-institutional implications of such an understanding are clear: the range and scope for political authority must be restricted, preferably by constitutional constraints that may be strategically introduced during the post-revolutionary moment and before particularized interests emerge. Explicit constitutional limits on the intrusion of politics into the market have the further advantage of providing expectational stability for persons and groups, internal and external, who might make long-term investments.

Constitutional Politics and Ordinary Politics

On many occasions, I have emphasized the necessity for a constitutional understanding, by which I mean an appreciation for and an understanding of the two stages or levels of political decision making that must describe the functioning of any political order that can claim either legitimacy or tolerable efficiency. There is, first, the design, construction, implementation and maintenance of the basic rules, the fundamental law, the constitution, that defines the parameters within which what we may call ordinary politics is to take place. And there is, second, the operation of such ordinary politics within these rules, so defined.

In some ultimate descriptive sense, there must always exist such a two-stage, or even perhaps a multi-stage characterization of politics as it is actually observed. But the explicit recognition of the distinction, and, more importantly, of the operational implications, is often neglected, with the result that ordinary politics is allowed to proceed as if there are no limits. It is critically important that the logic of the distinction between the stages informs thinking about politics, both during moments of constitutional choice and in the post-constitutional periods described by the workings of ordinary politics.

There are, literally, hundreds of familiar nonpolitical analogues to the two-stage structure of politics emphasized here and elsewhere. Consider word processing. The user must first choose a software programme and, second, choose what to write within the constraints imposed by the programme. Or, consider the purchase of any durable good, say, an automobile. The capacities of the car limit to some extent the activities that may be performed in using it. Or, consider planting a fruit tree, where the initial choice is among an apple, peach, plum or pear tree. Once this choice is made, it necessarily constrains the activities involved in cultivation, and also the type of output to be expected. For economists, the Marshallian distinction between the long-run choice of a fixed facility or plant and the short-run choice concerning the level of operation of the plant, as given, is familiar, and this distinction is directly analogous to the constitutional choice–ordinary politics choice introduced here.

Constitutional politics involves setting the rules, selecting the parametric framework within which ordinary political decisions are to be made and carried out. Such politics defines the manner of selecting those who seek to govern others, the extent of the voting franchise, the timing and procedures for elections, the voting rules, the terms for eligibility for office, methods of representation and many other procedural details that are necessary for democratic processes to operate at all. These constitutional parameters for democracy will be almost universally acknowledged both to be necessary and to differ in kind from the objects upon which ordinary politics operates, even in those settings where there exists no explicit constitution, as such. But the extension of constitutional parameters to include more than these formal procedures for governance must also be recognized to be important for ensuring stability of expectations. The range over which governments are allowed to act, even governments that are procedurally legitimate in the democratic features listed above, must be known, at least in terms of well-defined boundaries beyond which political intrusion shall not extend. Such constitutional limits may lay out protected spheres for personal liberties, as in bills of rights, and also for economic liberties, without which any market order remains highly vulnerable to piecemeal interferences generated by interest-motivated coalitions.

A domain for the exercise of constitutional politics may be described, but the existence of limits does not, itself, imply that there is little or no room left for the play of ordinary politics, the spaces within which the activities of governments, as we know them, may be observed. Clearly, governments may do many things, whether these qualify as good or bad by any criterion, that are within the constraints defined in almost any constitutional structure. But it is folly to think that governmental activities are appropriately constrained only by the feedbacks on voter attitudes that the formal procedures of democracy make possible.

Politics within Rules

Politics, as we observe it and talk about it, is, therefore, strictly a politics within rules or, in the reductionist classification of the preceding section, strictly ordinary politics. A well-functioning polity will, indeed, be described by stability in its basic constitutional structure, which translates into an absence of activity aimed towards continual constitutional change and discussion of such change. But the politics within rules that describe the well-functioning polity operates effectively only if the rules are themselves both understood and respected. A politics that seems to proceed as if a constraining set of rules does not and should not exist must fail in several dimensions. An imperialistic ordinary politics ensures the removal of stability-predictability from the whole political-legal-economic order and thereby guarantees both economic stagnation and the loss of individual liberties.

To suggest that the constraints on the operation of ordinary politics that are embodied in a constitution, whether these constraints be formal or informal, whether they emerge through an evolutionary process or as a result of deliberative design, are not subject to continual change does not, of course, imply that genuine constitutional politics, the politics involved in changing the basic rules, is out of bounds for discussion or that genuine constitutional reform is taboo. The suggestion is only that constitutional rules should be treated as "relatively absolute absolutes" by any comparison with the operation of within-rule politics and that these rules, if changed, be considered to be quasi-permanent, and that they be analysed as if they are and must become elements in genuine political capital.[1] Politics loses meaning if every moment becomes constitutional in the sense that efforts are made to modify the basic structural parameters of the system. Genuinely constitutional moments are identified in part by their singularity, by their extraordinary presence, by their intrusion of sorts into the ongoing compromises of conflicting interests that describe and define ordinary political experience.

Democratization may be introduced with reference either to constitutional or to ordinary politics, but it is essential that the domains be understood to be separate and apart. Democracy, defined as ultimate equality of influence over collectively determined results, may characterize procedures through which, at some appropriate moment, the structural parameters are chosen. On the other hand, and by contrast, these parameters may be imposed non-democratically, for example, the MacArthur constitution for modern Japan.

---

1. James M. Buchanan, "The Relatively Absolute Absolutes," in *Essays on the Political Economy* (Honolulu: University of Hawai'i Press, 1989), 32–46.

But independent of how the rules are themselves selected, these rules themselves may or may not provide for ordinary politics to operate democratically in the standard meaning. The rules may dictate that, within the boundaries specified in the constitution, individual citizens are guaranteed the exercise of equal ultimate influence over particular outcomes, with modern Japan again offering an example.

It is important to note, however, and as the discussion should have made clear, that there are limits to any democratization of constitutional politics imposed by the necessary quasi-permanence of the rules. If the parameters of structure are to remain in place over a sequence of periods during which the processes of ordinary politics are expected to take place, it is necessary that citizens, acting politically in any arbitrarily chosen period, cannot expect to exercise an influence comparable to that exercised in the ordinary politics that is bound within the existing constitutional rules. In a very real sense, the electorate for an effectively democratic constitutional politics must include participants over the course of many periods. Political equality may be retained as a normative democratic ideal, but individuals must reckon that the influences exerted spill over through time periods as well as among participants within any time period. That is to say, the set of participants who may claim idealized equality of influence is larger, in a temporal dimension, in constitutional than in ordinary politics.

Constitutional Misunderstanding: Examples from Modern United States

In the introduction, I stated that the United States has lost its constitutional way, that constitutional understanding has been allowed to slip from public consciousness and that modern experiences drawn from the United States may usefully serve as precautionary warnings to those who are actively engaged in constitutional design for countries that remain in a formative moment. In order to support this claim, it is necessary for me to summarize very briefly elements of the constitutional history of the American republic.

In James Madison's grand design, the central or federal government of the United States exercised extremely limited authority, but within such authority its sovereignty was unchallengeable. The separate state governments were not to restrict the free flow of commerce over the inclusive territory; the extensive internal market was to remain open, allowing for full exploitation of the specialization of labour, producing advantages that became relatively more important as technology developed. Because of this guarantee of a large internal open market, there was relatively little need for explicit and extensive constitutional constraints on the domain for ordinary politics of the several state governments. The competition, both actual and potential, among these several units within the large open market acted to ensure that any excesses of ordinary politics, motivated by coalitions of conflicting interests, be kept within reasonable bounds. The competitive politics of a viable federalism can substitute for the explicit constitutional politics that would be necessary in a unitary polity. (This is a simple principle that the nations of the European Community should learn and act upon. Unfortunately, the constitutional moment during which a viable federal structure might have seemed possible may already have been missed.)[2]

Madison and his peers overlooked the requirement for constitutional guarantees for openness in the external market, that is as between domestic and foreign traders. The central government was empowered to regulate external commerce, and the absence of explicit constraints allowed the ordinary politics of interest to generate welfare-reducing and regionally discriminatory restrictions on trade. These observable excesses of ordinary politics were at least in part responsible for the intense interregional conflict that provided the origins for the bloody Civil War in the mid-nineteenth century. And the outcome of this war itself ensured that the effective federalized structure of American governance would, over time, disappear. Over the course of a century, the central government, without any threat of secession on the part of states, predictably assumed increasing authority, with the result that the modern United States is, basically, unitary in a descriptive sense. The central government is overwhelmingly dominant in any and all potential conflicts with the states.

This change in political structure was not accompanied by any recognition that the demise of the competitive politics as among the several states should have dictated the imposition of additional constitutional constraints on the powers of the central government, over and beyond those that Madi-

2. James M. Buchanan, "Europe's Constitutional Opportunity," in *Europe's Constitutional Future* (London: Institute of Economic Affairs, 1990), 1–20.

son thought to be necessary at its formation. As the operation of the internal market of the United States came increasingly under the regulatory control of the ordinary politics of the single central government, there was no effective constitutional barrier to the intrusive interferences with the workings of the market, either internal or external. And the intrusion, once commenced, took on a dynamic of its own. Those interests that were successful in securing the artificially created profits or rents from politicized protection became attractors for other interests seeking, and getting, similar treatment. There were parallel extensions through the emergence of the transfer sector. The financing of genuinely collective functions from revenues raised from broad-based and general taxes was supplemented and expanded to include the financing of transfers, in money and in kind, to designated recipient groups, and taxes were deliberatively modified to ensure nongenerality in liability.

Many of these changes might have been tolerated without major damage to the constitutional fabric if they could have been considered as quasi-permanent. But, instead, the whole expenditure-tax structure in the modern United States has been allowed to become the primary object for the machinations of ordinary politics. The fiscal system is not treated as a part of the framework within which the decisions of participants in the market sector are made. The whole budgetary process reflects little more than the continuing compromises of the conflicting interests through ordinary politics. Everything seems up for grabs, and each legislative period is marked by proposed revisions in what should be structural parameters for the economy. Modern American political leaders, regardless of party, have no understanding at all of the need for, and the potential benefits from, stability in the rules, as applied to the whole of the regulatory-fiscal framework. The quasi-stagnation of the American economy in the 1990s is directly attributable to the failure of political and intellectual leaders to recognize that a more limited politics, as reflected in stability in rules, can be a more productive politics, if productivity is measured either in economic growth or in the liberties of citizens.

Conclusion

The U.S. constitutional experience must be avoided if the emerging democracies and market economies are to have reasonable prospects for success, especially with the past and recent history of the failed socialist experiments. It is critically important that the private property rights, as, if and when established, be guaranteed against politicized takings, whether in the form of direct seizure, the imposition of particularized punitive legislation or indirect and onerous burdens of taxation. It is imperative that the constitutions for the formerly socialist countries contain the guarantees for procedural democracy (elections, franchise and so on), for personal liberties (speech, press, religion and so on) and for protections against politicized (even if democratic) invasions of private property rights. Because of the historical memories of the politicized economy, property owners can be assured on the last point only by a specific constitutional listing of the allowed scope and range for the workings of ordinary democratic politics. The public goods that are to be financed by taxes must be specified, along with the basic structure of taxes to be used. A fiscal constitution is an essential element in any constitutional democracy, but it is more important in a setting where the distrust of ordinary politics and politicians is deeply imbedded in the psyche of citizens.

I am not so naive as to predict that any of the countries facing the constitutional moment of the 1990s will meet the ideal standards that I might suggest. Without a heritage of experience that embodies some understanding of the central logic of effective constitutionalism, any implementation of constitutional democracy will be difficult to achieve. But the logic remains, as does the tremendous and unique opportunity. The logic is simple, however, and appropriate leadership can influence public attitudes and opinions. And, once again, the force of potential competition cannot be overlooked. If only one of the countries in question should achieve the reforms required for a leap into genuine constitutional democracy, the exemplar offered to other countries in this age of instantaneous communication would almost guarantee generalization to other settings.

PART FIVE

Market Order

[Untitled]

I. Introduction

In this essay, I was asked to assess the state of economic science, necessarily from my own personal perspective, which is perhaps less representative of median or mainstream evaluation than those perspectives that may be offered by my peers in this series. I shall make no attempt to be comprehensive here, although the implications of my whole argument for the economist's stance as both a positive and normative scientist involve major shifts in attitudes toward the disciplinary subject matter. I shall concentrate discussion on my understanding of what an economy is, from which inferential criticisms of research programs, didactic instruction, and policy implementation emerge, more or less as a matter of course.

I may succeed in attracting your attention by stating two of these criticisms boldly at the outset. First, there is no place for macroeconomics, either as a part of our positive science or as a realm for policy action. Second, the appropriate mathematics is game theory rather than maximization of objective functions subject to constraints. These apparently unrelated criticisms emerge from understanding and interpreting the economy nonteleologically as an *order*, rather than understanding-interpreting the economy teleologically as an institutional arrangement that is to be evaluated in terms of relative success or failure to achieve assigned system-defined objectives. Were I to have a subtitle for this essay, it would be "The Economy as a Constitu-

From *The State of Economic Science: Views of Six Nobel Laureates,* ed. Werner Sichel (Kalamazoo: W. E. Upjohn Institute for Economic Research, 1989), 79–95. Reprinted by permission of the publisher.

I am indebted to my colleague Viktor Vanberg for helpful comments on an earlier draft.

tional Order." I would append the word "constitutional" to the word "order" so as to indicate that my perspective differs both from those evolutionists who do emphasize the economy as an order but who, at the same time, deny that such an order can be "constituted," and from those who fail to make the distinction between constitutional and post-constitutional levels of choice.

Before proceeding, let me also classify myself philosophically. I am a methodological and normative individualist, a radical subjectivist, a contractarian, and a constitutionalist. These descriptive attributes are familiar to those of you who may have been exposed variously to my published works over four decades. In a very real sense, these works are little more than my continuing and considered assessment of the state of economics or political economy. I have always been, and remain, an outsider, whose efforts have been devoted to changing the direction of the disciplinary research program. There is perhaps less reason for me to take a reflective look at where we are scientifically than there is for those of my peers who have remained inside the dominant research program that describes what economists do. You would scarcely expect me to take on some new colors at this stage, and I assure you that there has been no recent conversion to a new paradigm. No one has had, or will have, occasion to label me as a holder of the conventional wisdom.

I shall proceed as follows. Section II examines the relationships between scarcity, choice, and value maximization within the domain of economics as scientific inquiry. My aim in this section is to demonstrate how these concepts, by having been placed in too central a role, have generated intellectual confusion. Section III extends the perspective to examine the appropriateness of macroeconomics in the subject matter domain of our discipline. Section IV briefly treats the grand organizational alternatives and develops the notion that the conception of what the economy is does have normative implications. Section V compares and contrasts the two approaches in terms of the shift from individual to social choice. Finally, in Section VI, the argument is summarized.

II. Scarcity, Choice, and the Maximization of Value

I do not know what the 1989 instructors in economics tell their students about the content of the discipline. Perhaps they simply ignore definitional starting points. But I do recall that, in the 1940s, economic theory (price theory) courses commenced with something like Milton Friedman's statement to the effect that economics is the study of how a particular society solves its economic problem.[1] And, at least in the 1940s, everyone knew that "the economic problem" was defined by Lionel Robbins as the allocation of scarce resources among alternative ends.[2] Scarcity, the inability to meet all demands, implies that choices must be made, from which it seems to follow directly that a criterion for "better" and "worse" choices is required. This criterion emerges as some common denominator that allows the differing demands to be translated into a single dimension, which we then label as "utility" or "value." The "economic principle" offers the abstractly defined normative solution to the economic problem. Scarce resources are allocated among alternative uses so as to secure maximum value when a unit of each scarce resource yields equivalent value in each use to which it is put. Satisfying this norm maximizes value subject to the resource scarcity constraints. Economics, as a realm for scientific inquiry, does indeed seem to be reducible to applied maximization; the calculus seems surely to be its basic mathematics.

I want to suggest here that this economics, which is the economics that I learned both as a student and as a young professional, generates intellectual confusion and misunderstanding because it focuses attention inappropriately on scarcity, on choice, and on value maximization, while shifting attention away from the institutional structure of an economy, with the consequent failure to make elementary distinctions among alternative structures. Given the dominance of the Robbins formulation in the economic theory of mid-century, it is not surprising that market solutions were often modeled as analogous to planning solutions to the resource allocation problem. Economists proceeded as if "the market" embodies "social choices" among alternative allocations of resources, choices that may be compared with those that might emerge from the monolithic decisions of a single planner. Given the mind-set of mid-century, it is also not surprising that Arrow extended his impossibility theorem to the market as well as to political choice.[3]

As early as 1963, in my presidential address to the Southern Economic Association,[4] I criticized the central role assigned to the maximizing paradigm

---

1. Milton Friedman, *Price Theory* (Chicago: Aldine, 1962).

2. Lionel Robbins, *The Nature and Significance of Economic Science* (London: Macmillan, 1932).

3. Kenneth Arrow, *Social Choice and Individual Values* (New York: Wiley, 1951).

4. James M. Buchanan, "What Should Economists Do?" *Southern Economic Journal* 30 (January 1964): 213–22.

in economics, and I called for a revival of "catallactics" (or "catallaxy") as the core of our discipline. My argument was that economics, as a social science, is or should be about trade, exchange, and the many and varied institutional forms that implement and facilitate trade, including all of the complexities of modern contracts as well as the whole realm of collective agreement on the constitutional rules of political society.

In a basic conceptual sense, the exchange process remains categorically different from the choosing process. In exchange, there is a necessary inter-action between (among) separate actors (participants), no one of which can choose among "solutions." In exchange, each participant does, of course, make choices among alternative bids and offers (strategies). But these choices of any single participant are, at most, only a part of the interaction process. A solution to an exchange emerges only from the choices made, separately and independently, by all participants in the process. This solution, as such, is not explicitly chosen by any one of the participants, or by the set of participants organized as a collective entity. This solution is simply not within the choice set of either individual actors or the collectivity.

This elementary sketch of exchange provides the basis for my early asser-tion that game theory offers the appropriate mathematical framework that facilitates an abstract understanding of economics. In exchange, as in ordi-nary games, players or participants may be modelled as behaving so as to maximize their separately defined utilities, subject to the constraints sepa-rately faced, as defined by the rules, the endowments, and the predicted re-sponses of other participants. The standard maximizing behavior embodied in rational choice models may, of course, be accepted for this analytical ex-ercise. But, in exchange, again as in ordinary games, neither any single player-participant nor the set of players-participants, as a group, treats the outcome of the process as a maximand. The solution to the exchange pro-cess, simple or complex, is not the solution of a maximization problem, and to model it as such is the continuing source of major intellectual confusion in the whole discipline.

Equilibrium in any exchange interaction signals the exhaustion of the mutual gains, and this solution, as such, has behavioral properties that also describe positions of maxima for all choices. At equilibrium, no participant has an incentive to make further bids (offers) within the rules that define the structure of the interaction. In the equilibrium of the ideally competitive economy, there is no incentive, either for any single participant, or for any group of participants, including the all-inclusive group, to modify the results within the rules.[5] But what is maximized in this solution to the competitive "game"? That which is maximized, in any sense at all meaningful for behavior, is the value for *each* participant, as determined separately and subjectively, subject to the endowments initially possessed and to the expressed preferences of others in the nexus, as reflected in the bids (offers) made in markets. There is no "social" or "collective" value maximization, as such, in the exchange process, even in some idealized sense. Aggregative value, measured in some numeraire, is, of course, at a maximum in the solution, but this is a definitional consequence of the equilibrium. The relative prices of goods and services are themselves determined in the process of attaining the equilibrium, and it is only when these emergent prices are used that any maximum value, as an aggregate, can be defined.

Since an abstractly defined maximum for aggregative value cannot exist independent of the market process through which it is achieved, it is meaningless to refer to a shortfall in aggregative value, as such, except as some indirect identification of failure to exhaust gains from trade among participants somewhere in the nexus. Since participants are presumed able to make their own within-exchange choices, the political economist's hypothesis that value is not being maximized must be derived from observations that there exist impediments to the trading process,[6] whether at the simple level of buyer-seller exchange or at the level of all-inclusive complex "exchanges" in public goods. The observing political economist is unable, even conceptually, to construct a "social welfare function" that will allow him to carry out a maximization exercise analogous to that which the planner for a centralized economy must undertake. For such a planner, his choices are analogous,

---

5. In slightly more formal terms, the competitive equilibrium is in the core of the game. This conclusion holds only if the rules of the game are strictly defined and enforced, and especially in relation to the incentives offered to potential monopolizing coalitions.

6. James M. Buchanan, "Positive Economics, Welfare Economics, and Political Economy," *Journal of Law and Economics* 2 (October 1959): 124–38; "Economics and Gains-from-Trade," *Managerial and Decision Economics,* special issue in honor of W. H. Hutt (Winter 1988): 5–12.

even if at a different dimension of complexity, to those faced by any single participant in the exchange nexus.

III. Macroeconomics and Constitutional Political Economy

The basic and elementary distinction between the maximizing and the exchange paradigms supports the proposition advanced earlier concerning the suggested exclusion of macroeconomics from the domain of our disciplinary subject matter, at least macroeconomics as normally defined. That which is generated in the economic interaction process, whether or not represented as a formalized, abstractly defined equilibrium or solution, emerges from the separate and interdependent choices made by many participants, choices that are coordinated, whether efficaciously or not, through the institutional arrangements that define the economic structure. The economywide aggregated variables, such as national income or product, rates of employment, capacity utilization, or growth, are not variables subject to choice, either directly or indirectly, by individual participants in the economy or by political agents who may presume to act on behalf of all participants as a collectivity, or any subset thereof.

It is intellectually confusing even to model "the economy" as if its normative purpose is one of maximizing income and/or employment, or, indeed, as if "the economy" has normative purpose at all. As noted earlier, any failure of the interaction process to generate maximum value must reflect failure to exploit gains from trade, whether simple or complex. This putative diagnosis calls attention to the structure itself which may contain constraints that prevent the consummation of mutually advantageous trades.

Alternative structures are, of course, to be evaluated indirectly by observations of the patterns of results generated, and these results may be represented in terms of the familiar macroaggregated variables such as the level and growth of national product or employment. An economy that persistently generates wide swings in levels of income and employment would, appropriately, be deemed to be a *structural* failure, and such a pattern of results should offer incentives to investigate, locate, and identify the structural sources of the problem, leading ultimately to structural-institutional reform.

The tragic flaw in Keynesian-inspired macroeconomics lies in its acceptance and, hence, neglect of structure while concentrating almost exclusive attention on the prospects and potential for "guiding" the economy toward more satisfactory target levels of the aggregative variables. It is not at all surprising, when viewed in retrospect, that this monumental misdirection of scientific effort should have occurred, given the dominance of the maximizing paradigm during the critical years of mid-century. There was a general failure to recognize that the whole intellectual construction is inconsistent with a structure that allows for the independent choice behavior of many participants in the economic nexus. As Keynes himself recognized in his preface to the German translation of his book, the whole reinterpretation of the economic process in a normatively directed teleological model was more applicable to an authoritarian regime than to a democratic one.

I do not want to suggest, however, that the classical economists, at least those who were the targets of Keynes's direct criticism, were free of their own peculiar sort of blindness that led them, also, to neglect structural elements. In their implied presumption that results embodying satisfactory levels of the aggregative variables would emerge, independent of possible structural failures, these economists were ill-prepared to defend the discipline against the emotionally driven zealots for macroeconomic management.

The intellectual, scientific, and policy scenario should have been, and could have been, so different in those critical decades before mid-century. Little was really needed beyond an elementary recognition that the economic process functions well only within a legal-constitutional structure that embodies predictability in the value of the monetary unit, accompanied by a regime reform that would have been designed to guarantee such predictability. (In this respect alone, a unique window of opportunity was missed in the 1930s.) Macroeconomic theory, in both its lower and its higher reaches, need not have been born at all, along with the whole industry that designs, constructs, and operates the large macroeconomic models.[7]

---

7. Because of the near-universal failure of economists to look at structure, then and now, we face, in the 1990s, even more potential unpredictability in the value of the monetary units than we did in the 1920s. Given the inherent structural defect in our monetary regime, macroeconomic theorizing and the macro models may be useful, if for no other reason than that our discretionary monopolists of fiat issue may use such models for their own purposes. The macro money game that we all must play is cumbersome, complex, and confusing. It is sheer intellectual folly, joined with some jealousy for pseudo-scientific

IV. Socialism, Laissez Faire, Interventionism, and the Structure of an Economy

It is now widely acknowledged, both in theory and in practice, that socialism was (is) a failure. The socialist god is dead; the promise that was once associated with socialism, as an overarching principle for social organization, no longer exists. The romantic image of the state as an omniscient and benevolent entity, an image that had been around since Hegel, was shattered by the simple observation that those who act on behalf of the state are also ordinary humans, like the rest of us, who respond to standard incentives within the limited informational setting they confront. Centralized economic planning, with state ownership and control over means of production, has entered history as intellectual folly, despite the record of its having attracted the attention of so many brilliant minds in the first half of this century, and also despite the awful realization that efforts to implement this folly involved the needless sacrifice of millions of lives.

At the opposing end to socialism on the imagined ideological spectrum stands the equally romantic ideal of laissez faire, the fictional image of the anarcho-capitalists, in which there is no role for the state at all. In this model, freely choosing individuals, who have somehow costlessly escaped from the Hobbesian jungle, will create and maintain markets in all goods and services, including the market for protection of persons and possessions. It is as difficult to think systematically about this society as it is to think of that society peopled by the "new men" of idealized communism. Robert Nozick's derivation of the minimally coercive state was surely convincing even to those stubborn minds who held onto the laissez-faire dream.[8]

Any plausibly realistic analysis of social order, whether positive or normative, must be bounded by the limits set by these ideological extremes. The state is neither omniscient nor benevolent, but a political-legal framework is

---

inquiry, to pretend that a regime shift could not produce dramatic increase in well-being for almost everyone.

With predictability in the value of the monetary unit established (with any one of the several alternative regimes that might be the replacement for the discretionary authority in existence), economists could then get on with their appropriate social roles of analyzing the exchange process in detail, with identifying barriers to the implementation of value-enhancing voluntary exchanges, with advancing hypotheses concerning changes in constraints that allow individuals to exploit more fully all potential for mutual gains.

8. Robert Nozick, *Anarchy, State, and Utopia* (New York: Basic Books, 1974).

an essential element in any functioning order of human interaction. The analysis, discussion, and debate then center on the degree or extent of political control over and intervention into the interaction process. The extended interventionist state remains a viable alternative in the ongoing political argument, and proponents for such a state are found among scientists and citizens alike, and despite the general loss of faith in the socialist ideal. Opposed to the extended interventionist polity lies the minimal or protective state, tempered variously by acknowledgment of the appropriateness of both productive and transfer state elements.[9]

Questions may be raised at this point concerning how these issues relate to my evaluation of the state of economic science, which was, after all, my assigned task for this essay. I return to my central theme. My hypothesis is that the basic conceptualization of what "an economy" or "the economy" is, the paradigmatic vision of what it is that we are inquiring into and about, does, indeed, carry direct normative implications. In a real sense, my hypothesis suggests that divergent normative stances may reflect divergent *understandings* rather than differing ultimate values. If this hypothesis is descriptively accurate, genuine scientific progress may be made at the level of fundamental understanding (methodology) as well as at the apparent cutting edges of some presumed invariant empirical reality.[10]

Applied somewhat more narrowly, my hypothesis is that the normatively preferred scope for state or collective intervention will depend directly upon the conceptualization of what the economy is, as the subject for scientific inquiry. That is to say, the normative debate on the turf bounded between the socialist and the laissez-faire extremes will reflect the divergent models of the observed reality. In a certain sense, *the ought is derived from the presumed is.*

Let me try to be more specific. I suggest that an accepted understanding

9. A cynical observer might suggest that little, if any, scientific progress has been made since 1776, when Adam Smith first presented the antimercantilist argument from which modern economics emerged. Mercantilism (protectionism, interventionism) seems to have reemerged in the decades of the 1970s and 1980s in partial replacement for the acknowledged demise of socialism.

10. As my great professor, Frank H. Knight, once remarked at the end of an impressively presented empirical survey "proving that water runs downhill," which expresses my own verdict on much of what I see in the now-dominant empirical emphasis of modern economic research. I doubt if many economists are convinced by empirical evidence alone, although I acknowledge that the linkage between evidence and understanding remains mysterious.

of the economy as an order of interaction constrained within a set of rules or constraints leads more or less directly to a normatively preferred minimal intervention with the results of such interaction. By comparison and by contrast, an accepted understanding of the economy as an engine, mechanism, or means, organized for the achievement of specifically defined purposes, leads more or less directly to a normatively preferred stance of expediency in evaluating possible state or collective intervention with the interaction process.

Many textbooks commence with a discussion of the functions of an economy, as introduced by Frank H. Knight.[11] I have suggested that even so much as a listing of "functions" for an economy may generate confusion and misunderstanding.[12] If the economy, as such, is without purpose, how can we attribute functions to its operation? The economy-as-order conceptualization forces us to restrict evaluation to the relative success of the structure in facilitating the accomplishment of whatever it is that the separately interacting participants may seek. (Again, the basic game analogy is useful. We evaluate the rules that describe a game by assessing how successful these rules are in allowing players to achieve those objectives they seek in playing.)

The point here may be made emphatically in the simple example of two-person, two-good exchange. Two traders are presumed to hold endowments in two goods, and these endowments are assumed to be mutually acknowledged to be owned by the initial holders. The traders are observed to engage in exchange, and a post-trade distribution of endowments different from the pre-trade distribution emerges. How do observing economists evaluate this simple exchange process? The two interpretations or understandings involve quite different exercises. The mechanistic, functionalist, teleological understanding introduces a presumed prior knowledge of individual utility or preference orderings, and the post-trade positions are compared with the pre-trade positions, for each trader. If the comparisons indicate that each trader has moved to a higher level of utility, the exchange is judged to have been mutually utility-enhancing.

The economy-as-order understanding proceeds quite differently. The economist does *not* call upon some presumed prior knowledge of the utility or

11. Frank H. Knight, "The Economic Organization" (University of Chicago, 1934, mimeographed).
12. Buchanan, "Economists and Gains-from-Trade."

preference functions of the two traders to be able to conclude that the exchange has been utility-enhancing for each trader. He does not evaluate the results of exchange teleologically against some previously defined and known scalar. Instead, he adjudges the exchange to have been utility-enhancing for each trader to the extent that the *process* itself has embodied attributes of fairness and propriety. If there has been neither force nor fraud, and if the exchange has been voluntary on the part of both traders, it is classified to have been mutually beneficial. When the economist analyzes the behavior of the traders in entering into and agreeing on terms of exchange, he may, if desired, use the language of utility maximization, provided that the exclusive emphasis is placed on individuals' behavior in maximizing their separately identified utilities, which are not observable independently.

Important implications for potential intervention in voluntary exchanges stem from the contrasting interpretations here. If the economist bases his evaluation on the relative success of the exchange in moving the traders higher on an independently existing utility scalar, he may be led to recommend intervention even in the absence of observation of force, fraud, or coercion in the exchange process itself. This approach provides the basis for paternalistic, merit-goods arguments for collective interferences with voluntary market exchanges. The individual may not act so as to maximize his own utility. On the other hand, if the observing economist bases his evaluation exclusively on the process of the exchange itself, recommendations for collective intervention must be limited to proposals for removing barriers to trade inclusively defined.

We can remain with the simple exchange example to discuss the role of agreement in the two interpretations-understandings of economic interaction, along with the place of the Pareto criterion in any evaluative exercise. Exchange involves agreement on the part of traders, both upon entry into trade and upon terms of trade. The emergence of a post-exchange distribution of goods signals an equilibrium of sorts. The teleological interpretation of exchange does not call upon agreement for any critical purpose. The dual criteria are the separate utility scalars of our two traders, presumed known to the assessor prior to trade. If exchange moves each trader higher on the scalar assigned to him, the change is defined to have been Pareto superior. The welfare assessment can be positive without any necessary resort to interpersonal utility comparisons.

By contrast, the economy-as-order interpretation depends critically upon agreement as the criterion for assessment. Since there are no independently existent scalars, the only indication that traders have improved their position lies in their observed agreement. A positive welfare assessment becomes possible because the agreement has signaled mutually preferred change. Agreement is the means of defining Pareto (Wicksell) superiority, and it is the only means that exists.

V. From Individual to Social Choice: Utilitarian versus Contractarian Foundations

The economist who conceptualizes the economy as a potential welfare-generating mechanism or instrument may be unwilling to limit criteria of evaluation to separately imputed, individually identified scalars. Almost by necessity, and despite the acknowledged insupportability of a simplistic utilitarianism, some attempt will be made to derive meaningful measures for "social" or "collective" utility. This is the essential thrust behind the invention-elaboration-use of the social welfare function constructions in mid-century theoretical welfare economics, constructions that embodied both explicit introduction of ethical judgments and the relevance of the Pareto escape from direct interpersonal utility comparability. This whole exercise involved a search for a post-Robbins scalar against which the potential performance of the economy might be measured, a scalar that could be set up to exist independent of the performance itself. Success or failure of that which is evaluated, the economy or the market, is then determined from some comparison of observed results with those that might have been achieved. Modern economists who resorted to the social welfare function constructions, and despite all their methodological and philosophical sophistication, have really not succeeded in escaping from the utilitarian foundations from which the whole maximizing-allocationist paradigm emerged late in the nineteenth century.

If we shuck off the utilitarian trappings and simply abandon efforts to construct a scalar that will allow evaluation of performance for the economy or the market, as such, we are then forced into an acceptance of the alternative conceptualization advanced here, that of the economy as an order, or structure, or set of rules, the performance of which is not to be evaluated in terms of results that are conceptually divorced from the behavior of acting individuals within the order itself. Within the order or structure, individuals engage in trade. If we then generalize the trading interaction and extend its application over large numbers of actors, we may begin to explain, derive, and analyze social or political interdependence as complex exchange, i.e., as a relationship that embodies political voluntary agreement as an appropriate criterion of legitimation.

The contractarian tradition in political philosophy offers the intellectual avenue that facilitates the shift of inquiry from simple market exchange engaged in by two traders to the intricacies of politics. Many critics balk at this extension. They may accept the centrality of voluntary exchange in economic process but remain unwilling to model politics in the exchange paradigm. By simple observation, so say such critics, politics is about conflict and coercion. How can we even begin to explain political reality by an exchange model?

The contractarian response requires a recognition of the distinction between the constitutional and the in-constitutional or post-constitutional levels of political interaction, a distinction without which any normative justification for political coercion could not exist, at least for the normative individualist. Conflict, coercion, zero-sum, or negative-sum relationships among persons—these interactions do indeed characterize political institutions, as they may be observed to operate *within a set of constitutional rules,* that is, within a given constitutional order. The complex exchange model which embodies agreement among the many participants in the political "game" is clearly inapplicable here. But if analysis and attention are shifted to the level of rules, among which choices are possible, we can use potential and actual agreement among persons on these rules as the criterion for normative legitimacy. And such agreement may well produce rules, or sets of rules, that will operate so that, in particularized sequences of ordinary politics (single plays of the game) there may be negatively valued results for some of the participants.[13]

Note that there is a more or less natural extension from the simple model of market exchange to the complex model of constitutional politics. There is no categorical distinction between the economic and the political process; inquiry in each case centers on the choice behavior of individuals who act,

---

13. James M. Buchanan and Gordon Tullock, *The Calculus of Consent* (Ann Arbor: University of Michigan Press, 1962).

one with another, to choose rules that will, in turn, constrain their within-rule choices that will, in their turn, generate patterns of results. Note also, however, that this politics-as-complex-exchange derivation is not readily available to the economist who remains trapped in the maximizing straightjacket.

VI. The Political Economy as a Constitutional Order

I fudged a bit earlier in this essay when I indicated that my subtitle for it would have been "The Economy as a Constitutional Order." It should now be clear from my discussion that I define the institutions of both the economy and the polity as belonging to an inclusive constitutional order that we may designate as "the political economy." The political economy is described by the whole set of constraints, or structure, within which individuals act in furtherance of their own objectives.

Defined exclusively, these constraints include physical and technological limits, including those embodied in human capacities, that can be taken as invariant. These "absolutes" are beyond my range of interest, except to note that much of the folly of the socialist idea stemmed from a failure to recognize the relative immalleability of human beings. My concern here, however, is with the set of constraints that are subject to deliberative change, and, hence, to choice.[14] Because these constraints are general and extend over all participants in the political economy, any choice must be, by definition, public, in the classic public good sense of this term. A shift in constraints for any one actor must apply for all actors.

Let me now return to the distinction made earlier between the constitutional and the in-constitutional levels of choice. Given any set of constraints, individuals will, separately and jointly, act in pursuit of their own interests and objectives. For some purposes, it is useful to take the existing constraints as a set of relatively absolute absolutes and to direct inquiry to predictions about the emergence of patterns of results. This domain of positive econom-

---

14. I do not accept the implications of the analyses of some cultural evolutionists, who suggest that the basic institutions of social order evolve without conscious design and, by inference, suggest also that deliberate improvement in these institutions may be impossible, and, further, that attempts at improvement are harmful.

ics is productive, but it should not lead to the inference that these patterns of results can be modified to meet predetermined objectives, independent of any shift in the constraints themselves. Such effort must be paralleled by analyses aimed at predicting results that will emerge under alternative constraints, other rules of the game, other constitutional structures. As I noted earlier, the tragedy of the Keynesian enterprise lay in its failed effort to modify aggregative results directly due to its oversight of any prospects for institutional-constitutional change.

If the political economy is conceived as being described, in part, by constraints that can be subject to explicit collective choice, attention is immediately drawn to prospects for constitutional-institutional change. Once again the game analogy is helpful; we change a game by changing the rules, which will, in turn, modify the predicted patterns of outcomes. If we diagnose the patterns of results observed to be less desired than alternative patterns deemed to be possible, it is incumbent on us, as political economists, to examine predicted results under alternative constraint structures. It is not legitimate to criticize, for example, an existing distribution of income or allocation of resources as being unjust, inequitable, or inefficient, without being able, at the same time, to demonstrate some proposed alternative regime that can be expected to generate distributions or allocations that will do better by the same standards.[15]

No one will, of course, be surprised that I have used the occasion of this essay to present a varied reiteration of the case for "constitutional political economy" as the research program that should command the current attention of economists. As such, this research program involves both positive and normative elements. Some critics have often accused me of skirting dangerously close to, if not actually committing, the naturalistic fallacy, that of deriving the "ought" from the "is." I have never been concerned with such criticisms directly because, as noted earlier, in a certain sense we do derive "oughts" from our conceptions of what "is." The "is" that we take to be the economy does, indeed, have direct implications for how we ought to behave

15. Rutledge Vining, *On Appraising the Performance of an Economic System* (Cambridge: Cambridge University Press, 1984); Dan Usher, *The Economic Prerequisites to Democracy* (New York: Columbia University Press, 1981); Geoffrey Brennan and James M. Buchanan, *The Reason of Rules* (Cambridge: Cambridge University Press, 1985).

in our capacities as citizens who indirectly make collective choices among sets of rules. And let us be sure to understand that there is no "is" that is "out there" to the observing eye, ear, or skin. We create our understanding of the "is" by imposing an abstract structure on observed events. And it is this understanding that defines for us the effective limits of the feasible. It is dangerous nonsense to think that we do or can do otherwise.

The Minimal Politics
of Market Order

The economic progress of the twentieth century has fully con-
firmed that only a market economy is capable of ensuring high
efficiency in national economy.

—Leonid Abalkin, "What Hinders Reform?"

Introduction

The basic meaning of Abalkin's statement, which I have used as my opening
citation, is clear. As I have put the same point elsewhere, there is now general
agreement that the market economy works better than the socialist or centrally directed alternative. Further, we now agree on what is meant when we
say that an economy "works better." Such an economy produces a larger
bundle of goods and services, as measured by the evaluations of persons
who consume them. The economy organized on market principles produces more value than an economy organized on nonmarket principles.

Abalkin refers to "efficiency" in the production of value. A market economy is relatively more efficient for three reasons: It makes the incentives of
participants compatible with the generation of economic value; it exploits
fully the localized knowledge available only to participants in separated decentralized circumstances; and it allows maximal scope for the creative and
imaginative talents of all participants who choose to act as potential entrepreneurs.

From *Cato Journal* Special Issue, "From Plan to Market: The Post-Soviet Challenge,"
parts 1 and 2, 11 (Fall 1991): 215–26. Reprinted by permission of the publisher.

I shall not discuss these familiar, and now acknowledged, characteristics of a market economy further. My purpose here is to suggest that over-attention to, and over-concentration on, the efficiency generating features of the market economy may prompt neglect of the closely related corollary feature that is equally, if not more, important. The economy that is organized on market principles effectively *minimizes* the number of economic decisions that must be made *politically*, that is, through some agency that acts on behalf of the collective unit. In practical terms, we may say that an economy organized on market principles minimizes the size and importance of the political bureaucracy. If he had chosen to emphasize this feature rather than efficiency, Abalkin could have said: "The logic of the structure fully confirms that only a market economy is capable of allowing for a minimal politicization of the national economy." And should he have wanted to extend this statement, he might have added: "And only through such minimization of politicization-bureaucratization (or at least through some reduction) could meaningful individually based social objectives be secured, whatever these objectives might be."

In the second section of this paper, I shall describe the relationship between politicization and market organization as I develop the distinction between political pricing and market pricing. In the third section, I shall discuss the implications of political pricing for the whole set of relationships among citizens and groups of citizens in an economy. The analysis, which uses modern contributions of public choice theory, identifies sources of possible waste of economic value, as well as circumstances where persons are placed in dependency status in confrontation with others. The normative implications are evident. The fourth section discusses the necessary role of political or collective action in the design, construction, implementation, and maintenance of the structural framework within which any market economy is allowed to function. Collective choice among alternative sets of rules is required, but any such choice is constrained by feedbacks from value generation and from bureaucratic intervention. In the fifth section, I shall return to the distinction between political price and market price to illustrate how possibly agreed on "social" objectives might be advanced without overt politicization of markets. I shall also introduce the notion of a politically influenced market price, and I shall demonstrate the limits of applicability. The final section presents conclusions.

Political Price and Market Price

A characteristic feature of socialist regimes involves the use of politically determined prices for selected goods and services, presumably motivated by
both distributional and paternalistic considerations. The goods and services
so selected are made available to consumers at demand prices that reflect political judgments rather than the results that emerge directly from the interaction of demand and supply. The listing of such goods and services is empirically familiar: medical services, educational services, child care, urban
transport, housing, milk, bread, and so forth. Some or all of these selected
goods or services are made available to consumers or users at prices below
those that would be established by market forces.[1]

Consider a single and highly simplified example. Suppose a collective political decision is made to supply bread to consumers at a price of zero, which
may be called a "political price" because it is divorced from any relation between costs of production and demand. If political action is limited to an
announcement of this political price, the response is readily predictable. Potential consumers will demand large quantities of bread at the zero price, and
there will be no potential suppliers willing to put bread on the market at that
price. Political decisionmakers who initially try to meet potential consumers'
demands must direct large quantities of resources into bread production, either by direct requisition or by some scheme for subsidizing potential suppliers. That is, even if sufficient bread is available to meet all demands at the
artificial political price, some additional political action must be taken, over
and beyond the setting of price itself, to make the pricing operational. Resources must be drawn from other uses into bread production, and demanders are encouraged by the artificially low price to use bread wastefully. (The
illustration from Soviet experience that is often adduced here is the story of
peasants feeding bread to cattle.)

As noted earlier, however, I do not want to stress the wasteful or efficiency-
reducing effects of political pricing. Let us heroically assume, therefore, that
political decisionmakers, the planners who act on behalf of the collectivity, di-

---

1. Administrative inefficiencies in distribution may, of course, be so large as to make
the inclusive prices for such goods higher than free-market prices, despite the intent of
planners.

rect resources into bread production in some rough approximation of the quantity that would be forthcoming under market pricing. This combination of zero-demand price, along with roughly optimal supply, will ensure the presence of two results: There will be an excess demand for bread, and the costs of producing and supplying that quantity must be financed from sources other than people who consume the bread. Political decisions and political actions are required on two institutional dimensions over and beyond the setting of price.

We can compare such a regime of political pricing with a regime of market pricing by supposing that there is no politicized interference with the market for bread; thus the price is allowed to emerge from the interaction of demand and supply. In this setting, suppliers and producers may offer bread to prospective purchasers on terms of their own choosing, and potential consumers may choose to purchase or not, in whatever quantities they choose. We know that in this setting roughly the efficient supply of bread will be placed on the market ("efficient" as measured in terms of the value scales of demanders throughout the economy). In addition, under this regime of market pricing, the two results emphasized as characteristic of political pricing will be absent. There will be neither an excess nor a deficient demand for bread; there will be neither an excess nor a deficient supply of bread. And there will be no requirement that other persons in the economy, other than bread consumers, must finance the production of bread. The political decisions involved in (a) setting the political price, (b) allocating the available supply among potential demanders, and (c) financing the production of the available supply are unnecessary under the market pricing regime.

There are, of course, distributional differences between the two regimes. Those consumers who succeed in getting bread at zero price under the political pricing regime may be better off than they would be under the market pricing regime. (Although they need not be better off when the full price, including time in queues, is taken into account.) But these possible gains to consumers are fully offset by losses suffered by whoever in the economy must finance the supply that is made available. Political pricing must, in some sense, embody value transfers between users and nonusers of the goods that are politically priced. By contrast, no across-market transfers need take place under market pricing.

Political Pricing, Bureaucratic Discretion, and Social Waste

Market pricing incorporates two important coordinating functions that political pricing fails to perform. The available supply is rationed among potential demanders, and the quantity supplied is brought forth to meet the potential demand. If political price is set lower than market price, some means of rationing other than price must be brought into being, unless supply is adjusted to meet whatever demand emerges. In that case, massive waste of economic value must ensue.

Under excess demand conditions, nonprice rationing may take any one of several forms, singly or in combination. Available supplies may be allocated by some explicit rationing mechanism, for example, by issuing ration coupons that are required for purchase. Or rationing may be accomplished by some variant of a first-come, first-served scheme that involves waiting periods and long queues in shops. Or, finally, the people who control access to supply may ration goods through private pricing. In each scheme a necessary role emerges for a bureaucratic agency that market pricing would make redundant.

Similar implications for the necessity of a bureaucratic agency emerge when we examine supply-side coordination. If voluntary adjustment to market-related supply price is not allowed to take place, producers must, somehow, be encouraged to bring forth the politically chosen quantity of goods. Production may be directly organized through state enterprise, or private suppliers may be subsidized. In any case, some collection of revenues from other sources in the economy is required, collection that, again, depends on bureaucratic agency. Or production may be directly requisitioned, in which case suppliers must be subjected to coercive bureaucratic command.

Political pricing requires an extended supplementary bureaucratic agency to achieve plausibly meaningful coordination of objectives. Individual citizens, not only as demanders and users of the economy's end items but also as suppliers of the inputs that are combined to produce such items, are necessarily subject to the discretionary direction of the bureaucratic agency to an extent not present under market organization. This dependency of the citizen on bureaucracy exists quite independent of personal behavioral characteristics of people in bureaucratic roles. Even if all those bureaucrats should behave ideally in terms of widely shared criteria of fairness, the dependency relationship continues to exist.

As modern public choice theory suggests, however, bureaucratic agents are not likely to be different from other persons in the community; at least, models of behavior should not be constructed that presume totally different behavior. The bureaucrat will, as will others, seek to maximize his or her utility subject to the constraints that are faced. And because the institutional structure under a regime of political pricing places other persons in a dependency relationship, the bureaucrat can scarcely be expected to refuse, deliberately, to exercise this power of discretion so as to maximize his or her own utility. Favoritism, discriminatory treatment (both positive and negative), and arbitrary classifications—these features are almost necessary characteristics of any system that places people in dependency relationships with bureaucrats who are living, breathing human beings.

These characteristics will be present in regimes of political pricing even if there is no corruption in the ordinary meaning of the term. Bureaucrats who possess discretionary authority to allocate or distribute access to economic value will, of course, have opportunities for pecuniarily beneficial trades for the simple reason that the allocative-distributive authority itself has value. And there is surely some positive correlation between opportunities for, and the exploitation of, gain.

But the problems of bureaucratic discretion do not lie exclusively, or even primarily, with bribery. First, these problems exist because of bureaucratic discretion itself, which implies that choices must be made among claimants on some basis other than economic value. In this respect, the introduction of bureaucratic discretion made necessary by political pricing becomes a source of the relative inefficiency of the whole structure. Second, the dependency relationship introduced between those persons who hold discretionary authority and those who are subject to that authority creates arbitrary class distinction. Third, and perhaps most important, the artificially created scarcities under political pricing become objects of socially wasteful investments. People find it privately rational to invest resources in efforts to secure differentially favored access to the economic power inherent in bureaucratic discretion. This rent seeking on the part of those who compete for the scarce access to valued goods (such as those who demand bread at the zero price) represents wasteful investment on the part of all people who are unsuccessful in the competitive effort.

There should be little or no dispute concerning the positive analysis of effects of political pricing on the size, range, discretionary limits, and secondary behavioral repercussions of bureaucratic agency. There are no normative implications to be derived directly from the analysis, as such. Nonetheless, to the extent that analysts and observers can agree that these effects are, in themselves, undesirable characteristics of political pricing regimes, the relative advantages claimed for such regimes in comparison with market pricing regimes are reduced in significance. The minimization of politicization-bureaucratization of economic interaction, which market pricing makes possible, must be reckoned to be a relevant factor in the ultimate comparative judgment over and beyond the closely related and more familiar argument from efficiency.

The Political Constitution of Economic Order

Until now, I have referred to regimes of political pricing and market pricing without direct mention (other than in my introduction) of the constitutional structure that defines the framework within which any regime of economic interaction operates. It is important to emphasize that political or collective action is necessary in establishing and maintaining the regime's structure, under any and all circumstances. The minimization of the range and scope of bureaucratic discretion, discussed in the previous two sections, refers exclusively to the setting for economic interaction within the structure of rules, that is, within the constitution of the economic order. As the analysis suggested, market pricing tends to minimize bureaucratic discretion relative to that which is required under political pricing. But market pricing will function effectively only within a set of framework rules that must, themselves, be established or maintained collectively. At the level of constitutional choice, there is no escape from politicization.

I shall limit my discussion to an outline of those features of constitutional structure that will allow market pricing to emerge and to function. I shall not discuss how the basic constitutional choice among sets of rules is made. First, there must be a dispersed and decentralized distribution of the capacities to produce economic value, along with an explicit political and legal acknowl-

edgment of this distribution. Property or property rights, both in human capacities and in nonhuman assets, must be widely dispersed in ownership,
and the pattern of ownership itself must be afforded explicit legal protection.
Second, private owners must be allowed to exchange owned rights to property among themselves, and there must be political-legal enforcement of voluntary contracts made for the exchange of these rights.

Under such a dispersed, decentralized pattern of private ownership, along
with political and legal acknowledgment, protection, and contract enforcement, the basic elements for the constitution of a market regime will be in
place. Resource capacities will be allocated among separate possible uses;
production will be organized through combinations of productive inputs;
and goods and services will be produced, supplied, and priced to consumers
who demand them. Nobody in either a private or a political role is directly
required to attend to the particular features of the outcome, or pattern of
outcomes, of the interdependent market process. This outcome, or pattern
of outcomes, will emerge from the interactive, interdependent choice behavior of many persons. The allocative and distributive results will be chosen by
no one.

It is precisely at this point that an overemphasis on the efficiency criterion
for evaluating the performance of a market economy may be misleading.
The efficiency that is, indeed, achieved by market interaction is, itself, defined by such interaction. The value scale emerges from the market choices
made by all participants; such a scale does not exist independently. There
need be no relationship between the performance of a market economy and
the efficiency relative to a value scale chosen by the planner or political de-
cisionmaker. Only if decisionmakers are willing to allow the market itself to
define efficiency can Abalkin's statement be valid.

A market order, of sorts, will emerge once the basic elements are in place.
But the constitutional structure may be extended to include other rules or
institutions that may be expected to facilitate the inclusive exchange process.
The political agency, the state, may take on the responsibility of defining the
monetary unit for the economic order and may, ideally, seek to maintain stability in the value of such unit. There may also be specialized institutional
arrangements aimed at promoting competitive forces, especially those that
promote freedom of entry into production and that prohibit cartel agreements. Other collectively consumed or public goods (for example, protec-

tion of environmental quality) may be brought within the state's authority, and constitutional rules may be introduced that specify the means through which state supplied goods and services are to be financed.

Minimal Bureaucratization and the Social Market Economy

Attention to, and emphasis on, the relationship between the coordinating properties of market pricing and the range of bureaucratic discretion have implications for the efficiency of political intervention that may be undertaken in the furtherance of social objectives. Political decisionmakers, either those who act as agents for a ruling elite or those who claim to represent electoral constituencies in democracies, may reject the efficiency norm as defined by operation of the market economy, even if the collectivized sector is extended to include the financing of non-excludable, collectively consumed goods. These agents, for the same distributional and paternalistic reasons that motivated many of the socialist experiments in economic *dirigisme,* may seek to use political authority to modify, at least in part, the results of the market system.

At the same time, the advantages of market organization both in generating economic value and in minimizing the role of bureaucratic discretion may be accepted. How might the coordinating properties of markets be retained while using political authority to modify the distributive-allocative patterns toward those patterns more desirable to decisionmakers (planners)?

Suppose that the basic structural rules of a market economy are established. Property rights are then decentralized, and voluntary contracts are enforced. Recall my earlier discussion in the second and third sections. If supplies are sufficiently provided to meet all demands at the politically determined demand price that faces potential consumers-users, there is no need for a supplementary rationing scheme. If all supplies offered at the politically determined supply price are taken, there is no need for rationing sales permits among potential suppliers. Price may be used, therefore, both to ration demand and to stimulate supply. But the additional market equilibrium characteristic may be absent. The demand price at which a good is offered to consumers may not be brought into equality with the supply price offered to suppliers. As noted, under any scheme of political pricing, some cross-market transfers of value must take place. If the political decisionmakers encourage market participants to purchase more of a good than their preferences will dictate in an undisturbed market pricing structure, a wedge must be driven between the demand price at which the good is offered to consumers and the supply price that is offered to producers. The demand price must fall below the supply price. Even if these separate prices fully accomplish their rationing function, means must be found to finance the difference.

The political decisionmakers must, in this case, be willing to introduce a wedge of the opposing direction in the market for some other good (or goods). That is, the demand price must be made higher than the supply price in some other market (or markets) to generate the revenues sufficient to finance the subsidy for the favored good or service. As in the first market, prices can be used to eliminate the need for bureaucratic discretion in supplementary rationing roles. But recognition of the across-market transfer of value here suggests that the budget must balance. That is, the revenues collected from the disfavored good must be precisely equal to the subsidies paid to the producers and consumers of the favored good. Production and consumption of one good can be encouraged; production and consumption of the other good can be discouraged. The alleged social objective can be accomplished within the set of constraints imposed by participants' preferences in the economy in their roles as demanders and suppliers of the two goods (or bundles of goods).

A TALE OF BREAD AND VODKA

The discussion here may be clarified by a simple example. Suppose the political decisionmakers, whoever they may be, modify the allocative and distributive results of the market economy in a specific way. The declared social objective may be to encourage the production and consumption of bread, to discourage the production and consumption of vodka, and, at the same time, to minimize both efficiency loss and bureaucratic discretion.

Bread production may be differentially subsidized, and vodka production may be differentially taxed. Under such arrangements, both goods continue to be marketed at prices that are politically influenced although they remain, in one sense, market prices. For such a scheme to work effectively, the two sides of the account must balance. Further, the solution must be brought into adjustment with the demand and supply schedules of both goods, as revealed through the independent behavior of demanders and suppliers.

The political decisionmakers cannot simply impose a per unit tax on vodka independent of the per unit subsidy on bread. Given the behavior of vodka demanders and suppliers, any specified tax per unit on vodka will generate a defined revenue total that will be available for subsidizing bread. But the size of the per unit subsidy will depend, in this case, on the behavior of demanders and suppliers of bread. Political decisionmakers cannot simply select any per unit subsidy for bread, if they want to minimize the need for bureaucratic discretion in bread distribution. Conversely, any preselected per unit subsidy on bread will, given the behavior of demanders and suppliers of bread, require a defined revenue outlay. So that this outlay may be financed from the tax on vodka, the per unit size of this tax will be fixed, given the behavior of demanders and suppliers of vodka.

Political decisionmakers might desire many solutions that may simply be inconsistent with the behavior of participants in the economy. For example, revenues required to finance a full subsidy on bread, to allow it to be offered at a zero price as in our earlier illustration, may be beyond the limits that could be generated by a tax on vodka. The demand and supply behavior of participants in all markets, which must be allowed to take place without bureaucratic coercion, will place constraints on the ability of political decisionmakers to modify market results. Within such limits, the structure of market prices may be very substantially modified in presumed furtherance of social objectives.

Conclusion

In any economy, resources must be allocated and combined to produce useful outputs that must, in turn, be distributed to consumers. An economy that is organized on market principles will accomplish this set of tasks more efficiently, more economic value will be generated, than in a centrally directed economy. My purpose has been to emphasize the importance of the corollary feature of the market economy, which relates the organization of the economy to the range of political and bureaucratic discretion. If resources are not allocated and products distributed through the workings of a market system, then the allocative and distributive functions must be performed directly by a political-bureaucratic agency. In this direct and obvious sense, markets, to the extent that they are allowed to operate, constrain bureaucratic intervention into the lives of citizens.

This conclusion does not imply that markets or market organizations eliminate, as if by magic, the elemental constraints imposed by scarce resources. By increasing efficiency in resource use, markets may reduce the severity of these ultimate constraints. Yet the basic limits on resources remain; markets replace the implementation and representation of constraints through coercive intrusion of personalized bureaucracy by the impersonal price structure. The discretionary power or authority of the bureaucrat is replaced by the impersonal authority of prices, with the accompanying differences in interpersonal relationships.

The market order minimizes the range of bureaucratic discretion, but this order operates only within a constitutional framework that must be politically established and sustained. The basic elements—dispersed private ownership of property and enforcement of contracts—are necessary to allow markets to emerge and to generate patterns of outcomes upon which preferences of participants place the highest value, as expressed through market behavior.

Politics, as it operates and no matter how the decision structure may be organized and how decisionmakers are selected, may not willingly confine its activities to establishing and maintaining the constitutional framework. Politicians, both on their own account and as representatives of constituencies of citizens, may seek to modify some outcomes that would emerge from the uncontrolled workings of market process. Many citizens may share in categorizing certain goods as "worthy of encouragement" (sometimes called "merit goods") and other goods as "worthy of discouragement" (sometimes called "sumptuary goods"). In almost every polity, attempts will be made to modify the results of market interaction to encourage the first set of goods and to discourage the second set.

There are better and worse means of intervening in the workings of markets if minimizing bureaucratic discretion along with efficiency is accepted as a norm. The objectives for a social market economy may be furthered by schemes of appropriately selected taxes and subsidies that are adjusted to the demand and supply behavior of participants.

PART SIX

Distributional Issues

Distributional Politics and
Constitutional Design

This century has witnessed a veritable explosion in the size of the governmental or politicized sector of the economies of all states, and between two- and three-fifths of all economic value generated is politically reallocated. Despite the dramatic revolutions in Central and Eastern Europe and the former territories of the Soviet Union in 1989–91, revolutions that reflected the demonstrated failure of socialist organization in the large, there seems to have occurred relatively little spillover effect on the proclivity of governments in Western welfare states to intrude pervasively in the value-creating operation of market economies. The observed movements towards privatization that seemed emergent in the early 1980s do not appear to have exerted lasting effects.

Despite Fukuyama's challenging claim,[1] the "end of history," as represented by the triumphant victory of the idea of market organization of economic interaction, has not yet happened. "Economic science" has not won the day.[2] Despite what has been the most overwhelming falsification of an organizational hypothesis in history, the idea that market structures create value superior to that produced by politicization has not motivated the behaviour of political agents in Western welfare states. Why not? This simple

From *Economics and Political Institutions in Economic Policy*, ed. V. A. Muscatelli (Manchester, U.K.: Manchester University Press, 1996), 70–78. Reprinted by permission of the publisher.

1. F. Fukuyama, *The End of History and the Last Man* (New York: The Free Press, 1992).

2. J. M. Buchanan, "The Triumph of Economic Science: Chimera or Reality?" in *A Reforma Fiscal no Brasil: Sibsídio do Simposio Internacional sobre Reforma Fiscal*, ed. A. Delfim Netto (São Paulo: Fundação Instututo de Pesquisas Econômicas, 1993), 113–24.

question must stand as a test for the explanatory potential of social scientists everywhere.

In recent decades, there has been an increasing acceptance of the hypothesis that "institutions matter" in generating and in shaping the outcomes of all social interactions, whether economic, political, or otherwise. And many subdisciplines or research programmes can be inclusively summarized under the common rubric "comparative institutional analysis." But what is there in the institutional structure of modern democratic politics, in particular, that operates to ensure the continuing and successful efforts at politicized domination of economic relationships in the face of the evidence that much larger economic value can be created by policies that will allow markets to function within generally applied rules but without detailed political interferences?

Why are the French farmers, the U.K. coal miners, and the U.S. automobile workers successful in imposing costs on their fellow citizens much in excess of the benefits that these groups secure by politicized interferences with free markets? How does modern democratic politics allow particular special interests to replace any possible conception of "the public interest"? Olson's "logic of collective action" is helpful in understanding the results that we observe.[3] A coalition of special interests, each with concentrated benefits, can succeed in majoritarian settings in imposing generalized costs on all members of the polity, costs that may far exceed the sum of benefits enjoyed.

How may we design political constitutions such that the exploitation of the many by the few can be effectively forestalled or prevented? How can democratic politics be made to work for the "general" rather than the special interest? These are the questions I want to explore in this chapter. I shall do so through the use of abstract analytical models, although the discussion is not itself technical. I apologize for examining features of a political structure that must seem to be far removed from the observable realities, but this seems necessary to isolate and to identify common elements. Even with this proviso, however, I am quite willing to acknowledge that my whole treatment may be clouded by my familiarity with the U.S. republican structure of politics to the neglect of parliamentary systems.

There are basically three distinct ways that political constitutions in dem-

---

3. M. Olson, *The Logic of Collective Action* (Cambridge: Harvard University Press, 1965).

ocratic polities might be reformed so as to eliminate or at least to reduce substantially the domination of special interests. In this chapter, I shall discuss the first two of these only briefly because they are both more familiar generally than the third and because I have, personally, discussed these other approaches in earlier writings. I shall concentrate attention on the third way of reforming democratic constitutions if the objective is that of reducing the mutuality of exploitation among the many different special interest groupings that describe modern political interplay.

Exit

Why do we not observe the exploitation of all by each that seems characteristic of politics in the everyday working of markets? The most salient feature of market organization is surely the presence of the exit option that each participant in a market relationship faces, to some degree. In the idealized limit, as stylized in formal economic theory, each buyer (seller) confronts another person as seller (buyer) and either party can exit from the interaction at zero cost. By dramatic contrast, in the stylized case of an inclusive democratic polity, each participant confronts all others in every collective interaction, from which no participant can exit. The prospect of exit places direct limits on the amount of exploitation that is possible in a relationship. Exploitation is minimized in market exchanges to the extent that persons may shift among potential sellers and buyers at low cost. In politics, exploitation is much more likely to occur until and unless explicit means are introduced for its limitation.

One avenue for possible reform in political structure is that of introducing at least some of the exit features analogous to those present in markets. The devolution of political authority from central to local units of government, along with freedom of entry into and exit from such local units, introduces elements of competitiveness into politics and necessarily provides incentives for political agents to act in the generalized interests of members, as opposed to exploitative actions against minority coalitions within its membership. Increasing attention has been given to the efficiency-generating features of genuinely federal structures, motivated in part by prospects for effective federalism in Western Europe, but there remains a lack of widespread understanding of the indirect control exercised on the play of special interest

coalitions by the very existence of federal organization. Constitutional reform prospects for an effective European federalism seem less propitious at
the time of writing than they might have seemed in 1990. And in my own
country, the United States, the current policy thrust is presumably towards
more rather than less centralization of authority in the central government.

Unanimity

The exploitation of the many by the few, via special interest majoritarian
coalitions, can occur only with a decision-making structure that allows
political-collective action to be taken without the consent of the exploited or
potentially exploited parties. As Wicksell recognized a century ago,[4] one
route for constitutional reform would be the replacement or partial replacement of majority rule in legislative assemblies by a more inclusive rule—at
the limit, a rule of unanimity. The larger the majority that is required for
reaching decisions, the more difficult it becomes for a coalition of special interests to secure differential benefits at the expense of the whole citizenry. I
have written on the Wicksellian scheme in earlier works,[5] and I shall not
elaborate on the advantages and disadvantages of this approach to constitutional reform here.

Generality

I want, therefore, to examine the question posed earlier within a setting of a
single political unit in which all collective decisions are reached through the
operation of a majority rule. In this setting, how can constitutional reform
be directed so as to ensure that coalitions of special interests, seeking differential benefits, will not impose net costs on all members of the political community?

Initially assume that there are no constitutional limits on the range and
scope for political-collective action. The only constitutional requirement is
that majority coalitions are unable to install themselves permanently in power.
The constitution effectively ensures periodic elections along with universality

---

4. K. Wicksell, *Finanztheoretische Untersuchungen* (Jena: Gustav Fischer, 1896).
5. J. M. Buchanan and G. Tullock, *The Calculus of Consent* (Ann Arbor: University of
Michigan Press, 1962).

of the voting franchise. But once in authority for the designated electoral period, majority coalitions may enact any legislation. I shall concentrate attention on fiscal politics, largely for expositional purposes.

A majority coalition, once formed, may impose taxes differentially on all
persons who are not members of the coalition, that is, on members of the
opposing minority. And the ruling coalition may then use the revenues collected from the taxes either to finance public goods that yield generalized
benefits to all citizens or to finance transfers differentially paid out to members of the majority coalition. In such a setting, it is clear that the dominating
majority strategy will be that which involves taxes levied on persons in the
minority coalition and money transfers to persons who are members of the
majority coalition.

Consider an expectational setting in which each member of a political
community considers membership in a minimally winning majority coalition to be equally likely with membership in a losing minority coalition. And
all persons are aware of the fact that the winning coalition, once formed, is
empowered to implement political-collective action without constraints as to
either the type of action or the distribution of costs and benefits.

In this highly abstracted model, with some heroic simplifications, we can
analyse the political "game" as a simple two-person matrix relationship between the individual who is a member of the majority and the individual
who is a member of the minority. We assume that there does exist a general-
benefit public good that will yield aggregate benefits that exceed aggregate
costs. The ordinal pay-off structure is the one that is shown in Figure 1. The
effective majority, whether this be the As or the Bs, can choose among three
separate solutions or outcomes, each one of which specifies the projected

		B	
		Pays net tax	Pays no tax and receives transfer
A	Pays net tax	I 3, 3	II 1, 4
	Pays no tax and receives transfer	III 4, 1	IV (2, 2)

Figure 1. Ordinal pay-off structure for a two-party political "game"

pay-offs to each player. The fourth solution, shown in cell IV, is not possible by the logic of the structure. (Strictly speaking, the politics modelled here is not an interactive "game" at all, since only one of the players determines the solution. Nevertheless the matrix construction is helpfully explanatory for my purposes.)

Assume now that the As make up the winning majority coalition. The solution will be that shown in cell III in the matrix, which indicates the relative pay-offs to individuals who are members of winning and losing sides. Note that in this solution, the As will be exploiting the Bs, who will be made worse off than they would be with no collective action at all. For illustrative purposes, think of the status quo as yielding the bracketed pay-offs in cell IV. The majority will not select the cell I solution or outcome, the one that involves the sharing of the tax costs and the financing provision of a genuinely public good that would yield net benefits to all persons in the polity. The basic incentive structure in majoritarian decision-making is such as to generate the differential exploitation of one group by another, despite the presence of potential benefits for all parties.

The results are, of course, reversed if the Bs make up the winning coalition, in which case the solution is in cell II, with the As being exploited by the Bs.

If the expectations are fully symmetrical, as assumed here, the rotating sequence of results, as between the cell III and cell I solutions, will generate a "present value" pay-off set like that shown in cell IV. Although this result is logically contradictory in the single period, the expected value of the political "game" to the players, all players, is zero, that is, equal to the values expected in the status quo, with no political-collective action at all. This result is evident since the rotating majorities take turns exploiting each other, and to the same degree. The simple majoritarian politics modelled here does not take advantage of the opportunity presented by the presence of the public good.

Note that there is no feedback effect on behaviour emergent from the "continuous dealings" between majorities and minorities over the temporal sequence. The absence of an exit option manifests itself through the continuing dominance of off-diagonal or non-symmetrical outcomes. Contrast this result with that of the market game, in which exit is possible. In this game, the player who is exploited will not enter into further trading arrangements with the exploiter. The non-symmetrical solutions will tend to be eliminated as a sequence of market exchanges extends through time.

Towards Constitutional Reform

The model of unconstrained majoritarian politics sketched out above is extreme, but the model does, nevertheless, draw attention directly to the structural features that may generate the undesirable results, measured both by failure to achieve the potential co-operative surplus from collective action and by failure of the incentive system to facilitate the survival of non-opportunistic behaviour. Unconstrained majoritarian politics produces the "churning state," to employ de Jasay's descriptive term.[6]

The simplified analytical construction is helpful because it points to separate, but related, avenues for constitutional reform within a single polity, either one of which might mitigate, if not totally eliminate, the failures noted. Clearly, the non-symmetrical or off-diagonal solutions must involve the coerced imposition of the action on the minority by the majority. As Wicksell recognized, and as we earlier indicated, any shift in the decision rule towards a constitutional requirement beyond simple majorities will reduce the potential for exploitation, even if the requirement does not extend all the way to unanimity. But the matrix construction also points towards a separate avenue for reform that may well be more practicable. The construction suggests immediately that direct conflicts between sets of participants arise only because there exist potential solutions that incorporate differential or non-symmetrical treatment. The two players must be placed in non-symmetrical roles, defined in terms of actions taken or results achieved.

The prospect of "winning" by imposing net costs on losers becomes the attractor, and it is this prospect that diverts attention away from the potential mutuality of gain promised by symmetrical sharing of surplus. Constitutional reform may eliminate the off-diagonal solutions that embody differential treatment. In the highly simplified construction of Figure 1, it is clear that the elimination of differential treatment will produce the Pareto-optimal solution, regardless of the decision rule. If the majority coalition is not allowed

---

6. A. de Jasay, *The State* (Oxford: Basil Blackwell, 1985).

to treat the members of its own group differently from members of the minority, it will choose to share taxes and benefits and to achieve the surplus promised by the availability of the public good.

Any move towards reality must allow for the existence of a multiplicity of potential political outcomes, all of which may fall within the set that could be classified to be Pareto-superior to that achieved in the rotating sequence of exploitative outcomes produced by unconstrained majoritarianism. And within this Pareto-superior set, there will be distributional differences as between different members of the body politic. Distributional elements will not be eliminated totally by the constitutional reform that eliminates overt differentials in treatment among persons and groups. But the "distributional politics" that is constrained by constitutional limits on the off-diagonals is quite different from that which is non-constrained.

Criticisms, Applications, Extensions, and Implications

My whole discussion, to this point, may be criticized for the implied presumption that majoritarian politics, as it has historically evolved and as it operates, contains within its rules none of the constraints that the analysis indicates to be necessary. There are both formal and informal constitutional limits upon discriminatory treatment that find their origins in the rule of law, in the precept that all persons are to be subjected to equal treatment under the law. To an extent, these precepts must be appreciated and acknowledged to exist. There are constitutional limits that prevent majorities from going beyond certain overt barriers against discrimination. Any effort on the part of a legislative majority to tax, subsidize, or regulate differentially persons classified by personal characteristics such as gender, race, religion, or geography would be treated as unconstitutional. By dramatic contrast, almost any action by a legislative majority to tax, subsidize, or regulate differentially persons classified by economic characteristics, such as amount and type of wealth or income, occupational status, profession, industry, product category, form of organization, and size of group would be left constitutionally unchallenged. (I say this with assurance in relation to the United States, but I think it holds for other countries.) Many possible non-symmetrical solutions are constitutionally permissible, and these have become increasingly characteristic of modern democratic politics.

I shall not go into detail with illustrative examples here, but think of restrictive trade policies, pork-barrel spending projects, occupational licensing, and many others. Reform in the directions implied by the analysis of majoritarian democracy here will move towards generality, towards general taxation, towards general accessibility to the benefits of public spending, towards generality in the application of regulations across occupations, industries, and product categories.

In summary, my argument here is that politics has lagged behind law in its incorporation of the principle of generality, and that efforts must be made to bring politics into line. The rule of law—this generalized term still carries considerable moral approbation among members of the community. And the central content of this term is that persons should be treated equally before the law to the extent that this is possible, that any discriminatory treatment violates the fundamental principles for a liberal social order. But we have allowed our politics to intrude pervasively into economic life without recognizing that some constraints akin to that summarized under the generality precept of the rule of law should long since have been applied. Until and unless there is some constitutional constraint on the differential treatment of persons and groups, majoritarian politics will surely come to be increasingly distributional.

It is, of course, naive to think that nothing more is needed here than constitutional reform that will eliminate and reduce the discrimination among persons and groups that majoritarian politics embodies. As the historical experience of many countries suggests, constitutions can be reformed without being effectively enforced. Perhaps more important than formal constitutional changes are changes in ethical attitudes that would make attempted reforms workable. There must, first, be a generalized understanding that constitutions are necessary for the functioning of the liberal order, and that the great "game of politics" is not best conceived as a struggle between winners and losers, is not zero-sum, but a positive-sum game, in which all persons can be net winners. There must be some general understanding that exploitation implemented through politics is just as immoral as exploitation implemented in the private sector.

Finally, I should emphasize that the argument and analysis here do not imply that there is no redistributive political role that qualifies as legitimate. For example, a flat tax, with uniform rates applied to all sources of income along with a set of demogrant (equal per head) transfers, would generate net gains for the poor and net losses for the rich. Such a fiscal scheme would clearly redistribute value. But on both sides of the account, there is a sense in which the precept of generality is applied. There would be no singling out of particular groups either to penalize or to subsidize in a differential fashion.

Political Constraints on Contractual Redistribution

James M. Buchanan and Winston C. Bush

Modern contract "theories" of distribution represent significant advances over the value-laden statements of preference that were passed off as serious intellectual constructions by the utilitarians. The modern theories attempt to "explain" observed institutions on the basis of conceptual contractual agreement among members of defined political communities. These theories may be classified in three distinct sets: preconstitutional, constitutional, and postconstitutional.

In the first, a preconstitutional state of anarchy is postulated, and hypotheses are then derived concerning the types of property rights that might emerge. Given a property rights structure and assumptions concerning individual behavior, conjectures can be made concerning the distribution of property.[1] In the second set, the contractual process occurs at the constitutional level where the position of individuals (families) is not fully identifiable; here the alternatives for choice are institutional arrangements that are presumed to remain in being over a succession of time periods. In the third set, the contractual process occurs postconstitutionally, within a defined in-

From *American Economic Review* 64 (May 1974): 153–57. Reprinted by permission of the publisher.

The final draft of this paper was submitted before the tragic death of Professor Bush on December 1, 1973.

1. James M. Buchanan, "The Limits of Liberty: Between Anarchy and Leviathan" (Blacksburg, Va., 1973, unpublished monograph), or Winston C. Bush and Lawrence S. Mayer, "Some Implications of Anarchy for the Distribution of Property," *Journal of Economic Theory* (forthcoming).

stitutional framework, and the alternatives for choice are explicit transfers of income and wealth among individuals and groups in the community. In the second or constitutional category, we place John Rawls's difference principle and also the related insurance principle.[2] In the third set, we place the so-called Pareto-optimal redistribution models based on utility interdependence.[3] As a somewhat in-between model, we note the self-protection theory recently advanced by G. Brennan.[4]

We restrict our discussion to contractually derived institutions that might emerge at the constitutional stage. We postulate that individuals are wholly uncertain about their prospective income-wealth positions in the periods for which the institutional structure to be chosen is to be applicable. Individuals make their own decisions, each behind a Rawlsian "veil of ignorance." For our purposes, this is a positive assumption about the actual states of persons making constitutional choice; it is not a normative statement concerning how persons should conceive themselves in making choices.

We want to address ourselves specifically to the questions raised by the recognition, at the time of constitutional contract, that actual in-period transfers of income and/or wealth must be implemented within an institutional setting peopled by individuals whose income-wealth positions are known. In other words, our questions concern the potential viability of the "terms of constitutional contract," the difficulties that might arise in enforcing these terms in a practically working political process, and, importantly, the possible feedback effects that these latter considerations may exert on the constitutional decision itself. These are issues which have not, to our knowledge, been examined in the burgeoning modern literature on contractual distribution.

We define a potentially viable constitutional contract as one in which a majority of the individuals in the postconstitutional stage benefit when the terms of the contract are executed. Although the relationship between viability and majority rule is arbitrary, it does not substantially affect the results,

2. See John Rawls, *A Theory of Justice* (Cambridge, Mass., 1971); also, James M. Buchanan and Gordon Tullock, *The Calculus of Consent* (Ann Arbor, 1962).

3. See Harold M. Hochman and James D. Rogers, "Pareto Optimal Redistribution," *American Economic Review* 59 (September 1969): 542–47.

4. Geoffrey Brennan, "Pareto Desirable Redistribution: The Non-Altruistic Dimension," *Public Choice* 14 (Spring 1973): 43–68.

Table 1

Individual	1	2
	No-Transfer Income Distribution	
A$_1$	$10,000	$10,000
A$_2$	10,000	10,000
A$_3$	1,000	10,000
A$_4$	1,000	1,000
A$_5$	1,000	1,000
	Posttransfer Income Distribution	
A$_1$	$ 5,000	$ 6,333
A$_2$	5,000	6,333
A$_3$	4,000	6,333
A$_4$	4,000	6,000
A$_5$	4,000	6,000

and also conforms with the orthodox idealizations of the institutions of democracies.

Let us assume, first, that individuals in a constitutional stage reach agreement on an institutional structure that will generate in-period transfers from the relatively rich to the relatively poor, as measured against the no-transfer distribution that would emerge from pure market payments to resource owners under the constitutionally defined property rights in existence.[5] Initially, we assume that there is only one period in the postconstitutional sequence. Assume more specifically that the contractual agreement dictates that posttransfer incomes of the lowest income recipients shall be maximized in accordance with some Rawlsian-like difference principle. Table 1 presents two separate no-transfer and posttransfer distributions, for a community of five persons. (Note that measurable and adverse incentive effects are incorporated in these examples.)

As Table 1 suggests, the enforceability of redistribution schemes will depend significantly on the pattern of pretransfer market distribution. In Dis-

---

5. For purposes of this discussion, we are restricting the analysis to the "distribution branch" of government budgets, in Richard A. Musgrave's terminology (*Theory of Public Finance* [New York, 1959]).

tribution 1, the assumed contractual rule for income transfers would clearly be viable. A majority of the community's members would benefit from it; indeed, by definition, no other rule could be better for them. By sharp contrast, in Distribution 2 implementation of the constitutional rule for redistribution will require that a majority of the community's members suffer transfer losses. In the absence of direct utility interdependence, implementation of the previously agreed-on constitutional rule for redistribution will be difficult to secure.

We may now consider the obverse of the above example. Suppose that there is no agreement on transfer policy reached in the constitutional state, which is equivalent to saying that the market-determined shares are to be left unchanged. In this instance, note that the results may be viable only if Distribution 2 emerges. If Distribution 1 emerges, postconstitutional transfers will tend to emerge, regardless of the absence of constitutional agreement.

The single-period arithmetical example is extremely simple, but it demonstrates one central point. The enforceability and maintenance of any constitutionally determined institution for income-wealth distribution will depend on the actual pattern of pretransfer distribution. The individual's expectations about this pattern will, therefore, influence his choice among alternative constitutional rules on income-wealth transfers. Other things equal, he will be more egalitarian in his constitutional choice the larger the proportion of relatively poor members he expects to be in the pretransfer pattern of distribution since this implies an increased probability that he himself will be poor. Note particularly that his result depends only on the relative numbers of poor and rich and not at all on the relative income levels of the two groups.

We can now relax the single-period assumption and examine the applicability of the chosen constitutional rule over a sequence of periods. We assume, as before, that at the time of constitutional choice the individual is wholly uncertain as to his own position in the market distribution that will emerge in the first period of the postconstitutional sequence. We need to specify, however, the relationship of the distributional position of an individual in each of the several postconstitutional periods. If his position is the same in all periods, the multiperiod model is no different from the single-period one. At the opposite extreme, assume that individual positions in the separate distributions are wholly unrelated. The individual who finds himself in a favorable income position in the first period remains wholly uncertain about his position in the second, etc. Consider the model in which Distribution 1 is predicted to emerge in each of the several periods of the sequence. As suggested, the Rawlsian redistributional rule is viable in the one-period setting. It will continue to be viable in the multiperiod setting under these assumptions only if individuals maintain the same set of attitudes or tastes for redistribution policy that they held at the time of the initial constitutional contract. If individuals observe that their own positions are unrelated over separate periods, and that these shift among different income levels, this experience may itself modify attitudes. Individual members of a political majority, in a single period, may find themselves unwilling fully to implement the redistribution that is dictated by the Rawlsian constitutional precept. In more general and relevant terms, this is the effect of observed upward social mobility on attitudes toward redistributional alternatives. Individuals may be unwilling to transfer maximinal incomes (dictated by Rawlsian precepts) from the relatively rich to themselves if they expect that any policy, once introduced, will become permanent.

The introduction of a multiperiod sequence reduces somewhat the expected political viability of the extreme distributional rule postulated under the predictions that Distribution 1 will prevail in all periods. But the basic conclusion that a less extreme version of this scheme might well be selected and expected to be viable holds.

Consider now the prediction that Distribution 2 will characterize market results over the whole sequence of postconstitutional periods. As indicated, the redistributional alternative would not be expected to be maintained in the one-period model, and a no-transfer policy might be the only agreed-on rule. In the multiperiod model, however, something between these extremes might emerge. Individuals who are in the relatively rich majority coalition, but who are wholly uncertain as to their own positions in subsequent income periods, will have some incentive to build in transfer mechanisms on the expectation that, once established, these policies will tend to be accepted in subsequent periods.[6] To accomplish this, they may accept net transfer losses

6. The argument here is related to Peter Hammond's ("Charity: Altruism or Cooperative Egoism" [paper presented at Russell Sage Foundation Conference, New York, March 1972]).

during the period when income shares are known. In anticipation of this, there may be constitutional agreement on a redistributive scheme, even in the expectation that Distribution 2 will characterize each income period, an agreement that will be expected to be implemented by the majority coalition in the community.

The general point made with respect to the single-period model remains valid, however. More redistribution will be constitutionally agreed upon if Distribution 1 is predicted than if Distribution 2 is predicted. The principle may be more generally stated. If *all* members of a community agree on a redistributional scheme at the constitutional level, those persons who find their income positions settled even for a single period will find their postconstitutional preferences for redistribution inversely related to income position. In the multiperiod model, lifting of the "veil of ignorance" for even a single period will modify the costs and benefits of any previously agreed redistribution scheme.

In real-world circumstances, something between the two extreme models of income expectations surely prevails. An individual's income-wealth position in any one period is related to that which he expects to hold in subsequent periods, although there may well exist considerable uncertainty. In this setting, results that fall somewhere between the single-period and the multiperiod models can be derived.

The examples have remained unreal because of the assumption of two distinct income classes. Somewhat more realism may be introduced by adding a middle class of income recipients in an example that becomes slightly more descriptive of existing distributional patterns. Consider a nine-member community, with no-transfer or market incomes arrayed as depicted in Table 2, Column 2. Assume that this pattern of market distribution is predicted to emerge in each postconstitutional period, but that the individual remains wholly uncertain as to which position he will come to occupy as the actual pattern emerges.

Initially, assume that there will be only one postconstitutional period, or, what amounts to the same thing, that an individual's position in the distribution will remain unchanged once it is settled in period one. From Table 2 it is clear that if there are no incentive effects, a policy of full equalization will be politically viable. Since the mean income is above the median, at least a majority of the persons in the group will find themselves improved as a result

Table 2

Individual	Predicted No-Transfer Distribution	Idealized Rawlsian Rule
A₁	$10,000	$7,000
A₂	8,000	6,500
A₃	6,000	5,500
A₄	5,500	5,200
A₅	5,000	4,600
A₆	4,500	4,400
A₇	4,000	4,000
A₈	1,500	4,000
A₉	1,000	4,000
Mean Income	$ 5,167	
Median	5,000	

of the constitutionally selected redistribution policy. If incentive effects are allowed to enter the model, however, this conclusion need not follow. The set of transfers that would be required to maximize the position of the least-advantaged person in the predicted distributional array need not be consistent with the political structure.

Suppose for example that, ignoring incentive effects, a policy of full posttransfer equalization is adopted in the constitutional assembly. As individuals earn incomes in the market, however, they will be motivated in part by the knowledge of this equalization policy. As a result, total community income falls to such a level that the income realized by each person amounts to, say, only $3,500, as opposed to an average income of $5,167 when no transfers are anticipated.

The position of the least advantaged may be improved if some allowance of inequality is reintroduced. If a benevolent despot is controlling, the position of the least advantaged may, say, be increased to an income level of $4,000, with a posttransfer income array like that indicated in Column 3, Table 2. Note, however, that this posttransfer distribution would not be supported in a strictly democratic political process. Six of the nine members of the community find their own posttransfer incomes to be lower than those which they secure in the no-transfer setting.

The example suggests that the minimal political constraint on the implementation of any redistributional rule would be the requirement that at least one-half of the community's members find their own income positions improved over the no-transfer setting. Further consideration of the limits that political process may place on redistribution rules may suggest more restrictive constraints. Evidence suggests that the observed beneficiaries of income transfers in democratic structures are middle-income rather than low-income recipients, and public-choice arguments have been advanced to explain this observation.[7] As a plausible constraint reflecting something of this, models might be examined which require that the median members of the community receive absolute transfers at least as large as persons falling lower on the income scale.[8]

Our purpose here is not to examine alternative constraints in detail. We make the more general point that political constraints must be recognized to exist when the problem of implementing constitutionally approved rules on income-wealth redistribution is discussed. In any real-world setting, of course, the discussion of institutional rules affecting income-wealth distribution must take place in recognition of existing legal definitions of property rights, of existing political decision-making mechanisms, and of predicted patterns of income distribution as well as predicted positions of persons within these predicted distributions.

7. See George J. Stigler, "Director's Law of Public Income Redistribution," *Journal of Law and Economics* 13 (April 1970): 1–10, and Gordon Tullock, "The Social Dilemma" (Blacksburg, Va., 1973, unpublished monograph).

8. See James M. Buchanan, "The Political Economy of the Welfare State" (paper presented at Capitalism and Freedom Conference, Charlottesville, October 1972).

Subjective Elements in Rawlsian Contractual Agreement on Distributional Rules

James M. Buchanan and Roger L. Faith

Rawls[1] argued that individuals choosing institutions from behind the veil of ignorance would unanimously agree on institutions that maximized the imputations of the least advantaged persons in the post-choice social outcome. Critics have argued that the Rawlsian contract requires risk averse individuals. Our paper focuses on the contractual element inherent in constitutional choice when individuals have differing subjective estimates of the working properties of different institutions. We show that in genuinely Rawlsian contractual settings there may exist a general bias toward the selection of institutions that embody maximin solutions without the assumption of risk aversion.

John Rawls[2] argued that individuals participating in conceptualized contractual deliberations behind the veil of ignorance would unanimously agree on distributional rules or institutions that maximize the imputations of primary social goods to the least advantaged person in the community in periods subsequent to the initial construction of the social order. Presuming

From *Economic Inquiry* 18 (January 1980): 23–38. Copyright 1980 by Western Economic Association. Reprinted by permission of the Western Economic Association.

1. J. Rawls, *A Theory of Justice* (Cambridge, Mass.: Harvard University Press, 1971).

2. Ibid.

that Rawls' first principle, that of equal liberty, is simultaneously satisfied, there are two quite distinct stages in the establishment of this *difference,* or *maximin,* principle for the selection of distributional rules. First, there is the individual calculus of choice among alternative institutions or rules. Second, there is the agreement among all individuals on the rule or institution to be adopted by the whole community of persons. Despite Rawls' continued insistence that the second, or contractual, element is a necessary part of his logical construction, critics have concentrated on the individual calculus. And indeed, several of these commentators have suggested that the contractual aspect of the whole Rawlsian edifice is wholly unnecessary. Given the requirements of ignorance about the individual's prospects in the original position, all persons will, necessarily, make the same individual choice. Hence, the critical argument runs, agreement among separate persons becomes a redundancy. For example, Pence argues,

> To be fair to Rawls, there is a good reason for not justifying the unanimity constraint, since with the existence of the veil of ignorance, it is superfluous. . . . Since there is no possibility of conflicts of interest, there is no possibility of non-unanimity.[3]

If this criticism is acknowledged, attention comes to be concentrated on the calculus of the single person, and here the familiar questions concerning the reasons for the selection of maximin rules emerge. Why must an individual act as if he is extremely risk averse?

Our purpose in this paper is to demonstrate that an appropriate appreciation of the role played by the *contractual* element in the Rawlsian construction modifies substantially the strength of this dominant criticism. We shall show that, in genuinely Rawlsian contractual settings, the distributive rule selected may embody the difference principle without the introduction of risk averseness on the part of individual participants. In other circumstances, the rules chosen may not embody the maximin, but neither need they embody the maximization of expected utility in the manner that this alternative is normally introduced by the critics. We shall argue, however, that there will

3. G. E. Pence, "Fair Contracts and Beautiful Intuitions," *Canadian Journal of Philosophy,* supplementary vol. 3 (1977): 146–47.

be a general bias toward the maximin outcome. Central to our analysis are the necessarily *subjective* elements of individual choice. These elements, to our knowledge, have been almost totally neglected in the post-Rawlsian literature.

I. The Contractual Setting

The contractual setting requires the presence of more than one selector in any conceptualized original position. Furthermore, and quite importantly, each individual who considers himself to be a potential participant in such choice processes is directly influenced by the knowledge that the selection of any rule will emerge only from agreement among several persons. The individual will reckon on his participation in a collective choice process in which the preferences of all participants will be reflected. This creates a problem in interdependent decision-making, which we shall discuss in Sections III and IV of the paper.

Initially, we do not relax the rigid requirements of the Rawlsian description of the original position in any way. Each person places himself in a position where nothing is known about his particular role in the social order during the periods in which the institutional rule chosen is to remain in operation. He faces uncertainty over such a role, and, in choosing among the rules, every individual must consider the possible impact upon his own well-being in any and all positions that he thinks might emerge under the operation of the rules.

Our departure from the strict Rawlsian construction arises only with respect to the general knowledge possessed, or assumed to be possessed, by individuals with respect to the workings of the alternative institutions. As Robert Cooter[4] has suggested, the strict Rawlsian construction requires that an individual know nothing in particular and everything in general. But what does "know" mean in this context? Independent of the hypothetical nature of the choice problem posed behind the veil of ignorance, the individual can, at best, try to make some predictions as to the working properties of the alternative rules. He cannot "know" with certainty, just how any rule or insti-

4. R. Cooter, "What Is the Public Interest?" (Harvard University, 1974, mimeographed).

tution will function.[5] He may, of course, *act as if he knows,* while at the same time he may *act as if he does not know* in that aspect of his choice calculus dealing with his own particular role or position under the alternatives considered.

If, however, we acknowledge that the individual's generalized knowledge about alternative rules must be reflected in predictions rather than in objectively measurable and observable data, we must also acknowledge that these predictions are inherently *subjective.* This apparently innocent admission has, however, significant consequences for the Rawlsian choice problem since, once subjectivity is allowed, differences in predictions about the properties of alternative institutions or rules can be expected to emerge. There is no basis for the argument that from behind the strict Rawlsian veil all persons must agree on the results predicted to emerge under the operation of any institution or rule, or set of such institutions or rules. Even if each person considers himself to be completely ignorant about his own role or position, or acts as if he so considers himself, differing subjective estimates about the *general* results of the institutions, or rules, may emerge. Everyone may possibly see an equiprobable chance of himself (and everyone else) occupying each position under any institution. Everyone may also agree on the imputation associated with each position under each institution. But each person may have different subjective predictions regarding the frequency of occurrence of a particular position under each institution. The prospect for such differences in subjective predictions may be acknowledged, however, without necessarily producing differences among individual choices of institutions or rules. That is to say, different persons may assign differing predictions to the results of a single alternative, but all may agree on the same rank ordering of all alternatives. If this should be the case, the contractual element in the Rawlsian construction, although conceptually present, becomes inessential. Any person will array or rank institutions or rules in the same manner as any other individual.

In order to demonstrate that the introduction of subjective elements in the individual calculus elevates the contractual process to center stage, it is necessary to show that differences in predictions can lead to differing arrays

5. G. L. S. Shackle, *Epistemics and Economics* (Cambridge: Cambridge University Press, 1972).

of institutional alternatives. Without some potential for disagreement on the alternatives from which a collective or group selection is to be made, the contractual process loses its relevance. Rawls himself is ambiguous in this part of his discussion. Such ambiguity is understandable when we recognize that Rawls seeks to derive a unique outcome from the hypothesized contractual process, and to do so without the introduction of bargaining theory. We shall discuss bargaining aspects further below, but, first, it is necessary to show that individuals' choices among institutions may differ once we introduce subjective elements, even if each person acts as if he remains strictly in the Rawlsian setting.

II. A Numerical Example

Consider the evaluation of two institutions or rules, A and B, each of which will operate to produce and to distribute primary goods among persons in the community. We shall initially limit our examination to the choice calculus of only two persons, i and j, although for expositional clarity of the example we shall place these persons in a ten-person community. If desired, each person may be treated as a representative member of one of two classes of persons in the whole group.

Despite the fact that neither i nor j has any notion as to what his own role or position will be under the operation of either A or B, their predictions as to the "social productivity" of the institutions may differ. Let us assume that both i and j act as if they expect all persons in the community, under the operation of either A or B, to be in only one of two possible positions, *Rich* or *Poor*. For person i, he predicts that Institution A will generate a total product of 5200 units of income (Y), distributed among 3 Rich persons and 7 Poor persons, with the former securing income of 1500 Y each and the latter securing income of 100 Y each. For institution B, person i predicts the same ratio of Rich to Poor (3:7), but he predicts that this institution will produce an income of only 1200 Y for each Rich person, while generating incomes of 200 Y each for the Poor persons. Person i's evaluations of the two institutions are depicted in the first row of Figure 1. Note that if i, behind the Rawlsian veil of ignorance, assigns an equal probability of his being in any one of the ten positions in society, and if he is risk neutral, he will maximize expected utility of income by selecting A over B.

Institutions

	A	B
i	3 Rich 7 Poor Rich $Y = 1500$ Poor $Y = 100$ Total $Y = 5200$	3 Rich 7 Poor Rich $Y = 1200$ Poor $Y = 200$ Total $Y = 5000$
j	2 Rich 8 Poor Rich $Y = 1500$ Poor $Y = 100$ Total $Y = 3800$	2 Rich 8 Poor Rich $Y = 1200$ Poor $Y = 200$ Total $Y = 4000$

Individuals

Figure 1

Consider now person j, whose predictions are depicted in the second row of Figure 1. For simplicity, we assume that the expected income levels of Rich and Poor in the two settings are predicted to be the same by j and i, that is $1500\,Y$ and $1200\,Y$ for the Rich, and $100\,Y$ and $200\,Y$ for the Poor. The subjective predictions of j differ from those of i only in the relative number of Rich and Poor persons who are expected to emerge in each setting. For j, he expects only 2 Rich persons and 8 Poor persons in each case. Under the assumptions of the example, note that if j assigns an equal probability to the chances of being any person, and if he is risk neutral, he will maximize the expected utility of income by selecting Institution B rather than A. Hence, i and j will differ as to the institutional arrangement that will maximize expected utility of income despite the fact that each chooses as if he remains strictly behind the Rawlsian veil of ignorance.

In order to generate a difference in preferred rules or institutions, it is useful to assume that individuals assign probabilities to potential positions, and given risk neutrality, that they try to maximize expected utilities. This procedure should be useful in countering some of the expected-utility criticism that has been directed against Rawls.[6] In presenting the results in this way,

6. See, for example, S. S. Alexander, "Social Evaluation Through Notional Choice," *Quarterly Journal of Economics* 88 (November 1974): 597–624.

however, we are explicitly violating Rawls' own admonition against assigning probabilities behind the veil of ignorance. In one sense, our argument may be interpreted as an alternative line of reasoning that Rawls "should" have adopted, one that might have forestalled unnecessary and digressionary criticism peripheral to his primary purposes. We shall simply proceed on the "as if" assumption that probabilities are assigned in some subjective sense.

Note that, in the numerical example, if the objectively observed results should be those predicted by j, the selection of Institution B would satisfy Rawls' criterion and that of expected value maximization. Once subjective elements are introduced, it becomes difficult to ascertain just what is implied by the maximization of expected values. Note, however, that, in the example, the selection of B will meet the maximin criterion regardless of the relative accuracy of the two predictions; under either i's or j's predictions, B will maximize the position of the least advantaged.

Under the conditions of the example, there is no internal quarrel between criteria as to j's preferred institution (B). There is no need to make any assumption about risk aversion in j's calculus. But can it be argued that B will tend to emerge from the contractual agreement process? There are three distinct arguments that may be offered here in support of the claim that B will, in fact, tend to emerge. First, since i maximizes expected value by selecting A, it might be argued that his choice will switch to B under sufficiently strong risk aversion. In this argument, the Rawlsian agreement on B must embody strong risk aversion on the part of some of the contracting parties, even if not on the part of all persons. There are, however, two additional, and quite different, arguments that are not so familiar, and it is these arguments that we want to develop more fully in this paper. We shall first discuss a "bargaining model" in which we demonstrate that particular outcomes are more likely to emerge. Following this analysis, we shall, in Section IV, introduce an argument based on sustainability, which reinforces the conclusions of our earlier analysis.

III. A Two-Person Bargaining Model

While insisting that contractual agreement is a necessary part of his theory of justice, Rawls also insists, in what seems an apparent contradiction, that no "bargaining" takes place among the parties. Unanimous agreement emerges more or less spontaneously. In a sense, Rawls is correct. In orthodox bargaining theory, the conflict between two or more parties takes place in a context where each party has an identifiable position and where each party seeks to maximize his personalized share of the total gains that are to be realized. Clearly, there can be no bargaining of this sort in the Rawlsian setting since, by construction, each party is behind a veil of ignorance concerning his own position. There is no meaning to be attributed to "maximizing his own share of potential gains." In another sense, however, Rawls is incorrect. If there is genuine disagreement among the parties, some process of reconciliation is required for group selection of a single outcome, and, if defined broadly enough, "bargaining" can be used to refer to this process.

Return to our two-person example. Let us assume that neither i nor j is risk averse. In this case, there must arise genuine disagreement between the two on the preferred institution or rule to be chosen for the group. There is a range of conflict; in the qualified sense noted, there exists a bargaining range. In this setting, however, a specific result can be predicted only if we can demonstrate that one of the parties will be determining or controlling in the contractual process. Our purpose is to construct a model which will identify the conditions in which person j will "drive the choice process," by which we mean that j's initial preferences rather than i's will tend to be reflected in the outcome. In this reasoning, the maximin criterion is met because of the particular nature of the contractual process and not because it must reflect the maximizing choice for *every* person.

In order to develop the argument in somewhat more detail, it may be useful to attach descriptive labels to the persons who enter the contractual process. We may designate individual i as the "optimist" and individual j as the "pessimist" in our two-person example. We should note, however, that, in doing so, we are not violating Rawls' description of a person in the original position who cannot know "his liability to optimism or pessimism."[7] Rawls seems here to be defining the prospective attitudes of a person concerning his particular role or position vis-à-vis others in the post-choice sequence of periods. He is not referring to attitudes about the generalized social productivity of alternative arrangements. Each individual, regardless of his subjective attitudes regarding the future, is not making predictions about himself *relative* to others. The likelihood of occurrence of each potential position in

7. Rawls, *A Theory of Justice*, 37.

the post-veil setting is predicted by the individual to hold for *all* individuals.[8] He does not see himself as smarter, stronger, or luckier than his contemporaries behind the veil. There is no sense of oneself being treated, or likely to be treated, any differently from anyone else in one's subjective view of the world. Individuals have differences of opinion only with respect to how all individuals will be treated under various institutions.[9]

We shall show that the pessimist, by our definition, can dominate the institutional selection process and that the optimist will acquiesce in the pessimist's initial preferences. The result will be that *under many sets* of circumstances, the Rawlsian difference principle will emerge as the predicted outcome.

Let us examine more carefully the choice calculus of each person in our two-person, two-institution example of Figure 1.

If individual *i* prefers Institution A while individual *j* prefers Institution B (see Figure 1), how is this conflict reconciled? Each individual faces two alternative actions. He can agree to accept the other man's preferred institution or he can refuse to accept any institutional choice save his own.

If an individual holds out—refuses to accept the other individual's institutional offer—he may expect to gain only the difference in subjectively expected income between the two institutions. One can always assure himself the expected income of the other man's preferred institution by simply giving in. The cost of holding out—not reaching an agreement—is the loss of the subjectively expected income associated with the alternative institution, on the assumption that subjective income in the original position is reckoned at zero. Potential gains and losses for the other individual are computed in like manner.

---

8. The situation is analogous to but not completely identical to that confronted by the individual who is choosing among quantities of a genuinely public good, defined in the Samuelsonian sense. He does so in the knowledge that the quantity finally selected, however and by whomever chosen, will be equally available to all members of the relevant group. The "bargaining" is not over identifiable "shares," but rather over differing quantities. In the setting discussed in this paper, individuals prefer differing institutions because of differing predictions about their working properties, which will, of course, affect all persons simultaneously.

9. If one insists that such subjectivity is not permissible under the veil of ignorance construct, then there are no distinct "individuals." This is analogous to pure exchange models in which all traders have identical endowments and preferences. Pragmatically speaking, there are no "traders."

To understand better the outcome of this "bargaining" situation, it is convenient to think of the subjective incomes as flow-rates of wealth, say, daily incomes. Let Y_x^k denote individual k's subjectively expected daily income under Institution X. Individual i may reason as follows: "each day that j and myself fail to reach agreement, I will lose Y_B^i, whereas if the bargaining resolves itself in my favor, I will gain $Y_A^i - Y_B^i$ per day. It would take me, therefore $Y_B^i/(Y_A^i - Y_B^i)$ days to recoup my losses from one day of nonagreement." For individual j, a similar computation yields a "payback" period of $Y_A^j/(Y_B^j - Y_A^j)$ days. Assuming identical, low rates of time preference, that institution would emerge which has the *shorter* payback period. As both individuals know the payback periods of the other, no holding out or overt bargaining need even occur; both individuals will rationally move to adopt the "winning" institution. Hence, in general, the individual who "will drive the rules" is that individual who can hold out longer, who can recover his opportunity losses of holding out in a shorter time. For j, the pessimist, to drive the rules it must be the case that

$$\frac{Y_B^j - Y_A^j}{Y_A^j} > \frac{Y_A^i - Y_B^i}{Y_B^i}._{10} \tag{1}$$

We note that so long as within each person's evaluation the differences between the two institutions are identical, $(Y_A^i - Y_B^i = Y_B^j - Y_A^j)$, as they are in our numerical example, condition (1) always holds. The pessimist will dominate the outcome of the contractual process, producing the Rawlsian or maximin result.[11] We do not argue that the maximin outcome will always emerge from such veil of ignorance "bargaining," but we do suggest that there is a distinct bias in favor of such an outcome due to the structure of the

10. This is very similar to J. C. Harsanyi, "Approaches to the Bargaining Problem Before and After the Theory of Games," *Econometrica* 24 (1956): 144–57. It is different, however, in that the players do not, at the solution, agree on the amount of income each is to receive. Indeed, they cannot since this is subjective and the basis of the bargaining to begin with. Hence, expression (1) need not end up as an equality. Further, players do not iterate, by a series of concessions, to a stable outcome. This is because if one were to rank on the axes the respective expected utilities of the two players under various institutions, the utility "frontier" would be inherently nonconvex since the institutional ranking giving the utility ranking for one individual will be different for the other individual.

11. There can, of course, be ties in which case expression (1) is a strict equality. In that case, the selection of the contractual institution may be made by simply flipping a coin.

process itself.[12] It should also be pointed out that when subjective institutional differences are equal across the various preferred choices of all individuals, the result readily extends to the *n*-person case.

As both the numerical example and the algebraic formulation should make clear, the introduction of sufficiently strong differentials in evaluations for the two persons, as between the two alternatives, could reverse the order of the predicted outcome, and could place the optimist in a position of dominating the choice among rules. If, for example, the pessimist, who, by assumption, assigns lower productivities to both A and B, should predict relatively little differences in income as between A and B, while the optimist

---

12. Some other implications of the bargaining model may be briefly noted. First, let us rewrite expression (1) in the following manner.

$$Y^j_B \; Y^i_B > Y^i_A \; Y^j_A. \tag{2}$$

Inequality (2) says that the institution which will emerge from the Rawlsian contractual setting is that institution for which the *product* of the perceived subjective social productivities over all institutions is maximized. How might we interpret this? Think of *i* and *j* as being faced with a choice of an institution from a set of feasible institutions. Suppose Institution U yields the same subjectively expected income to *i* as Institution V but V yields higher subjectively expected income for individual *j*. Then, Institution V would be selected. Hence, *i* and *j* will agree implicitly on that institution which is jointly efficient from their subjective points of view. It is as if each person is fully respectful of the other's subjective feelings and seeks to maximize his expected income given the expectations of the other person. In this sense, the model generates a Pareto optimal choice from the viewpoint of the two individuals.

Second, note that if the sum of *i*'s and *j*'s subjectively expected incomes is equal over all alternatives, then the institution which has the smallest difference between expected incomes will be selected. Hence, if there is a continuum of institutions which differ from one another only in the degree of income distribution, maintaining the same total perceived income, then the most egalitarian institution will be chosen via the "bargaining" process outlined above.

Third, it is clear that equiproportional change in an individual's subjective gross income for all institutions will not affect the choice of institutions. However, this does not imply that if one alters his subjective feelings by expecting there will be one more Rich person and one less Poor person under all institutions, the percentage change in subjectively expected incomes will be equal for all institutions.

Fourth, it is clear that if the pessimist's subjectively expected income approaches zero in the preferred state of the optimist, $(Y^i_A \to 0)$, the pessimist will tend to dominate the outcome regardless of *i*'s and *j*'s subjective evaluations of the other institutions.

A brief discussion extending the model explicitly to *n* individuals and m institutions can be found in the Appendix.

should predict substantially large differences, the latter may be recognized to be willing to invest more time in attempting to get his preferred arrangement.

We should suggest, however, that the likelihood of widely different intensities of preferences as between the institutional alternatives seems much lower here than in the orthodox bargaining models, where individualized positions and opportunities are fully identified. In the setting analyzed here, the differences in the personal evaluations of social rules or institutions are differences in subjectively estimated working properties. In a sense, such predictions are akin to those of scientists who disagree over the outcomes of particular experiments. The subjective predictions are untested hypotheses about how alternative rules or arrangements will work. As we have emphasized, differences among persons will emerge, and preferred rules will differ as among persons. But the situation is not analogous to differences in preferences over, say, the shares of the spoils of modern politics. There are no differential gains or losses, as among persons, involved in the Rawlsian setting. The differences in preferences could, at most, reflect differences in the predictions about generalized results, applicable to all members of the community. For this reason, we should argue that our general proposition to the effect that the "pessimist tends to drive the rules" holds in most genuinely Rawlsian settings.[13]

IV. Institutional Choice and Sustainability

We have suggested that there may be a bias toward selection of Rawls-like rules in veil of ignorance settings, even when quasi-formal bargaining behavior is allowed to take place and even when something like risk neutrality is assumed to characterize all participants. In a sense this bargaining analysis has been aimed to counter some of Rawls' critics and, as noted earlier, any discussion of overt bargaining behavior is somewhat at variance with the argument in *A Theory of Justice* itself. In this section, we develop an argument

13. We remind the reader that our purpose is to build a bargaining model which produces the Rawlsian maximin solution as a rational outcome. Other bargaining models which either expand or constrain an individual's strategic possibilities could be constructed, and such models could conceivably generate outcomes different from ours. It is, of course, up to the reader to decide if our model is a reasonable description of bargaining in a Rawlsian environment.

that reinforces and supplements that which emerges from the bargaining model, and one that is more in keeping with the spirit of Rawls' own discussion, although he does not develop such an argument in any explicit way.[14]

In our two-person example, the optimist, i, prefers Institution A in the absence of risk aversion, but he will also recognize the prospect that j may rank the alternative institutions differently. How "should" i behave in terms of incorporating risk averseness, risk neutrality, or risk preference? Because of the inherently subjective nature of the choice set, there is no way that he can relate his options one to the other in terms of their relationship to some idealized "fair gamble." He cannot rationally act as if his subjectively estimated predictions are objectively determinate facts. As Rawls insists, risk attitudes, as such, cannot enter the calculus, at least in the orthodox manner. But what can be done? Person i can, in the hypothetical contracting process, presumably commence by comparing his own subjectively estimated predictions against those of j, which is more pessimistic about the social productivity of both arrangements in the example. Person i can reason as follows: "If j's predictions rather than my own are accurate, I, too, should choose B regardless of any attempt to treat risk explicitly in my calculus. On the other hand, if my own predictions rather than j's are more accurate, then j could be induced to select A only if I can convince him that my predictions are superior and if he can be persuaded to act as if he is risk neutral."

But what about the *sustainability* of the two institutions? Suppose that i should succeed in convincing j that i's predictions are superior and that j agreed to go along with the selection of A. Further, suppose that, in periods subsequent to the choice between institutions, j should end up on the short end of the stick; that is, j finds himself among the Poor in A. In this setting, j would, of course, be extremely unhappy with his lot, and especially so as he recalls the persuasion by i which initially had convinced him to agree on A as the basic institution. This situation is, however, to be sharply contrasted with its obverse. Suppose that i agrees to B, and, in periods subsequent to the

14. The analysis of this section has some relationship to that contained in a paper by Buchanan. J. M. Buchanan ("A Hobbesian Interpretation of the Rawlsian Difference Principle," *Kyklos* 29, Fasc. 1 [1976]: 5–25) introduced the importance of predicted sustainability or enforceability into the Rawlsian contractual deliberation, but he did not allow for the subjectively derived differences in predictions as to the workings of alternative institutions, which are central to our analysis in this paper.

initial choice among institutions, suppose that i ends up among the Poor in B. In retrospect, i will be indeed *grateful* to j for having persuaded him to acquiesce in the selection of B. There will be no "sour grapes" feedback at all; quite the opposite.

Is it meaningful to assign some weight to predicted sustainability of the contract in the individual's own calculus at the time of agreement?[15] Note that no such question could be raised if contractual elements could be wholly eliminated from consideration. If everyone should rank alternative institutions identically from the outset, agreement would emerge without the necessity of contractual discussion, and, in periods subsequent to choice, each person would be living with the consequences of his own wisdom or his own folly, as the case might be. No one would have grounds for recrimination because of some initial failure to "carry the day" with his privately preferred institutional arrangement. However, if contractual agreement necessarily involves some departure from initially preferred arrangements, at least on the part of some persons, the post-choice consequences are to be reckoned with. If we plausibly attribute a positive and differentially higher prospect to nonsustainability in those settings where initial institutional preferences are somehow overruled, the dominance of the relatively more pessimistic party to an agreement in the quasi-bargaining process may be readily predicted.

In the context of our example, suppose that i, over and beyond the subjectively estimated predictions depicted in Figure 1, assigns some positive value to the prospect that A, if selected, will be less sustainable or enforceable than B, due to the possible defection of j in A. Reasonably low values here might well lower the expected value of income in A, even for i, below the expected value of income in B.

No such calculus can be traced out for j in the obverse situation. If B is agreed upon, and, hence, if the initial preferences of i are overruled, then i will, in post-choice periods, willingly support the continuance of B if he finds himself among the Poor, even if i's own subjective predictions prove to be

---

15. This has some relation to the bargaining model of J. R. Hicks (*The Theory of Wages* [London: Macmillan, 1932]) and the synthesis by R. L. Bishop of Zeuthen and Hicks where the length of time in which the settlement will last will have an effect on the behavior of the bargainers ("A Zeuthen-Hicks Theory of Bargaining," *Econometrica* 32 [July 1964]: 410–17). In our model, however, sustainability is a purely subjective construct, while in Hicks' model it is a prior datum.

accurate. On the other hand, if *i* finds himself among the Rich under Institution B, he will experience regrets that A was not chosen. Barring extreme risk preference, he will not, however, take action or even threaten to take action toward defection that will undermine the structure of social order. Individual *i* as the "regretful Rich" will simply have too much to lose in defecting. The alternative to any institution, once selected, is some reversion to the initial state where neither set of rules prevails, at least for some period. The differences in attitudes toward the prevailing institution of order, whether this be A or B, on the part of the Rich and the Poor are dramatic. In our example, the Rich person stands to lose 1200 *Y* per period if he finds himself Poor in A.

The prospect for nonsustainability is nonsymmetrical. Only the relatively Poor, or disadvantaged to use Rawls' term, can be predicted to embody a viable threat to the stability of social order, and then they can be predicted to embody such a threat only when they find themselves in arrangements which they do not consider to be "fair," defined in the specific sense as belonging, at least conceptually, to the set of arrangements that "are of their own choosing."[16]

In the preceding analysis, the contractual calculus of the two parties is the focus of attention. A categorical distinction must be made between this calculus, from which a contractual agreement emerges, and the post-choice operation of some chosen institution, an operation that may be objectively observed and recorded. In the original position, and behind the Rawlsian veil of ignorance, the individual who is to be party to a potential contract will not have, indeed cannot have, either empirical records of institutional or personal experiences upon which to draw. He must make decisions on the basis of subjectively estimated predictions, and the solipsist extreme is to be avoided only to the extent that comparable predictions of other parties may be allowed to influence choice.

---

16. Some problem of sustainability will, of course, always be present. Even if a person's preferred institution is selected, he may seek to defect if he loses out in the lottery. He may seek a new game, one in which the expected value is the same as that he faced in the initial contractual setting. Our argument suggests only that the proclivity to defect from agreed-on rules is higher in those institutions where those who lose the lottery are not playing with their own preferred rules than in those situations where the game is of their own choosing.

Objection may, of course, be raised to the example that we have introduced to illustrate our analysis. We may be charged with having deliberately contrived an example that will demonstrate our results, with the inference that their results cannot readily be generalized. In a sense, we are guilty of this charge, although the inference is unwarranted. Our example was contrived in order to allow us to remain strictly within the Rawlsian definition-description of the original position, while producing the maximin outcome from the contractual process without requiring universalized risk aversion. Our analysis becomes much more general, and perhaps plausibly more realistic, if we modify the Rawlsian constraints very slightly. If we are willing to drop Rawls' insistence that a person in the original position does not know his own liability to optimism and pessimism, our results can be produced more straightforwardly and be essentially the same argument. In the two-person, two-institution example, we can now allow each person to make the same subjective estimate of social productivity of the alternative institutions. We can introduce differences only in their subjective predictions as to their own prospects for being located in the more-favored or less-favored positions. The optimist thinks of himself as being personally lucky and assigns a higher prospect to his own expected value than does the pessimist. For precisely the reasons already discussed, in such a setting the pessimist will tend to dominate the contractual process.

V. Concluding Remarks

Our analysis has shown that the maximin criterion is satisfied as an emergent outcome of the contract in certain settings, independent of universal and extreme risk aversion. Our purpose is *not* that of arguing that the contractual process will always produce the institution or rule that will satisfy the maximin principle. It should be clear that no such proof could be offered by the analysis.

The analysis does, however, have general implications for what we may label as "veil of ignorance bargaining," implications that have not, to our knowledge, been fully recognized. As the examples indicate, there is a bias toward "pessimist" control of the selection of the basic rules in such settings. The parties to a "veil of ignorance bargain," all of whom acknowledge their ignorance about particular positions, but all of whom make their own subjective predictions about the working properties of the alternative institutions, are *not* equals in terms of their predicted abilities to influence the group choice that can be predicted to emerge.

Our own speculations on this problem arose from a real-life situation. Five persons make up a minimal-sized group for a pleasant game of poker. They meet and discuss the rules prior to any knowledge as to the fall of the cards on later plays under whatever rules may be chosen. It is evident that in such a setting, the person who is most pessimistic about his own chances of winning will tend to be most influential in settling upon the rules, since he has, in the net, the least to gain from participating in the evening's play. The costs of exit for the pessimist are uniformly lower than for anyone else in the group, and, because all parties recognize this at the time the rules are selected, all will tend to accept, or at least move toward, the pessimist's preferred set of rules.

Appendix

Consider a generalization of the bargaining model discussed in Section IV to m institutions, or sets of rules, and *n* individuals. Again, the chosen institution, if any, must be agreed upon by all participants behind the veil of ignorance. Individuals differ only in their subjective predictions of the social productivity of each feasible institution. The "winning" institution is that institution, preferred by at least one person, which has a shorter (or equal) "payback period" than any other feasible institution preferred by at least one individual.

To illustrate, consider the five-person, five-institution example shown in Figure A-1.

The elements in each row correspond to a particular individual's subjective predictions of the expected income under each of the five institutions, A through E. The last column denotes each individual's predicted distribution at Rich and Poor states; the last row denotes the objectively known incomes of the Rich and Poor under each institution. Notice that the cells along the main diagonal correspond to the subjectively expected incomes under each individual's most preferred institution. Figure A-2 shows the winners of each comparison of any two individually preferred institutions.

	A	B	C	D	E	Subjective distribution of rich and poor
i	820	808	750	620	505	8R 2P
j	640	656	650	565	485	6R 4P
Individuals k	460	504	550	510	465	4R 6P
l	280	352	450	455	445	2R 8P
m	190	276	400	427.5	435	1R 9P
Objective incomes of rich and poor in each institution	1000	960	850	675	535	Rich
	900	200	350	400	425	Poor

Figure A-1. Subjectively expected incomes

For example, compare i's preferred institution, A, to k's preferred institution, C. Individual i has a payback period of $750/(820 - 750) = 10.7$ days while individual k has a payback period of $460/(550 - 460) = 5.1$ days. According to the bargaining model in Section III, k's preferred institution, C, would be mutually agreed upon by i and k. Hence, the entry in the first row and the third column of Figure A-2 is "C." The remaining entries in the figure are derived in like manner. One can readily see that Institution D, the preferred institution of individual i, will be selected unanimously by the group—i.e., there will be no hold-outs.

This example illustrates a number of characteristics of the solution. First, it shows that the two most likely-to-be-chosen institutions, C and D, need not be those preferred by either the extreme optimist or the extreme pessimist (i and k). All that can be said for certain is that the final choice of institution will come down to a conflict between a *relative* optimist and a *relative* pessimist. Note, however, that the relatively pessimistic individual, i, drives the rules in this example.

Second, there need not exist an institution which beats all others in a pairwise comparison. Consider the three-person, three-institution example in

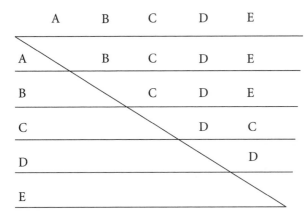

Figure A-2. Pairwise winning institutions

Figure A-3. Here, Institution A beats B, B beats C, and C beats A. However, it is still the case that there is one individual who can hold out longer than any other individual. Consider individual *i*. In order to calculate his payback period he must make a prediction as to which institution would emerge if his preferred institution does not. Since in a pairwise comparison B beats C, he would figure on B as the rival institution, and *i* would calculate his payback period as $780/(816 - 780) = 21.6$ days. Individual *k* has the shortest payback period, 4.2 days, and, consequently, since all individuals know one another's propensities to hold out, Institution C would emerge victorious.

		Institutions			Subjective distribution of rich and poor
		A	B	C	
	i	816	780	636	8R 2P
Individuals	j	632	660	636	6R 4P
	k	448	540	554	4R 6P
Objective incomes of rich and poor under each institution		1000	900	800	Rich
		80	300	390	Poor

Figure A-3. Subjectively expected incomes

That is, individual k is willing to hold out longer to ensure that B is not chosen than individual i is willing to hold out to ensure that C is not chosen.

Finally, even if examples can be constructed where no equilibrium exists, this need not bother us. There is nothing in the Rawlsian model which assures that society will take the leap from anarchy to orderly society. Not all constitutional conventions result in new states. Sometimes the proposed poker game just never gets off the ground.

PART SEVEN

Fiscal and Monetary Constitutions

Procedural and Quantitative Constitutional Constraints on Fiscal Authority

Economists of the garden variety seem to have little or nothing to contribute to the discussion of the various proposals to impose constitutional limits on the powers of government to tax and to spend. This is paradoxical, since clearly the basic impact of the proposals would be, and is intended to be, economic. But most economists are inhibited because constitutional "policy," as distinct from ordinary legislative policy, lies outside their familiar framework for discussion. Economists are usually quite willing to advise or to criticize officials in making ordinary, postconstitutional policy. But constitutional constraints are viewed negatively because they would necessarily restrict the ability of policy makers to follow the proffered advice of economists.

Public choice economists, those of us who have concerned ourselves with the processes of political decision making, are at some advantage in confronting issues of constitutional policy. Of necessity, collective decisions must be made through some process, some rules for combining separate individual values or preferences, whether of voters, groups, parties, or members of legislative assemblies. And such rules are necessarily "constitutional" in the sense that they are chosen separately from and independent of the particular choices we might make on particular issues. Indeed, these rules are pre-

From *The Constitution and the Budget: Are Constitutional Limits on Tax, Spending, and Budget Powers Desirable at the Federal Level?* ed. W. S. Moore and Rudolf G. Penner (Washington: American Enterprise Institute, 1980), 80–84. Reprinted with the permission of The American Enterprise Institute for Public Policy Research, Washington, D.C.

sumed to remain invariable over a whole sequence of separate policy issues. In our initial work on what may be called an "economic theory of the political constitution," Gordon Tullock and I concentrated on the choice of decision rules. In this, we were following the lead of Knut Wicksell, who looked to economic policy reform through reform of the constitutional decision rules through which economic policy emerges. However, neither Wicksell nor Tullock and I fully explored the possible substitutability between decision rules and other kinds of constitutional constraints intended for comparable purposes.

Before discussing possible substitutability, I should emphasize that any constitution, any set of rules selected independent of the particularized choice setting, necessarily restricts the range of options available to the decision-making unit, whether this be an individual, a committee, a firm, or a legislative assembly. The very purpose of rules, of constitutions, is to prevent us from making decisions in an overemotional or overpragmatic response to particular situations. Constitutional choices are presumably made at a more "rational" level of consideration, with situational distractions at least partially subordinated to long-term interests. Constitutional choice in politics is analogous to the long-run planning decision familiar in the neoclassical theory of the firm, whereas postconstitutional choice is akin to short-run output decisions. The short-run options are necessarily constrained by the prior long-run commitments.

Now let me return to the specific issue of fiscal limits—proposed constitutional constraints on governmental powers to tax and to spend. We have always had such constraints in our political history, although economists, for the most part, have ignored them. The very institution of taxation, for instance, stems from the acknowledged constitutional constraint against arbitrary discrimination in "taking" resources from citizens without due process of law and without due compensation. If government could simply take what it needs, why should it bother to tax? Further, even within the taxing power, governments are further prohibited from arbitrary discrimination. As we know, a *constitutional* amendment was required, the Sixteenth, to grant government the discriminatory tax treatment embodied in the progressive income tax.

Those who favor additional constraints are, therefore, merely proposing that we add to the constitutional constraints that exist and that have always existed. But why are additional constraints considered to be necessary? This question brings me back to the relationship I mentioned earlier between constitutional rules for decision making and constitutional rules on the powers to tax and spend. The need for additional fiscal constraints did not become apparent until the empirical-historical record began to suggest that the nonfiscal constraints had failed. Nineteenth- and twentieth-century political thought, as expressed by scholar and citizen alike, embodied a blind faith that, somehow, the competitive pressures of electoral politics made explicit consideration of further constitutional constraints unnecessary. That is to say, the prevailing mythology about politics was that so long as politicians and political parties were required to submit their record to the voters periodically, the overall results could not really get out of bounds. "Democracy at work" meant government by congressional majorities, and any constraint on majorities' freedom to work their will could only reduce the flexibility of response to "needs." (This attitude was expressed clearly by Justice Felix Frankfurter with respect to economic legislation.) The very notion of what I have elsewhere called the "constitutional attitude"—the vision of the Founding Fathers of a society in which government, too, would be kept strictly within *constitutional* limits—was lost to the consciousness of the dominant American political mind.

Fortunately, in my view, residues of such an attitude had not entirely disappeared. And the accumulating fiscal record in the decades after World War II suggested that government had clearly overstepped any reasonable bounds. Even the most ardent defender of public sector growth is hard put to account for the post-1965 explosion, in particular, solely in terms of a democracy's response to the demands of the citizenry. Increasingly, the growth patterns came to be understood and interpreted as the outputs of a political sector that has an internal dynamic of its own, subject to relatively indirect and incomplete electoral control.

The time came, in the late 1970s, for a reassessment of constitutional limits. Again, the prospect for two different approaches should be recognized. Wicksell wanted to allow full flexibility in tax-sharing schemes, but he wanted to require more than simple majorities for spending authorizations. He also wanted to reform the decision processes in legislatures to require simultaneous consideration of items of spending and of the taxing necessary to finance them. Wicksell wanted legislators to be forced to confront the benefits and the costs of each spending proposal on its own.

As we know, Congress itself recognized that its own processes had got out of hand and passed the Budget Reform Act of 1974 in an attempt to restore some order. But this was legislative rather than constitutional reform: Its long-term results cannot be estimated, and it takes little or no political sophistication to recognize that the structure through which fiscal decisions are made is a long way from the Wicksellian ideal. Many of the proposed constitutional limits can, therefore, be interpreted as attempts to modify procedures so as to move closer to Wicksell's ideal, where taxing and spending decisions would, indeed, reflect rational benefit-cost responses to citizens' demands for government action. Alan Greenspan, among others, has called for two-thirds majorities on all spending legislation, clearly a Wicksellian reform; and the neglected part of Proposition 13 also calls for a qualified legislative majority for the enactment of new taxes.

The balanced budget amendment can also be interpreted in these terms. Considered at its simplest, this proposal is based on the readily understood notion that governmental decision making should be required, in the large, to balance out the two sides of the account. Indeed, the widespread support for this proposal stems from its place in citizens' logical understanding of their own affairs. Interestingly enough, budget balance was a part of the pre-Keynesian fiscal constitution, even if it was implicit rather than explicit. The effect of Keynesian economic policy was to destroy this part of the fiscal constitution. Keynesian economics told politicians that deficits were good. Since politicians always want to spend and never to tax, the regime of deficits followed. The amendment is an attempt to undo much of the resulting damage. Since I have written a book on this, I shall not elaborate the argument here.

Another existing procedural constraint, one that has historical-legal origins in the U.S. Constitution, is the legal recognition of the federal structure, with units at each level being assigned and restricted to the exercise of specific fiscal powers. This and other procedural constraints have in common that they seek not to operate upon specific outcomes, but to modify the processes or rules through which fiscal decisions are made. Clearly, there is some relationship between the procedural reforms suggested and the directions of change in the predicted sequence of results. But procedural reforms do have the advantage that they do not directly restrict the potential for response to the demands of citizens, either in relative or in absolute terms. None of the procedural constraints places a ceiling on the share of GNP that might be collected in taxes or appropriated for public or governmental use.

It is precisely this characteristic that distinguishes the procedural from the quantitative constraints that have been variously proposed. If the processes through which governments make budgetary decisions are considered not amenable to constitutional change, because amendments either may not pass or may not be effective if they did pass, then attempts to impose constitutional constraints more directly on the results may seem justifiable.

The set of proposals that seem to have gained widest favor among the subset of economists who support any constitutional changes falls within this category. These are proposals to impose constitutional limits on the share of income and/or product that might be collected in taxes or expended for public uses or, alternatively, to set limits on the increase in this share in relationship to increases in income and/or product. This set of proposals has the apparent advantage of bypassing or ignoring the processes through which fiscal results might be generated within the governmental structure. Their disadvantage lies in the rigidity they would necessarily impose on the potential response to demands. In recognition of this disadvantage, most specific proposals of the share or ratio type embody escape clauses which allow departure from the constraint by a modified decision rule. In total, therefore, these proposals embody both quantitative and procedural limits.

Geoffrey Brennan and I have found, in analyzing alternative constitutional constraints on fiscal powers, that constraints on the bases for taxation allowed to government may have much to recommend them. These constraints allow for flexibility in response to spending demands within relatively wide limits, but, at the same time, act to keep government's fiscal appetites within certain limits.

The quantitative constraint that is most widely known is, of course, Proposition 13—the constitutional lid imposed on California real property tax rates. An advantage, and indeed one of the success secrets of this sort of constraint, lies in its directness. An offsetting disadvantage is its rigidity with regard to rates, along with the accompanying temptation offered to governments to choose other tax bases and to shift fiscal responsibility upward to higher-level units.

This brief review of some of the proposals for constitutional fiscal constraints, though cast in general terms, has probably revealed my own attitudes toward them. I support almost any and all proposals, and I would not reject any proposal on the ground that there may be better ways to accomplish similar results. It seems to me that the need for constraining government is so urgent that we must capitalize on the momentum that Proposition 13 has set off.

Tax Reform in
"Constitutional" Perspective
The Case for a Fiscal Constitution

Within modern memory there has never been general agreement that the tax system functioned even tolerably well. Year in and year out, almost continually, we find tax lawyers, tax economists, journalists, bureaucrats, and politicians talking about and agitating for "tax reform." In a sense, this is understandable and predictable. Within popular as well as political discourse, taxation is fully analogous to a never-ending zero-sum game. A decrease in the tax share of some person or group can be achieved by an offsetting increase in the tax share of some other person or group. Hence, it remains always in the interest of any person or group to agitate for "tax reform," provided only that this can be translated to mean specific change in the tax-share distribution that will redound to his or its own benefit. We should not, therefore, be very much surprised that "tax reform" becomes a blanket rubric within which the underlying political struggle over the assignment of tax shares takes place. Nor should we be shocked to observe that this struggle has become more acute as the revenue requirements of government have increased dramatically during the years since World War II.

Nonetheless, "tax reform" agitation does vary in intensity over time, and we have been riding a crescendo in the late 1970s. In 1976, Jimmy Carter traveled throughout the land castigating the United States tax structure as a "disgrace to the human race." And President Carter promised to deliver a com-

From *Invited Essay*, 1977, 1–6. Reprinted by permission of the publisher, Beta Gamma Sigma.

prehensive tax-reform package to the Congress in late 1977. This package will, in its turn, insure discussion and debate into and beyond 1978.

I shall not discuss the details of Mr. Carter's, or anyone else's, tax-reform proposals in this paper. I want, instead, to examine the desirability of "tax reform" itself, independent of how this might be defined. That is to say, I want to discuss the relative efficacy of *changing* the distribution of tax shares via a partisan political decision process and of *leaving the existing distribution alone,* regardless of what the latter happens to be. I shall argue that there is, indeed, something "disgraceful" to be observed, if we choose to employ such emotive rhetoric. In this context, it is "disgraceful" to subject the basic tax structure to the continuing struggle of majority-rule politics, with the accompanying wastage of untold billions in attempts either to reduce or to forestall unduly discriminatory tax treatment or to initiate or to increase the favorable treatment of this or that source or use of income, this or that class, industry, region, or occupation.

More constructively, I shall argue that the tax system can be meaningfully discussed only in a *constitutional perspective.* By this I mean that the basic structure of taxation, the distribution of tax shares among persons and groups, should be considered to be a part of an ongoing *fiscal or tax constitution,* defined as a set of quasi-permanent rules or arrangements within which individuals can anticipate making appropriate behavioral adjustments, including those made over a long-term planning period. From such perspective, structural changes in the tax system should be discussed as, and treated as, changes in basic constitutional law, and hence should be potential outcomes of a categorically different process of decision-making than that which generates ordinary legislation. I shall argue further that meaningful criteria for a "good" tax system can be derived only from this constitutional perspective, which offers the only escape from the zero-sum implications of the conventional tax-reform exercise.

I shall suggest that there is no "scientifically best" or "scientifically ideal" tax structure in any objectively measurable sense that would be accepted by separate observers. More importantly, it is relatively easy to demonstrate that, even should an "ideal" tax structure exist, the vagaries of majority-rule legislative politics could not be expected to generate even an approximation to such an "ideal." We should predict that such politics would generate more or less the results that we now observe; continual changes in structure, along with unceasing clamor for still further changes.

The implications of the argument are conservative in the literal sense. *Stability* in the basic rules for taxation has a value in itself, and stability is not achievable through continual manipulation. While interrelationships exist, the basic *structure* of taxation must be conceptually distinguished from the *level* of taxation. "Tax reform" is relevant to the allocation or distribution of tax *shares* among persons and groups. It is not directly relevant to "tax reduction" or "tax increase," determined by the overall level of tax rates, within any given structure of tax sharing. The argument for stability in tax structure can be developed simultaneously with an argument that the level of taxation is excessive (or deficient). My discussion in this paper is limited to tax-share distribution.

What Is a "Good" Tax System?

Almost all of the traditional literature of normative tax theory could be summarized under the title of this section, extending at least as far backwards as Adam Smith's canons of taxation on the one hand and including the highly mathematical modern theories of "optimal taxation" on the other. Such a summary is not my objective here. I shall distinguish two sets of criteria for evaluating a tax structure, or any part thereof. First, there are those criteria which require resort to norms that are *external* to the preferences of potential taxpayers themselves. Second, there are those criteria that are *internal* to, and hence derivable from, these preferences. With the single exception to be noted below, traditional normative tax theory falls within the first, or external criteria, category. That is to say, the orthodox procedure is to adjudge a tax structure, or a part thereof, to be "good" or "bad" in terms of its standing against externally defined criteria. Some of the latter are such things as: allocative efficiency, redistributive potential, equal treatment for equals, taxation related to ability to pay, convenience in collection. The normative tax analyst, the lawyer, economist, or bureaucrat, looks at a tax structure, in whole or in part, and concludes that it is "good" or "bad" because it does or does not generate "least price distortion"; or because it does or does not reduce sufficiently the disparities in incomes and wealth; or because it does or does not treat equally situated persons equally; or because it does not impose sufficiently high burdens on the rich relative to those imposed on the poor; or because it is or is not progressive; etc.

It should be clear from this summary recital that the procedure cannot be expected to result in general agreement, even among the so-called expert analysts. "One man's meat is another man's poison." Separate "experts" can look at the same tax structure, either existing or hypothetical, and place it in widely differing positions or ranks in an institutional ordering of "goodness." And there are simply no instruments for the "evaluation of values" which might produce the divergent orderings here. Because fundamental norms differ, it must be expected that "experts" can usually be located to label almost any conceivable tax-share system, or any part thereof, to be "inefficient," "unjust," or "inequitable," or, contrariwise, "efficient," "just," or "equitable," or several of these combined.

This sort of disagreement would emerge, with its consequent implications for "tax-reform" discussion, even if all of the parties to an evaluation should be high-minded, disinterested, and charged with the pure pursuit of the public interest, defined, of course, in their own terms. But such disagreement becomes more acerbic when there exists mutual recognition that the evaluations of tax systems, or particular features of tax systems, will also be affected by the private rewards accruing to those who are most successful in the persuasive effort. Once again, the zero-sum features of the tax game must be stressed. Is it really so surprising when we find Harvard professors tending to justify the charitable-educational deduction under the income tax, or to find Brookings Institution representatives seeking ways to extend the tax base and hence the gross revenue potential for the federal government? Or to find economists for the AFL-CIO justifying the shift from payroll to income taxes for the financing of social security? Or to see the economists for the National Association of Manufacturers (NAM) arguing that the personal income tax structure is overly progressive?

The tax-reform game should be seen for what it is, an interrelated set of attempts by various parties, both those directly interested and those allegedly "disinterested," to persuade others, and especially political decision-makers, that their own private version of the "good" tax structure is, somehow, unique, and, therefore, the proper benchmark or target for institutional change. Confronted with the array of conflicting testimony from the parties adversary to one another, with arguments that appear plausibly persuasive on all sides, should we then wonder that experienced politicians who actually write the tax laws soon come to be somewhat cynical about the process of "tax reform"? There is no "best" tax system in terms of evaluation by external criteria for the simple reason that there is no single set of criteria upon which agreement exists or can exist.

To say this, however, is not equivalent to saying that one tax system is as good as another. Means of evaluating a tax structure or system can be developed on *internal* criteria, that is, on the basis of the desires of the taxpayers themselves, independent of external norms, and with no necessity of resorting to such norms. Such internal criteria can be discussed at two separate levels, the nonconstitutional and the constitutional. We shall postpone our more elaborated treatment of constitutional criteria for tax systems until a later section of this Essay. It will be useful here to summarize the development of internal criteria in only a nonconstitutional setting.

Taxation as One Side of Fiscal Exchange

Suppose that we simply refuse to invoke external ethical norms for evaluating a tax-sharing scheme. How can we possibly judge one tax to be better than another? An answer is found in the "fiscal exchange" approach to taxation, pioneered by Knut Wicksell, a famous Swedish economist, whose important work on taxation was published in 1896.[1] What is the ultimate purpose of taxation? Surely a primary purpose must be that of financing goods and services desired by the taxpayers themselves. In this sense, tax payments can be looked on as having most of the characteristics of prices paid for goods and services purchased in the marketplace. A person pays money for shoes because he values the product more than he does those things that he might otherwise purchase for the same money. A tax can be treated analo-

---

1. Knut Wicksell, *Finanztheoretische Untersuchungen* (Jena: Gustav Fischer, 1896). The major portion of this work is published in an English translation as "A New Principle of Just Taxation," in *Classics in the Theory of Public Finance,* edited by R. A. Musgrave and A. T. Peacock (London: Macmillan, 1959), 72–118.

gously. A taxpayer may value a good and service provided by government more highly than he values the alternative goods or services that he might otherwise secure with the money measured by the tax he pays. Looked at in this way, there are elements of "voluntary exchange" in many taxes.[2]

What is the "best" assignment of tax shares under this fiscal exchange conception of taxation? Since the benchmark is voluntary exchange, it follows that *all* persons must secure net benefits. That is to say each taxpayer must get back from governments goods and services that he values more than the tax payments made. Wicksell moved quickly to the direct conclusion that *any* tax-sharing scheme that could be agreed on by *all* taxpayers is acceptable, although he also recognized that many arrangements might be possible. But through this process of looking for agreement among taxpayers themselves Wicksell was able to evaluate tax arrangements *without* bringing in external ethical criteria.

At a conceptual level, the Wicksellian framework for looking at taxes gets high marks indeed. But the realities of politics get in the way. We do not observe tax rules and political rules that require the consent of all persons and groups before taxes are imposed. What we do observe is governmental decisions taken by a majority coalition in a legislature with the outcomes coercively imposed on all taxpayers. In this real-world setting of politics, there is no assurance that all parties gain in their "exchange" with government. And this becomes notably true when we recognize, further, that tax revenues are not used exclusively to provide goods and services. Tax revenues are also used to finance transfers directly from taxpayers to recipients. Income and wealth redistribution is an inherent part of the fiscal process that we observe. For practical purposes, therefore, the Wicksellian criterion for evaluating tax arrangements does not work. We are back where we started; we have no apparent means of evaluating tax structures unless we are willing to invoke external ethical norms. I shall show that things are not nearly so bad as they seem here when we introduce a genuine constitutional perspective. The detour into this brief discussion of the Wicksellian approach will be helpful when this perspective is discussed in detail.

2. For an extended discussion of this approach, see my paper "Taxation in Fiscal Exchange," *Journal of Public Economics,* 6 (1976), 17–29.

The Instability of Majoritarian Politics

The fiscal exchange conception model for taxation fails because political decisions are not made unanimously. General consent is not required before governments invoke their residual "powers to tax." Perhaps this suggests only that there are flaws in the constitution. Wicksell proposed that all taxing and spending propositions should require the unanimous or near-unanimous agreement of all members of a legislative assembly. Through this political or constitutional reform, Wicksell aimed to generate "tax reform" indirectly.

The political decision process is costly, however, and any move toward requiring that decisions on taxes be made more restrictive and inclusive might involve dramatic increases in costs. Recognition of the cost of decision-making itself—which includes the costs of inaction, of strategic maneuvering, of shifting coalitions, of political trades, deals, side payments—suggests that the Wicksellian route to reform would be limited in applicability.[3]

It is important to understand just why general agreement on tax arrangements would be so difficult to secure. To show this, let us suppose that a specific tax-sharing scheme, along with a proposed budgetary pattern, would, in fact, insure that *all* taxpayers gain by the "fiscal exchange" with the government. This generality of net gain would not, however, make agreement easy to obtain for the simple reason that taxpayers and taxpayer groups would still find it profitable to seek differentially advantageous shares in the total gains available. Under one sharing scheme, a taxpayer might be insured of a net fiscal gain of, say, $100. But another arrangement might promise him a net gain of $1000. In this situation, he will never agree on the first arrangement; instead he will invest time and resources in attempts to get politicians to adopt the second.

If general agreement is too costly and time-consuming, there is some rational basis for having political decision structures that do not require general agreement. What we observe, of course, are variations on majority voting rules—in voting on candidates and/or referenda by the general electorate, in voting in legislative bodies, in voting in committees of such bodies. But the

---

3. For a generalized discussion, not limited to taxation, see James M. Buchanan and Gordon Tullock, *The Calculus of Consent* (Ann Arbor: University of Michigan Press, 1962).

same reasons that make general agreement so difficult to reach also emerge to insure that decisions reached under majority-rule institutions will tend to be highly unstable. Even if there exists a fixed number of alternatives to be voted upon, and even if individual voters' preferences are well organized, majority voting may produce a cycle.[4] There may be no single alternative that will secure majority approval against all proposals. The outcome that finally emerges may well depend on just how the items to be voted upon are placed on the agenda and on how the rules for stopping the voting are made. This tendency toward instability in voting outcomes under majority rule becomes more pronounced when the range of effective alternatives may be readily modified. Clever manipulation can almost always produce amendments to agreed-on majority results that will be preferred by some other majority coalition. Furthermore, persuasive arguments, along with side deals and agreements, may modify the preferences of voters, or of legislative representatives, during the decision period.

"Tax-reform" discussion, debate, and review, as we observe them to operate in the United States, exhibit all of these properties. Indeed we might say that the functional purpose of tax-reform advocacy is that of organizing new alternatives that might command majority assent in the Congress. The turnover in representatives, even if this has been severely limited in recent decades, tends to allow for shifting coalitions. And the very electoral term structure of Congress itself almost insures that "tax reform" will always be on the agenda for action.

The Case for a Fiscal Constitution

To this point my argument has been largely negative. I have argued that there is no "best" tax system in terms of any agreed-on external criterion. Further, I have suggested that the internal criterion advanced by Knut Wicksell, that criterion which utilizes the agreement among taxpayers themselves as the

---

4. The now-classic works developing the implications of this majority-voting paradox are Kenneth Arrow, *Social Choice and Individual Values* (New York: Wiley, 1951), and Duncan Black, *Theory of Committees and Elections* (Cambridge: Cambridge University Press, 1958).

signal for desirability, will not work effectively. Finally, I have shown that under the politics that we see, outcomes are likely to be highly unstable, with "tax reform" being a continuous process.

From this point, I want to develop a constructive argument. I shall show that a genuine constitutional perspective on taxation can do much to mitigate the difficulties suggested. There seem to be at least three major advantages to be expected from treating taxation as a part of a genuine fiscal constitution. First of all, the value of institutional predictability could be fully captured; the efficiency gains would surely be great. Secondly, the related and obverse side of this relationship would be equally, if not more, productive; individuals and groups would reduce substantially the major investment in "rent-seeking" which, socially considered, is wholly wasteful. Thirdly, and most importantly, only with a constitutional perspective could something akin to the Wicksellian criterion be introduced; agreement on tax changes might become possible, both conceptually and in actuality.

These three promised advantages of a constitutional perspective stem from the implied shift between the treatment of tax rules as ordinary, year-to-year legislation, subject necessarily to ever-changing political-ideological winds, and their treatment as permanent or quasi-permanent institutions, beyond the immediate and expedient control of ordinary legislation, as a part of the set of legal rules which are expected to remain in being for a long period. Indeed, this is the very meaning of the words "constitutional" and "constitution." By the latter, I refer to the basic rules and institutions within which choices are made, publicly and privately, rules and institutions which are expected to remain in being for periods sufficiently long to enable behavioral plans to be made and long-term adjustments to be completed.

Tax Rules as Public Capital

The efficiency of establishing and maintaining quasi-permanence in the basic structure of taxation should be obvious. To the extent that modern levels of taxation are tolerable at all, they are so because elements of the structure are relatively immune to change. In this sense, these elements have been treated as "constitutional." Suppose that Congress should have switched, year-to-year, between the tax on corporation income and a value-added tax as a major revenue source. These taxes would require differing adjustments on the part of firms, and the uncertainty about which tax would be levied in which year or period would produce major waste in the economy.

Tax rules or arrangements are no different in this respect from other rules and institutions of the society. The importance of some long-term predictability in the "rules of the game" within which individuals and groups are allowed to make choices can hardly be stressed too much. Consider the following simple example, which I owe to my colleague Geoffrey Brennan. Two passengers arrive simultaneously on adjacent platforms, A and B, in a station. Both persons seek to change trains quickly, and to do so, each must run across a narrow bridgeway across the tracks. The bridgeway is just wide enough for two persons to pass while running in opposite directions, *provided* that there exists a generally recognized "rule of the road" that dictates right-side or left-side movement. If such a rule exists, and both passengers are fully informed as to its existence, both can change trains successfully during the stop. If no such rule exists, or if one or both of the passengers is badly informed, both persons may miss the connection and remain stranded on the platform. In this example, the efficiency of having a widely known and stable rule, any rule, is clear, and here, as in many instances, it is the very existence of a stable rule rather than the particular form of the rule itself that assumes critical importance.

Predictable rules within which individuals may rationally plan their activities are part of the "public capital" of any society. Tax rules are similar to other legal rules in this respect. To change a tax rule that has long been in existence, and to which individuals have adjusted their long-term plans, is analogous to tearing down a permanent structure. Any new, or replacement, rule will necessarily require a long period before some sort of behavioral-institutional equilibrium is reestablished. The worst of all situations would be one in which basic tax rules are subject to continual modification, such that individuals and groups could neither approach some sort of equilibrium adjustment nor even make rational plans toward such adjustment. There is genuine economic content in the adage that "an old tax is a good tax."[5]

5. For a specific discussion of the economic content of this adage, see my *Public Finance in Democratic Process* (Chapel Hill: University of North Carolina Press, 1967), es-

The argument suggests that "tax reform," in and of itself, is undesirable, and especially if the changes are to be made through a political game characterized by majority-rule partisan maneuver. This is not to say that taxes should never be changed, or that the distribution or assignment of tax shares should literally be permanent, as if somehow fixed in concrete. The argument implies only that the costs of changing the structure be accurately estimated, and that a tax system should not be modified merely because some other system "might have evolved" which would now seem "better." There is a positive value in "that which exists" for the simple reason of its existence, and quite independent of whether or not rational defenses can be worked out on *carte blanche* assumptions. To be rationally justified, therefore, "tax reform" must be shown to have taken the full costs of change into account, costs which must also include those involved in the transition between tax schemes.

"Tax Reform" and "Rent-Seeking"

There is another side to the argument against "tax reform," which is perhaps more important than the "rules as public capital" point. The predictability of taxing arrangements can increase the productivity of the economy by making personal planning more efficient. But, also, the stability in tax rules, along with the generalized understanding that these rules are quasi-permanent, will also reduce substantially the socially wasteful investments in "rent-seeking" that continual change and discussions of change will insure. To the extent that tax arrangements can come to be considered as quasi-permanent features of the economic environment, individuals will divert resources from wasteful to productive investments.[6]

Consider, first, a setting in which particular tax-share rules are literally "up for grabs" with each congressional session. Consider the position of a particular group of persons, representing a specific industry, occupation, or

---

pecially Chapter 5. For a more general discussion of rules as public capital, see my *The Limits of Liberty* (Chicago: University of Chicago Press, 1975), especially Chapter 7.

6. For a general discussion of "rent-seeking," see Gordon Tullock, "Rent-Seeking," mimeographed, Center for Study of Public Choice, Virginia Polytechnic Institute and State University, Summer 1977.

region that might be favorably or unfavorably affected by specific congressional action on whether or not, say, a certain tax deduction or tax credit is allowed. There may be millions of dollars in the balance with the action of Congress meaning the difference between superior short-run profits and near-bankruptcy. In such a situation, it becomes privately rational for the group potentially affected to spend time and money in efforts to persuade members of the administration, the Congress, and notably the relevant members of the key committees that favorable treatment is in the "public interest," and, at the least, to convince such politicians that unfavorable treatment is clearly immoral. At the appropriate margins of decision, investments of this sort may be privately more rational than comparable investments in improved technology, in research, and even in purchases of new plant and equipment.

It is clear, however, that in some overview of the situation, when the comparable activities of all those who are seeking to secure favorable tax treatment and to avoid unfavorable treatment are taken into account, the net investment in "lobbying" is wasteful. Only the group which successfully wins the tax-persuasion game finds that it earns a positive return on its investment in time and money in "politicking." Those groups that lose have invested their time and money without return; these groups end up paying higher tax shares in addition to the unproductive investment in "rent-seeking."

How would the constitutional approach to tax-share arrangements modify this sort of behavior? If tax rules are generally expected to be unchangeable, there would be no gain to be secured from investment in lobbying for differentially advantageous treatment. But the constitutionalist approach does not imply an absence of change; it implies only that change be treated as quasi-permanent, and that institutions should be expected to have reasonably long lives. In this case, however, there may seem to be more profits from securing a favorable rules change than from comparable political action in a situation where any profits are anticipated to be short-lived because of shifting political coalitions. From this it seems that more rather than less lobbying effort might be forthcoming under a constitutionalist than under a legislative approach to tax reform.

Suppose, for illustration, that tax rules were changed only one time each decade, and that a particular feature of the tax system, once installed, was known to have a minimum life of ten years. The present value of a tax advantage is clearly higher than the comparable value of the same advantage without the temporal guarantee. Suppose that the differential advantage is initially worth $1000 per year. In a year-by-year legislative consideration of tax changes, the $1000 prospect will attract investment in lobbying effort each year, which may be less, equal to, or more than the $1000 in promised gain, which, in this case, will be reasonably certain to the successful "bidder." But if continued for a period of ten years, the differential gain from the same tax feature may be much less than $10,000 because of the mobility of resources in the economy. A tax advantage will offer differential short-run profit potential to those owners of resources employed in the "successful" industry. These differential profits will attract new investment; as investment moves in and output expands, profits are reduced. Over a ten-year span, the rate of return on new investment in the industry or group affected may return to the level that would be present in the absence of the tax advantage. Those within the industry who might seek the tax advantage initially will, of course, recognize that new entrants will quickly dissipate the differential profits owing to the tax feature. They will, accordingly, reduce their efforts to secure the tax advantage in the first place. It seems clear that, for this reason alone, the overall investment in "rent-seeking" will be much less than ten times that which would be anticipated to take place in any one-year legislative consideration of the same tax feature.

Over and beyond the long-term uncertainty about differential profitability due to the attraction of new investment, there is the related, but conceptually different, uncertainty that temporal extension of the planning horizon necessarily introduces. A person may be less willing to invest in effort to secure a quasi-permanent and long-term change in tax institutions than in effort to implement short-term change, because he may be unwilling and/or unable to "identify" his own future position so well in the former case as in the latter. A diversified corporation, for example, may know pretty well just what tax gimmicks will redound to its profitability given its current product line. But what will be its product line ten years down the road as it responds to changing tastes and technology? That particular tax arrangement which looks highly profitable in the short run may well prove to be a hindrance to expansion in the longer term. This argument from temporal uncertainty is the same that underlies the positive argument for constitutionalism in tax reform, to be discussed further in the following section. But for this as well as the first reason examined above, it seems intuitively clear that the total investment in "rent-seeking," in attempts to secure differential profits from favorable tax treatment, will be inversely related to the average length of life of particular features of the tax system. And, as noted, any reduction in this sort of investment represents pure social gain.

Constitutionalism and a Partial Veil of Ignorance

I have stressed the zero-sum aspects of the tax-sharing game, of "tax reform" discussion as this is generally observed to take place. The argument seems to be among groups that seek to reduce their own shares in total tax burden, with each group calling down familiar and somewhat tiresome slogans about "justice," "equity," "efficiency," etc. As I suggested, agreement is not possible in such a setting because individual positions in the economy are well identified. With fixed total revenue projections, most rich men know that an increase in the allowable standard deduction accompanied by a closing up of loopholes will increase their own tax shares; most poor men know that their shares will be reduced. It is folly to expect these two groups to "agree" on any change, one way or the other.

But the prospect for general agreement, for genuine consensus, may change dramatically if we allow for some introduction of ignorance and uncertainty into the individual's calculus. Suppose that a person confronted with a prospective tax change does not really know, and cannot accurately predict, whether he will be a rich man or a poor man. Suppose that his position in the economy is not fully identified. In this setting, he may genuinely try to choose features of a tax structure, a tax-sharing scheme, that will be "fair," in the sense of acceptability under either one of the two positions.

A person who does not know what his own position will be under the rule to be chosen is behind a "veil of ignorance"; this is the construction that has been used by John Rawls in the derivation of his notion of "justice as fairness."[7] Rawls did not discuss the tax system in particular, but his construction was used to derive "principles of justice" generally, and without resort to criteria external to the evaluations of persons within the group. To the ex-

---

7. Rawls developed his analysis in a series of papers published in the late 1950s, but the analysis has been very widely discussed only after the publication of his major work in 1971. See John Rawls, *A Theory of Justice* (Cambridge: Harvard University Press, 1971).

tent that a person does not know where he will be located in some final distribution, he will tend to opt for rules that are "fair," and that will be considered to be "fair," no matter just what his final position might turn out to be.[8]
In its idealized version, the veil of ignorance must be total; any ability of a
person to predict his own future position will bias his own choice of rules
and make agreement difficult to achieve.

In any conceivable real-world setting, however, persons would have at
least some idea as to where their own economic positions might be in any
future operation of the economic environment. If the Rawlsian criterion is
to be applied directly to any practical problem, something less than the idealized setting must be introduced.[9] A partial rather than a complete veil of
ignorance is the best to be expected. It is precisely at this point, however,
that the distinction between the constitutional and the nonconstitutional
approach becomes critically important. In the here and now, in 1977 or
1978, individuals may be able more or less fully to identify their own economic positions, and, because of this, may be able to translate the direct effects of any proposed tax-share change on their own pocketbooks. The current tax game is strictly zero sum; agreement remains impossible. But this
conclusion must be modified if a proposed change in tax shares is lagged in
effect so that it will be implemented only after a period of, say, ten years,
twenty years, or even fifty years. The increased difficulty in making any accurate prediction about one's own economic status over such a long period
is evident. Think of the poor but bright young man with confidence in himself. Increased rates of progression in the income tax may be beneficial to
him in the immediate future, but such increases in rate of progression may
prove harmful if the rate structure remains frozen, say, until 1990. The young
man, if he knows that the change being discussed is to be quasi-permanent,
may be very reluctant to support measures designed to impose punitive rates

8. I have found it useful to present the central idea here in terms of an analogy with
ordinary games. Consider a group of persons planning an evening's poker. They must
first decide on the rules for the evening's play. Since there is no means of predicting just
how the cards might fall on particular rounds of play, each person will be motivated, in
his choice among rules, to select rules that will generally be "fair." Furthermore, it seems
clear that *agreement* among all potential players on a set of rules will be much easier in
this setting than in one where the precise run of cards should be predictable.

9. A less-than-idealized setting was used to evaluate rules for political decision-making
in James M. Buchanan and Gordon Tullock, *The Calculus of Consent*.

on the currently rich. In similar fashion, the person who is now rich may consider the prospects of his family's own lapse into poverty. He may be willing to raise personal exemption levels, despite the fact that such change will increase his current tax share.

The prospects of general agreement, for consensus, on change in the tax-sharing scheme will be directly related to the predicted length of life of tax rules. To the extent that the tax structure is "constitutional," in the sense that we have used the term, there are opportunities for agreement that simply do not exist when the structure is known to be "up for grabs" with each congressional session. And, if there can be no external ethical criteria upon which agreement might be reached, the demonstration of internal agreement among potential taxpayers or their representatives in a legislative assembly becomes the only test of "improvement" in tax structure, the only proof that a shift in tax shares does, in fact, reflect genuine "reform."

"Tax Reform" in the Late 1970s

What about the current discussion of tax reform? What does the constitutionalist argument imply for President Carter's proposals for changes in tax structure? To the extent that the proposals are treated as "President Carter's," or as "the administration's," or as the "Democratic Party's platform obligations," they should be categorically rejected. A tax measure was enacted in 1976, and the tax structure that exists in 1977 has surely not been around long enough for individuals and firms to make adjustments to it. To open up the whole structure for reconsideration in 1978 must be counter-productive in many respects.

This is not to suggest that the tax-sharing scheme which exists in 1977 or 1978 is "ideal," and that changes should never be considered. There is room for "tax reform," properly interpreted. But for any set of proposals to qualify for evaluation under this rubric, it must emerge from a nonpartisan dialogue and it must be discussed as if it were designed to effect long-term institutional change. If "tax reform" is to be meaningful, if this term is other than empty rhetoric, the designers must think of changes, if adopted, that will remain in being for ten, twenty, or thirty years.

The question to be asked is: What "should" the tax structure of the United States be over the remaining years of this century? As the alternative schemes are examined in the light of this meaningful "constitutional" question, some approach to general agreement is within the realm of the possible. The question to be avoided is: What "should" the tax structure of the United States be over the years of the Carter administration, when the Democratic Party retains control over both the executive and the legislative branches of government? To the extent that this latter question informs those who advocate "tax reform," the scope for meaningful improvement in the tax system is necessarily eliminated.

Our society faces a critical choice. The tax system can be treated as a part of the general rules of order within which we live, rules that allow us to make rational long-term plans, or the tax system can be used as the institutional means through which members of a dominant political majority secure profits at the expense of others in the community. If we observe the current political discussion, it may seem that the second of these images dominates the scene. But if we value the liberties of persons, interacting with one another in a free society bound only by general rules of order, we must retain some faith that the current confusion will soon be dispelled, and that Americans will yet recover some of the wisdom of their Founding Fathers.

The Relevance of
Constitutional Strategy

It would be erroneous to interpret Peter Bernholz's paper as another argument for a commodity-based monetary standard, and it would also be amiss to interpret the paper somewhat more generally as an argument for monetary rules (that is, for some monetary constitution) as opposed to nonconstrained discretionary authority on the issue of modern central banks.[1] The paper is, of course, both of these; it does contain a powerful argument for monetary rules, and it does come down in favor of a commodity-based standard. These two strands of discussion are imbedded in a genuinely massive array of data from the monetary histories of many nations, an array that will in itself insure the paper's longevity. Peter Bernholz has established himself as perhaps the world's leading authority on the comparative history of inflations.

I want in my comment, however, to emphasize a feature of the Bernholz paper that is more important than any of those noted above. I refer to the innovative integration of what we may call "constitutional strategy" into the discussion.

A Methodological Schema

I propose to examine the Bernholz discussion in terms of a general methodological schema that can then be used in particular applications, including monetary policy. There are two categorically distinct classifications: *the theory of economic policy* on the one hand and *constitutional political economy*

From *Cato Journal* 6 (Fall 1986): 513–17. Reprinted by permission of the publisher.

1. Peter Bernholz, "The Implementation and Maintenance of a Monetary Constitution," *Cato Journal* 6 (Fall 1986): 477–511.

on the other. In the first category, analysis (whether positive or normative) is limited to the constraint that the basic institutions through which policy actions are taken are considered invariant. In the second main category, these institutions are considered to be variable, and alternative regimes are subject to examination.

There is a further breakdown within the two main categories. Within each category, I separate positive analysis from normative, and, further, I distinguish two types of positive analysis and two types of normative analysis under each main category.

A Methodological Schema

I. Theory of Economic Policy

A. Positive

1. Incidence and effects of alternative policy choices under given institutional arrangements.
2. Analysis of the predicted behavior of agents empowered to make choices under given institutional arrangements.

B. Normative

1. Argument in support of policy choice norms preferred by analyst independent of possible constraints derived from analysis under IA-2.
2. Argument in support of policy choice norms preferred by analyst as constrained by behavioral predictions derived in IA-2.

II. Constitutional Political Economy

A. Positive

1. Incidence and effects of alternative rules, regimes, or institutions within which policy choices are made by designated agents.
2. Analysis of the predicted behavior of persons and groups involved in making changes in the basic rules or institutions.

B. Normative

1. Argument in support of rules or institutions preferred by analyst independent of possible constraints derived from analysis under IIA-2.
2. Argument in support of rules or institutions preferred by analyst as constrained by behavioral predictions derived from analysis of IIA-2.

Theory of economic policy

Consider first, subcategory IA-1 of the schema (see below), the domain of the traditional theory of monetary policy. Here the analyst examines the effects of alternative policy actions that the authorized agents may take under existing institutions. This sort of analysis is conceptualized as offering potential input into the actual policy choices of agents empowered to make decisions. Bernholz is essentially unconcerned about this type of inquiry.

At the outset of his discussion, Bernholz focuses on the inquiry under subcategory IA-2, namely, an analysis of the incentive structure faced by agents empowered to act within existing institutions and an explanation-prediction of those agents' behavior. Bernholz suggests that existing monetary regimes exhibit an inflationary bias due to the vulnerability of agents to the unidirectional political pressures toward inflation. He backs up his prediction with a carefully prepared exhibition of data drawn from the experience of many countries over long periods of time.

As the shift is made into the normative theory of policy, Bernholz pays little or no attention to the idealized policy pattern that might characterize perfect adherence to the dictates of some agreed-on or postulated social welfare function. The possible content of discussion under IB-1 does not interest him because it is deemed to be irrelevant. The prior analysis under IA-2 offers the essential input into that of IB-2, and here the normative argument comes down clearly for rule-directed behavior of monetary agents.

Constitutional political economy

The second major category, constitutional political economy, is subdivided analogously to the first category. Under subcategory IIA-1, I have included positive analyses of the operations of alternative sets of rules, arrangements, or regimes. In monetary matters, this area of inquiry involves comparisons of the predicted working properties of commodity-based standards, competitive money regimes, discretionary fiat issue by governmental agencies, rule-constrained fiat issue, and others. Analyses here must, of course, draw on and use that summarized under IA-2. Most of the positive analysis that has emerged under constitutional economics could be classified as falling within subcategory IIA-1.

The innovative feature of the Bernholz paper lies in the specific inclusion of the inquiry that I have labelled under subcategory IIA-2, that is, the attempt to explain and predict the choices among regimes, and the analyses of the processes through which constitutional-institutional changes or reforms are made. Almost no research has been devoted to this area of inquiry. As I have noted in the schema, the analysis in IIA-2 is analogous to that in IA-2, where an attempt is made to explain and predict choices among policy actions within existing institutions. In IA-2, analysis concentrates on the incentive structure faced by agents empowered to make choices, and it is from this structure that the prediction of the inflationary bias emerges. In IIA-2, by comparison, analysis concentrates on the pressures toward constitutional changes in existing institutions.

Toward a Positive Theory of Constitutional Choice

Why has this area of inquiry (under IIA-2) been neglected? In part the answer lies in the generalized failure of economists to consider constitutional rules, that is, to examine the institutions through which policy must be implemented, and to undertake the research summarized in the second major category of the schema. Modern public choice theory has been instrumental in correcting this neglect, but, within public choice itself, we may still ask why so little attention has been paid to what may be called the "positive theory of constitutional choice."

The answer to this more specific question is complex. Those of us who have long held that policy reform can come only through changes in the rules of politics and who have called on economists to shift their attention to the constitutional stage have implicitly assumed that such a shift, in itself, largely eliminates the dilemma-like setting that prevents preferred policy patterns from emerging at the level of choices dictated by given institutional arrangements. In a sense, we have implicitly assumed that there is a total transformation in the choice setting when we shift from choices within given institutional regimes to choices among the regimes themselves. If the incentive structure for persons in identified roles is such as to prevent normatively preferred patterns of outcomes from being realized, then it is deemed necessary to change the incentive structure by placing choosers in positions where precise identification of roles becomes impossible. The Buchanan-

Tullock veil of uncertainty and the Rawlsian veil of ignorance are familiar devices that tend to accomplish this total transformation of the choice setting as between the two levels.

In effect, Bernholz pulls us up short and suggests that, after all, we are caught up in our own histories. We cannot consider constitutional change *carte blanche,* and, hence, we will tend to react to proposals for changes in the rules in terms of an incentive structure that can be subjected to examination by economists. While we may want to acknowledge that there are categorical differences between choices among alternative policy actions within existing institutional arrangements and choices among the arrangements themselves, we need not go all the way to postulate that there is no positive analysis relevant to institutional choices—that is, to the choices of rules shaping individual choice sets. We need not presume, as our practice might have suggested, that subcategory IIA-2 is empty of potential content. If, however, we bypass IIA-2, there is no relevant content in subcategory IIB-2, the second of the normative subcategories that I have included under constitutional political economy. If the second major category here is restricted so as to eliminate IIA-2, then analysis in IIA-1 allows the analyst to shift directly to IIB-1 when he seeks to advance arguments in support of preferred rules, quite independent of the rule-feasibility set that the analysis of IIA-2 might allow him to define.

Conclusion

I apologize for what is surely an overly taxonomic comment. Let me conclude by summarizing the Bernholz argument. There is an inflationary bias in the operation of existing monetary arrangements. This bias stems from the incentive structure that agents confront when making policy choices. Analysis of alternative institutional structures suggests that such bias can be eliminated only under some commodity-based monetary standard. As historical examples and analysis indicate, reforms in monetary rules in the direction indicated to be preferred can be predicted to occur only in specific circumstances defined by the incentives faced by relevant interest groups in modern democracies. In particular, Bernholz suggests, only after periods of moderate, but not hyper-, inflations can sufficient political support be mustered for the directionally preferred basic shifts in monetary rules.

The domain of strategy for constitutional reform must be opened up for intensive inquiry by constitutional economists. In a very real sense, the strategy of constitutional reform must be prepared well in advance so that when circumstances are right, those who recognize them to be such can indeed "seize the day."

PART EIGHT

Reform

The Economic Constitution
and the New Deal
Lessons for Late Learners

The following is an analysis of the Roosevelt New Deal and its consequences in "constitutional" perspective. I interpret the economic legislation of the 1930s and 1940s as changes in the basic "rules of the game," whether or not these changes may be discussed in narrow, legalistic meanings. In effect, the New Deal rewrote the political economic constitution. We are living with the results, and the implications for social order and stability are still emerging. However, we have yet to learn the larger lesson that the New Deal experience should have taught us.

Constitutional Failure

Did the pre–New Deal economic constitution of the United States fail? By "economic constitution" I mean the rules of the game, or the constitution, the set of generally expected working properties of institutions of the economic-political order. This constitution was best described in minimal-state, *laissez faire* terms before the New Deal era. The role of the central government was severely circumscribed. This is not to suggest that the motives and ideas in the New Deal were without precursors or that legal and political precedents were wholly absent. The Progressive Era had laid some of the ideational ground-work for New Deal change, and the legal gates had been partially ajar at least

From *Regulatory Change in an Atmosphere of Crisis: Current Implications of the Roosevelt Years,* ed. Gary Walton (New York: Academic Press, 1979), 13–26. Reprinted by permission of the publisher.

since *Munn* v. *Illinois,* and, perhaps most important, the Federal Reserve Board had been emplaced with some elements of national monetary coordination.

To some extent I refer to prevailing public attitudes about the economic order. I think that J. R. T. Hughes had presented convincing evidence that the American attitudes never did embody much positive faith in the working of markets.[1] However, I think that pre–New Deal attitudes about the efficacy of political interference with the economic order were dramatically different from the attitudes that followed. The governmental habit, according to Hughes, was one of piecemeal, pragmatic restriction. The price of milk might be legislated by New York, there being no prevailing public philosophy that said that it should not be, but this was not the same as, nor was it conceived to be the same as, an attempt to coordinate milk pricing and milk marketing nationwide, much less to coordinate the pricing and allocative structure of the existing economy. The latter action was simply not dreamt of in existing public philosophy, again excepting the establishment of the Federal Reserve Board. The economic constitution prior to the New Deal was described as being *laissez faire* in the literal sense; it was not *laissez faire* in its publicly conceived philosophical foundations. Markets were expected to coordinate activities across sectors and regions, because a governmental role in such activity was inconceivable.

In retrospect, we may view the New Deal as having made such a governmental role conceivable to public consciousness. However, this does not suggest that there was a positive motivation for the political coordination of the economy. When we ask, first, why the New Deal made forays beyond the pale previously defined, and, second, why it was at least partially successful in securing acceptability in the public mind, we must look to the negative side of motivation—the almost complete absence of alternatives.

Considered in toto, the economic constitution of the 1920s failed with the Great Depression; coordination broke down. The system did not deliver, and it was seen not to deliver. Normal expectations were not met. The New Deal moved in by default. In the setting of the Great Depression, and without a prevailing public philosophy or understanding of the relative successes and failures of the system's several parts, is there really much surprise that, like a

---

1. J. R. T. Hughes, *The Governmental Habit* (New York: Basic Books, 1977).

wounded animal, the body politic should have launched out into ill-conceived, mutually contradictory, and self-defeating policies? The economic policies of the New Deal were simplistic in the extreme and were naively conceived. In short, they were confused reactions to particular institutional circumstances when there seemed to be urgent need for corrective action. Prices had fallen— so why not try to raise prices by legislative-administrative fiat? Men were unemployed—so why not introduce work-sharing schemes? What harm could be done by setting floors on wages and restricting hours? Why not "plow under all the little pigs" that were in surplus? Since employers did not provide jobs, why not give unions more power? The coal industry was in trouble— so why not cartelize the structure and encourage industry-wide unionization of its labor force? If the price level was tied to gold, why not devalue and improve everything? If full employment was desired, why not have the government guarantee it?

As the aforementioned questions suggest, the New Deal policy responses made up a motley set. In part, they reflected positive reactions to pressures from special interests. In part, they reflected the legislative versions of wild-eyed professors' dreams. In part, they represented the best intentions of legislators who had neither the time nor the competence to examine their long-range consequences. The absence of effectively presented alternatives was perhaps the characteristic feature of all New Deal policy.

There was no sense or understanding of the vital distinction between the constitutional framework of an economy and the operation of the interdependent markets within this constitutional framework. We now know, in retrospect, that a modicum of discrimination would have led to the diagnosis that *only* the monetary elements in the economic constitution had somehow failed and that these elements should have been the direct target for improvement and change.

But this was not to be. In the absence of an offsetting public philosophy and relying on the governmental habit of piecemeal interference with markets, the New Deal placed on the governmental-political structure tasks that it should never have been expected to perform. The failures of the administrative bureaucracy were not, however, to be recognized for decades; and moreover, there was widespread conversion to the socialist-inspired doctrine that governments know best and can solve all problems. Arms and agencies of the central government proliferated, and Washington became the American capital city. In all of this, it is perhaps not surprising that, along with the confusion, some genuinely constitutional improvements were made, some changes in the rules of the game that proved to produce greater stability and efficiency.

What Might Have Been

It is indeed interesting for us to speculate on the half century of history that might have taken place if the distinction between the organizational-constitutional framework and the operation of markets within such framework could have been clearly conceived and if policy could have been based on such a conception. What might have been accomplished? What permanent damages to our social fabric might have been avoided? Suppose that the political leaders of the early 1930s, Hoover and/or Roosevelt along with their advisers and the leading members of Congress, could have recognized early that the monetary framework was in shambles. Suppose they could have seen that the breakdown in the American economy could be traced directly to the failures of the fractional reserve banking system interlinked with a national monetary standard tied to gold reserves and with powers of interference resting with the Federal Reserve Board. Suppose that the system's extreme vulnerability to waves of contraction and expansion could have been identified, along with the accompanying recognition that the Federal Reserve authorities were empowered to act without knowledge of what they were about. Suppose that, upon such diagnosis, action could have been taken, early in the 1930s, to sweep away the residues of monetary disaster and to start afresh with a genuinely new "monetary constitution." Suppose that United States currency issue could have been wholly and finally divorced from gold with the limits of fiat issue defined either by a monetary growth rule or by some linkage to a price index. Along with these changes, suppose that 100% reserve banking could have been introduced. It boggles the mind to think what might have been, especially if we assume that the political leaders could have possessed the wisdom that would have allowed them to shun multifarious political interferences with the market process.

Aside from the latter constraint, we may be surprised when we look at the record to see how close we might have been to the enactment of basic components of genuinely permanent reform in the monetary constitution. We know that there were some economists, notably Irving Fisher as well as several members of the University of Chicago group, who were, at the time, calling for monetary-policy reform along the lines sketched. However, these ideas were also in the forefront of discussion and action in the Congress, and, in the almost-anything-goes atmosphere that must have been characteristic of those exciting days, it might have been only an accident that prevented our getting more effective revision in our economic constitution. Robert Weintraub's recent paper on Wright Patman is of great interest in providing historical detail.[2] Citation at some length is warranted here, both for the intrinsic value of the factual record and for the support that this record lends to my argument that New Deal policy emerged from confused blundering rather than from rational action by political men or from some quasi-mysterious, efficient, institutional response to historical events.

> During the early 1930s, Congress worked its will on a number of bills providing for the issue of additional currency by open market and other operations in such amount as was necessary to increase the index of wholesale prices *back* to the 1921–29 (or, alternatively, the 1926) average, and thereafter to control the issue of currency (sometimes the reference was to currency plus check deposits) so as to stabilize the index at that level. . . . [The Goldsborough] bill declared it "the policy of the United States that the average purchasing power of the dollar as ascertained by the Department of Labor in the wholesale commodity markets for the period covering the years 1921 to 1929 inclusive, shall be restored and maintained by the control of the volume of credit and currency."
>
> The House passed the Goldsborough bill by a vote of 289 to 60 on May 2, 1932, Mr. Patman voting aye. The bill was killed by the Banking Committee of the Senate. It was vigorously opposed by the Hoover Administration and the Federal Reserve. Fed witnesses (Mayer and Miller) questioned the validity of indexing prices and denied the Fed had powers to fix and stabilize (even approximately) the purchasing power of money. Carter Glass, now a Senator, played the crucial legislative role killing the Goldsborough bill. Goldsborough was scathing in his denunciation of Glass.

2. R. E. Weintraub, "Some Neglected Monetary Contributions: Congressman Wright Patman (1893–1976)," *Journal of Money, Credit, and Banking* (November 1977): 517–28. Reprinted by permission of the Ohio State University Press.

Addressing the House on June 8 after his bill had been killed, he said, "Some 10 days ago the distinguished Senator from Virginia stated on the floor of the Senate that he would not be willing to give the power provided in this bill to any seven men that God ever made. Does not the Senator from Virginia know that the Federal Reserve System is now exercising these vast powers in an absolutely uncontrolled manner, and does he not know that this legislation would be a limitation upon their powers and their discretion?"

Wright Patman introduced a stable money bill on June 4, 1934. His bill called for redeeming Federal Reserve notes and all other outstanding currency with Treasury notes (greenbacks) and issuing the new currency "in payment of the ordinary expenses of the Federal Government" until there is substantially full employment at the wage and price levels of 1926, and thereafter restricting issue to "a rate not to exceed four percentum per annum." In addition, commercial banks would be required to keep 100 percent reserves in Federal Reserve banks behind demand deposits (and 5 percent behind other deposits) and under the direction of a new Federal Monetary Authority. Federal Reserve banks were to buy and sell securities . . . if the wholesale index fell or rose by 5 percent above or below the 1926 level.

That bill never got off the ground. The Patman (Bonus) bill did. It was an end run that almost succeeded in incorporating variants of the two main principles of the stable money movement of the 1930s into law. First, it provided for reflation. The Treasury would be required . . . to pay for the Adjusted Service Certificates, by having engraved and printed new noninterest-bearing, tax-exempt legal tender Treasury notes; i.e., greenbacks. Second the Patman (Bonus) bill provided for contracting Federal Reserve notes upon a finding by the Secretary of the Treasury that it was necessary to do so to maintain the index of wholesale prices at the 1921–29 level. His bill did not, however, provide for any subsequent currency expansion "beyond implementing the bonus." It was focused on current problems and fears.

The bill passed the House on March 22, 1935, and the Senate on May 7. President Roosevelt vetoed it on May 22. The House overrode the veto the same day by a vote of 324 to 98 against. However, the president's veto was sustained by the Senate the next day, 54 voting for overriding but a 2/3 vote being necessary to override. [Weintraub, "Some Neglected Monetary Contributions," 520–21.]

What Was

What might have been, indeed. But, out of the lashing about, there did emerge a basic change in the monetary constitution, one that has survived the tests both of time and of critical evaluation. Although it did not seize the day and create a full-reserve banking structure, the Congress in 1933 went for the next-best option and introduced governmental insurance of bank deposits. As it has turned out, the results have not been too different from those that might have been generated under the 100% reserve system, although, characteristically, more bureaucratic supervision and control necessarily accompanies the insurance scheme. Deposit insurance has modified the economic history of the half century more than many other measures, and it stands in an extremely confined set of institutional changes that must be adjudged to have proved beneficial.

Aside from this single measure, however, the crisis-generated opportunity to reform the monetary constitution constructively was muffed, and the emergence of the Keynesian theory in 1936 simultaneously distracted attention away from monetary institutions and laid the foundations for the gradual destruction of an important part of the fiscal constitution, the rule of budget balance. Economists were reasonably quick to support fiscal policy, which in practice meant deficit spending, and to give it a predominant role in demand management. The politicians were slow learners, but ultimately they were converted to an economics that played directly to their natural proclivities. Economists remained blithely unaware of the implications of their teachings concerning the constraining rule of budget balance, with consequences that are now available for all to see.[3] As with so many of depression-inspired changes in the basic economic constitution, however, these consequences would not emerge full blown for decades.

The opportunity to amend the nation's monetary constitution faded into

---

3. For an elaboration of the history and an analysis, see James M. Buchanan and Richard E. Wagner, *Democracy in Deficit: The Political Legacy of Lord Keynes* (New York: Academic Press, 1977).

limbo after 1936, and the elementary confusion between constitutional structure and the system operating within that structure continued to characterize public and political reality. At this point, my critics may appropriately ask, "But was not macroeconomics born in 1936, and is this not precisely the sort of distinction that you emphasize?" There are both similarities and differences between the constitutional-operational distinction that I stress and the more familiar distinction of post-Keynesian macroeconomics-microeconomics. Some comparative discussion is warranted, and it may be argued that the Keynesian impact was to add to the confusion rather than to the enlightenment. In my own conception, a constitutional rule defines a process or structure within which certain results, sometimes referred to as end states, emerge from the behavioral interaction of many persons, each one of whom acts independently, subject to the constraints that he privately confronts. Consider the example that was discussed by the Congress in the early New Deal period, a proposal that would direct a monetary authority to stabilize the general price level. This proposal qualifies as a constitutional rule because it establishes the absolute price level as a predictable component of an economy within which the allocation of resources and the setting of relative prices emerge from the independent actions of many decision makers interacting in many interrelated markets. In one sense, we may say that stability in the absolute price level is an end-state characteristic, desirable in itself. However, in the larger sense, and relevant to my argument, this price-level stability is a *facilitative condition* for the effective functioning of the economy, a functioning that allows the specifically desired results to be generated. Such a rule may be compared and contrasted with the full-employment objective that emerged directly from Keynesian economics and that found its political embodiment in the Full Employment Act of 1946, an act that must be included in any comprehensive catalog of New Deal policy.

Full employment is in itself a highly desirable end state, and its attribute as an end state dominates any facilitative role that its achievement might otherwise play in the functioning of the economy. The desired end state, full employment, *should* emerge from the operation of the market process, provided that the constitutional framework which constrains this process is correctly designed and implemented. However, to direct governmental policy instrumentally toward the attainment of the full-employment end state is necessarily to distract attention from the facilitative conditions that might be required to generate the same result. If the government may instrumentally legislate full employment, what logical consistency remains in an argument that government should not legislate particularized end states for resource use, for prices, for income shares, for rates of growth, for regional economic performance, and for urban and rural development? The post-Keynesian policy emphasis on the employment objective seemed congenial to the natural proclivities of the American politicians to restrict markets pragmatically, and its effects were largely to expand both the public and the political willingness to interfere on increasingly grandiose scales. The post–New Deal conventional wisdom essentially reversed the standing orders of American politics. "Don't just stand there, do something" emerged to characterize both New Deal and post–New Deal political history. The public's measure of political progress came to be discussed in terms of the number of bills passed by the Congress rather than the opposite, and, even in skeptical 1978, the absurd implications of this legislative-quantity criterion seem hardly to be recognized.

I shall not trace in detail the history of post–New Deal follies that were inspired by the threshold piercing patterns of the early federal interventions of the 1930s and 1940s. While Eisenhower slumbered with us through the 1950s, the bureaucratic empire expanded, agencies matured, and attitudes ossified. Few recognized that these were but the cocoon stages for the New Frontier–Great Society activism, surely the apogee for all those who dared to dream of a federally orchestrated and controlled national economy. However, the politicians had finally learned that Keynesian economics had made them free; they could spend without either taxation or guilt. Economists played fine tunes as inflation's fires began to kindle. Johnson's Great Society program was a blunderbuss attempt to implement the New Deal promises that were never intended to move beyond politicians' rhetoric. The transfer society emerged to pass a critical inflection point around 1965.

Environmentalism moved in to capture the romantic fancy of those for whom the New Deal promises had become stale. The established bureaucracy was ready to oblige; regulatory agencies again proliferated, with the costs largely left out of any decision calculus. The arrogant presumption that there is such a thing as free air dominated discussion.

What Is

So much for a selected and personalized sketch of the American history of earlier times. It is now appropriate to freeze the lens and to examine critically the situation that we confront in 1978. I shall discuss only three features: (a) the bureaucratic paradox, (b) the institutional lock-in, and (c) monetary-fiscal disarray.

THE BUREAUCRATIC PARADOX

Federal benevolence, the predominant image from the 1930s through the 1960s, became federal bureaucracy in the 1970s, with the implication that words in the public philosophy do have meaning. In this respect, the New Deal attitudinal syndrome has disappeared; the faith has gone.[4] Was not the January 1978 funeral celebration for Hubert Humphrey the final acknowledgment that the New Deal flame was not eternal?

We now live with an absence of public confidence in politicians and bureaucrats along with the absence of belief that political-bureaucratic institutions can accomplish results that are either desired or intended. This loss of public confidence in government is solidly grounded. At the level of ordinary observation, political institutions seem to have failed. This perception is supported by sophisticated empirical test results. Accompanying this empirical assessment of the record, there has been the growing acceptance of a theory of political and bureaucratic process that allows us to predict results closely resembling those that we can directly observe.[5] The romantic image of politics as the pure pursuit of public interest has been shattered, perhaps beyond repair.

A paradox arises when we observe the continuing proliferation of federal regulatory bureaucracy simultaneously with the shift in public attitudes toward it. New and expanded tasks are assigned to politics and to administra-

4. This shift in public attitudes is acknowledged and discussed from a perspective quite different from my own in Henry J. Aaron, *Politics and the Professors* (Washington: Brookings Institution, 1978).

5. The theory of public choice can be interpreted in this sense of a "theory of governmental failure" akin to the "theory of market failure" that described the theoretical welfare economics of the 1930s through the 1950s.

tive bureaucracy while, at the same time and at other levels of consideration, there is little or no expectation that these tasks will be, or possibly could be, accomplished satisfactorily. How do we explain this?[6]

Three separate explanations may be advanced. Each is partially correct, but, in my view, the first two are subsidiary in relevance to the third. First, the pattern of events does seem to support those who say that government acts and expands its range of controls quite independent of the desires of the citizenry. The observed increase in the size and scope of the political sector may be due to the internal dynamics of a bureaucracy that has attained a life force of its own, subject only to some ultimate threshold constraints imposed by its ability to squeeze resources from the productive elements in the economy. In such a vision of our world, there is really no paradox to be explained.

In a second view, as in the first, there is no anomaly in the results that we observe. The so-called paradox emerges only when we try to impose a unified order on what must be a very complex set of collective-choice institutions. In this second model, unlike the first, there is no independently acting government at all. There is only a complex and interrelated set of institutions, constrained by intricate rules and standing orders. Out of this structure, results emerge that may embody little or no internal coherence, either from the viewpoint of the citizenry or of the bureaucracy itself. It is, therefore, not surprising that some extensions of regulatory control occur simultaneously with other thrusts toward deregulation. It is not a source of wonder that political leaders espouse constraints on the dominance of federal government while actively promoting increasing federal intrusion into economic activity.

As was suggested, there is surely explanatory power in each of these alternative models of modern governmental process. My emphasis here, however, is on a third explanation or model, one in which the "paradox" terminology takes on a more acceptable meaning. We observe a continuing expansion of the political-governmental-collective sector of the economy at the expense of the private market–individual sector. We recognize the presence of an increasing public consciousness of political-governmental failure because to-

---

6. For a treatment that parallels this discussion in some respects, see James M. Buchanan, *The Limits of Liberty* (Chicago: University of Chicago Press, 1975).

day, as in the 1930s, there is simply no positive public philosophy that contains a nongovernmental alternative. As contrasted with the first explanation above, the third model does allow generalized public preferences to be met via political-bureaucratic institutions, at least in broad directional terms. Further, as contrasted with the second model, the outcomes predicted need not be internally inconsistent. In the third model, however, the coherence of outcomes critically depends on the presence of an integrating philosophy of social order. One of the central themes of this chapter is that the United States has lacked such a philosophy for at least a century. The crisis atmosphere of the Great Depression allowed for a basic revision of the economic constitution, but this revision was scarcely conscious, and its occurrence was sensed only by members of a Supreme Court who were made to seem mental fossils by the onrush of events. The constitutional revolution of the New Deal was implicit, and, because it was so, the results were not coherent. The New Deal amounted to revolution by default.

The dreams of the New Deal–New Frontier–Great Society have faded because, in a real sense, there was no system to those dreams. The pragmatic patchwork has clearly failed. We find ourselves in a situation somewhat analogous to that of the early 1930s, but there is no crisis, at least not yet, and constitutional revolution does not seem likely to occur by default again. In the 1930s, the system had failed, and, in emergency, we turned to untested, untried, socialist-inspired alternatives, as packaged pragmatically by New Deal advocates. In the 1970s and 1980s, by contrast, there is no untested option that commands more than minimal public support. There is no "Old Deal" waiting in the wings, a movement that might sweep away the political-bureaucratic maze created by a half century of history. Those persons who see hope in the current thrust toward deregulation should look at results, not at rhetoric. Surely the energy policy of 1978 reflects the paradox in unalloyed form. There is little or no public understanding of or faith in the ability of the market process, which offers the only alternative to bureaucracy. Politically, we struggle to choose between two institutional forms, neither one of which commands public respect or engenders public confidence.

THE INSTITUTIONAL LOCK-IN

It is much easier to explain why political-bureaucratic structures, once created, are unlikely to be dismantled than it is to explain why new empires are started. Once a governmental program is instituted, a specific clientele is born, with clearly defined interests in both the maintenance and the expansion of the program's benefits. These interests make themselves felt politically, with the familiar concentration of pressures toward expansion as opposed to the dissipated opposition reflected in the generality of the taxes used to finance the benefits. Even if the structure of a program is widely acknowledged as producing undesired results, it may prove politically impossible to work out the set of compromises and compensations that would be required either to replace or to reform the program in accordance with the promotion of shared objectives.

The OASI (social security) program offers the single example worthy of brief discussion. The Roosevelt New Deal was the political vehicle for this Bismarkian transplant onto hitherto alien American ground. Initially, all was promise; little was delivered. The pie was in the sky in the 1930s, but even future pies require resource commitments, and the initial notion was that there would be gradual accumulation of tax-financed fund reserves to meet future benefit commitments. But who could have been so naive as to expect elected politicians in a democracy to tax the citizenry in the absence of currently observed benefits? The 1939 changes in the legislation were telegraphed from the start. The system became an unfunded, pay-as-we-go transfer mechanism, shifting funds from currently productive taxpayers—wage earners to currently retired beneficiaries. However, so long as the labor force was expanding rapidly relative to those who were made eligible for benefits, the tax-transfer costs seemed negligible, and pie remained in the sky for most of those who paid the taxes. New benefits were added, at little apparent political cost and with great political payoffs, and social security was, for decades, acclaimed as one of the New Deal's shining monuments.

What happened? In 1978, it is difficult to find articulate, informed defenders of the massive tax-transfer system that currently exists. Almost everyone will say, "How nice it might have been had it been differently organized." The tax-transfer mechanism now in place is widely acknowledged to have a major adverse impact on the rate of productivity growth in the American economy, both from its direct effect on labor inputs and its indirect effect on capital formation. Claims against the system represent the most important item in national wealth in behavioristic terms, yet there is no real stock of wealth existent to meet such claims. To dismantle the system would amount to disavowing these claims; to continue the system amounts to sapping the nation's productive potential. Through time, the tax-transfer system will force American workers to transfer more of their incomes to the provision of retirement stipends than their own preferences would dictate. Conceptually, reform should be possible that would embody compensations such that all persons might be made better off than they are under the current system. However, such reform may be impossible to implement politically.[7]

MONETARY-FISCAL DISARRAY

Earlier I noted that the 1930s were characterized by an absence of any understanding of the distinction between the constitutional structure of an economy and the operation of the related markets within that structure. It would, indeed, be satisfying if I could, at this point, assert that intellectual progress has been great, that such an understanding has now become much more widespread. Such an assertion would reflect wishful thinking rather than reality. We need only look to the 1978 public, political, and academic discussion of employment and inflation to see that the confusion is almost as prevalent now as it was then.

Keynesian economics effectively destroyed an important part of the previously existing fiscal constitution: the rule of budget balance. This rule, which was interpreted to be a constraint on budgets except during emergencies, forced decision makers to measure the opportunity costs of governmental spending programs with reasonable accuracy. In the absence of this rule, these costs are lowered; spending programs seem less costly than they are. Government spending expands disproportionately. Deficits have become permanent and are accelerating in size with time. Politically, however, it has become impossible to achieve a regime of budget balance regardless of the macroeconomic setting.

Even this obvious flaw in the fiscal-monetary constitution might be contained with little other than a pronounced public-spending bias if there should exist an offsetting monetary constitution, a rule or set of rules that would allow for predictability in the structural macroeconomic setting. However,

---

7. For a discussion of the problems here, see James M. Buchanan, "Comment on Browning's Paper," in *Financing Social Security,* ed. C. Campbell (Washington: American Enterprise Institute, 1979), 208–12.

no such set of rules describes the post-Keynesian economy of the 1970s. Budget deficits place on monetary authorities the conflicting requirements to maintain reasonable stability in interest rates and in the general price level while, at the same time, being charged with concern for both the full employment objective and the position of the dollar in international currency markets. Stagflation has become the observed result, and the developing expectation seems to be that the discretion of the politicians and of the monetary authorities can be counted on only to keep both inflation and unemployment within tolerable bounds, with the acknowledged resource costs that both of these phenomena embody.

Implications for Reform

What are some of the implications of the New Deal experience, considered in its totality, for our time, for potential reform in the 1980s?

Several elements of my answer to this question have been evident in my discussion of recent history. We must learn to make the distinction between the constitutional structure or framework of an economy and the operations of institutions constrained within this framework. We must learn that the market process does present a viable alternative to bureaucratic chaos, provided only that the framework, the laws and institutions, are properly constructed. We must learn, and learn better, the central principle of economic theory, the principle of the spontaneous coordination achieved only by market process. We must learn the simple lessons of public-choice theory, which teach that politics and the political man cannot be predicted to promote some vaguely defined public interest.

We must learn these lessons in order to better design and control the political economy. Economics is not like astronomy, in that the movement of the stars is not within man's powers of control. In economics, we learn to predict how an economy operates under alternative institutional constraints, and these constraints do not evolve naturally in some ineluctable process of history. We learn about them in order to design improvements, and we look to the political-governmental process to implement and to enforce change. We learn economics in order to make better political decisions and in order to use our intelligence to reform the constitutional setting within which we are to operate as economizing agents.

In our blundering efforts as professional economists, we have been far too preoccupied with efficiency as the end-state characteristic in the operation of an economy. We have talked about "market failure" and "market success" almost exclusively in efficiency terms. We have said far too little about the political function of market organization, about the liberty of markets, and about the voluntary features of trade that are necessarily removed by the shift to any collective alternative. Democratic politics, too, must be constrained within a constitutional framework, and such politics can function only if their operational tasks are severely limited. The market's primary role is to allow depoliticization of major areas of allocative choice. We have said far too little about the "justice of markets," despite the fact that Adam Smith put much stress on this element in his historic book. It is a violation of "the justice of his natural liberty" to restrain the teen-aged black from employment through a minimum-wage law, quite apart from and beyond its effect on efficiency.

If the "we" in my answers here referred only to professional economists, there might be some grounds for cautious optimism. Some solutions are to be found here and there in our literature, and other elements may be found lurking between the lines. But professional economists are not likely to be assigned roles as philosopher kings, and they are equally unlikely to be called upon to give advice to genuinely benevolent despots. The "we" must refer, not to the professional economists, but to the general public, and, in some more inclusive sense, to all those who act in various ways to influence policy and politicians. What should the experience of 50 years have taught us, as professional economists, about the potential for the attainment of wisdom on the part of the public?

To the naive among us, the results might suggest the need for more and better economic education, carrying more or less the content that our curricula now embody, but here we run squarely up against the evidence that modern university economics does not provide the normative understanding that I have called for in the foregoing. Instead, the evidence suggests that such instruction provides no understanding for students that is retained for periods sufficiently long to make the whole exposure relevant. Indeed, perhaps the cynics who offer that the best to be said for instruction in economics is that it is better than instruction in sociology are right, at least in their low opinion of university economics. In any case, let us acknowledge that the elementary textbooks must be rewritten; the courses and curricula redesigned. We must cease our efforts to make students into imaginary social engineers on the one hand or into empty empiricists on the other. It is more important that law and ethics enter economics than it is that economics enter law and ethics.

Nevertheless, we must not be apologetic for our subject matter or demeaning to the normative philosophic position that defines it. We are the keepers and the transmitters of intellectually respectable arguments that defend the structural features of the only societies in history that have been free and prosperous. Without renewed efforts at explicit articulation of this defense, pragmatic and unprincipled politics will generate results desired by no one. If the New Deal and its consequences teach us anything at all, it surely must be that a society lacking a public philosophy must drift toward its own Sargasso Sea.

Acknowledgment

I am indebted to my colleagues Robert Tollison and Gordon Tullock for helpful suggestions.

Sources of Opposition to
Constitutional Reform

In this chapter I seek to examine the sources of opposition to constitutional reform, independent of the specific form or direction of proposals for change.[1] For me, this task is difficult because the constructivist-contractarian-constitutionalist position has always seemed sufficiently self-evident to make methodological defense unnecessary. I continue to be surprised when I encounter persons, whose intellectual stature commands respect and attention, who explicitly take an anticonstitutionalist stance. What are the sources of their ideas? How do they conceptualize sociopolitical order? How do they model their own roles in social interaction?

It is necessary at the outset to clarify an important distinction between straightforward opposition to general constitutional change, as such, and opposition that stems from what may be called a genuine anticonstitutionalist mentality. The sources of opposition discussed in the first two sections of this chapter need not reflect anticonstitutionalism in some conceptual sense. In the third section I examine a particular position that is broadly summarized under the term *majoritarian*. The fourth section introduces what I call a *rights* position, which embodies constitutionalist elements while at the same time reflecting anticonstitutionalism in political argument. In

From *Constitutional Economics: Containing the Economic Powers of Government*, ed. Richard B. McKenzie (Lexington, Mass.: D. C. Heath, 1984), 21–34.

1. I am indebted to Peter Bernholz, Geoffrey Brennan, and Viktor Vanberg for helpful comments on earlier drafts. The important debates between proponents and opponents of this or that proposal for constitutional reform are outside the scope of this chapter. Arguments may, of course, be advanced in opposition to particular proposals for constitutional reform, while remaining within the general constitutionalist perspective.

the fifth section I examine the fundamental element of the anticonstitutionalist mind set, that which involves conceptualization of democratic process. The last section represents my attempt to collect the several strands of the argument into a coherent summary that may offer some basis for elaboration.

Constitutional Reform and the Constitutional Perspective

The constitutional perspective embodies a two-stage (or multistage) conceptual model of behavior, whether the acting entity is the person, the voluntary association, or the inclusive collectivity. Decisions or choices over alternative *outcomes* or end states are made within the constraints of well-defined operating *rules* (institutions). In the deliberations over choices of outcomes, the rules are provisionally fixed. But decisions or choices may also be made over alternative rules or processes that define constraints within which subsequent choices over outcomes may be made.[2]

It is possible to make the constitutional distinction between rules or processes within which postconstitutional or within-rules choices are made and the actions made within such rules without, at the same time, accepting the possibility, and hence the desirability, of making changes in the rules in any explicitly chosen sense. That is to say, a person may respect the importance of established rules and institutions but reject the full constitutionalist position, if the latter is interpreted in a constructivist manner. Whether or not the nonconstructivist who does respect processes can appropriately be called a constitutionalist is not important for my argument. It will suffice to say that, in my own interpretation of the constitutionalist perspective, rules and institutions of social order are treated as variables subject to modification, but at a very different stage from the within-rules decisions over end states.

Opposition will arise to almost any conceivable proposal for change in sociopolitical arrangements. Some persons are, by nature, conservative in their subconscious evaluation of change. They will acquiesce in institu-

2. For an early discussion, see James M. Buchanan and Gordon Tullock, *The Calculus of Consent* (Ann Arbor: University of Michigan Press, 1962).

tional change that emerges without deliberative decision; but their reaction to history is passive. They refuse to acknowledge man's power to make his own history, and they explicitly reject the notion that observed institutions of interaction are, in themselves, products of intended human action. I shall discuss the evolutionist version of this perspective in the following section. My concern in this section is with the unthinking conservative stance that does not inquire into the origins of institutional change, simply accepts that set of rules in existence, and evaluates this set as good only because such a set exists and has endured. In a somewhat bizarre use of the term, such a position might be called one of extreme constitutionalism because of its elevation of the status quo to sacredness; but it should not be classified as such in my perspective.

As proponents of this position are observed, however, they are difficult to separate from persons who oppose constitutional reform out of genuine constitutional illiteracy. The latter simply cannot enter into constructive discussion about the rules for socioeconomic order. They cannot be engaged by those who seek to suggest explicit changes in the rules. Such persons react only to perceived short-term benefits that are promised by this or that politician or party. It is impossible to ask such persons to think of their long-term interest, and it remains folly to ask them to think of the interests of the more inclusive community. These individuals tend to oppose changes in basic rules because they cannot translate the benefits that changes may offer into measurable short-term gains. The status quo tends to be supported out of ignorance rather than any adherence to the principles of conservatism outlined above. Unfortunately, most of the U.S. politics that we observe, circa 1982, seems to be based implicitly on the hypothesis that large numbers of the electorate belong to the group of persons just described.

Opposition to constitutional reform may also stem from economic self-interest in a direct sense, and need not reflect more fundamental proclivities, in either one of the types. Members of the other groups to be identified may well recognize that the basic rules (institutions) are subject to modification and change, that differing sets of rules generate differing patterns of outcomes, and that some comparative evaluation of alternative rules is possible and meaningful. Members of the groups to be mentioned here benefit or think they benefit explicitly from the operation of the status quo set of rules. I include this source of opposition to reform in my general examination because, generally speaking, the arguments advanced by members of these groups will seem indistinguishable from those that may be made by disinterested anticonstitutionalists. In a real sense, members of these groups become anticonstitutionalists in debate discussion because at a fundamental level they are indeed constitutionalists.

Included in these groups are those who administer the existing rules, the agents of the bureaucracy who have job-specific and role-specific human capital invested in the status quo. They oppose any attempt to modify institutional structure since this amounts to erosion in the value of their own endowments. A second category includes those who think themselves to be differentially advantaged by the operation of existing rules or to be especially well informed about the potential exploitability of such rules. Agents of political organizations, as well as individual politicians, may have learned the ropes, or think that they have done so, and hence may be reluctant to modify the rules as the game is being played. The uncertainty about how any changed rule will work creates possible opposition even among persons and groups who might, if they could foresee how alternatives might work, secure differential gains.

A third, and influential, category of persons who oppose reform out of economic self-interest includes the interpreters of the status quo set of rules, the constitutional lawyers in the academy, at the bar, and on the bench. The intellectual capital of the constitutional lawyer is heavily invested in the rules that exist and that have evolved through standardized thought processes and value norms of the legal insiders. Members of this group will resist any effort to shift the constitutional margins by nonjudicial means, including resistance that takes the form of attempts to choke off discussion of basic constitutional issues by those who are not accepted in their group. The in-group of constitutional lawyers is acting in this respect precisely as any protected monopoly would act; it is seeking to preserve rents. It is not surprising, therefore, when we see how few constitutional lawyers and legal scholars advocate explicit constitutional reform.

I have identified several sources of opposition to constitutional reform in this section largely to dismiss their various arguments as irrelevant to the discussion of the genuine anticonstitutionalists. These sources of opposition are included only because it is useful to be able to recognize the origins of the arguments advanced.

Institutional Evolutionists

In recent years, and notably arising from interpretations of the position of F. A. Hayek, social scientists have advanced what I shall call an *evolutionist* theory of basic social institutions.[3] In this construction, the institutions that exist are those that have somehow spontaneously evolved and survived. Because they have done so, they are efficient in at least one sense. Note that this position does offer intellectual support for the more naive conservative stance previously discussed. It does so from the presumption that it is essentially impossible to construct social rules and institutions; hence, any attempt to do so is doomed to frustration. The evolutionist position embodies respect for those rules and institutions that are observed to exist, indeed even to the extent of generating an attitude of quiescence before any of the potential proposals for reform.

Fortunately, however, many of those who seem to adopt the evolutionist perspective in some generalized methodological sense do not really act in accordance with these implications. Hayek himself is a strong advocate of fundamental constitutional change, presented in terms of very specific proposals. In practice, therefore, Hayek combines the evolutionist with the constructivist-constitutionalist perspective. Appropriately constrained, more or less as it is in Hayek's usage, the evolutionist perspective on social institutions can offer helpful counters to the sometimes romantic urges of the constitutional reformers. For those who seek, through the design and the implementation of new rules, to modify the essential nature of man, as this nature has evolved culturally through the ages, it is well that they be called up short by those who insist on the nonmalleability of basic elements in human motivation and behavior.[4] There remains nonetheless the danger that the evolutionist perspective will dampen enthusiasm for genuinely viable reform

---

3. See Buchanan, "Law and the Invisible Hand," in *Freedom in Constitutional Contract* (College Station: Texas A&M University Press, 1977), 25–39; and "Cultural Evolution and Constitutional Reform" (mimeographed for presentation at Liberty Fund Conference, Savannah, Georgia, March 1982). For a statement of Hayek's position, see the epilogue to his *The Political Order of a Free People,* vol. 3 of *Law, Legislation and Liberty* (Chicago: University of Chicago Press, 1979), 153–176.

4. For an attempt to reconcile Hayek's perspective with my own along essentially the lines suggested here, see Viktor Vanberg, *Liberaler Evolutionismus oder Vertragstheoretischer Konstitutionalismus?* (Tübingen: J. C. B. Mohr, 1981).

prospects that are consistent with human behavior, and particularly on the part of social scientists and social philosophers who might otherwise tend to be broadly supportive of reform proposals advanced by modern constitutionalists.

Majoritarianism

My discussion to this point has really been preliminary to the examination and analysis of what I consider to be more important sources of opposition to general constitutional reform, sources that can much more directly be classified as anticonstitutionalist. Why do respected social scientists and philosophers, who are not natural conservatives and who do not seem motivated by self-interest, reject, almost categorically, any argument for constitutional change?

One apparent source of an anticonstitutionalist mind set arises from a naive commitment to democracy, without any underlying examination of what this term means. Implicitly, democracy as a political, governmental form of decision making is equated with majoritarianism, with majority voting rules being placed in a central and critical institutional role. When carefully analyzed, however, this majoritarian stance is peculiar with respect to its implied constitutional foundations. The will of the majority is to be paramount, and any limits on the exercise of this will are deemed to violate territory that is sacrosanct. At the same time, strict constitutional protection is presumably required for those institutional elements that define the operation of majority voting rules themselves. Simple majorities are not to be allowed to act so as to abolish majoritarian processes of decision making; they are not allowed to prohibit new elections at periodic intervals with any view toward freezing permanently the power position of a specific coalition.

Members of majority coalitions will, quite naturally, be inclined to maintain the powers they have achieved. To prevent majoritarian abolition of majoritarian processes, constitutional guarantees presumably become legitimate, but only if these guarantees are strictly limited to the protection of voting–electoral processes. Aside from these procedural guarantees, however, the will of the majority to do as it pleases becomes the essence of democracy.

What majority is to count? The generalized majoritarian response to this question seems highly ambiguous. There is no clearly defined relationship between majoritarianism and representation. If all adults are franchised, but if plebiscitary methods of ascertaining majority resolution of all issues are not feasible, how are persons to be represented in a legislative assembly? There is no natural bridge between majority voting under universal franchise, as an abstract ideal, and majority voting in a specifically defined legislative assembly. It is relatively easy to show with the simplest of analytical models that the majority will of the legislature may not be consistent with the majority will of the electorate under a wide variety of circumstances.

Even if the problem of effective representation is neglected, there remains the familiar difficulty that arises because of possible inconsistency in majority decisions. In the presence of voting cycles, there is no majority will, which then prompts the question: When should voting stop?

Quite apart from the questions raised above, and even if it is assumed that somehow these might be satisfactorily answered, any simplistic majoritarian position founders on the shoals of limits. Almost all of those persons who argue that the exercise of majority will in duly elected legislative assemblies should not be restricted, do so only with reference to potential changes at the margin of current political order. That is to say, few persons, whether they be scholars or laymen, will openly and avowedly defend the rights of legislative or electoral majorities to do whatever they please to do, even within the constitutional guarantees of the majoritarian process itself. Would it not be legitimate for a duly elected and constituted majority coalition in a legislature to make speech or publication illegal? To make association unlawful? To take valued goods from members of a political minority in a discriminatory way? To jail opponents for their political opinions?

Almost all announced majoritarians will invoke constitutional protections and guarantees as the appropriate means of checking or limiting the will of majority coalitions. In so doing, however, have not the majoritarians really emerged from what seems to be an anticonstitutional stance? If constitutional protections for both electoral-majoritarian institutions and basic human rights are acknowledged to be necessary and legitimate, what is there left in the standard majoritarian opposition to constitutional dialogue, other than possibly pragmatic disagreement concerning the location of the constitutionally protected margins? And need these margins correspond with some historically determined status quo?

The Domain of Constitutional Rights

We do not normally associate what can roughly be called a rights position with anticonstitutionalism. There would seem to be relatively little intersection between the sometimes intense discussion among political philosophers about rights and the reactions of that set of economists, political scientists, and lawyers who reject contemporary proposals for constitutional reform for general rather than specific reasons. It is possible, nonetheless, to assign to some members of the second group what seems to be a strongly held, even if not explicitly stated, rights position. If we take this step, it becomes possible to explain this group's seemingly contradictory stance on constitutionalism on the one hand and rights-imposed limits on majoritarian democracy on the other.

The set of basic freedoms of speech, press, assembly, and franchise are not, in the outlook suggested here, constitutionally protected or guaranteed for the same reasons that justify constitutional limits to the constitutionalist-cum-contractarian. The rights position does not derive those protected spheres of individual activity, even at the most abstract level of consideration, from generalized consensus among members of the polity. In other words, there is no constitutional choice that is conceived to have been made. The basic personal liberties that are to be constitutionally protected are natural rights, which are presumed to be known to all persons, and which are also naturally beyond the boundaries for the exercise of majoritarian discretion. In this rights perspective, there is no rational basis for constitutional limits as such.

The fundamental liberties are constitutionally protected, and legitimately so, because these liberties represent rights that are self-evident to all who seek wisdom and truth. Persons have rights to free speech, transcendently defined natural rights, that governments, whether majoritarian or otherwise, dare not abridge. The argument for the protection of such liberties is moral rather than rational. In this view, it is immoral for a legislative majority to restrict free speech; it is equally immoral for a military junta to do the same thing. There is no widely accepted rational basis for morality, however, and once the argument has been shifted to moral grounds, effective dialogue with the contractarian-cum-constitutionalist may become impossible.

The constitutional moralist, whose attitudes are under examination here, feels no tension between his sometimes extreme opposition to proposals to restrict or expand majoritarian powers over areas of social and economic behavior and his sometimes equally passionate defense of a specified range of human liberties against any and all governmental intrusions. There is no inner psychological conflict because the constitutional moralist does not regard the line between the protected and the nonprotected spheres of human activity to be subject to analysis and discussion. This line is given externally, by God as it were, and who is to question its location?

Insofar as the moralist interprets existing constitutional rules as embodying basic rights, he may make a sharp and indeed categorical distinction between these rights and ordinary political activity that goes on within the unprotected spheres. In this limited sense, the rights advocate may seem constitutionalist in many of his overt arguments. As Bernard Siegan has demonstrated, however, the set of rights that are deemed to deserve legal protection may shift dramatically over time.[5] The Lockean notion of rights to property dominated our legal history for decades, and these rights were accorded constitutional protection. However, the protection was based on a perspective that included property rights as morally deserving of legal protection. Rights to property were not derived from a conceptualized contractarian process in which individuals make rationally informed constitutional choices. In other words, the status of economic rights in the early years of this century in the United States was evaluated on essentially the same grounds that are now accorded to human rights. This rights-based support of economic liberties proved to be unsustainable in the shifted moral climate of midcentury. It seems plausible to suggest that a genuinely derived constitutionalist argument for these economic liberties might have fared somewhat better.

The Conceptualization of Politics

The argument that is based on rights, as this argument is used to oppose constitutional change on general grounds, does explain important parts of the dialogue. The moral precepts of the late twentieth century do not include

5. Bernard Siegan, *Economic Liberties and the Constitution* (Chicago: University of Chicago Press, 1980).

economic liberties in the empirically accepted set of rights that warrant constitutional legal protection. Hence, those who interpret the legitimately protected spheres of activity to be those that are coincident with morally based rights cannot become enthusiasts for constitutional-reform arguments. At best, they may become pragmatic supporters for specific reforms, which they may reluctantly treat as constitutional.

To those who adhere to the rights position, however, the set of proposed restrictions on the powers of government and on the range of activities over which majorities may exercise their wills, does nothing to violate the basic rights that are within the moral boundaries. It is far-fetched to suggest that majorities hold rights that are justified in some moral sense. The person who does acknowledge the need for constitutional protection for a morally legitimatized sphere of human activity will not be outraged at proposals for shifts in the margins allowed for the working of majoritarian politics. The rights advocate seems quite unlikely to classify those who do advance such proposals as fascist.[6] To understand this extreme form of anticonstitutionalism, it is necessary to examine carefully the conception of politics and government that such a position must embody.

What is there in the constitutionalist position generally, or even specifically, when its advocates advance proposals for constraints on the taxing, spending, and money-issue powers of modern governments, that provokes the fascist charge? We may recognize, of course, that *fascist* is an emotionally loaded scare word. But there is a serious question to be answered here. What is it in the constitutionalist reform position that generates the apparently genuinely felt fear and loathing? The various elements of anticonstitutionalism previously discussed in this chapter cannot possibly provide the basis for the emotional intensity that seems to be aroused.

My hypothesis is that the anticonstitutionalist mentality embodies an inability to enter into a conceptual political dialogue in which all persons are assigned equal values. This position does not, and cannot, locate the ultimate source of values in individuals who make up the polity with separate persons

6. I have personally been so classified at least indirectly. See John Foster, "Review Note," *Economic Journal*, 91 (December 1981), 1105. In a more general context, Paul Samuelson has introduced the fascist epithet in discussing proposals for constitutional change. See Paul A. Samuelson, "The World Economy at Century's End," *Bulletin of the American Academy of Arts and Sciences*, 34 (May 1981), 35–44, especially page 44.

counted as equally weighted units. In this very real sense, the position I am describing here is antidemocratic and antiliberal.

In its crudest formulation, the position seems avowedly elitist. If persons are not to be given equal weights in constitutional discussions concerning the rules under which they must live, some persons must count for more than others. Discrimination and differentiation among persons is necessary, and the straightforward elitist simply assigns differentially higher weights to the values of his own group.

Unfortunately, the elementary elitist model is not sufficiently explanatory for the position I am trying to analyze. At a meaningful level of self-consciousness, the anticonstitutionalist need not think that he or she is assigning higher weights to his or her own values than to those of others in the community. Unless this step is taken, however, what is the origin of the observed reluctance to allow all values to count equally in some individualist-democratic-constitutionalist perspective?

My secondary hypothesis is that the basic difference lies in the conceptualization of what politics is all about. The anticonstitutionalist does not (cannot) think of political collective interaction in an exchange or contractarian paradigm. That is to say, individuals are not modeled, even conceptually, as forming and maintaining a polity analogously to entering a complex set of exchange arrangements aimed at securing mutually demanded and jointly consumed goods.[7] The political, governmental process is conceptually divorced from human interaction.

Politics is, instead, conceived as an institutional process through which those in designated roles search for truth, which, when found, comes to be embodied in solutions for the body politic as a community. The whole institutional apparatus (elections, politicians, parties, bureaucrats, legislatures, agencies) may or may not be efficient in discovering or in implementing the

---

7. It is ironic that Paul A. Samuelson, in particular, should be among the anticonstitutionalists discussed here, since the modern normative theory of public or collective goods owes so much to his seminal papers of the 1950s. As these papers, and subsequent writings, indicated, however, Samuelson was never interested in the processes of decision making, as such, but rather in the formally defined properties of outcomes or end states. See Paul A. Samuelson, "The Pure Theory of Public Expenditure," *Review of Economics and Statistics,* 36 (November 1954), 387–389; "Diagrammatic Exposition of a Theory of Public Expenditure," *Review of Economics and Statistics,* 37 (November 1955), 350–356.

true results. Nonetheless, such uniquely true or right results exist, and the never-ending quest of politics is one of coming closer to the desired objective reality.

In this idealist conceptualization of politics, individual evaluations are useful only insofar as they offer a means for arriving at a *truth judgment*. Individual evaluations are not incorporated as value weights that count because they represent persons' own values or opinions or interests. In this conceptualization, truth is not located by counting heads, and agreement itself is not a criterion for the rightness of an outcome.

I can perhaps best illustrate the profound differences in the two opposing conceptualizations of politics by introducing the contrasting examples of the jury and the market. Consider first the decision process of those individuals who find themselves on a jury assigned the task of determining the guilt or innocence of a person charged with a specific crime. These jurors are chosen because they are disinterested in the result; overt conflict of interest would tend to disqualify anyone from jury duty. The jurors are directed to find the truth, to ascertain the correct answer to the question of guilt or innocence. The presence of several persons on the panel, rather than a single person, reflects an understanding that such an institutional arrangement offers a more desirable means of securing correct results than alternative structures, because this arrangement provides protection against biased insights and because, historically, it has been held to assure disinterestedness. Similarly, the voting rule used by the jury, whether this be unanimity, qualified, or simple majority, is evaluated solely in terms of its efficacy in generating patterns of outcomes that are independently defined to be desirable.

By contrast, consider a simple two-person, two-commodity exchange. Persons A and B enter into potential trade with separately owned endowments of apples and oranges. Trade takes place. When trade ceases, the final imputation of apples and oranges differs from the initial or pretrade imputation. It would seem highly unusual, indeed inappropriate, to classify the posttrading set of endowments, the results of trade, as true or right. On the other hand, the results may be classified to be efficient in economists' terminology, provided only that the trade was seen to be voluntary on the part of both parties and provided that no fraud was seen to be present. The results here are classified by criteria applied to the *process*. In the jury example, by contrast, the process is evaluated by criteria applied to the *results*.

These examples allow me to illustrate the profound difference in the two conceptualizations of politics. The constitutionalist-contractarian interprets the political process as a *generalization of the market*.[8] The anticonstitutionalist, truth-judgment conceptualist interprets politics as a *generalization of the jury*.[9]

My purpose is not to discuss in depth the implications of these dramatically differing conceptualizations of politics. I introduce the difference here only to explain the intensity of anticonstitutionalist argument as it seems to be encountered when proposals for reform are presented. For the persons whose mentality embodies the truth-judgment conceptualization, any overt limits on politics as an activity must serve only to close off preselected avenues of possible exploration and discovery. To such persons, politics as an activity or experience to be constrained within rationally chosen rules makes no sense. From this perspective, there follows naturally the view that those advocates who seek to impose limits on the exercise of political authority must proceed from some motive aimed at preventing true judgments from being allowed to emerge. Constitutionalists, viewed in this light, are basically immoral, since they stand opposed to truth and right.[10]

Additional insight may be gained here if we think of the social scientist or social philosopher who adheres, either explicitly or implicitly, to the truth-

8. Geoffrey Brennan has objected to my treatment of the constitutionalist as necessarily contractarian. As noted earlier, there is a sense in which the distinction between rules and politics within rules can be appreciated without, at the same time, accepting the notion that rules are themselves subject to explicit change. In this variant, contractual origins of rules may be rejected, while, at the same time, politics within rules can be modeled in an exchange paradigm. It is difficult for me to define a coherent position that would model within-rule politics as a generalization of exchange and constitutional politics in a truth-judgment perspective. At best, therefore, the Brennan critique would seem to suggest that all those who reject the exchange paradigm for constitutional politics need not be classified as within the group that adheres to the truth-judgment paradigm.

9. The general attractiveness of this second interpretation is enhanced because it fits descriptively with the development of science. Even with science, however, the interpretation may be seriously misleading, and the extension that models politics as science is surely misplaced. On all these issues, see Buchanan, "Politics and Science," *Ethics,* 77 (July 1967), 303–310.

10. For a paper that deals with related issues, see Geoffrey Brennan and James Buchanan, "Is Public Choice Immoral?" presented at the March 1982 meetings of the Public Choice Society (mimeographed, Center for Study of Public Choice, VPI).

judgment conceptualization of politics as he examines his own role. In such an intellectual setting, the scholar does not, and indeed cannot, model himself directly in a participatory capacity. The activity of politics is clearly one to be carried out by professional politicians and bureaucrats, who are modeled as disinterested seekers after solutions to political problems as these emerge. These persons are not agents, or even representatives, who act on behalf of franchised citizens, as such, and the observing scholar does not treat his own interests to be relevant in some indirectly participatory sense. Almost by necessity, the truth-judgment perspective requires the social scientist to model his behavior as that of a disinterested adviser or consultant to those who are the active participants. Like the professionals, the observing consultant scholar seeks only to promote truth through politics.

The scholar I am here describing remains almost totally immune to Knut Wicksell's charge that he behaves as if he is proffering advice to a benevolent despot.[11] If he cannot model politics in some ultimate exchange paradigm, in which outcomes must reflect some amalgamation of separate individual and group interests and values, there is simply no way that the scholar can envisage a role for himself other than that of the disinterested scientist whose evaluation of truth may be somewhat more heavily weighted than that of the ordinary citizen.[12] This perception rules out any search for a compromise among separate interests, and makes the scientist-scholar unwilling to look closely at processes as means of placing judgments indirectly on outcomes.

If he assumes the advisory role, the scientist-philosopher must oppose suggestions for constitutional reform if these involve additional limits on the exercise of political authority. For the same reasons, he should support suggestions for relaxing existing constitutional barriers on political action. Any restriction on political authority directly impinges on the scholar's freedom of choice once removed. In his idealized search for political truth, such a scientist-philosopher needs to keep his possibility set as inclusive as observed

11. See Knut Wicksell, *Finanztheoretische Untersuchungen* (Jena: Gustav Fischer, 1896).

12. The long-continuing tension in the social-choice literature, and one of the features of this subject matter that seems to attract scholars, lies precisely in the opposing pulls of the two disparate conceptualizations of politics discussed here. The social-choice theorist wants simultaneously to array social outcomes in some relationship to individual evaluations of those outcomes and to be able to evaluate those outcomes that are so arrayed in accordance with some nonprocess criteria.

environmental parameters allow. He must be concerned especially about the emergence of unforeseen events, and about the ability of political authority to respond effectively to such events unconstrained by previously imposed constitutional limits, always on the presupposition that such authority, if unconstrained, can indeed locate and implement the right action.

In Praise of Political Philosophy

In preceding sections of this chapter, I have tried to uncover several elements of what I have called the anticonstitutionalist mentality. These various elements may be, but need not be, combined in the attitudes of particular persons. It seems quite possible that the truth-judgment conception of politics may be overlaid on a rights position, especially if the latter remains largely implicit. A truth-judgment conception is not totally congruent with majoritarianism; the truth-in-politics adherent can scarcely applaud the populist strains of majority rule where each man does seem to count as one. On the other hand, majoritarianism is broadly consistent with a rights position so long as majority coalitions work their will along the peripheries appropriate to the stage of cultural history and well outside the range of rights deemed appropriate for protection. Neither majoritarianism nor rights advocacy is fully consistent with the evolutionist perspective on institutional change. But there may be congruence between the latter and the truth-judgment conceptualization.

Even to list the possible sources of opposition to constitutional reform that are generally based and not specific to the proposals advanced suggests the magnitude of the challenge that the constitutionalist faces, even at the most fundamental level of ideas. I now think that many of us, myself included, who have tried to advance practical suggestions for constitutional change, have been guilty of oversight and neglect of challenges at the more basic level. We have been negligent because of an implicit assumption that the constitutional-postconstitutional distinction is widely and readily understood and that arguments are concentrated on the particular proposals for change.

We have been successful in gaining a few adherents among academics and among those whose political influences are closer to the realities of practical affairs. But we are likely to remain unsuccessful in the large until and unless we win more converts in the continuing battle of basic ideas. It is in the realms of political philosophy that the struggle must be waged. At base, what is at issue here is how persons conceive themselves with respect to their interactions one with another and with respect to the collectivities that attempt to command their loyalties. As of any chosen moment in time and space, a people's attitudes in these respects may be empirically described. There are no universal constraints in such descriptions, temporally or locationally. Ideas may be changed, however, and ideas that persons have about their own positions in the social order may be influenced by articulated statements of the alternatives.

The U.S. citizenry has surely come closer to an embodiment of a set of constitutional attitudes than any other people in the history of the world. I have often noticed and remarked about the clearly observed differences between the acceptance of constitutionalism by U.S. citizens and foreign citizens. My admonition here is that the constitutional mentality that so many of our fellow citizens possess almost unthinkingly is a precious heritage that we must do everything within our powers to preserve. At the sheer level of prediction, I am not at all hopeful in this respect.

The constitutionalist vision suggests that free men and women may impose constraints upon themselves and live within these constraints, both in their private and in their political capacities. This is indeed a noble vision, but those of us who hold it will be the fools of history if we fail to recognize that the vision is neither natural to the human psyche nor universally accepted as part of our modern culture. Frank Knight often asked the question: Was (is) the free society an accident of history? He did not answer his own question. I might ask: Is (was) the constitutionalist mentality an accidental constrained framework for ideas that shows little evidence of staying power? I do not answer my own question, but, to me, the two questions are the same.

Achieving Economic Reform

Economists, along with others, agree that economies "work better" when governments keep out of the way and allow voluntary market exchanges to operate within a legal framework that protects property rights and enforces contracts. And to "work better" means to produce a higher valued bundle of goods and services. But governments do not restrict their activities to protective functions; governments, everywhere, in greater or lesser degree, interfere with the workings of markets. Economic reform, then, becomes the inclusive term that refers to institutional changes in the direction of liberating free exchange from politicized intervention.

What is the starting point? Why is economic reform needed at all? Why is it so difficult to achieve? What are the prospects for economic reform in the 1990s? These questions dictate the organization of my efforts in this chapter.

1. Here and Now

As many of you know, I have always insisted that would-be reformers of economic and political institutions acknowledge the simple existential fact that reform, improvement, or change is tethered to the "here and now" as a starting point. I continue to be surprised by those romanticists among us who advance policy nostrums in blissful ignorance of this fact. But "here and now" embodies a multiplicity of dimensions and this cautionary warning gets us nowhere in itself. We need to go further and to specify what we are talking about. That which exists in the "here and now" which is relevant for my discussion is described in a set of individuals who are organized variously in an interlinked set of institutional arrangements, including a polity, normally a nation-state. These individuals have, in turn, a set of rights, claims, duties, and obligations to or against the other participants-members through the institutions in which they cooperate, and these rights, claims, duties, and obligations are themselves defined in the same set of rules or procedures that specify both constraints on individual and institutional behavior and procedures for changing the rules. In summary, we can say that a "constitution" offers a comprehensive description of the rules within which the socio-economic-political game is played. The constitution that exists defines the "here and now" that becomes relevant for my purpose, and effective improvement or reform must involve changes in this defined structure of rules.

2. But How Do We Know That Improvement Is Possible?

Let it be acknowledged that change commences with the status quo. But how do we answer Dr. Pangloss? Why does not the very existence of the rules for social order imply their functional rationality? Absent some rational role, why would the rules that we observe have ever evolved into everyday usage or have been explicitly chosen and maintained through time? And, indeed, is not the primary task for social scientists, and especially political economists, one of locating explanations for observed institutions of order? And does not any diagnosis of structural defects reflect the presumptive arrogance of "rationalist constructivism," against which Hayek has warned us?[1]

I place myself on record here in opposition to this element in Hayek's thought, and, more specifically, in opposition to other modern political economists (many of whom have Chicago moorings) who invoke "transactions costs" barriers to explain the absence of the complex trades or agreements on rules changes that might seem to be mutually beneficial by the criteria of theoretical welfare economics. But I also, and at the same time, place

---

1. F. A. Hayek, *Law, Legislation and Liberty,* 3 vols. (Chicago: University of Chicago Press, 1973, 1976, 1979).

myself on record alongside William H. Hutt, who never ceased from diagnosing putative structural failures when he observed the existence of politicized barriers to voluntary exchanges.

In a 1959 paper,[2] I suggested that the analysis derived from theoretical welfare economics did offer the political economist the bases for advancing hypotheses for changes in rules, hypotheses that could find confirmation only
in the attainment of consensus, hypotheses that would be effectively falsified
in the absence of such attainment. This stance allows the political economist
to infer, by hypothesis, a shortfall in potential well-being when he or she observes politicized barriers to voluntary exchanges among persons, but it does
not allow the derivative normative inference that such barriers should necessarily be removed by a presumed benevolent government. The stance here
forces upon the economist the secondary chore of working out schemes of
compensations between potential net gainers and potential net losers that
any changes in rules must involve. The distributional elements of any proposal for reform are necessarily combined with allocational elements in any
search for prospective consensus.

3. The Simple Logic of Agreement on Pareto-Relevant Reform

In this section, I shall first present the basic logical principles of the Pareto
optimality construction in abstract terms, but applied to the stance of the
political economist outlined above. I shall then proceed to illustrate these
principles through a simple and familiar example, that of politicized control
over the price of rental housing.

The political economist observes some politicized interference with the
freedom of persons to engage in voluntary exchange transactions. The existing situation is adjudged to be nonoptimal, or inefficient, in the Pareto sense.
There must then exist some alternative situation in which all persons could
be made better off, by their own evaluation, or some persons made better off
and no others worse off than in the existing setting. From this definitional or
classificatory starting point, there follows the conclusion that there must also

2. James M. Buchanan, "Positive Economics, Welfare Economics, and Political Economy," *Journal of Law and Economics* 2 (October 1959): 124–38.

exist some means of moving from the initial, nonoptimal position to an alternative, optimal position in a way that will damage no one in the economic nexus. This allows the further inference that there must then exist some means of securing agreement on the part of all parties to make the shift in question.

Let us now apply this analysis to rent control. The economist diagnoses rent control to be inefficient. The rental price on old housing is below equilibrium levels, there is a shortage of such housing, and waiting lists and various "key price" arrangements have become substitute rationing devices. The price of new housing, which is exempt from control, is above the price of old housing by more than any meaningful equilibrium price differential.

If presented as a simple proposal to abolish rent control, there would be immediate opposition by those persons who claim rights to existing old housing units. This opposition would prevent the emergence of consensus on the proposal for change. The task for the political economist is to work out the minimal set of compensations that would be required to "buy out" the claims held by those who live in the old housing subject to control and, at the same time, work out some scheme whereby these compensations may be voluntarily financed by others in the community. Owners of old housing could be a major source for such "taxes," and prospective tenants who have previously been denied easy access to such housing would also be willing to meet some share of these financing requirements.

The logic is straightforward. If the rent control rule is Pareto inefficient, or nonoptimal, there must exist some scheme of potential compensations and payments that will prove possible and upon which consensus may be attained. If there is no such scheme possible, the observing political economist must acknowledge that his initial classification of the rule as inefficient is in error.

4. Why and How, Then, Can Inefficient Arrangements Continue to Exist?

The reasoning is impeccable, and there is little or no disagreement among economists in the classification of politicized interferences into value-reducing and value-enhancing sets. Why, then, do we observe pervasive and continuing politicized restrictions on voluntary exchanges among persons, restrictions that almost all economists would label value reducing, like rent controls? And why do such restrictions persist once they are in place? And, further, why do new intrusions into the liberty of persons to make voluntary exchanges continue to emerge from political process? If such intrusions are genuinely value reducing, as economists agree, what prevents the working out of agreed upon schemes that will both eliminate existing interferences and prevent new ones from arising?

I shall discuss these two questions separately. First, I shall address the issues that arise in attempts to secure economic reform by removing existing interferences with voluntary exchanges. Second, I shall extend the analysis to efforts to forestall or prevent the politicization of markets that are operating without specific controls. I shall, in both cases, use the rent control example where applicable.

Suppose that an observing political economist adjudges an existing regime (for example, rent control) to be value reducing. Accepting the stance outlined above, this economist advances a reform package that includes removal of the controls along with compensation payments to those who claim rights or entitlements in the status quo, and, also, tax payments or contributions from those members of the community who could expect to secure net gains from the removal of the restrictions. (With rent control, the package would involve removal of controls over rental housing prices, along with compensations to those who claim "tenant rights," financed by tax payments from those who are expected gainers, owners of controlled units and others who are denied access to the stock.) The elementary logic suggests that there should exist many such schemes that could command generalized assent.

The economist, whom we presume has done his or her work well, is likely to be shocked by the negative reactions to this proposal, when it is advanced as a hypothesis for general approval. And this economist is likely to face continuing frustration when, as, and if differing schemes for effecting the reform are put forward. Persons and groups whose well-being would be predicted to increase, and perhaps substantially, may nonetheless reject, out of hand, any and all schemes that involve their payment of compensation to other persons who would be predicted to lose, and perhaps substantially, from the proposed change in market restrictions.

To understand the central problem in achieving economic reform it is necessary to examine the bases for the apparent refusal of potential gainers to participate in the "complex exchange" that promises to yield net benefits to all members of the community. Why do such persons (such as the owners of controlled housing units) act in ways that seem contrary to their own economic interests?

Two separate but somewhat related explanations may be suggested. The potential gainers from suggested reform may refuse to acknowledge the *entitlements* or *rights* of those who would be damaged by removal of the restrictions on market exchanges. To offer compensations to those who seem to be unfairly advantaged by existing arrangements, even if it is recognized that such compensations would be required to secure the agreement needed to make the reforms, would violate canons of rough justice. And these canons or principles may dominate the straightforward calculus of economic self-interest.

A separate, but somewhat related, reason why potential gainers from proposed economic reform may refuse to participate in any overall scheme that requires any contribution toward the financing of compensations to potential losers emerges when we examine the political calculus of the former. Full treatment here would require an intellectual excursion through much of elementary public choice theory; a summary description must suffice. Most politicized restrictions or controls over the liberties of persons to enter into voluntary exchanges emerge from the workings of ordinary democratic politics, within which decisions are reached by *majority* coalitions in legislative assemblies or parliaments, decisions which are then imposed on the full membership of the polity. Those who are losers, in some opportunity cost sense, from prior enactments of market restrictions, may consider themselves to have been coerced by the will of an opposing majority coalition. And these losers, who would be the potential gainers from the removal of the restrictions, may hold out positive prospects for the organization of a different and politically successful majority coalition that will, in its turn, impose its own will on members of the majority that enacted the restrictive legislation in the first place. In this imagined scenario, those who stand to gain by economic reform may anticipate securing the desired reform without compensation paid to those who stand to lose. And a rational calculus may dictate that investment in efforts to build new majority coalitions may be more productive than investment in the direct payment of compensation designed to secure the agreement or acquiescence of the potential losers from the proposed change.

The effects of this political choice calculus in preventing agreement on economic reform measures that promise to yield benefits to all parties, given appropriate compensations, are related to differentials in expectations among the separate groups of participants. If prospective gainers from removal of market restrictions anticipate the effective formation of a new majority coalition which will act to repeal the restrictions, why should they pay compensations to the losers? But if these expectations are in error, and those who are in place and protected by existing controls (for example, tenants in old housing) anticipate continuing political dominance, the status quo can surely be predicted to prevail. In contrast, to the extent that prospective gainers become less hopeful of being able to form successful new majority coalitions, they become more willing to finance compensations. And, conversely, to the extent that prospective losers become less secure in their maintenance of majority support, they become more willing to accept compensations that are within the relevant choice-set of those who must finance them.

We now shift attention to the different, but related, set of questions involving possible ways and means of preventing the interferences that seem to be characteristic of the working of democratic politics. If, in some way, political behavior could be constrained to insure that value-reducing restrictions on exchanges would never be imposed, there would never arise the need for economic "reform" of the sort under discussion here.

Again, we can locate a source of difficulty in a failure of majoritarian politics to allow a separation to be made between allocational and distributional objectives. A majority coalition may impose economic control measures that clearly reduce value in order to attain desired distributional results. (For example, if tenants in old housing units form a majority coalition, they may impose rent controls simply to keep their own housing costs down, with no regard to the overall waste in economic resources that the control generates.) If, before any such measure could be enacted, prospective beneficiaries should be required to get the agreement of prospective losers, no value-reducing restrictions could be put in place. But, or so the argument might go, why should members of an effective majority coalition, or their legislative representatives, feel obliged to attain the consent, through appropriate compensations or otherwise, of those who are members of the opposing minority? Does not "democracy" mean "rule by majority"?

So long as such an attitude describes both public and intellectual-academic understanding of what "democracy" is all about, we can predict only continued, politically motivated interferences with the liberties of persons to enter freely into exchanges one with another. Until and unless *constitutional* constraints are placed upon the authority of legislative majorities to intervene in the workings of the economy, there will be no means of forestalling the continuing need for economic "reform," defined as the dismantling of prior interventions.

To suggest that political actions aimed at intervening in economic exchanges must pass a constitutional test need not rule out, in any way, all such interventions. Constitutions contain within their rules further rules that define how changes in rules are to be made. But constitutional politics is necessarily more inclusive than within- or postconstitutional politics. A simple majority is not (or should not be) sufficient to implement genuine constitutional change. Hence, proponents and advocates of economic intervention would be required to secure the assent of something more than a bare majority. And in an idealized, and admittedly limiting, case, constitutionally authorized political interventions into markets could take place *only* if such interventions are value enhancing rather than value reducing.

Merely to suggest that intervention into the economic process should be placed out of bounds for majoritarian legislative politics may be labeled subversive, especially in view of a century of socialist inspired and romanticized misunderstandings about the relative efficacies of markets and politicized alternatives. But this century of confusion has surely come close to running its course. It is time to restore an understanding of the relationship between effective democracy and constitutional order.

5. Economic Reform and Distributional Conflict

The discussion to this point suggests that the central problem of achieving economic reform, or of preventing institutional changes that would make future reform desirable, is not, in itself, *economic*. The problem is, instead, that *the economy* (by which term I refer to the interaction of persons and groups in an interlinked nexus of market transactions) becomes the institutional setting within which *distributional* conflicts are resolved through *political* means. The logic of the Paretian welfare economics sketched out in section 3 is based on the implicit presumption that such conflicts have been resolved or, alternatively, have been relegated for resolution to some arena that is independent of economic process. This logical exercise is helpful in suggesting that a separation between the basic conflicts over claims to value among persons and groups and the voluntary contractual exchanges of values among persons and groups is conceptually, and also institutionally, within the possible.

The political economist, as such, can contribute nothing directly to the dialogue concerning conflicting claims and rights to shares in value. The political economist can, however, provide a measure of the social waste of value that is involved when conflicts over claims are settled through politicized intervention into markets. (Return to the rent control example. The political economist cannot offer a scientific judgment concerning whether or not the tenants of old housing units should be subsidized at the expense of other groups in the community. The political economist can, however, demonstrate that the subsidization in the form of rent ceilings destroys potential value.)

The possible achievement of economic reform through some institutional conversion of indirect subsidization of particular groups through market intervention into direct subsidization through fiscal transfers faces much the same difficulty discussed earlier with reference to the payment of compensations. Groups that benefit through indirect subsidization or protection by market distortions recognize that direct fiscal subsidization intended to generate equivalent distributional patterns will secure relatively less political support. Arbitrary and discriminatory programs of direct fiscal transfers designed to match the distributional effects of piecemeal interferences with market exchanges would not stand scrutiny when evaluated against generalized criteria of fairness or justice, no matter what ultimate form these criteria may take. And the political economist can, indeed, offer some assistance here in pointing out the discrepancy between the attainment of idealized distributive norms and the arbitrary patterns that emerge from politicized markets, quite apart from the demonstrable resource waste. Through such an exercise, the advocates of continued market distortion can be forced into blatant expressions of particularized distributional objectives and away from arguments cloaked in terms of advancing generalized norms.

6. Economics, Politics, and Prospects

The logic of Paretian welfare economics tells us that the removal of politicized intervention in voluntary market exchange can be orchestrated in such a way that everyone in an economy can be made better off, and by his or her own reckoning. This theorem provides the economist with both a scientific raison d'être and a basis for hope. The economist need not take sides among gainers and losers since, by the Paretian logic, all persons can become gainers from economic reform. And because persons can be presumed to pursue their own interests, there must always remain the hope that, ultimately, rationality will prevail in the choice among institutions.

At the same time, however, the logic of democratic politics, and especially majoritarian politics, tells us that the separation between the operation of the market economy and persisting distributional conflict is unlikely to be secured, thereby insuring that the economist's hopes will remain unfulfilled. It does remain possible, however, to say something further about the prospects for reform, at least in terms of an attempted identification of those situations and settings in which economic reform seems most likely to occur.

First, consider a setting where major shocks have essentially destroyed and disrupted the legal-economic-political order; specifically, consider the upheavals generated in the aftermath of major war or revolution. In this setting, there exist no effective rights and claims to values in a status quo; hence, there can be little overt opposition to the emergence of relatively nonpoliticized exchange arrangements that may not have been present prior to the disruption.

And, if there are economists in the wings who have prepared a reform agenda, we might predict that a market order substantially free of political encumbrances might emerge, with the predictable consequences of economic prosperity and growth. Mancur Olson has used this argument persuasively to explain the economic rise of Germany and Japan in the years following World War II, a war that destroyed the institutional base in both countries.[3] William H. Hutt also relied on the disruptions of the institutional arrangements in Great Britain during World War II to make possible his proposed plan for reconstruction which did involve compensatory adjustments

---

3. Mancur Olson, *The Rise and Decline of Nations* (New Haven: Yale University Press, 1982).

for groups that might make claims against some return to the prewar status quo ante.[4] As we know, Hutt's proposal did not succeed.

It is important to emphasize that, even when possibly favorable conditions for economic reform exist, there must be an available agenda for action ready for implementation, an agenda that has been prepared by political economists. The Freiberg or Ordnungspolitik school served this function admirably in postwar Germany, as did the so-called Chicago boys in post-Allende Chile.

Prospects would remain bleak indeed if economic reform could take place only in the upheavals of major wars or revolutions. We can identify a different, and nonwar, setting that offers the opportunity for effective removal of politicized controls over the workings of markets. If a national economy undergoes a historical experience during which, due both to falsified theoretical principles and to the workings of interest-group majoritarian politics, many separate markets have come to be politicized, either by direct interferences with freely established prices or, alternatively, by direct governmental enterprise operation, a "constitutionlike" shift toward the opening of markets may come to be feasible. The economy that has come to be overburdened with a whole set of restrictions will be inefficient in a readily demonstrable sense, and especially so in comparison with other national economies. Participants even in politically protected markets will be able to reckon the general costs of continued widespread politicization. Resistance to depoliticization (privatization) will be less acute on the part of members even of protected industry and consumer groups if the proposed reform is presented as a "package" that embodies similar treatment over a whole set of industries. That is to say, generalized economic reform that incorporates changes in the organization, operation, and control over many sectors may offer more prospects for political success than piecemeal reforms that pick off one or a few industries at a time. If stated as a hypothesis, we could say that the more socialized is the economy, the higher the prospects for economic reform.

I noted only in passing the relevance of the openness of an economy to international comparisons. Almost regardless of internal distributional pressures, a nation cannot long retain inefficient politicized controls over those

---

4. William H. Hutt, *Plan for Reconstruction* (London: Kegan Paul, Trench, Trubner & Co., 1943).

sectors of its economy that produce for foreign markets. And, further, to the extent that inefficiencies in nonexport sectors exert spillover effects on economies generally, we should predict that small national economies with important export sectors should experience fewer difficulties with securing effective depoliticization than large national economies. This sketch of an analysis yields a hypothesis. If, as, and when the small national economies of Eastern Europe (for example, Hungary, Poland) come to be increasingly opened, we can expect more by way of growth-producing economic reform than elsewhere over the ensuing decades. By comparison, in large internal economies where conflicts among domestic distributional interests dominate international considerations, and where socialization-politicization has not been extended to absurd limits (for example, the United States), we must, I think, remain relatively pessimistic about the implementation of economic reform.

To this point, I have not mentioned ideology or conversion to organizational principles as a source or motivation for economic reform. But the influence of ideology should not be totally left out of the account. The depoliticization of the British economy that occurred during the late eighteenth and early nineteenth centuries was surely due, in part, to the conversion of political leaders to the normative principles advanced by the classical political economists. Sober assessment of the modern mind-set in the academies of the 1990s suggests that there is scant prospect for any intellectually led rediscovery of laissez-faire as an explicit normative ideal for social organization. This negative assessment must, however, be accompanied by an acknowledgement of near total uncertainty about the direction to be taken by the intellectuals of the world in the post-Marxist, postsocialist epoch that has so suddenly emerged upon us. Confronted with the discredited socialist alternatives, where are the intellectual critics of free markets to turn?

It seems at least to be within the possible that the leading centers of effective economic reform will be the postsocialist economies, which may well outdistance those mixed economies where extensive politicization did not describe the middle century but where, at the same time, the politicization that did occur is held in place by the exigencies of domestic distributional conflict.

Pragmatic Reform and
Constitutional Revolution[1]

James M. Buchanan and Alberto di Pierro

None of thy wholesome counsels have escap'd me, but nature's
force subdues my better reason.

—Chrysippus

When ventured at all, predictions of permanence and stability in sociopolitical institutions are now made with caution. General malaise seems to characterize modern attitudes about civil order, and revolution is more widely
discussed than at any other time in the last half-century. The aging positivist
idol, the benevolent nation-state, neither commands obedience nor inspires
respect, and men search for a new god. Materialist ideals are challenged by
young and old alike, and the clichés of middle-aged and liberal politicians are
treated with near-contempt. The individual suffers alienation, social claus-
trophobia, and frustration in a congested, collectivized civilization that he
feels powerless to control. Democratic process seems out of kilter, and faith
in political leaders seems almost wholly extinguished. Fundamental values
are being questioned, even by those who do not claim to be philosophers; yet

From *Ethics* 79 (January 1969): 95–104. Copyright 1969 by The University of Chicago.
All rights reserved. Reprinted by permission of the publisher, the University of Chicago
Press.

1. Thanks should be extended to Professors William Breit and Roland McKean for
helpful comments and criticisms.

policy making and policy advising move piecemeal along predetermined and predictable patterns.[2]

There is no need to expand this familiar description of the age, a description that is itself riddled with facile images. Description is at best only a faltering first step toward the intelligent understanding that is required for improvement. We propose to contribute to such understanding by applying the professional tools and the approach of economists. These provide an "explanation" of historical experience which may complement other explanatory hypotheses. We claim neither exclusive nor primary causal significance for the models that we develop.

Our hypothesis has its foundations in economic theory, but it is not "economic" in the restricted sense that denotes a pre-eminence of materialist motivation in man. The analysis has three sources: the theory of opportunity cost, the theory of externalities (of public goods, of common property resources), and the theory of collective decision making. The basic methodology is individualistic. We examine the behavior of an individual who participates in a sequence of collective or political choices over a finite period of time. We demonstrate that patterns of behavior that seem privately rational at each point in time may produce results that generate inefficiencies over time. Somewhat differently from orthodox analysis, however, our model does not necessarily converge to an inefficient equilibrium. Indeed, one of the more interesting aspects of our model is its ability to explain the major swings in political organization that may take place upon recognition of inefficiency or non-optimality. Quantum changes in organization, derived from the behavioral choices of individual participants, are not inconsistent with our model. The results of choices made over a whole sequence of time periods may be reversed at one fell swoop, and the cyclical pattern of events may be repeated only after such "revolutions."

Although developed in a broader framework, our analysis is related to the "incremental" approach to policy analysis and policy making developed by C. E. Lindblom.[3] In a positive sense, we accept Lindblom's proposition that political changes normally take place incrementally and in small stages. Our

2. See C. E. Lindblom, "Policy Analysis," *American Economic Review,* 48 (June, 1958), 298–312.
3. Ibid., 302.

hypothesis, however, does not produce the normative or quasi-normative implications suggested by Lindblom, because the genesis of non-incremental or quantum changes is to be located precisely in the cumulation of distortions that piecemeal policy making generates. In fact, our hypothesis allows no room for an "invisible hand" that insures either efficiency or stability from evolutionary step-by-step political reforms.

In a general sense, the argument is very simple. The state extends its control over society through a gradual process of usurpation, stretching over a long period. Society reverses this process and re-establishes its freedom from the state only through "revolution."[4] The cycle is non-symmetrical. Our analysis grounds this general argument in the choice behavior of individuals who participate simultaneously as citizens of the state and as members of society. Our analysis does not invoke differential power structure hypotheses; we do not discuss usurpation of power by particular groups or "active" minorities. On the contrary, we attempt to map one possible "democratic" Road to Revolution.[5]

Specifically, we develop a model of rational choice behavior in which the individual pragmatically approves the collectivization of a series of activities over a sequence of time periods. As he takes these separate decisions, one at a time and separately, he fails to include relevant intertemporal and interpersonal externalities in his cost-benefit calculus. At some critical stage, however, the environmental changes imposed by earlier-period decisions begin to exert influences on behavior. At this point, rather than remain in a non-efficient and overcollectivized "equilibrium," the individual may support political reforms aimed at dramatically reversing the collectivization process. Under some conditions, paradigmatic or constitutional revolution may ensue. Again overadjustment is possible, and the whole cycle may be recommenced.

Section I develops the framework of an extremely restricted model within which the pattern of results suggested is not possible. Section II begins the progressive relaxation of the extreme assumptions. In Section III, the relaxation is continued, with the emphasis on the indivisibility of freedom. Sec-

4. For a provocative treatment of the current situation along with some discussion of prospects, see Ignazio Silone, "Rethinking Progress, II," *Encounter* (April, 1968), 27–40.

5. For some introductory remarks about limitations in the rationality of democratic choice in a dynamic setting, see C. Tisdell, "Some Bounds upon the Pareto Optimality of Group Behavior," *Kyklos*, 19 (fasc. 1, 1966), 81–105.

tion IV introduces the peculiar problems emergent from collective decision processes. Our summary conclusions are presented in Section V.

I. The Symmetrical Community of Equals

We shall initially describe a pattern of rational choice behavior that will embody no trace of the effects that we emphasize in this paper. The extreme assumptions that are required to generate such a result negatively illustrate the generality of our explanatory hypothesis. First of all, we assume that the person whose decision calculus we examine has perfect knowledge of all the alternatives that he confronts, both at present and in all future periods, and that this knowledge includes information about external events as well as his own utility function. Second, the individual behaves in terms of an infinitely long planning horizon; he acts as if he will live forever. Third, he is hypersensitive; his choice behavior exhibits no threshold phenomena. The individual cannot, of course, be considered in isolation, since our whole purpose is to analyze collective action. We add the restrictive assumption that the community is made up exclusively of persons who are identical in all respects. Collective decisions are made upon agreement among all citizens.

In this rarefied setting, no relevant externalities are produced by collective community action, either intertemporally or interpersonally. To show this, assume that initially all activities are in the private sector; no collective "goods" are provided. Members of the community will recognize that net efficiency gains are promised through joint production-consumption of some "goods." They will unanimously agree to collectivize these activities. Since all persons are identical, agreement will be reached easily on both quantities and cost-sharing.

The collectivization of any activity will reduce to some extent the individual's freedom of action. Collectively imposed results must be applicable to everyone, which is the obverse way of saying that the options open to anyone are diminished.[6] In each instance, however, the individual's private cost-benefit calculus suggests to him that the efficiency gains from joint effort

---

6. Emphasis here is on what Sir Isaiah Berlin calls "negative freedom," "the area within which a man can do what he wants." This is to be distinguished from what Berlin calls "positive freedom," centered on the idea of self-realization. On these, see Sir Isaiah Berlin, *Two Concepts of Liberty* (Oxford: Clarendon Press, 1958).

outweigh these restrictions on freedom as well as the more explicit costs that he must bear under collectivization. When he casts a positive "vote" for shifting an activity to the public sector, the individual is, of course, aware that he is participating in a collective or group choice. In so doing, he is generating a potential external economy or diseconomy on his fellow citizens. He is "voting" to impose costs on all others, including restrictions on their freedom of action. This inherent externality in collective decision making is not eliminated even in this extreme model. This does not, however, generate inefficiency in results because of the precise symmetries that the restrictive assumptions guarantee. The individual who "votes" for the collectivization of an activity faces a decision alternative in which the Pigovian divergencies between private and social marginal cost and private and social marginal benefit are large indeed. His calculus leads him to efficient results, however, because proportionately his share in community costs is symmetrical with his share in community or social benefits. There are no differentials among individuals either on the cost or the benefit side of the account.

The organization of activities that will emerge from collective decision making in this model will be fully efficient. All interdependence among separate activities will be taken into account, and no individual will experience regrets about any organizational decision that has been taken. The organization need not, of course, settle to an unchanging equilibrium, descriptively speaking. Individual utility functions may change over time, but so long as the shifts here are predicted in advance, the appropriate adjustments in structure will be made, again on the basis of unanimous agreement.

II. Imperfect Foresight, Opportunity Cost, and Institutional Rigidity

Only when we relax our restrictive assumptions do we begin to approach realistic choice situations. Initially, we drop only the assumption of perfect foresight on the part of the individual; other conditions of the model, including the world-of-equals, are retained. Imperfections are now allowed to emerge in the foresight of events in future periods, including foresight about the individual's own utility function.[7] This change dramatically converts the

7. Even in the simplest of decision models, complexities arise when individual utility maximization over time is introduced. On some of these, see Robert H. Strotz, "Myopia

model into one where decisions made in one period can exert relevant externalities on individuals in other periods. In effect, unless he has perfect foresight, the individual becomes a different person in each period. Choices made at one time may not reflect the preferences of another time.

If we could assume, with any degree of plausibility, that organizational decisions could be made anew at the onset of each time period, that individuals could start from *tabula rasa* with unbiased choice alternatives before them, the absence of foresight in the still-restricted model would not create major difficulty. But such an assumption would make the whole analysis absurd. Individuals do not participate in a "social contract" that involves organizing everything from scratch. They do participate in social decision processes that involve changes in organizational structure, changes from what exists to what might be. Once this simple fact is acknowledged and the notion of opportunity cost is fully grasped, the bias of all organizational choice toward non-reversibility becomes evident.[8] The cost of making any change in structure from what was to what is has been borne *in past periods*. The cost involved in making a change to something different must be borne *at the time of decision*. There is always a bias toward the status quo, toward continuing in existence the set of organizational rules that exist.[9]

To illustrate, let us assume that after careful consideration of the alternatives, the individual "votes" for a shift in the organization of some activity from the private to the public sector. He does so rationally; the anticipated benefits at the time of decision exceed anticipated costs. Since all persons in the community are identical, the collective decision is made unanimously. Consider, now, some time period after that during which the organization choice is made and the collectivization of the activity implemented. Assume that either the course of external events or the individual's own utility function is now different from that which was foreseen in the initial period. Further, let us specify that the subjective "terms of trade" have shifted against collectivization and that this shift is significant enough to have caused the

---

and Inconsistency in Dynamic Utility Maximization," *Review of Economic Studies*, 23 (January, 1956), 165–80.

8. J. R. Schlesinger and A. Phillips, "The Ebb Tide of Capitalism? Schumpeter's Prophecy Re-examined," *Quarterly Journal of Economics*, 73 (August, 1959), 448–65.

9. This argument has been developed in relation to the familiar fiscal adage, "An old tax is a good tax," in James M. Buchanan, *Public Finance in Democratic Process* (Chapel Hill: University of North Carolina Press, 1967), 68–71.

individual to reverse his initial-period decision had the new information been properly anticipated. Note, however, that the alternatives confronted in the later period will not be the same as those initially faced. Therefore, the individual may not actually reverse the organizational decision that has been made. The reason is that the opportunity cost involved in collectivization was borne at the time of the initial choice; the opportunity cost of reversing this decision remains to be borne in the later period. Clearly, the value placed on the anticipated stream of benefits may fall substantially before a reversal of an earlier-period organizational decision can rationally take place, even if the earlier-period decision should have been precisely marginal in that anticipated benefits barely exceeded the anticipated costs. The individual's choice behavior, as observed, would exhibit characteristics that are analogous to threshold-sensitive responsiveness despite the assumed hypersensitivity in his cognition pattern.

It is perhaps useful to contrast the relevance and importance of "bygones" or "sunk costs" as features of *organizational* decisions, whether these be private or collective, and as features of the standard decisions discussed in economic theory. In the latter, the consumer or entrepreneur is faced with given choice alternatives in a specific period. The commitments made can, of course, extend over a time sequence. But there takes place, in each instance, a using-up process over time that makes resort to new decisions necessary. Goods purchased are consumed; the consumer must return to the supermarket each week. Capital goods wear out; the entrepreneur must replace his old equipment. The continuing necessity for making new or replacement choices through time produces a quickly and smoothly adjusting convergence toward long-run equilibrium even in the face of constantly changing environmental conditions and utility functions. Long-run equilibrium may never be achieved, of course, but where choices are *by their nature* bounded in time, the system is described by a continuing process of readjustment.

With organizational choice, or the choice of rules more generally, there is no "using up"; there is no "natural" or "behavioral" time limit placed on commitments that are made when a rule is modified. There is no physical necessity which requires the explicit making of new or replacement decisions; constitutions do not "wear out." The choice of an organizational form modifies the environment and does so *permanently*. In the light of imperfectly foreseen events, therefore, the individual must look on the organizational structure inherited from past-period choices as embodying externalities analogous to the ordinary sort. Previous choices have affected his level of utility, and even if he made these choices himself, he still experiences "regrets," even though, given the environment that he confronts, it remains irrational to change. But he muses over what "might have been."[10]

To this point, we have relaxed only one of the central assumptions of our extremely restricted model, that which requires perfect foresight. It is evident that the effects noted will be enhanced in significance as relaxation proceeds. If we impose limits on the planning horizons of individuals and no longer assume that they act as if they live forever, the intertemporal externalities become intergenerational. For any existing "generation," the environmental structure will seem to have been imposed by others than themselves. This will surely produce an even greater sense of frustration than any sense of regret over past mistakes that were of one's own choosing. While it may remain fully rational for existing organizational structure to be continued in being rather than overthrown, individuals may be acutely sensitive to the distance of this structure from that which we may call the "long-term equilibrium," by which we mean the constitutional pattern that would be optimally desired.

Nor does it seem probable that the departures from optimality in organizational structure will fall symmetrically on either side of the arbitrary and existing private-sector, public-sector line of division. If the subjective terms of trade have shifted against collectivization for one activity, they seem likely to have shifted in the *same* direction for other activities, and vice versa. This suggests that the discontent experienced by the individual may have important implications for political reforms that might be observed to take place. If the departures from long-term equilibrium are in the same direction over a whole set or range of "goods," and if the changes in external events or in utility functions are also unidirectional over some reasonable time span, the

---

10. The features of organizational choice that exert the bias toward the status quo and which allow the intertemporal externalities to be introduced even in our still-restricted model apply to individual private choices as well as to group collective choices. There is a categorical difference, however, in the significance of organizational rules as between individual private behavior and group collective behavior. An individual may, and often does, institutionalize his own behavior through time by adopting rules to which he more or less routinely conforms. To the extent that he does so, the analysis sketched here holds. When groups of individuals are concerned, however, organizational rules become essential.

effective decision threshold may be crossed sequentially, even if not simultaneously, for a whole set of activities. Hence, even in this near-perfect world of equals, the absence of foresight alone, supplemented by some limitation on planning horizons, may generate broad and general shifts between private and collective organization in the supply of goods and services. The line of division between the political and the market sectors may not remain at or even near the long-term equilibrium position, which will itself, of course, be changing. The equilibrating forces set in motion by departures from equilibrium here operate only with significant time lags and then only when significantly large thresholds are surmounted.[11]

III. Freedom as an Indivisible but Exhaustible Good

In this section we examine more carefully one element of cost that arises from joint or collective action, the restriction on personal freedom to which the individual must submit when his behavior is subjected to community controls. The indivisible nature of personal freedom, the difficulty of making specific imputation of this cost to particular collective activities, may produce an interdependence among separate individual decisions that cannot be fully incorporated in the results of a sequential choice process where foresight is imperfect.

Consider the person who must make an organizational choice when the line of division between individual and collective activity (between the private and the public sector) is on the non-collectivist extreme of the scale. Rational consideration may suggest that the limitation on personal freedom that collectivization might involve is not sufficient to warrant either careful estimation or undue value weighting. Individual freedom of action may re-

---

11. We have not explicitly incorporated threshold-sensitive responsiveness in the behavior of individuals in our model. As noted, however, a threshold-sensitive pattern of behavior is exhibited because of the "sunk cost" aspects of organizational choice itself. The explicit introduction of threshold sensitivity would make the effects predicted more pronounced.

On the introduction of threshold sensitivity in economic theory generally, see Nicos Devletoglou, "Threshold and Rationality," *Kyklos* (forthcoming).

main open over so wide an area, over such a large number of options, that the restricting of only one of many avenues for private behavioral expression becomes insignificant for choice. As more and more activities are subjected to collective control, however, the limitations on personal freedom are cumulative. At some stage, these become relevant in any rational consideration of cost, and this cost may increase exponentially as the range of collectivization is extended. Because of the indivisibility of personal freedom, however, the individual may find attribution of this cost to separate activities difficult. In one sense he may feel schizophrenic when he confronts new organizational choice alternatives. If he neglects the limitations on personal freedom embodied in collectivization of an activity, the anticipated benefits may substantially exceed anticipated costs. If, on the other hand, he tries to include this aspect of cost, he will recognize that he is really loading the one activity with the burden arising from the general narrowing of his options and not with the specific closing off of one avenue of free behavior. More importantly, the individual may feel that the activity in question offers considerably higher net efficiency gains from collectivization than many activities that were organized governmentally during earlier periods when the added cost element seemed irrelevant. For reasons already discussed, however, these now inefficient activities may not be rationally decollectivized. In the struggle here, the Galbraithian elements seem likely to dominate the Goldwaterian, at least until some substantial departures from an ideally desired state of affairs are made. At some critical stage, however, the individual will begin to attribute the cost in personal freedom to all activities that are collectivized, and again because of the indivisibility of freedom itself, he will neglect the interdependence among separate activities. As a result, he may support drastic political reforms, amounting to constitutional revolution.

An economic analogue is provided in the behavior of a person who exploits a natural resource that he considers initially to be inexhaustible. He proceeds to use the resource as if the supply were infinitely large with respect to his own demands. At some stage, however, the individual discovers that the resource is exhaustible; he then recognizes that his earlier exploitation rate has been inefficient, that he has wasted a scarce resource. He may at this point dramatically reduce his rate of use, and, if he thinks it possible, he may also take measures that are aimed at renewing the stock. At the point of rec-

ognition, the individual may be observed to undergo a revolution in his behavior. The analogy with freedom does not seem farfetched here. As more
and more avenues for free individual behavior are closed, the individual may
quite suddenly realize that his options are not limitless.[12] Collective controls
become stifling at this point. Not only will the person refuse to support further collectivization; he may actively support measures aimed at reversing
the organizational pattern. Hence, this feature of choice behavior tends to
reinforce the more general features discussed in Section II.

IV. Interpersonal Externalities and Collective Decision Making

To this point, discussion has been deliberately restricted to the extreme world-
of-equals model. This has been designed to emphasize that even if interpersonal externalities of the familiar sort could be wholly disregarded, intertemporal externalities may arise when an historical sequence of organizational
choice behavior is examined. It should be clear, however, that the whole analysis becomes much more plausible and its results more meaningful when we
drop the world-of-equals assumption and when we allow for collective decisions under some non-unanimity rule.

If persons differ, they will not exhibit similar preferences about the organization of an activity. Some will prefer collectivization; others will prefer to
leave the provision of the "good" in private hands. Differing attitudes will
prevail about any demarcation line between the private sector and the public
sector. In the face of such individual differences, the requirement of unanimity in collective decision making may create unacceptable delays. The community may, with general agreement on the part of all members, settle for
some less inclusive rule, and, of course, democratic process is normally analyzed as if its institutions embody majority rule.[13]

If a non-unanimity rule is operative, however, political decisions inher-

12. For a corresponding view as regards sequential market choices, see A. E. Kahn,
"The Tyranny of Small Decisions: Market Failures, Imperfections and the Limits of Economics," *Kyklos,* 19 (fasc. 1, 1966), 23–47.

13. For a general discussion concerning the derivation of collective decision-making
rules from individual choice behavior, see James M. Buchanan and Gordon Tullock, *The
Calculus of Consent* (Ann Arbor: University of Michigan Press, 1962).

ently embody externalities, even if we now limit attention to one period of time. The dominant majority, the members of an effective coalition for any particular decision, imposes net costs on the dissident minority. Therefore, even before the intertemporal changes in the choice situation take place, a minority of citizens may disagree with decisions that have been made collectively. This tends to reinforce and to strengthen the probability of wide swings in organizational structure that we have already derived from the choice behavior of the individual decision maker. As more and more members of a dominant majority coalition become disaffected, as these persons come to experience regrets over past-period organizational choices, the possible attractiveness of their shifting to a new coalition increases. At some point, the exploited minority is converted into a majority, and a new value pattern typifies the average or representative decision maker for the community. There is, in one sense, a quantum difference in the utility function of the effective chooser as between two periods of time surrounding this critical switching point. For reasons noted, there will remain a bias toward the status quo in organizational structure, but once the effective threshold is crossed, shifts in the composition of the majority coalition may generate quantum variations in constitutional patterns.

V. Conclusion

Our general hypothesis is that dominant majorities will choose decision-by-decision and piecemeal to collectivize activities over a wide constitutional-organization range from rather extreme reliance on spontaneous interaction processes to substantial conscious collectivism. At some critical point in this historical sequence, the limitations on individual freedom that collectivism embodies will be sensed by a majority of the community. Equilibrium in the marginal sense may be established, and the disadvantages of further collectivization may be held to offset the advantages. However, this equilibrium will be inefficient; it will tend to embody an excess collectivization due to the forces that we have discussed. The potential exhaustibility of freedom has been neglected, and the political decision process itself may have imposed relevant external diseconomies. "Long-term disequilibrium" may be suffered for a considerable period of time due to the bias toward non-reversibility of organizational decisions, but during this period frustrations will increase and a

new majority coalition will come into being. At a critical stage in this sequence, a proposal for a genuine constitutional "housecleaning" will command widespread support.[14,15] Due to the indivisibility of freedom itself,
there may be an abrupt and dramatic shift away from collective controls and
an attempt to start again from an institutional *tabula rasa*. This constitutional revolution may not take on violent form, but it will be revolution
nonetheless.

Social scientists have often used the pendulum in discussing historical
change, and especially in their discussion of collective controls. The swing
between extreme laissez faire and collectivism has been interpreted in this
manner. In the early part of the nineteenth century, signs were evident that
the non-collectivist end of a swing was being approached. At first the discussion of intellectuals, and later public policy, began the turning back; the collectivization process was commenced. In this pendulum analogy, we may
now be in the stage where the end of the collectivist swing can be foreseen. A
turning back and gradual reversal might be predicted over the remaining decades of this century. Our analysis does not depend on specific predictions
about identifiable stages in the historical cycle. Our hypothesis does involve
a rejection of the pendulum analogy. The symmetry is absent, although the
cyclicity remains.

14. The possibility of quantum changes in behavior when the environment challenges
exceed certain critical limits is discussed briefly in Arthur Koestler, *The Act of Creation*
(New York: Macmillan, 1964), 554.

15. In theoretical welfare economics, private or independent behavior in the presence
of external effects will generate an equilibrium. As the theorems prove, however, this
independent-adjustment equilibrium is inefficient or non-optimal. It becomes relatively
easy to demonstrate that all persons may be made better off in terms of their own preferences through some collectivization of the activity, if certain costs of organization are
neglected. In this literature, however, relatively little attention seems to have been given
to the quantum jump from individual adjustment behavior to collectivization that must
take place when the externalities are internalized. Presumably, welfare economists consider that such "revolutions" take place through the ordinary collective decision processes
when and if the externalities are widely sensed by individuals and when these are of significant importance.

The analogy between this quantum jump from independent adjustment to collectivization in the context of a single activity that embodies externalities and the quantum
jump from excessive collectivization over a whole range of activities that have been collectivized over a historical sequence seems close. The point is that collectivization itself
embodies external diseconomies which, at some critical state, will come to be recognized.

Analysis of individual and collective choice behavior is greatly facilitated when it can be limited to instantaneous or one-period models. We have discussed choice phenomena that extend over a long historical sequence. Of necessity, therefore, the analysis is less rigorous and more heuristic than that which can be more appropriately restricted. Nonetheless, the economist's approach yields an hypothesis that is conceptually testable. With two-thirds of the twentieth century behind us, societies in both East and West seem to be characterized by persons who are in the process of awakening to the realization that collective controls have been allowed to exhaust dangerously the scarce stock of personal freedom. If this is descriptively relevant, our hypothesis predicts first a slowing down of the collectivization process, the signs of which may be already apparent. More importantly, we should expect to witness a growing disaffection with the institutions of collective control, with bureaucratic procedures generally, and an increasing discussion of major constitutional changes. This, too, may be characteristic of the late 1960's. If our hypothesis remains valid, this may produce genuine constitutional revolution which, hopefully, may take place non-violently but which will, regardless, represent genuine "revolution." There is, of course, nothing in our analysis which leads us to predict the paradigmatic content that such "revolution" might embody. If any specific prediction were asked from us, we should answer with Émile Durkheim's assertion: "The stages that humanity successively transverses do not engender one another."

Lagged Implementation as an Element in Constitutional Strategy

Give me chastity and continency—but not yet.

—St. Augustine, *Confessions* (Bk. VIII, Ch. 7)

Abstract: Lagged implementation may be an important element in a strategy of constitutional choice. By shifting the temporal dimensionality of a proposed rule, the present or current bias stemming from sensory perception may be reduced. Choice among lagged constitutional alternatives may allow for a more "reflective" personal evaluation.

1. Introduction

In this paper, I argue that lagged implementation is an important element in any strategy for constitutional change, and for reasons that are over and beyond the familiar facilitation of agreement among individuals and groups whose identified interests may conflict. I suggest that, particularly for choices among constitutional constraints, individuals may be better able to make meaningful evaluations among alternatives when the time sequencing of the effects of these alternatives is postponed or delayed beyond the period of choice itself. One way of putting the point here is to say that the individual

From *European Journal of Political Economy* 10 (1994): 11–26. Copyright 1994. Reprinted with permission from Elsevier Science.

I am indebted to my colleagues Roger Congleton and Viktor Vanberg for helpful suggestions.

chooser may find it advantageous to establish some measured distance from current-period impact in any choice of a plan that extends over several periods. By so doing, an individual may be able to make "better" choices, by his or her own ex post reckoning, than those that would emerge from choice settings in which the rejected alternative necessarily embodies an immediate or current-period initial impact.

In one sense, the whole argument may be interpreted to carry the straightforward normative implication that persons should "plan ahead," provided that the process of planning involves the making of commitments that cannot be readily circumvented by situational responses in periods subsequent to that in which the planning choice is made. My central argument is based on the claim that an individual, whether in a private or a collective constitutional choice setting, will find it "easier" to weigh alternatives that involve differing temporal characteristics in their effects when it is possible to eliminate the "privileged" role that is necessarily occupied by the immediate or here-and-now impact that bears on the psyche in a manner that is necessarily unique.

Section 2 introduces the logic of lagged implementation in a setting of individual choice over ordinary end-items of final usage ("goods"). Section 3 briefly refers to related work on temporary preference theory in psychology. Section 4 extends the analysis to choices among constraints. Section 5 compares and contrasts the analysis and argument of the paper to the familiar veil-of-ignorance/uncertainty device that is widely introduced in contractarian discourse. Section 6 introduces the notion of constitutional strategy and outlines the role of the political economist in those constitutional settings that may be described to embody unexploited gains-from-trade, as interpreted in familiar conceptual terms, even if the institutional structure of reform remains quite complex. Section 7 applies the argument to an issue of constitutional change that is important in current policy discussion in several countries in the 1990s. Section 8 concludes the paper.

2. The Present as Privileged

Economists tend to model choice as if there is no lag between choice and implementation and, also, as if all of the alternatives for choice have identical temporal features. Both of these implicit assumptions must be abandoned in the exercise that I am undertaking here.

Let me consider the first feature in isolation. Consider an individual's choice between two ordinary end-items of consumption, say apples and oranges, that are temporally identical in the sense that whichever one is chosen is to be consumed or used up during the same period. It is still possible to describe a process in which choice itself is not simultaneous with consumption. I may purchase fruit for dinner during a morning shopping excursion. And my choice, once made, will effectively constrain my dinner menu.

It seems clear that there is a sense in which we may claim that such a temporally detached choice may be more likely to be evaluated positively (as "rational") in some post-consumption perspective than would be a comparable choice made contemporaneously with consumption. In the latter, choice is more likely to be influenced by qualities that appeal directly to sense perception "on the surface" rather than those qualities that emerge as dominant in a plan that involves time-displaced utility maximization.

I am not suggesting that impulse buying is eliminated by temporal displacement. In choosing this morning between apples and oranges for this evening's dinner, I may still be influenced, and perhaps unduly, by the manner of display and the location of the alternatives in the shop. What is eliminated is the immediate linkage between the choice calculus and its effects, a phenomenon that may reduce impulse behavior of only one particular sort.

I do not, however, want to make too much of the possible importance of lags between the moment of choice and the period of final consumption of one utility-yielding "good" that is temporally identical to other "goods" in the feasible choice set. My primary emphasis is on the second of the implicit assumptions noted to be descriptive of the economists' model, that which assumes that the alternatives for choice do not differ along some relevant time dimension. I want to suggest that the modification of this assumption in the analysis of choice has relevant and important consequences, and particularly for choices among rules or constraints.

My concern centers on the setting in which one of the options in the choice set embodies implementation that is simultaneous with the moment of choice itself, at least in part, while the remaining option (or options) involves implementation only at a later time. For now, remain with an illustration that uses ordinary end-times of consumption. The relevant choice that the individual faces is that between choosing and eating an orange now and choosing the orange for eating later, say, tomorrow. It is evident that this choice is not "unbiased," as might be the case if the choice should be between a "plan" to eat an orange tomorrow and a plan to eat an orange on the following day. The immediacy or simultaneity of one of the choice options in the first setting described allows for the presence of attractors exerted in part by direct sense perceptions, attractors that necessarily remain pure mental imaginings with respect to the other of the options. The individual can, of course, imagine how an orange tomorrow would smell and taste, and this imagination can be translated into a present utility value that will be matched against that which is represented in the more immediate taste and smell of the orange to be currently experienced. But clearly the "orange now," as one of the choice alternatives, occupies a sensorially privileged position in the choice calculus.

Any trade-off between the present values of the utilities of the alternatives that differ temporally in final usage may reflect a time preference that places some premium on usage closer to the moment of choice. The orange that is to be eaten in t_2 stands higher in the ordinal utility ranking (at t_0) than the orange to be eaten in t_3. But the time preference between t_2 and t_3, as exhibited in choices made at t_0, seems categorically different from the sensorially biased time preference that would be exhibited between projected end-uses at t_0 itself and t_1 or any later period.

3. Temporary Preference Theory

In this Section, I shall discuss briefly the analytical and experimental work that has been done and is being done, primarily by psychologists, on what is called "temporary preference theory," and especially as this research program is summarized by Ainslie.[1] Various versions of a "matching law" have been advanced, and, although controversy remains, these have been widely observed to describe behavior in both human and animal experimental subjects. The relationship states that there tends to be an inconsistency in the temporal discounting of anticipated rewards, even in the absence of uncertainty. When choice is made among rewards sufficiently displaced in time, subjects tend to select the larger, later, values. But as the time for realization of reward approaches, the earlier, smaller reward generates an apparent switch in preferences, and subjects modify behavior accordingly. In sum,

1. George Ainslie, *Picoeconomics* (Cambridge: Cambridge University Press, 1992).

more immediate opportunities tend to be discounted at higher rates than less immediate or longer term opportunities.

The results of this research program in psychology can, I suggest, be interpreted as lending empirical support to the argument that I have advanced in this paper. The counterclaims to the effect that, in repeated choice situations, there is a tendency for time-consistent discounting to emerge is not relevant for my purposes. Constitutional applications tend to be unique; participants in constitutional choices do not have the luxury of repetition.

In the discussion of Section 2, above, I mentioned the difference between choices made when one alternative appeals to the senses directly and choices made when all alternatives are temporally detached so as to eliminate immediately experienced influences on evaluations. This distinction has been noted, but it has perhaps not been stressed sufficiently in the psychology literature. As Ainslie put the point: "Abstraction occurs downstream, as it were, from where motivation occurs."[2] Or, "(the person) is more likely to use the bank rate in calculating the value of distant goods than the value of nearer ones, because he will not have to overcome a spontaneous hyperbolic value function."[3]

Choices, as observed, must, of course, be made at the moment and under the influence of the perceptions that exist. It is only as attention shifts to the prospect for choices among constraints on future-period choices that explicitly defined lags in implementation can offer a means of partial escape from the necessity of evaluating immediately experienced cost and benefit flows.

4. Extension to Choices among Constraints

My purpose is not to concentrate attention on the individual's choice among alternatives within a defined set of constraints, even if temporal differences among these alternatives create specific problems that are not often incorporated adequately into the economists' analytical apparatus. The discussion above in Sections 2 and 3 was intended as a lead-in to a more careful examination of the individual's choices among constraints or rules for behavior,

2. Ibid., 83.
3. Ibid., 318.

choices in which the temporal characteristics of the alternatives become much more significant.

In what follows I shall presume that the individual can indeed choose constraints or rules that will effectively place limits on choices and actions in periods subsequent to that in which the constraint is chosen. That is to say, the individual can impose binding constraints over future behavior. But why would a person choose to restrict his or her own future-period choice? Such a choice of constraint may be preferred when nonconstrained patterns of future-period behavior are predicted to generate results that involve undesirable consequences during periods still further removed in time. The behavior that may be constrained is behavior that affects individual well being over a temporal sequence.

Examples are familiar. The individual may predict a situational response that will be regretted in later periods. Ulysses chose to constrain his predicted situational response to the song in order that he might continue his voyage beyond the sirens' shore.[4] By adopting a plan that was predicted to require utility loss, as experienced during the periods when the constraints were to be operative, Ulysses sought to insure that the predicted utility gain in subsequent periods would be realized. The choice of the constraint involved a necessary trade-off among anticipated utility flows in differing periods.

This example is also helpful in allowing me to stress the main point of this paper. Recall that Ulysses adopted the plan before he set sail on the voyage. The constraint was put in place prior to the time when it was predicted to come into play as limiting behavior. The implementation of the rule was lagged in time. The choice of the constraint was made when the temporal utility trade-offs, as anticipated, were viewed dispassionately, as alternative choice options, each of which was temporally detached from the period of choice itself. Ulysses did not wait until his ship approached the sirens' shore and only then try to constrain his response behavior. The whole point of the constraining exercise was to prevent the sensory response that was predicted to take place.

A "constitutional choice" necessarily involves some lag in implementation, and, therefore, to an extent at least, the person chooses at a moment in

4. Jon Elster, *Ulysses and the Sirens* (Cambridge: Cambridge University Press, 1979).

which there is no sensorially biased alternative, as there is in the immediate usage illustration introduced earlier. There remains, however, a categorical distinction to be made between the selection of a constraint that is to be implemented *immediately* upon choice, and to continue over a time sequence, and a constraint that is delayed in its commencement until some time has elapsed after the moment of choice itself. My central argument here is that such delays or lags in implementation can be important elements in facilitating an unbiased consideration of relevant alternatives.

Again, consider an example. An individual has, within the feasible choice set at t_0, the selection of a constraint that will effectively prevent the behavior in future periods that is deemed to be harmful and will be so assessed, say, beyond period t_3. One alternative form of this constraint is "cold turkey"; the chooser imposes a constraint that is effective immediately, in t_1. Or a second alternative may be in the form that becomes effective only after a one period lag, that is, in t_2. It may be much easier for the second form of the constraint to be chosen over the "do nothing" option than the first form. The attractor exerted by the immediacy of the utility loss may be too great to overcome, but some time lag in the realization of this loss may prompt more "rational" consideration of the options.

In the example here, the potential chooser's ordering of the options at t_0 may be as follows:

1. Binding constraint on behavior, at t_2.
2. No constraint—or "do nothing."
3. Binding constraint on behavior immediately, at t_1.

If we assign a zero value to the utility level anticipated at t_1, we can depict the ordering in utility flows as follows:

	t_1	t_2	t_3	$\ldots t_n$
1.	0	–	+ + +	+
2.	0	0	0 0 0	0
3.	–	+	+ + +	+

As the ordering suggests, the choice-relevant time preference (or rate of discount) is different as between t_0 and t_1, and t_1 and t_2. If the rate of discount should be uniform over time, option 3 must always rank higher than option 1.

It is clear from the discussion here that more sophisticated and more complex analyses may be introduced which include varying lengths of implementation lags and varying differentials between immediate and lagged time rates of discount. These complexities may serve to distract attention from the central argument. But a single illustration may be helpful.

Consider a person who is observed to discount rewards (income) that are distanced further in time at a lower rate than more immediate rewards. Assume that the relationship here is that shown by the smooth curve, D, in Fig. 1. The individual now confronts a choice between two courses of action: between (C) continuing to use up or consume all income currently received in each period, and (S) adopting a rule or constraint that will set aside some share (S/Y) of income per period for saving, which, when invested, yields a positive net return. The all-consumption regimen, C, must involve a forward time displacement relative to the saving regimen, S. Assume that at t_0, the moment of choice, the person values the all-consumption option (C) more than the saving option (S). And since the person will confront essentially the same choice in each period, he will not embark on the saving plan in any later period so long as the rule or plan requires immediate implementation.

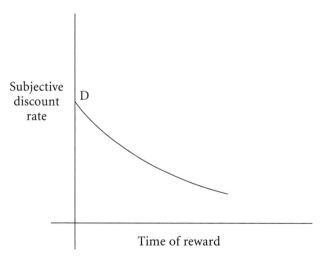

Figure 1

Consider, however, the evaluation, *from* t_0, placed on the alternatives (incomes, rewards) at t_1, and beyond. The rate at which income (reward) is discounted is *lower* (by the relationship of Fig. 1) than that applied to the incomes from the alternatives at t_0. As the discount rate falls with time displacement from t_0, the two alternatives, as evaluated from t_0, must converge in value. As shown in Fig. 2, the curves C and S must intersect at some point, from the general shape of the relationship depicted in Fig. 1.

Suppose now that the individual is offered a "contract" that involves a binding commitment, *to be chosen at* t_0, that requires the commencement of the saving regimen, not immediately at t_0 but at t_7, or beyond (Fig. 2). The lagged implementation feature will make the rule acceptable, whereas no immediately applicable rule would ever be chosen. And note that, so long as the curves C and S intersect at any point, there must exist an implementation lag that will reverse the preference ordering to the two alternatives.

Only one feature of the analysis warrants further discussion. The question at issue concerns the individual's intertemporal utility trade-offs that are involved upon the imposition of binding constraints on behavior, constraints to be chosen in some period, the "here and now," and to become effective either immediately or with some explicitly defined time lag. The individual's ordering of the choice alternatives will necessarily require a discounting of

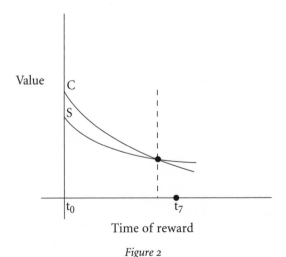

Figure 2

anticipated utility flows, and any ordering will reflect a set of subjectively generated intertemporal discount rates. These rates will remain strictly internal to the choice calculus of the individual, and there is no objective standard against which any external observer can adjudge results to be or not to be "efficient." Although intertemporal trade-offs are central to any such choice calculus, there is no analogue here to the present-value maximization that can be applied as a criterion for assessing the intertemporal exploitation of a marketable asset or the income stream therefrom. That is to say, the external observer does not have available any basis for evaluating behavior like that present in the judgment that the owner "cuts the trees too soon" in a maturing forest.

The economist, as external consultant or adviser to the chooser, is limited to a possible role in suggesting that any listing of precommitment or planning options should include behavioral constraints that explicitly incorporate lags in implementation. A rational calculus need not be restricted to the choice set that either leaves behavior nonconstrained or involves immediate limits on situational response. Time displacement and detachment from the "tastes" that exploit personal vulnerabilities may be necessary components in any inclusive rational strategy selection.

5. Veils and Lags

The feature of the individual's choice setting examined in this paper is related to, yet remains categorically distinct from, the feature that has entered modern contractarian analysis as the "veil of ignorance," as introduced by Rawls, and also as somewhat differently used (as a "veil of uncertainty") by Buchanan and Tullock, and even earlier and more normatively by Harsanyi.[5] The placing of the individual chooser behind or within a veil of ignorance and/or uncertainty is designed for the purpose of removing or at least substantially reducing potential conflict between an individual's fully identified

5. John Rawls, *A Theory of Justice* (Cambridge: Harvard University Press, 1971); James M. Buchanan and Gordon Tullock, *The Calculus of Consent* (Ann Arbor: University of Michigan Press, 1962); John Harsanyi, "Cardinal Welfare, Individualistic Ethics, and Interpersonal Comparison of Utility," *Journal of Political Economy* 63 (August 1955): 309–21.

interest and what may be called his or her "general" or "constitutional" interest.[6] The inability to predict what one's own position will be in the social interaction process, including the distribution of both initial endowments and final goods, and/or the particular impact and effect that particular rules or institutions will have on the position of the individual, even as identified, leads the chooser to prefer options that embody general criteria. And since such criteria are, by definition, generalizable over all participants in the stylized constitutional choice process, agreement or consensus on rules is brought within the range of possible achievement.

The lagged implementation feature of one of the choice options does not involve any veil; the person who faces choice knows precisely who he or she is and will be over the relevant sequence of time periods. But lags in implementation do allow a divorce, of sorts, between a currently sensed impact of a constraint and the impact or effect that will be sensed only by the person who lives in future periods. If we face up to the ontological reality that "personal identity" changes through time, lags in the implementation of a constraint introduce choice options that allow for a removal of that "person," who is strictly identified by the moment of choice. If I can choose between a constraint on behavior and no constraint, and if both of these alternatives are postponed until some well-defined future period, I am able to make trade-offs among anticipated utilities to be enjoyed by "separate persons," no one of which enjoys a privileged position. Criteria that may be akin to "fairness" in treatment as among these "persons" in the separate time periods become meaningful here.

In the conventional discussion, the veil of ignorance and/or uncertainty has been employed exclusively as a device aimed at facilitating agreement on constraints among separate potential contractors. The implicit presumption has been that the constraints within the choice set are to be implemented once they are chosen to be preferred. Of course, the very nature of any constraint or rule does involve a continuing sequence of applicability during which time behavior is to be restricted. In this sense, the timing of the effects has been analyzed. There has been a general recognition that the length of the period over which the constraint is to be applied and enforced will affect

6. Viktor Vanberg and James M. Buchanan, "Interests and Theories in Constitutional Choice," *Journal of Theoretical Politics* 1 (January 1989): 49–62.

the prospects for reaching agreement among participating contractors.[7] This argument can readily be extended to allow for lags in the initial implementation with the implication that any postponement will tend to facilitate agreement.

The basic difference between the veil of ignorance and lagged implementation is best understood, however, by concentrating attention on the individual's internal choice calculus independent of any participation in a multi-person contractual process. In considering whether or not to impose a constraint privately on his or her own behavior, any attempt to impose a veil becomes self-contradictory. The individual who chooses, or who might choose, a constraint is the person to whom the constraint is to be applied, within the limits of personal identity continuity mentioned earlier. There is no way to escape personalization by retreat behind a veil. By contrast, opening up the choice set to allow for a constraint with a lagged implementation may allow a chooser to adopt a plan of self-control that promises long-term utility gains, a plan that might prove impossible to adopt under any other terms.

6. The Economist and Constitutional Gains-from-Trade

In my initial response to the invitation to contribute to the set of papers honoring Peter Bernholz, I suggested that I examine "Problems of Constitutional Strategy." Bernholz stands almost alone in his early recognition and emphasis that genuine constitutional change is likely to take place only when the opportunities are propitious, and that one role of the political economist is to recognize the presence of such "constitutional moments," and to influence, if possible, both the shaping and the timing of reform proposals.[8]

I had scarcely commenced my effort before I realized that any discussion and analysis of strategy of constitutional change requires preliminary diag-

7. A. S. Pinto Barbosa, "The Constitutional Approach to the Fiscal Process: An Inquiry into Some Logical Foundations" (Ph.D. diss., Virginia Polytechnic Institute and State University, Blacksburg, Va., 1978).

8. See Peter Bernholz, "The Implementation and Maintenance of a Monetary Constitution," *Cato Journal* 6 (Fall 1986): 477–512, along with my comment, "The Relevance of Constitutional Strategy," *Cato Journal* 6 (Fall 1986): 513–17.

noses, and a subsequent taxonomy, of "constitutional failure." If we define "the constitution," inclusively and generally, as the laws, rules, institutions, and conventions within which persons in organized communities act, in their capacities as private individuals, as members of groups (firms, clubs, parties, etc.), and in their capacities as public choosers (voters, elected politicians, bureaucratic agents, etc.), we must first identify the circumstances under which an existing set of such rules and institutions, or any part thereof, can be described to exhibit failure. This step, in itself, is by no means simple, and economists, along with others, are often naive in their proclivity toward too-early diagnosis.[9]

Political economists who do concentrate their attention on constitutional structures (constitutional political economists), as contrasted with those who pay attention to policy alternatives within existing structures, tend to interpret failures in terms of a relatively straightforward extension of the Pareto-Wicksell criterion to the level of choices among rules. That is to say, an existing set of rules or constraints is classified as failing when there seem to exist at least some proposals for change upon which all of those who participate in the interaction process can agree. In this enterprise, the role for the political economist can be outlined with ease.[10] The preliminary stage is that which involves hypothetical identification of a failed rule, followed by the presentation of an alternative, or alternatives, that might secure consensual support. The ultimate test is agreement, and the secondary stages of the economists' effort involve the working out of possible package deals, compensations, compromises, side payments, appeals to ethical norms, and other effective schemes that may make potential agreement possible.

Any change in operative constitutional rules is difficult to secure, and more so in a stable than in an unstable order, since only in the former do constitutional structures effectively constrain action, and especially action taken by political agents. And even if we, as political economists, find instances of presumably failing rules in all polities, our conceptual task in any overall strategy of constitutional reform remains straightforward. Almost all

---

9. Rutledge Vining, *On Appraising the Performance of an Economic System* (Cambridge and New York: Cambridge University Press, 1984).

10. James M. Buchanan, "Positive Economics, Welfare Economics and Political Economy," *Journal of Law and Economics* 2 (October 1959): 124–38.

polities fail in elements of what we might call the "economic constitution," and the role for the economist is the never-ending one of analysis, discussion, and suggestion of rules changes that promise benefits for all persons and groups.

The examples are familiar. Politically imposed restrictions on trade, whether domestic or foreign, must, save in exceptional circumstances, be value-reducing rather than value-enhancing, and constitutional rules (or the absence thereof) that allow such restrictions to be legislatively enacted can be classified to be in need of correction. Special benefit (pork-barrel) spending projects financed from the revenues collected by general taxes and enacted by rotating legislative majorities tend to be inefficient, and quite possibly harmful to all citizens. Constitutional failure is evidenced in the absence of effective constraints on such excesses of distributional politics.

The strategy for constitutional change that can be brought within the Pareto-Wicksell construction, stylized as required, calls upon the economist to exercise familiar tools and to use familiar language. Basically, the economist here does little more than to say "I think that there exist mutual gains from trade or exchange." The exchange in question involves all parties subject to existing rules (or the lack thereof) coming into agreement on a change; in the process each party gives up or trades away some element of own behavior, actual or potential, in exchange for like behavior on the part of others. In the standard PD illustration, each player gives up the off-diagonal option of trying to secure differential gains from strictly opportunistic behavior in exchange for similar action by the other player. So long as the enterprise of potential constitutional reform can be brought into the generalized exchange paradigm, even as applied to exchanges of constraints, the economist is perhaps too complacent in considering that there are no further elements to be introduced in a strategy of constitutional reform.

Two points deserve attention. First, constitutional failures that may be brought within the generalized and extended Pareto-Wicksell umbrella may not exhaust the set, and, indeed, these may not be the most important. If other sources of failure exist, something other than the standard effort of the political economist may be worth examining. Second, for all constitutional failures, the timing patterns of proposed changes may be critical in affecting acceptance or rejection by choosers.

My particular concentration in this paper is on the intertemporal utility trade-offs that are within the choice sets of individuals. My concern does not extend to that which prompts examination of exchange prospects among separate individuals, even in some indirect and complex sense. But what can the economist say about the trade-offs among "goods" (and "bads") that are strictly internal to the individual's choice process? And the limits on economists' competence here would seem to be equally applicable to choices among constraints (constitutional choices) and choices among alternatives that are within the feasible set as defined by the constraints in existence, whether these be "natural" or "artifactual."

I want to suggest, however, that the economists' retreat, when confronted by individuals' preferences, either as postulated or as revealed by behavior, has often been hasty and ill-conceived. The discussion in earlier sections was intended to suggest that there is more to be said, once we explicitly recognize that the moment of choice may be temporally displaced from the period of final implementation of the effects, and, also, that the separate alternatives in a relevant choice set may embody quite different temporal dimensions.

7. Constitutional Application

In Sections 2, 3, and 4, individual choice among options that include constraints on behavior was examined independent of any constitutional setting. The discussion in Sections 1 and 5 was prefaced by references to constitutional choices faced by members of an ongoing political community and to elements in a strategy that might be aimed toward making constitutional reform easier to accomplish. Two points warrant repetition. Not all cases of alleged constitutional failure can be brought under the economist's familiar gains-from-exchange analytical umbrella, and for both such cases and other alternatives, lags in implementation of constraints on behavior may be helpful in achieving change, and for reasons that are like those that were developed in the more detailed examination of the private choice calculus, as outlined in the preceding sections.

We can apply the analysis to a real-world example of alleged constitutional failure that cannot be brought readily within the mutuality-of-gains framework. The inability of democratic governance in many modern polities to maintain fiscal responsibility is widely adjudged to reflect constitutional failure. And efforts are made to reform constitutions so as to constrain the profligate fiscal behavior of politicians and governments, but these efforts continue to fail. Governments continue to operate with deficit financing of substantial proportions of public outlays, and operative constitutions do not include effective constraints on such operation.

Note that this particular constitutional failure, as alleged, need not reflect any self-evident presence of nonexploited gains-from-exchange, even if the notion of exchange is extended to include exchanges of agreement on constraints. Each and every adult citizen in a polity may appear to be quite satisfied with the collective choice process that involves the financing of a substantial share of governmental outlay by borrowing rather than by taxation. A somewhat different way of putting this point, and more related to the earlier examination of individual choice, is to say that such an alleged constitutional failure might be observed to occur even in a polity where all persons are equally positioned in terms of all of the relevant economic and demographic characteristics.

The political agents in the community may respond directly to the demands of constituents, and suppose that we observe a continuing response that generates a substantial shortfall between revenues produced by approved rates and tax and approved outlays on governmental programs (including transfers). The deficit is, however, observed to remain within the limits of creditworthiness; the government remains able to market its debt obligations. In this scenario, the annual interest charges increase through time, and an increasing share of tax revenues collected must be dedicated to meeting these charges.

We observe some discussion of proposals to replace the regime of continuous deficits in the government's budget by the enactment of a constitutional change that will require that the fiscal account be kept in balance, with projected outlays kept within the limits dictated by projected revenue flows. But we also observe that such discussions, and proposals for change, fail to secure much public support.

How is it possible in such circumstances to claim that there is any constitutional failure? The evidence seems clear that persons are unwilling to trade off the current or short-term utility losses that any shift toward a balanced-budget regime would involve in exchange for the future-period utility gains that would ensue from the removal of the interest charges (or any part thereof) from future-period incomes. The alternatives for constitutional choice may not, however, be exhausted by the pairwise comparison between the (1) no change option and (2) approval of a budget balance constraint. An additional constitutional option may be approval *now* of a binding constraint that is explicitly lagged in its implementation, and over a sufficient number of time periods, to enable individuals to escape from the pressures on their choice calculus by the immediacy of the promised utility losses consequent on the enforcement of the constraint. Note that, in such a scheme, although the anticipated utility losses are advanced in time over the anticipated utility gains, both streams (losses and gains) are distanced from the moment of choice itself, and sufficiently so to allow for an unbiased trade-off in anticipated utilities to take place.

At this point, a critic of my argument might suggest, and especially in the context of the fiscal example, that the value of lagged implementation has always been recognized, and, indeed, that almost all proposals for constitutional fiscal reform allow for a relatively long period of transitional adjustment before the final objective of budget balance is to be achieved. But gradualism, as a distinct element in a constitutional strategy, is categorically different from the element that I have tried to discuss in this paper, although there remain subtle relationships between the two worth some clarification. To suggest that a proposal to require budget balance should be introduced gradually, over, say, a five-year period, involves an unwillingness to require adjustments that exceed certain threshold limits in any single period. Within these threshold adjustment limits, there is no lagged implementation of the sort that is discussed in this paper.

For numerical illustration, take the United States setting in the early 1990s. Suppose that the annual deficit is measured at roughly $300 billion, and that a proposal for constitutional change requires budget balance after six years, with an annual $50 billion adjustment downward in the size of the deficit. Approval of this proposal would require acceptance of the immediate utility loss involved in the $50 billion adjustment in exchange for the later-period utility gains that this adjustment would produce in reduced interest charges. For the later years in the transition, the lagged implementation argument would become effective in influencing choice. The implication of my argument here is that some *combination* of lagged implementation and gradualism might succeed; perhaps the proposal should take the form of, say, a three-year lag, to be followed by a six-year period of transition. A proposal for a constitutional amendment to be approved in 1993, to commence to be implemented in 1996, with final achievement of budget balance by 2002 might secure general support.

8. The Reality of Constraints

The discussion in this paper has been grounded in the presupposition that in their capacities as private individuals, as members of groups or associations, or as members of a politically organized community, persons can choose constraints upon their own behavior, and that of their selected agents, and, further, that the constraints, so chosen, can act so as to restrict or limit behavior. There is no requirement that any and all imagined constraints could be totally effective; the issue is not properly treated in all-or-none terms. There may well be efforts to impose constraints that fail; persons may adopt rules that they cannot follow, and other rules may prove to be unenforceable. And there may be some constraints that affect behavior, but only to some lesser extent than initially intended. Any overall constitutional strategy must of course reckon on the prospects for the workability of any set of rules.

The sometimes encountered argument to the effect that constitutional rules cannot constrain behavior should be rejected as absurd. We live always within constraints that we acknowledge to limit our behavior, and we acknowledge that many of these constraints are artifactual. There is no "natural" constitution that defines the limits on our behavior, whether with reference to private or public activities. The constraints within which we act are in part natural, in part the product of an evolutionary process, and in part the result of constructive choices made both privately and publicly in prior periods. As of any given time, these constraints are exogenous, but there should be no presumption that the set that is in existence is optimal. Within limits, we are able, privately and publicly, to construct our own future by selecting the parameters within which we and our agents will act in future time periods.

In any planning process that involves consideration of alternative rules, the temporal displacement among the separate effects becomes important. And the immediacy of the utility losses promised by the choice of constraints that might prove ultimately beneficial may cause such constraints often to be rejected. Lags in the implementation of such constraints may provide the means to remove the privileged position of the immediate. Plans may be made, and choices exercised, as among alternative futures.

Prolegomena for a Strategy of
Constitutional Revolution

This chapter amounts to an extended discussion stimulated directly by a paper presented by Professor Peter Bernholz at a Washington, D.C., conference in 1986, followed by comments of my own. Bernholz's paper was on prospects for reform in monetary constitutions, and my comments were entitled "The Relevance of Constitutional Strategy."[1] In this further discussion, I shall examine prospects for genuine constitutional reform in the early 1990s. Is the time at hand when genuine constitutional revolution in Western countries may be possible? How could we recognize the elements of the socio-economic-political interaction process, including the attitudes of the participants, that might bring constitutional reform within the realm of the feasible? Can we identify steps that the political economist might take to direct or to channel discussion toward mutually beneficial changes in the rules of the political game?

In his paper, Bernholz limited his attention to prospects for change in monetary regimes, and he introduced a discussion of how separate interest groups might converge in support of regime change during specifically identifiable phases or stages of cycle described by differential rates of inflation. That is to say, the Bernholz argument suggested that the prospects for constitutional reform may vary with the situational setting and that an exami-

From *The Economics and the Ethics of Constitutional Order* (Ann Arbor: University of Michigan Press, 1991), 89–97. Copyright 1991 by The University of Michigan. Reprinted by permission of the publisher.

1. Peter Bernholz, "The Implementation and Maintenance of a Monetary Constitution," *Cato Journal* 6 (Fall 1986): 477–512; James M. Buchanan, "The Relevance of Constitutional Strategy," *Cato Journal* 6 (Summer 1986): 513–18.

nation of the convergence and/or divergence among the separate interest groups may generate, for the observing political economist, a basis for a constitutional strategy. I propose here to go even further back in analysis, so to speak, and to examine the basic features of the "dilemma" that exist, pre-reform, in each of three "constitutions," the regulatory, the fiscal, and the monetary. Once these elemental features or characteristics have been identified, the problems faced in any reform strategy are more readily subject to analysis.

It will first be necessary to define, very briefly, what I mean by constitutional change, reform, or revolution. I shall, of course, be covering material here that I have discussed in many earlier books and articles. But a short summary, presented in section 1, seems essential in order to insure that my subsequent argument is understood.

After the summary statement of the constitutional perspective, I shall, in sections 2, 3, and 4, examine the distinct features in the separate diagnoses of the regulatory, the fiscal, and the monetary constitutions.

1. The Economy as a Constitutional Order

Those who conceptualize national economies as networks of macroaggregates that can be managed or manipulated for the purpose of promoting the achievement of macroeconomic objectives cannot understand what the terms *constitutional reform* or *constitutional revolution* mean. In this conceptualization, economic policy is straightforwardly teleological; there exist objectives worthy of achievement that are recognized by the authorities, and the economy must be guided toward such ends.

The constitutionalist perspective differs dramatically in its fundamental conceptualization of what the "economy" is. Here, the political economy is conceived as a *constitutional* order that, in itself, and, as such, embodies no independently defined objective or goal and has no function. The order is best described as a set of rules, or constraints, within which individuals, and organizations of individuals, interact, one with another, in promoting their own, individually initiated purposes. Patterns of outcomes or results (allocations, distributions, utilization, and growth rates) depend critically on the rules that constrain both private and public choices. And persons, generally, may judge some patterns of outcomes to be less desirable than others that might be generated under alternative rules. In such circumstances, there may be general agreement on a change in the rules, or constitutional reform.

It is essential to recognize that the choice of a rule (or a set of rules) within which a pattern of outcomes may emerge over a sequence of interactions is categorically distinct from the choice of an outcome or result that has well-defined characteristics. Policy is misdirected to the extent that it is motivated by the notion that specific outcome targets can be achieved. Even an ideally omniscient and benevolent authority could not choose an allocation of resources, a distribution of income, a rate of resource utilization, or a rate of economic growth. This proposition holds even if we totally ignore issues relating to the definition of what the ideals would look like in each case.

The social interaction process necessarily involves choices made by the many separate individuals and organizations in the economy-polity, each one of whom chooses subject to the constraints that are separately confronted. The many choices generate one outcome from among a whole set of outcomes that might emerge within the same set of constraining rules. To model policy as if the alternatives for "social choice" are outcomes amounts to a denial that participants retain independent powers of choice. Those who choose rules for games do not, in doing so, choose solutions; rather, solutions *emerge* from the choices of players made within the rules that constrain them.

Regardless of the ultimate location of political authority, whether this be concentrated in a single person, party, or class or dispersed among many persons who act through some collective decision-making institutions, any imposed, politically directed action or law must modify the constraints for all those who choose in any of the many capacities or roles. In this narrowly defined sense, any political action must be "constitutional." It seems preferable, however, to restrict the use of the term *constitutional* to those actions that have rules changes as their primary purpose.[2] The "economy as a constitutional order" is described by the set of rules within which individuals

---

2. Taxation offers an example. Any tax will modify the constraints faced by individuals in the polity, even the lump-sum tax that is often used for benchmark comparisons by public finance theorists. But a tax levied for the purpose of financing public outlay, which will change constraints for individual choice, is not exclusively aimed at accomplishing the behavioral change induced by the modification of constraints. In the terminology suggested here, only the latter tax is to be considered "constitutional."

and organizations (including government) make choices and implement them in subsequent actions.

An existing constitution is evaluated through reference to the relative desirability of the pattern of outcomes that it allows the choices of participants to generate stochastically over a temporal sequence. The problems that arise in diagnosing "constitutional failure" are difficult and not well understood, even if we restrict attention to evaluation by a single person, whether this person be an active participant or an outside observer. My concern here is not, however, with such problems, as difficult as these may be.[3] My concern is with the comparative evaluation of an existing set of rules made by the many separate persons in a constitutional democracy, where basic changes in structure are made, ideally, only upon consensual agreement.

It is, first of all, self-evident that any agreement on the diagnosis of a constitutional order is enormously more difficult to achieve than the making of a diagnosis itself by a single person, or even by a group of persons who share evaluative norms. In particular, if the status quo set of rules, or some part thereof, is consensually diagnosed as needing reform or change, players must not only agree that the "game" played out within the existing rules is negative sum, in some appropriately defined opportunity cost sense, but, also, there must be agreement upon the alternative set of rules that is predicted to yield higher utility levels. The monetary regime offers a good example. There may be general agreement that an existing regime "fails" in comparison with some alternative regime, but agreement may break down on the identification of the alternative with which the existing regime is compared. The discretionary authority of national central banks may be judged to be nonpreferred by all parties, but the preferred alternative may be a gold standard by some and a rule-directed fiat system by others.

Is it not absurd to think that the required consensus could ever be attained? Will not there be at least some major groups in a polity that will consider any existing rules preferred over any alternative? I do not underestimate the magnitude of the challenge here. But, by way of precaution, we must keep in mind that, if there is no agreement possible on any change, then

---

3. See Rutledge Vining, *On Appraising the Performance of an Economic System* (Cambridge and New York: Cambridge University Press, 1984), for a concentrated treatment of some of the issues in constitutional diagnoses at the level of the individual evaluator.

the existing set of rules is, in this sense, to be considered optimal. The simple logic of Pareto criteria tells us that if an existing state of affairs is to be evaluated as Pareto-inferior, there must exist at least one alternative that is Pareto-superior. The challenge to the political economist is to locate the set of changes that will command general agreement.[4]

2. Features of the Regulatory Dilemma

I propose to examine, in turn, three areas where constitutional failure seems to be present in Western democratic nations, three "constitutions." I shall try to outline, in each case, elementary features of the prereform setting. This step is required *before* any discussion-analysis of possible change in rules.

In this section, I consider the general area of "regulation," by which I refer to the direct intrusion of politicized controls over market interaction. The familiar examples are political controls over (or interferences with) terms of potential voluntary exchanges of goods and services: controls over wages, prices, interest rates, rents, entry into and exit from occupations, industries, and locations. In each case, the political controls are motivated by producer group interests, which seek to secure benefits (monopoly rents) at the expense of the citizenry generally. Any change in rules that prohibits such political control is clearly not to the particularized interest of any such potentially favored group if the policy issues affecting that group are taken one at a time and in isolation. The potential or actual beneficiary group or class will never freely assent to piecemeal constitutional change. The particular interest of the group will be damaged in the process.

By contrast, each group that finds itself the beneficiary of the regulation that protects its own particular interests is itself damaged by regulations that serve to generate particularized benefits to other groups and interests. Each group would, in its *constitutional* interest, prefer that all of the other regulations be removed and that exchanges be allowed unrestricted domain over these sectors of economic life. If this generalized conflict between the indi-

---

4. For a statement of this general methodological position, see James M. Buchanan, "Positive Economics, Welfare Economics and Political Economy," *Fiscal Theory and Political Economy* (Chapel Hill: University of North Carolina Press, 1960), 105–24. Also see W. H. Hutt, *A Plan for Reconstruction* (London: Kegan Paul, Trench, Trubner & Co., 1943).

vidual's particular interest and his or her constitutional interest is acknowl-edged, then the way seems open for a general agreement that will prohibit, constitutionally, any political interference with the freedom of voluntary ex-change. If the number of producer groups that secures political protection becomes sufficiently large, the losses suffered, even by a protected producer group, may outweigh any gains from the protection. In this setting, the members of all protected producing groups, along with nonproducers in the economy, will agree on a change in rules that eliminates protection over *all* groups.

The essential feature of this prereform regulatory setting is described in the classical Prisoners' Dilemma. Given the constitutional rules of the game, as they exist, producer groups maximize utility by seeking protection under the state's regulatory umbrella. As more and more groups succeed in this ef-fort, a point is reached where members, even of those groups that are pro-tected by regulation, are worse off than they would have been or would be in the absence of political regulation generally. But the generalization feature is worthy of emphasis here; it would not be in the utility-maximizing interest of any protected group to seek removal from the protective umbrella of regu-lation in isolation from the other protected groups. Constitutional reform can be successful only if it is sufficiently *general* to bring in large numbers of separate producer interests and remove all of these, simultaneously, from the regulatory umbrella.

3. The Potential for Reform in the Fiscal Constitution

The central flaw in existing fiscal constitutions lies in the absence of any con-straint on the debt financing of current public consumption. The impact of the Keynesian revolution in economic policy was to repeal effectively the bal-anced budget norm for fiscal prudence. Post-Keynes, political decision mak-ers have felt free to exercise their natural proclivities to spend without taxing currently, proclivities that are based on the desire to meet demands of con-stituents. As I have argued on numerous occasions and in many forums for three decades, the suggested constitutional reform is simple and straightfor-ward and represents the implementation of a central principle of classical public debt theory. The constitution should be changed to include a prohibition of debt financing of outlay on currently consumed publicly provided goods, services, and transfers.

Note, however, that the basic features of the prereform status quo here, with the observed regime of continuous deficit financing, are quite different from those that are present under the protectionist regulatory regime discussed in section 2. The fiscal status quo cannot be modeled in terms of the classical Prisoners' Dilemma, where individuals' particular or operational interests may conflict with their more generalized constitutional interests. Any argument for constitutional reform must incorporate recognition of the distinct structural features. In the ongoing deficit regime, persons living now, in their capacities as current recipients of publicly financed benefits or in their capacities as current taxpayers, secure net utility gains at the direct expense of persons who will occupy beneficiary-taxpayer roles in future periods. (There will, of course, be some overlap between these groups.) Deficit financing of current consumption is a pure intertemporal transfer. And, like all transfers, no efficiency gains are available that, even conceptually, would allow the potential gainers from a change in the rules (future-period taxpayers-beneficiaries) to compensate the potential losers (current-period taxpayers-beneficiaries). The argument for constitutional change must, therefore, be grounded differently from the interest-based logic of regulatory reform.

There are two separable features of the argument here, each of which is derived from a feature that is familiar in nonfiscal applications. In the first, we ignore the collective decision aspects of fiscal choice and concentrate exclusively on the individual. Here any change in the rules that will restrict debt financing of current consumption must call upon some argument from the "economics of temptation." The individual who recognizes his or her own possible "weakness of will" in future periods may choose to impose upon himself or herself binding constraints that will effectively prevent his or her situational responses, as those responses might be dictated by in-period utility maximization. This precommitment logic has been discussed by Elster, Schelling, Thaler, and others in such examples as forbearance from tobacco, alcohol, food, and sex. Somewhat more generally, the argument may be extended to personally derived norms against pure consumption borrowing.

A second part of an argument for change in fiscal rules requires the introduction of the collective aspects of choice. Even in settings where an individual might not, upon reflection, choose to bind himself against consumption borrowing, he or she may well agree to bond or precommit the collective of which he or she is a member. Individuals may do so because they do not "trust" fellow members to refrain from "temptation," and because they recognize that, in majoritarian settings, they cannot effectively forestall *undesired political* choices.[5] One or both of these elements may generate a consensus that a balanced budget rule should be adopted, despite the recognized current-period loss.

There is, however, an implication of the constitutional reform logic here that is not present in the regulatory example. Because rule changes here do, indeed, impose acknowledged current-period utility losses, relative to utility levels enjoyed in the absence of the change, consensus building may require that implementation be lagged over several periods. This time lag requirement is not central to reform in the regulatory constitution, as previously discussed.

Also, as the discussion suggests, the moral or ethical dimensions of the comparative evaluation of the status quo and the alternative regime become important in the fiscal constitution, whereas such dimensions may remain relatively insignificant in the thrust for regulatory depoliticization. Deficit financing of current public consumption involves a more blatantly unjust transfer from future-period to current-period taxpayers-beneficiaries than the more diffuse transfer from consumers to producers in the regulatory setting. Quite apart from this difference in generality, there are also "excess burdens" produced by politicized interference with voluntary exchanges, the elimination of which offers a "cushion" for working out agreed upon compromises on rules changes. No such "excess burden" exists in the pure intertemporal transfers reflected in deficit financing. Only some introduction of a moral argument can oppose the play of self-interest here.

4. Potential Change in Monetary Rules

In the paper referred to earlier, Bernholz suggested that the dynamics of the inflationary process offer opportunities for implementing change in the mon-

---

5. For elaboration of the argument here, see chap. 21 in James M. Buchanan, *Liberty, Market and State: Political Economy in the 1980s* (New York: New York University Press, 1986), 229–39.

etary structure. In his analysis, nonconstrained discretionary authorities exhibit consistent inflationary bias due to pervasive political pressures. As the authority responds by reducing the value of the monetary unit, the interests of government and of debtors, both existing and potential, are promoted at the expense of creditors. As potential creditors (lenders) recognize the inflationary patterns and make predictions concerning their continuance, they will demand and be able to secure protection of value through modified terms of intertemporal exchange. As this adjustment takes place, the earlier gains from inflation, to the government on the one hand and to debtors on the other, may be squeezed out, and, in some cases, converted into net losses. At some appropriate point in the dynamic sequence, there can be a genuine convergence of debtor and creditor interests on a shift in structure toward a regime that embodies predictability in the value of the monetary unit.

Predictability, in and of itself, implies pure efficiency gains to all potential transactors who use money as a medium of exchange or store of value. There is an "excess burden" in nonpredictability that is analogous to that involved in politicized interferences with market exchanges, and this "excess burden" can provide a cushion for securing agreement among different interests. Note here that the efficiency-based argument for predictability is not the same as the argument for *stability* in the value of the standard, at least in any direct sense. On the other hand, if a change in regime insures predictability in the value of the monetary unit, there should arise no conflict among interests (for example, debtors and creditors) as to the direction or rate of change in this value through time. If all transactors make the same prediction as to the temporal path of change in the standard's value, and if the regime insures that these expectations are fulfilled, there is no difference in first-level efficiency between inflationary, stable, and deflationary patterns. Efficiency differences here, which may be minimal, arise only from differences in the resource costs of using money relative to other standards for storing value.

5. The Welfare Politics of Constitutional Change

I have entitled this chapter "prolegomena" for a strategy of constitutional revolution. My central point has been that we must understand the characteristic features in the diagnosis of regime failure in each of the three cases examined before proceeding to suggest specific reforms. This approach suggests, in turn, that the prospects for securing constitutional change need not be so dismal as pessimistic political economists sometimes seem to accept. With reference to both the regulatory and the monetary constitutions, there can arise some convergence of special interests in support of change; the thrust need not come from some effective representation of the generalized and diffuse interests of nonorganized and nonorganizable consumers. In regulatory reform, the very multiplicity of special interests who seek, and get, regulatory protection from the state may, at some point, insure that these interests, in their roles as consumers, will recognize the negative-sum aspects of the rent-seeking game in which they are all involved. In monetary reform, the dynamics of the inflationary sequence will possibly generate a convergence of interests on basic structural change at the appropriate point in the sequence.

In the fiscal constitution, the reform in the rules that will replace the regime of permanent deficit financing with one of balanced budgets is not as amenable to any convergence of interests as the other constitutional sectors examined here. The overt conflict of interests here is not between groups within the existing population (between producers and consumers in the regulatory case, between debtors and creditors in the monetary case), but between "generations," or between temporally defined sets of taxpayers-beneficiaries. Some motivation other than the current interests of persons, whether organized in special interests or diffused and generalized, must describe any thrust toward the introduction of constitutional checks.

It may seem, in some respects, surprising that the agitation for constitutional change seems to be greatest precisely in this area where the interest-based thrust for change would seem weakest. On the other hand, the observed agitation seems to have produced relatively little effective change. Perhaps we can explain the differences in the three regimes, along with the prospects for dramatic constitutional change, by the characteristic features of the diagnosis after all. Because both the regulatory and the monetary rules are ultimately vulnerable to pressures from interest-driven coalitions in support of change, the excesses of departures from the dictates of efficiency-defined ideals may have been more limited. The protectionist intrusion of the modern state may be limited by the recognition that, if it extends beyond certain limits, it becomes self-destructive in the interest-driven polity. The monetary authorities, seeking always to protect their own bureaucratic interest, may reckon on the interest group feedback from too extensive an exercise of the inflationary engine. There is no such limitation internal to the fiscal profligacy that describes the financing of modern states; the relatively greater agitation for change in fiscal rules arises precisely because there are fewer constraining internal checks.

The Structure of Progress

National Constitutionalism in a Technologically Opened World Economy

---

I. Introduction

As you know, I am not sufficiently familiar with the history of Spain to speak from an informed perspective about political and institutional changes that have taken and are taking place or about further changes that might be generated from explicit policy choices. Secondly, even with reference to my own country, the United States, I am not the sort of political economist who acts as social engineer by participating actively in normative discussion about alternative directions for hands-on management of national economic parameters. By the nature of both my externally and internally restricted capacities, I am forced to concentrate on very general themes that may be no more relevant for Spain than for many other countries in the world of 1996.

In one sense, a necessary recognition of nonparticularity may be treated as an overreaching motive of the whole lecture. The separate nation-states of the world, described variously by differing racial, ethnic and religious compositions; by diverse political histories; by differentiated cultural traditions and by empirically distinct legal and economic structures, are far from homogeneous on many descriptive dimensions. Modern pluralist philosophers who stress the differences can scarcely be challenged empirically. And they are surely on target when they issue warnings against the naive application

From *Doctorado "Honoris Causa" del excmo. sr. d. James M. Buchanan* (Valladolid, Spain: University of Valladolid, 1996), 19–29. Reprinted by permission of the publisher.

of the same nostrums everywhere, whether these be political, economic or cultural in nature.

Nonetheless, and despite the differences, when we compare the international scene from the beginning to the end of this century, there has surely been substantial convergence among the separate national units. The world today is more homogeneous than it was in 1900; this straightforward proposition can scarcely be denied. And a major element in generating convergence has been technological development that has threatened to swamp politics, economics and culture. The separateness of the nations has been quite substantially reduced, quite apart from explicit policy steps aimed at economic and political integration.

I propose, in this lecture, to examine the role of the single nation-state, as reflected in possible choices confronted by political leaders, acting as agents for citizens, in the turn of the century setting described by the technologically determined openness of the world, derivative from the information-communication revolution that remains ongoing. My subtitle in this respect is explicitly descriptive; I suggest that separate national economies are necessarily open, to greater or lesser degree, due to technology itself and, further, that internally motivated efforts to manage or control such economies are severely constrained by instant access to cross-national comparisons.

The words *national constitutionalism* in the lecture's subtitle are inserted to suggest that, as the constraints are recognized, political agents will be forced to rely primarily, if not exclusively, on "constitutional" parameters in any efforts to further the objectives of national policy. And the word *constitution* in my usage here includes any and all rules that constrain behavior, publicly or privately, whether these rules be legal, political or ethical in content.

The openness of the single nation-state, and, here, especially the openness of the recently developed and emerging states, carries with it potential warning signs that must be heeded. There are very real dangers that states will be led to maintain institutional patterns which have inhibited, rather than enhanced, economic growth. Particular reference is made here to the institutional climate described as "welfare dependency"—a climate that is now eroding the economic potential in many European countries as well as the United States.

It is useful to distinguish between the socialist and the mercantilist mind-sets. Both reject the constitutional or structural framework orientation for political economy that is derived from eighteenth-century classical liberalism, exemplified in the stance of Adam Smith and James Madison. Socialists and mercantilists alike remain unwilling to allow the forces of market capitalism to work freely, limited only by those constitutional or structural parameters that define and enforce property rights and contracts, foster competition and insure monetary stability. The socialists have suffered defeat, ideological and practicable, through the major revolutions of 1989–1991. But the mercantilists remain alive and well despite the absence of an overreaching ideology. Because mercantilist policy thrusts are fully consistent with, and in part generated by, internal interest-group pressures, major damage may be done, if the natural limits imposed by the openness to the world trading network are not explicitly respected.

Separate sections of this lecture will elaborate and extend the several points summarized in this introduction.

II. Technology and the Nonisolated State

An early nineteenth-century German economist, von Thünen, entitled his major work *The Isolated State*,[1] in which he analyzed the workings of an economy that was wholly separated from interaction with other economies, or, in modern terminology, that was completely closed. I use von Thünen's title only to instance its opposite, the nonisolated state, and to suggest that it is now almost impossible, in these final years of the twentieth century, to think of a totally closed polity that is economically viable.

In the world of modern technology, persons, anywhere, can virtually be everywhere, and instantaneously. The magic of satellite technology, implemented through CNN and other enterprises, allows persons everywhere to observe what is happening everywhere else. This modern technology is institutionalized through legal political economic structures that allow electronic transfers of capital value across the whole world at the speed of light. As McKenzie and Lee have emphasized,[2] the technological revolution surely

---

1. The first part of this work was published, in German, in 1826.
2. Richard B. McKenzie and Dwight R. Lee, *Quicksilver Capital* (New York: The Free Press, 1991).

makes it more difficult for persons to be controlled, directed and manipulated by whoever is in a position of political authority.

Openness, defined in terms of information flows, is not, of course, a direct guarantee of openness in the flow of valued goods and resources. But we do know that television imagery was an important factor in generating the discontent in central and eastern Europe and in areas of the former Soviet Union before the revolutions of 1989–1991. The individual who can actually see the low-price availability of valued goods in other countries is not nearly so likely to acquiesce in the sacrifice she is asked to undergo for the sake of achieving historically determined ideological purpose. The fact that we now think of North Korea and Cuba as exceptional cases serves to reinforce my point of emphasis here.

The technological revolution witnessed during the last third of this century is by no means complete. And this ongoing revolution implies a twenty-first century in which the whole world must, almost necessarily, become increasingly open, in all respects. Both the opportunities offered and the constraints imposed by this technologically determined openness of the world to come are presumably more natural to the thought patterns of those of you who are citizens of nations that are in the process of achieving Europe-wide integration than they are to those of us who still think in isolated state patterns, due to the large scale of our internal national economies. Nonetheless, I suggest here that more attention be paid, by all of us, to the impact that the technologically driven openness must exert on any pursuit of strictly national policy goals.

III. National Constitutionalism

History has dictated how we are politically organized. With some exceptions, peoples of the world think of themselves as citizens, or subjects, of well-defined nation-states, defined in part by the institutions of legal structure. (In one sense, Europeans are now at some in-between stage, with historically defined national loyalties, but, increasingly, identifying themselves as Europeans.)

Persons in, say, Brazil, think of themselves as Brazilians because they are subject to the dictates of Brazilian law. And despite divergent individual and group interests, Brazilians share a potential common interest in either maintaining or changing this legal framework, which, inclusively considered, incorporates and embodies political structure and political action. What I am saying here is only that each person, no matter where she lives, has an identifiable national interest because of the political-legal division of the world into national political units. The individual may speak, metaphorically, of a world interest, but this remains categorically distinct from national interest because of the absence of institutional links between the person and the world, as such. (Again, Europeans now occupy an in-between position.) When a person, any person, thinks about changes in the institutional setting that might be aimed at the furtherance of his or her privately identified well-being, attention still turns primarily toward the nation-state, the institutional setting that is shared collectively by all its inhabitants and organized as the unit that, potentially, can act for the benefit of all members, as a collective unit. Persons, whether individually or as members of organized groups, will, of course, differ among themselves as to what the national interest might dictate, as reflected in their separate evaluations of alternative politically implemented changes that are within the feasible set of possibilities, including the no-change or status quo alternative. My concern here is not primarily with how these internal political differences may be reconciled or resolved through the operation of some collective decision rules. My focus here, as in much of my earlier published work,[3] is on the categorical distinction between political changes made within the structure of accepted constitutional rules and changes in these rules themselves. More specifically, I want to concentrate on the relationship between within-constitutional change and constitutional change itself and the increasing and necessary openness of the separate national economies, as dictated by modern technology.

I suggest that in an open economy, constructive political reform should be largely, if not exclusively, constitutional. The collective attention should be placed on the parameters within which economic interaction takes place on the structure rather than directly on the terms of trade that emerge in particular markets. Efforts to direct and control resource allocation and usage in this second sense are likely to be thwarted by exposure to the external constraints of the world economy.

---

3. James M. Buchanan, *The Economics and the Ethics of Constitutional Order* (Ann Arbor: University of Michigan Press, 1991).

Let me use modern New Zealand as an example of the argument. Within its basic institutional patterns, described as a majoritarian-parliamentary democracy with English common-law protection of individuals' rights, New Zealand's leaders chose, in the mid-century decades, to embark on a mixed socialist-mercantilist program of economic development. Domestic industries were protected from foreign competition by tariffs and quotas. Some industries were subsidized directly from tax revenues. Some markets were cartelized, with legally enforced restrictions on entry and exit. Whole sectors of the economy were politicized through the organization of national public enterprises. Deficits in these enterprises and in other sectors were financed by government funds, secured from money issued by the central bank. The government budget was used as a tool to redirect resources to chosen targets.

Given the economic sophistication of the 1990s, we now know that the results should have been predictable. New Zealand's economy stagnated at low or negative rates of growth; unemployment increased and remained high; the exchange rate moved sharply against the local currency; budget deficits increased; inflation soared.

The state of play in the early 1980s was recognized to be undesirable by almost all New Zealanders, quite independent of party affiliation. What could be done? At this point, Roger Douglas, Finance Minister under a Labor Party government, was the leader in implementing a series of reforms that were, effectively, constitutional in nature and which were consistent with the principles of time-tested economic science. Tariffs and quotas were reduced or eliminated; whole industries were depoliticized or privatized through the selling off of national enterprises; domestic cartelization of markets was reduced; regulated prices were allowed to find market levels; the currency was floated; controls over capital movements were eliminated; the budget was balanced; total government spending relative to GDP was reduced; the central bank was subjected to rules that offered incentives for the maintenance of monetary stability. Yet again, to modern economic science, the results should have been predictable: the aggregate growth rate increased; unemployment fell; investment increased; the exchange rate stabilized; inflation disappeared. These reforms continued over the course of a decade and have made New Zealand, in 1996, the envy of much of the world.

I could go on with the story, but this is not a lecture about New Zealand or even about the triumph of economic science. I use New Zealand merely to suggest the difference between nationally directed reform in the constitutional parameters, changes in the structural framework of an economy and efforts at hands-on interferences into the workings of markets. The first set of reforms, those that modified the economic constitution in ways consistent with economic science, succeeded beyond expectations, generating results that we now observe—results that are universally acknowledged to have been beneficial to all persons in the nation-state that is New Zealand. The earlier efforts at socialist-mercantilist manipulation of markets failed demonstrably to achieve the desired purpose.

This example surely supports my central thesis. New Zealand was unable to achieve its internally generated, and socialist inspired, goals for two interrelated reasons. The crude politicized efforts at micromanaging the market violated elementary canons of economics. And, importantly, the opportunity costs of this mismanagement were made clear to everyone, because the economy was not isolated from the world; it could not carry out national economic policy as if the country existed in isolation. The costs simply were too high, as measured in losses in levels of living for its citizens. (Essentially the same series of events occurred in France, a much larger economy, during and after the early months and years of the Mitterrand presidency. And was not the same pattern descriptive, in less extreme form, of the early Gonzalez leadership in Spain?) What New Zealand could, and later did, do, and very successfully, was to implement general constitutional reforms, consistent with economic principles, that allowed the forces of national and international markets to work, thereby generating overall economic growth and stability, while at the same time removing regulatory and tax shackles on its citizens. In sum, New Zealand adjusted its constitutional parameters to reach accommodation with the open world economy.

The same process will work for any nation-state, large or small. But the effects of relative size should be noted here. As a very small economy, it was surely more difficult for New Zealand to act as if it were isolated from the world than might have been the case for, say, the United States, where the internal market is large relative to its external trade. In Spain, you are somewhere in between; your economy is large relative to that of New Zealand, but small relative to that of the United States. But any and all efforts to impose economic direction that do not embody recognition of the technologically driven international interdependence seem foredoomed to failure.

The ongoing technological revolution will insure that internal market manipulation can become only more, rather than less, difficult as time passes. My general normative counsel is clear: Political leaders, and the citizenry, in any nation-state at century's end should concentrate on genuine constitutional changes, which can themselves be strictly national in origin and motivation, but which can, at the same time, remain compatible with the continuing integration of markets worldwide.

I suggested earlier that, in my usage here, the term *constitution* referred to the whole set of rules that constrain behavior, whether these rules be formalized constraints, embodied in legal structure, or informal conventions, practices or social norms, including those often summarized under the rubric moral codes. Even the most scientifically informed structural reform may fail in a setting where individual behavior is unduly opportunistic, and where there is an absence of minimal standards of interpersonal trust.[4] In this respect, the nation-states of eastern Europe and the former Soviet Union face greater difficulty in effectuating genuine constructive change than those countries with a legal tradition of property and contract. My main point here is to indicate that the moral constitution cannot and should not be neglected, even if the difficulties of explicitly directed reforms are acknowledged.

IV. Emergent Nations and Western Welfare Statism

Some of the emergent nations, those that have dramatically moved toward achievement of the universally acknowledged objectives of high growth, low unemployment and budgetary-monetary stability over the last third of the century, are fortunately placed in comparison to the nations of Western Europe and the United States—nation-states that developed earlier in the century and before. The recently emerging nation-states do not find their economies burdened with the excessive costs of extended welfare-transfer systems—costs that are reflected both in the incentive incompatibility between high taxation and economic progress and in the social climate of welfare dependency that undermines traditional value standards. Western welfare states were constructed more or less deliberately in response to fears of

---

4. Francis Fukuyama, *Trust* (London: Hamish Hamilton, 1995).

Marxian ideas. Prince Bismarck of Prussia invented the system of cradle-to-grave social security as a sop to members of the working classes, whom he feared would be fatally attracted to the Marxist-socialist idyll. What Bismarck, the Prussian autocrat, failed to foresee was that, as transposed to a setting of populist democracy, the welfare-transfer state embodies a self-generating momentum that makes control or limitation effectively impossible. The welfare-transfer share in government budgets increased dramatically throughout the century, especially after 1960.

Western nations now find themselves unable to dismantle or even to reform cumbersome and growth-retarding institutional mazes, despite the disappearance of the ideological challenge that provided the initial impetus.

With the accelerating increase in politically driven welfare-transfer activity, potentially productive members of these states have, in increasing numbers, chosen to become "welfare dependents," to subsist on tax revenues coercively extracted from productive earners. The effect has been to reduce the rate of growth in Western economies from both potential and earlier patterns, to make maintenance of budgetary-monetary stability more difficult and to generate internal political conflict between classes.

To the extent that any emerging political economy succumbs to the demands for the maintenance and extension of Western style welfare-transfer programs, its own growth potential will, of course, be undermined. Such a polity will lose, relatively, to other nations who do not respond positively to the siren's call. It now seems unlikely that Western nations will be able to reduce substantially their own welfare-transfer sectors or to correct the climate of welfare dependency.

V. Socialism, Mercantilism and National Constitutionalism

Socialism, both as an ideological norm and as an organizing principle for socioeconomic order, has collapsed. There exists in 1996 almost no movement, anywhere in the world, toward increased politicization of national economies in the explicit sense of centralized direction and control. The Marxian slogan, public ownership of the means of production, has totally vanished from academic as well as political discussion. Socialism, as a political system, demanded the isolated state; by contrast, economic participation in an open world order can occur only if the scope of politics is structurally limited.

Mercantilism has by no means disappeared, for Spain, Europe or anywhere else. I use this term inclusively to refer to any and all politically motivated efforts to interfere piecemeal with the workings of markets, and for whatever reasons. The central principle, if it could be so called, is that political or governmental interference can, in some fashion, improve on the allocative-distributive patterns that emerge from the market interaction processes. Mercantilist policy can, for the most part, be explained in terms of the conflict among domestic political groups, representing separate economic interests.[5] The game is negative sum; an interest group secures a subsidy or protection against entrants, foreign or domestic; members of this group gain, at least temporarily, while others in the economy suffer losses, and the losses exceed the gains in total magnitude. Mercantilism is, however, rarely justified on blatant arguments advanced in support of differential private interests.

Mercantilist policy may be presented to the citizenry under some guise of overriding national purpose. The arguments of modern economic theorists may be utilized to suggest that governmental selection and subsequent subsidization of specific sectors (those of potential growth) of the economy may accelerate rather than retard overall aggregate rates of growth.

Within some limits, and to the extent that mercantilist policy choices are both well-informed and lucky, the mercantilist interferences may seem successful. Again, however, the constraints imposed by the openness to international competition must be kept in mind. Mercantilist policy thrusts are, to a major extent, kept within bounds that prevent major economic loss if the economy remains open to the world market. And the relative success in achieving aggregative objectives should never be attributed falsely to market interferences, as such, when the primary causal factors remain the adjustment of constitutional parameters that insure open markets, legal stability and financial predictability. Within a set of well-designed and well-functioning constitutional parameters, the potential damages that specific interferences

5. Robert B. Ekelund, Jr., and Robert D. Tollison, *Mercantilism as a Rent-Seeking Society* (College Station: Texas A&M University Press, 1981).

with market processes can generate must remain limited. And, if the apparent gains seem concentrated whereas the opportunity losses are spread out over the whole citizenry, the policy thrust may often be deemed successful.

Modern mercantilism is not, however, different in kind from its seventeenth- and eighteenth-century counterparts. The principles of classical political economy, articulated by Adam Smith in 1776, remain alive and well. Modern technological developments, which create the pressures toward the openness of markets worldwide, make adherence to these classical principles easier to accommodate within the broadly democratic structures of governance. The objectives of growth, stability and personal liberty, which I call the structure of progress in my title, are shared by citizens of any nation-state. These objectives can best be secured and maintained by adjustments in the constitutional rules that insure compatibility between national institutions and the technologically interdependent world. But quiescence before the forces of history will not suffice. The national constitutionalism that is dictated by the emergent technological opportunities requires both an understanding of economic science and the sublimation of the distributional conflicts inherent in the politics of majoritarian democracy.

Notes on the Liberal Constitution

No existing or proposed political constitution contains sufficient constraints or limits on the authority of the agencies of government over the activities of individuals and groups, and most notably over their economic activities. There is no *liberal* constitution in existence or in prospect. In this sense, all existing constitutions are failures, and almost all serious proposals for reform fall short of any promise of full success. I advance this blanket criticism of existing and proposed constitutional structures without knowledge of particular details but in full and conscious awareness of the historical fact that, for well over a century, all political discourse has been informed by, and the institutional results thereby influenced by, the "fatal conceit"[1] that political direction can facilitate rather than retard economic progress. All constitutions that have been put in place since the 18th century, and all that have been "reformed" either explicitly or by usage and interpretation since that time, must reflect, to some degree, the romantic image of the benevolent state, whether actual or potential, the image that was introduced by the political idealists on the one hand and by the visionary socialists on the other.

The constitution that embodies "politics without romance"[2] exists nowhere today, and no reform proposals that reflect such a realist model of politics enter directly into any ongoing dialogue. Residues of such a vision may be found only in some of the Madisonian elements that remain in the United States documents and records, and in the arguments of the relatively

From *Cato Journal* 14 (Spring/Summer 1994): 1–9. Reprinted by permission of the publisher.
1. F. A. Hayek, *The Fatal Conceit* (Chicago: University of Chicago Press, 1989).
2. J. M. Buchanan, "Politics without Romance: A Sketch of Positive Public Choice Theory and Its Normative Implications," *Zeitschrift des Instituts für Höhere Studien, Wien* 3 (1979): 1–11.

small number of classical liberals now extant. Despite this negative assessment, which may seem to be nearly total in its condemnatory sweep, there may be bases for some optimism as we look far enough forward into the post-revolutionary epoch, and especially into the next century. Ideas do have consequences, and we have lived with the consequences of false ideas for almost two centuries, far too long to have expected shifts to occur by the early 1990s. But consequences, or rather events, also feed back on ideas, and, after the unpredicted revolutions of 1989–91, the romantic image of the benevolent and capable state must prove increasingly difficult to sustain. The theories of political failure, advanced sparingly by classical liberals throughout the period of socialist hegemony only to have been treated with scorn and derision, have been corroborated by history in what was perhaps the grandest of all experiments in social science. And unless we totally despair of human capacity for rational action, we must anticipate that, sometime in the post-socialist century, men and women will exhibit constructive constitutional capabilities that can now be scarcely imagined.

In this sense, Francis Fukuyama is surely right.[3] Call it what one will, something of historical note did effectively end with the great revolutions of 1989–91. And Fukuyama is also correct in suggesting that economic science, which explains how the market economy operates independent of politicized direction and control so as to produce the largest bundle of goods and services available within given resource constraints, has finally been vindicated. But is Fukuyama also right when he predicts that this scientific result will be incorporated into institutional-constitutional reform? To agree with him here, we perhaps must think beyond the horizon of a few decades.

As a start, it may be useful to extend our hindsight into the pre-romantic, pre-socialist epoch, back to the 18th century, and to try to recapture the constitutional understanding that so excited the philosophers as well as the politicians. Until and unless such a shift in the modern mind-set is somehow achieved, all efforts at constitutional dialogue aimed at basic reform will essentially be wasted. Governments, no matter how organized, will remain basically unchained, and the politicians-bureaucrats will continue to facilitate the mutual exploitation of each by all, in Anthony de Jasay's "churning

3. F. Fukuyama, *The End of History and the Last Man* (New York: The Free Press, 1992).

state."[4] Economies will founder, and, increasingly, potentially valued product will disappear into the "black hole"[5] of that which might have been.

The Constitutional Order of Classical Liberalism

The classical liberals of the 18th century, whether represented by the members of the Scottish Enlightenment or by the American Founding Fathers, were highly skeptical about the capability and willingness of politics and politicians to further the interests of the ordinary citizen. Governments were considered to be a necessary evil, institutions to be protected from, but made necessary by the elementary fact that all persons are not angels.[6] Governments, along with those persons who were empowered as their agents of authority, were not to be trusted. Constitutions were necessary, primarily as means to constrain collective authority in all of its potential extensions. State power was something that the classical liberals feared, and the problem of constitutional design was thought to be that of insuring that such power would be effectively limited.

The devices aimed to accomplish this purpose are the familiar ones. Sovereignty was split among several levels of collective authority; federalism was designed to allow for a deconcentration or decentralization of coercive state power. At each level of authority, separate functional branches of government were deliberately placed in continued tension, one with another. In some polities, the dominant legislative branch was further restricted by the constitutional establishment of two bodies, each of which was organized on a separate principle of representation.

It is important to recognize that these basic organizational-procedural elements of political constitutions were designed, discussed, and put in place by the classical liberals within the context of a shared aim or purpose, which was that of checking or constraining the coercive power of the state over in-

4. A. de Jasay, *The State* (Oxford: Basil Blackwell, 1985).

5. S. P. Magee, W. A. Brock, and L. Young, *Black Hole Tariffs and Endogenous Policy Theory: Political Economy in General Equilibrium* (Cambridge: Cambridge University Press, 1989).

6. J. Madison, *The Federalist No. 51, The Federalist Papers* (1787), ed. Roy P. Fairfield (New York: Doubleday, 1966), 160.

dividuals. The motivating force was never one of making government "work better" in the accomplishment of some arbitrarily selected "public good," or even one of insuring that all interests were somehow "more fully represented."

The organizational-procedural elements of the classical liberal constitution, those listed above and others, were deemed to be less important than those provisions that laid out the range and scope of activities that were appropriately to be undertaken by collective authority. That is to say, the constitutional instructions as to what governments might and might not do were always considered to be much more important than how governments do whatever it is that they, in fact, do. This critical distinction, which was central to the whole classical liberal conception of social order, was essentially lost to the public consciousness during the ascendency of electoral democracy, especially during the 19th and 20th centuries. There was generalized acceptance of the fallacy that equated the emergence of electoral democracy with a reduced need for explicit constitutional constraints on the range and scope of governmental activity.

In the classical liberal constitutional order, the activities of government, no matter how the agents are selected, are functionally restricted to the parameters for social interaction. Governments, ideally, were to be constitutionally prohibited from direct action aimed at "carrying out" any of the several basic economic functions: (1) setting the scale of values, (2) organizing production, and (3) distributing the product. These functions were to be carried out beyond the conscious intent of any person or agency; they were performed through the operation of the decentralized actions of the many participants in the economic nexus, as coordinated by markets, and within a framework of "laws and institutions" that were appropriately maintained and enforced by government.

This framework-maintenance role, properly assigned to government in the classical liberal order, included the protection of property and the enforcement of voluntary contracts, the effective guarantee of entry and exit into industries, trades, and professions, the insured openness of markets, internal and external, and the prevention of fraud in exchange. This framework role for government also was considered to include the establishment of a monetary standard, and in such fashion as to insure predictability in the value of the designated monetary unit. (It is in this monetary responsibility that almost all constitutions have failed, even those that were allegedly motivated originally by classical liberal precepts. Governments, throughout history, have almost always moved beyond constitutionally authorized limits of their monetary authority.)

A central principle inherent in the classical liberal constitution dictated that, regardless of what governments do, and whether or not collective activities are contained within the indicated limits, all persons and groups are to be treated equally. The generality principle, applicable to the law, was to be extended also to politics. There was no role for governmental action that explicitly differentiated among separate factions or classes of persons. In the classical liberal conception, successful majority coalitions could not impose differential taxation on members of political minorities, even for purposes of "doing good."[7]

The Constitutional Order of Socialism

The classical liberal vision of a constitutional order did not command widespread public and philosophical acceptance for more than the several decades that straddled the turn between the 18th and 19th centuries. In small part, the reaction against this vision was due to the zealotry of those advocates who extended the central laissez-faire precept too enthusiastically, even to the rejection of a collective-governmental role in setting the parameters for economic interaction. But, primarily, the reaction against classical liberalism stemmed from the generalized unwillingness of participants in the body politic to accept the spontaneous allocative and distributive results generated in the operation of a market economy. These results were not taken to be "natural"; they were not understood to be the working out of the whole complex of separated choices made by persons in their many capacities. The results of market process were taken to be "artifactual"—produced rather than emergent, and hence subject to direct manipulation, change, and redirection by politicized collective action.

The reaction against classical liberalism was specifically stimulated and fueled by two separate sources. First, the genius of Karl Marx lay in his ability to isolate, identify, and publicize those elements in the operation of market capi-

---

7. J. M. Buchanan, "Markets, Politics, and the Rule of Law" (Center for Study of Public Choice, George Mason University, Fairfax, Va., 1992, mimeographed).

talism that seemed most open to criticism, especially in the intellectual context of an incompleted classical economic theory, along with prevailing confusion as to the distinction between constitutional and within-constitutional operations of governments. Marx concentrated on the vulnerability of capitalism to financial crises, on the tendency toward concentration in industry, and on the alleged distributive exploitation of the proletariat. Secondly, political idealists for many centuries had implicitly used models of the state that involved presumptive benevolence and omniscience. Any failures of markets could, under this presumption of the idealized collectivity, be fully corrected by directed political action. The generalized Marxist critique, along with the presumption of idealized political governance, essentially destroyed the intellectual-scientific basis that had been constructed in justification of the classical liberal constitutional order.

From the middle of the 19th century, some vision of a socialist order emerged to capture, in varying degrees of enthusiasm, the minds of persons in all developed societies, even in those societies where Marxism, as such, was able to secure relatively little direct support. At base, the socialist vision categorically rejected the classical liberal conception of a self-regulating economy that operates within a set of constitutional limits enforced by government which, in turn, is itself limited largely, if not totally, to the enforcement role. And, if the self-regulating, or nonpoliticized, economy is rejected as the basic organizing principle, the controlled or regulated economy becomes a necessary component of any alternative model for social organization. This shift from the self-regulating model of an economy to that of a controlled or regulated economy may be, but need not be, directly related to issues that involve organizational-procedural changes involving ways and means that agents and agencies of governance are selected, along with constitutional dictates concerning how the control and regulatory functions are to be performed.

The socialist constitutional order, whether this be defined in application to a single party, a self-appointed authoritarian regime, or a social democratic parliamentary majority, necessarily extends the range and scope for politicization well beyond the narrowly defined limits of collective authority under the classical liberal order. If the whole economy is opened up for control and regulation "in the general interest," there can be, by definition, little or no prior constitutional constraint on the definition of what such interest is by those agents and agencies charged with the responsibility for allocative and distributive results. Whereas governments in a classical liberal constitutional order have only a limited responsibility for the results that emerge from the interaction of persons in many capacities, governments in the socialist constitutional order have full or total responsibility for all results, including the size, composition, and the distribution of the "bundle of value" generated in the whole system. This ultimate responsibility remains with government even if the market, as a means of organization, is allowed to operate without detailed direction over wide areas of interaction. In the socialist model of government, there is, and can be, no constitutional guarantee offered to economic actors, whether persons or firms, against politically generated intrusions into liberty of commerce, whether this be marginal or total. In a genuine sense, with reference to the structure of the economy, the very term *socialist constitution* is oxymoronic. At best the constitutional order of socialism embodies constraints only on the procedures of politics and the behavior of political agents in carrying out those procedures; it cannot extend to include constraints on politicization of the economy, as such.

As we now know, as we have been informed by the great revolutions in central and eastern Europe in 1989–91, as well as by the cumulative historical experience from other parts of the world, as supplemented by analytical argument, the central principle for socialist order is fatally flawed and has been from the outset of its promulgation. The presumption that politicized control-regulation of economic relationships can, and will, generate a satisfactorily large bundle of goods and services, as valued by participants themselves, has been shown to be grounded in fallacy. In sum, the grand socialist experiments of the century did not work, and improved variants on these experiments cannot work, given the motivational, epistemological, and imaginative limits of the human animal. There is now generalized acceptance of the proposition that only market organization of the economy, which exploits the human potential, can produce an acceptably adequate aggregate of economic value.

The Post-socialist Constitutional Contradiction

The set of public, professional, political, and philosophical attitudes that seem most descriptive of the immediate post-socialist years of the 1990s is internally contradictory. The socialist vision of politicized control-regulation of economic interaction has by no means been exorcised from the modern mind-set despite the evidence from reason or from history. The belief that persons, acting jointly through their membership in collectivities, can effectively "improve" on the spontaneously generated outcomes of market processes remains imbedded in the modern psyche. Despite the overwhelming strength of the evidence, and despite supporting argument, persons cannot readily acquiesce in the stance suggested by post-socialist reality. The romance of socialism, which is dependent both on an idealized politics and a set of impossible behavioral presuppositions, has not yet disappeared.

Whether or not the romance will, in fact, fade away as we move further beyond the post-revolutionary turbulence of the 1990s and into the next century, cannot be settled outside futuristic speculation. Several questions may be posed: Will truth finally triumph over romance? Will the constitutional order of classical liberalism return, in some form, and come to command acceptance as the only order that combines personal liberty and economic prosperity? Will the public's interest in aggregative economic growth, in economic progress itself, finally carry the day and be reflected in genuine constitutional reforms? Or, may we expect the emergence of some new ideology that will offer renewed sustenance to a romantic image of collectivized utopia? Without the emergence of such an ideology, can we expect public acquiescence in authoritarian grabs for power? Without some equivalent of the Marxist class struggle as an ideological crutch for sloganeering, can the politicians escape skeptical censure by the public, even if there is little understanding of the functioning of the market? Is some tacit knowledge of constitutionalism likely to surface as the 21st century approaches?

The politics of my own country, the United States, in 1993 does not offer much basis for short-term optimism in putative response to these questions. The rhetoric of class warfare is now used to generate support for an enlargement of the already swollen governmental sector of the economy, and the provisional skepticism of the 1980s about the efficacy of regulatory efforts seems to have been replaced by reversion to nostrums of a half-century past. "Socialism in the small" is on the ascendency, as if the demise of "socialism in the large" is totally irrelevant. Politics aimed at "improving" on the outcomes of market processes is presumed capable of succeeding, despite the working of the selfsame incentive incompatibilities, knowledge limitations, and entrepreneurial disregard that produced the background for the great revolutions of 1989–91.

As noted earlier, if we are to find grounds for constitutional hope, it may be necessary to extend our sights, both temporally and locationally. We must recall Keynes' insistence on the long-range influence of ideas. Perhaps the post-socialist period is simply too short for us to have expected shifts in public and political attitudes, and especially in those societies that did not themselves go through the revolutionary upheavals. Perhaps any rebirth of classical liberalism must be expected to occur in those societies that did indeed suffer the revolutions; perhaps only in those countries has there been a sufficient loss of belief in politics and politicians to allow some reconstruction of the 18th-century ideal of constitutional order. Only one prediction seems safe here. The constitutional prospect for the next century will be one of surprises.

Conclusion

I have discussed only briefly the whole set of constitutional issues that involves organizational and procedural alternatives of governance. I have not addressed such issues as republican versus parliamentary forms of government; proportional representation versus two-party structures; effective federalism versus political centralization. But my neglect of these issues has been quite deliberate. All such organizational-procedural matters fade into insignificance by comparison with the constitutional challenge of placing constraints on the authority of government over the operation of the economy. Until and unless the government is severely constrained in its economic overreaching, along more or less classical liberal principles, including the principle of generality, the particular choices made among the organizational and procedural alternatives become relatively insignificant.

A democratically elected parliamentary majority imbued with socialist ideas and vision can destroy the potential value that might be forthcoming from an unfettered market economy as much as or more than the activities of an authoritarian regime. To the extent that constitutional constraints do effectively limit governments in their regulatory, financial, and taxing powers, the particular constitutional form for governance itself assumes secondary rank. To the extent that the powers of government remain open-ended and nonconstrained, the forms of government may seem to matter. But in some final sense, the overextended politics must surely fail, regardless of structural particulars.

In almost all countries, the continuing dialogue and discussion is centered on the establishment, maintenance, and preservation of "constitutional democracy." My central argument may be summarized in the statement that "constitutional" is the critically important one of the two words here. Economic prosperity and progress, as measured in value produced and consumed, can occur only in settings where the activities of government are constitutionally constrained, quite independent of how governmental agents are selected.

Dismantling the Welfare State[1]

I. Introduction

During the middle years of this century the welfare state has emerged full grown in all Western nations. There is widespread agreement that many of the consequences were unintended and undesired. When viewed from the perspective of the 1980s, we can agree that things "might have been" better had the course of history been different from what it was. To agree on this proposition is *not,* however, equivalent with agreement on an apparent corollary proposition that steps should *now* be taken to dismantle the set of social institutions that describe the modern welfare state. This corollary proposition is much more controversial than the mere assessment of history, and not only at a level of actual implementation. To defend the corollary proposition it is necessary to bring to bear wholly different intellectual arguments.

Let me offer a simple example. A man (or woman) may arrive at the conclusion that a marriage was a mistake; it "would have been better" if the marriage had never happened. Nonetheless, the man (or woman) may, at the same time, decide that, given the fact of the marriage, divorce is *not* a rationally desired step to take. Failure to distinguish between the identification of a past mistake and the inference from this identification that the institution once established should be replaced has marred constructive discourse by both scholars and practical men of affairs. My concern in this chapter is ex-

From *Liberty, Market and State: Political Economy in the 1980s* (Brighton, England: Wheatsheaf Books, 1986), 178–85. Copyright 1986 by James M. Buchanan. First published in Great Britain in 1986 by Wheatsheaf Books Ltd, Brighton, Sussex. Reprinted by permission of Pearson Education Limited.

1. Material discussed in this chapter was first presented at a Regional Meeting of the Mt Pelerin Society in Stockholm, Sweden, in August 1981.

clusively with the apparent corollary proposition related to the modern welfare state. I address the question that given the welfare state *as it exists,* should it be dismantled, and, if so, how should the process be implemented?

II. Some Preliminaries

A first step is to define terms. I shall distinguish between the *socialist state* and the *welfare state.* The socialist state embodies collective ownership and operation of productive enterprise. The welfare state, in its pure form, involves no such ownership and operation. Instead, it imposes a set of collectively determined coercive income and wealth transfers upon the operation of a private-ownership, market directed economy. Until the middle of the 1970s, Sweden offered the closest real-world approximation of the pure welfare state. By the 1980s, Sweden, along with most other Western nations, was best described as some mixture of a welfare state and a socialist state.

In this chapter, I shall discuss only the welfare state, as if it exists in its pure form, and independent of its socialist state counterpart. (It is much easier to make out an argument for dismantling the socialist state than for dismantling the welfare state. The efficiency gains promised by the shift from public to private enterprise are sufficient to dominate other elements in any relevant decision.)

Within the welfare state rubric, as I have defined it, there are many varied kinds and types of income and wealth transfers to be observed. It is impossible to treat all of these as if they were identical in effect and as if they present the same difficulties in making constructive reforms. I propose, therefore, to limit my inquiry further. I shall confine direct discussion to the single most important set of transfers in the modern welfare state; namely, the set of transfers from the currently productive members of the economy to the currently unproductive members, primarily to pension recipients. For purposes of exposition and understanding here, we may think of the analysis as applying to a large, growing, unfunded scheme of retirement pensions (what we call in the United States the social security system).

III. Criteria for Reform

I promised to address the questions of whether the welfare state should be dismantled, and, if so, how the process should be implemented. It is evident that I cannot answer such questions without some normative criteria. I might, of course, state simply that the welfare state should be dismantled because I do not like it, for reasons of either private interest (I am a net loser) or ideological commitment (I do not like collectivized pension schemes). I might go further and suggest that government should simply follow my advice and abolish the transfer system, and that is that. Arguments of this sort would deserve what they get, little or no attention from anyone.

I propose to rely on the advice and counsel of the greatest of all Swedish economists, Knut Wicksell (and I am tempted to leave out the modifying word "Swedish"). If an existing institutional structure is genuinely inefficient, there must exist some means of changing or reforming elements of this structure so as to benefit *all* persons and groups in society. And if the observing economist tries and fails to locate some such means (there may, of course, be several), he is not allowed to say that the existing structure "should" be changed. The Wicksellian test of conceptual unanimity offers the only defensible normative criterion for evaluating reform proposals. (Professional economists will recognize the similarity between Wicksellian and the more familiar Paretian criterion. I prefer to use the Wicksellian criterion because it concentrates attention on potential agreement as well as upon institutional-constitutional change rather than upon more formal allocative requirements.) The conceptual unanimity test allows me to seek answers to both of the questions simultaneously. If I can locate a means of changing the existing structure so that *everyone* benefits (or at the least no one loses), and hence should agree to the change, I have both validated the argument that change should be made and indicated one way it might be implemented. If I cannot come up with some such proposal for change, I should be forced to acknowledge that the existing state of affairs is "Wicksell-efficient" (Pareto optimal) no matter how much my own dislike for this state of affairs may be.

IV. Entitlements and Claims

The first step in any search for possible reform involves a careful description of the existing structure of entitlements and claims against the welfare state held by separate persons in the society. Under tax-transfer structures, the "contract" made between government and claimants (those already retired or those who have accumulated credits towards retirement pensions) is implicit rather than explicit. The contractual basis is, nonetheless, widely acknowledged, and current and potential recipients make life-cycle plans on the expectation that the implicit commitments will be honoured by governments which hold ultimate taxing and spending powers.

Any proposal for reform or change that aims to meet the Wicksellian test must embody the meeting of all legitimate claims. Governments cannot, and should not, simply violate their implicit contracts with citizens. If this basic principle for reform is accepted, it then becomes necessary to identify and compute the net entitlement or claim of each person at some specified point in time, say, 1 January 1986. A person's claim against the system may be positive or negative, with the precise amount depending on the structure of taxes and benefits, on the age and status of the potential recipient, and on many other variables. Once a claim is specified for a particular person, we then have a benchmark against which the effects of all proposals for change may be measured. If a person's properly computed net claim (present value of anticipated benefits minus present value of anticipated tax payments) is, say, $10,000, any modified or changed structure must yield this person a net present value of at least this amount. If the properly computed net claim is negative, say (−) $10,000, then any proposed structure must represent a net obligation of less than $10,000 for this person.

V. The Aggregate Liability of Tax-Transfer Systems

The tax-transfer systems of modern welfare states are not in what we might call "actuarial balance." As they exist today, these systems are characterized by massive net liabilities, defined in the aggregative sense. That is to say, if we compute the net claims of all persons in the manner indicated in section IV above, the aggregate value of currently anticipated benefits would far exceed the aggregate value of anticipated tax payments under the systems. In the United States social security system, for example, the aggregate net liability amounts to several *trillions* of dollars.

This aggregate net liability of any tax-transfer system represents implicit national debt that cannot be forfeited or cancelled, even by inflation. It should be explicitly recognized to be such, and this debt should be entered into any national balance sheet accounting. Each holder of a net positive claim should be treated equivalently with the holder of an indexed governmental security.

The aggregate net liability of modern tax-transfer systems increases over time because none of these systems has ever attained, and can never expect to attain, a steady-state equilibrium. A major principle for constructive reform must be that the aggregate net liability should be stabilized at current levels, say as of 1 January 1986. *Additional "issues of implicit national debt" must somehow be avoided.*

VI. Paying Off Individualized Claims and the Issue of Explicit National Debt

If government is to honour all implicit claims of current and potential benefit-payment recipients, and if the aggregate net liability of the system is to be stabilized at levels of some specified date and not allowed further to increase, there must be an abrupt halt to taxes and benefit flows within the system as of the chosen effective date. As of this date, say 1 January 1986, the government must pay off all individual claims; the implicit national debt must be retired. Persons with positive net claims should be compensated in terms of cash capital values. Persons with negative net claims should be billed for the capital value of their net obligations. From the specified point in time, the system, as previously organized, would simply cease to exist. No taxes would be collected within the system; no benefit payments would be made.

As noted above, however, the aggregate net liabilities of modern pension schemes are of tremendous magnitude. How can governments finance the horrendously large claims? How can governments retire the implicit national debts that the pension schemes represent?

I propose that those who hold claims be "paid off" individually in capital sums. I do *not* propose that the burden of payment be saddled onto the current generation of taxpayers. I propose that funds for meeting the individual claims within the system be raised by the explicit issue of general-purpose national debt, with the perpetual interest charges on this debt to be levied equally against current and *all* future generations.

The modern welfare state represents the mistakes of almost a century. It is fully analogous to the failure of a nation to accumulate a capital stock over a comparable period of time. Having made such mistakes, however, we must live with them, and the nation must carry forward, *forever,* the annual costs of these mistakes it has made. *Reform involves stopping the net increase in ag-*

*gregate liability; it does not involve the imposition of differentially onerous bur-
dens of taxation and/or inflation on the particular generation of persons who
are producing income at the time of the structural change.* Clearly, any attempt to impose such differential burdens would violate the Wicksellian
unanimity test. Current-period taxpayers can, of course, meet the annual
interest charges on the aggregate net liability since this group, even before
any structural change, is bearing at least this cost of the system.[2]

After the tax-transfer pension system is abruptly closed down, and all
compensations are paid, there will be demonstrable increases in the productivity of the economy due to the reductions in excess burdens generated by
both taxes and benefit payments. This productivity gain will allow the economy to carry forward the annual interest charges on the accumulated welfare
state overload (which would then be represented by explicit national debt)
with a gradually decreasing weight relative to annual gross product in the
economy.

VII. Provision for Pensions after the Welfare State Tax-Transfer System Is Abolished

To this point, I have said nothing at all about provision for retirement pensions *after* the existing structure ceases to operate. The reform measures
sketched out above offer a means of closing down the old system without
harm to anyone in the society. The reform proposals do not address themselves to the establishment of some new, replacement structure of retirement
pensions.

Nonetheless, after the old system is closed down, the way is cleared for the
construction of a fully funded, actuarially sound pension scheme with separated and identified individual accounts. Persons can be offered the option of
making their own private provision for retirement through market-organized
insurance schemes or joining a government insurance enterprise. In either
case, their payments would be directed into a fund from which *their own* re-

---

2. For a more detailed analysis, with numerical examples, see James M. Buchanan,
"Comments on Browning's Paper," in *Financing Social Security,* ed. Colin Campbell
(Washington: American Enterprise Institute, 1979), 208–12.

tirement pensions would eventually be financed. These genuine "retirement contributions" should be categorically separated from any coercive taxes imposed to service the national debt made explicitly necessary by the closing down of the old system.

VIII. Redistribution

An actuarially based, individualized system cannot of course embody within it redistribution among separate persons and groups. The abolition of the old welfare state system carries the major advantage of providing the opportunity of separating, once and for all, genuine retirement pension schemes from redistributive schemes. There is, of course, no reason why redistribution schemes may not be set up along with the efficient pension schemes if these are deemed desirable by the citizenry.

The closing down of the mixed-up, unsound, and confused system of retirement pensions and redistribution arrangements will offer societies the opportunity to modify, perhaps dramatically, the whole redistributive apparatus of the welfare state. Under the approach suggested here, all potential recipients of net transfers will have their accumulated claims (entitlements) fully satisfied. Their expectations of possible "cradle to grave" support from government will be validated. But there is *no* implication in the set of proposals for reform that any *future* members of society, those who have not entered adulthood or even have not been born, should be able to accumulate *new* claims against the productive members of the economy. The critically important feature of the reform proposals advanced lies in the stabilization of the aggregate net liability. Implementation of the reforms suggests that persons born at different points in time must be treated differently. A person born in the first half of this century may have been allowed to accumulate net positive claims against the society. These claims must be paid off. But a person, in a similar relative economic status, who is born *after* the existing welfare state structure is abolished, need not be allowed to accumulate comparable claims. Whether or not such a person might or might not qualify as a net transfer recipient under a newly chosen redistributive scheme would be determined in the post-reform stage of revaluating all redistributive objectives as well as the costs of attaining them.

IX. Compensation and Agreement as Bases for Politically Attainable Reforms

I have sketched out an approach to reform of the modern welfare state by concentrating on the retirement-pension example. The approach utilizes the Wicksellian test of conceptual unanimity to determine the possibility of genuinely efficient or desirable changes in the existing institutional structure. To secure unanimity, even in some proximate sense of consensus among most persons and groups in society, those who are positive claimants under the existing structure must be "paid off." Compensation is necessary for agreement. This compensation approach to reform admittedly involves major costs that might seem to be avoidable if the ruling political coalitions could be induced to renege on the implicit contractual obligations that governments have made over the decades of the welfare state. Such a policy of open default would, however, involve major costs of quite a different sort. The sense of unfairness generated might be such as to undermine severely the sense of legitimacy without which modern governments could not survive.[3]

It seems highly unlikely, however, that ruling political coalitions would ever choose to default in any important measure on the implicit contracts made under the guise of the modern welfare state. Faced with the stark choice between continuing to allow the net liability of the ongoing welfare state to increase, even with its admitted consequences, and closing down the system by default, democratically influenced governors will almost surely opt for continuation. Those economists who advise governments to proceed with action contrary to the political interests of the actors in the process are likely to experience repeated frustration.

Political leaders need not be faced with the dichotomous choice between

---

3. As Gordon Tullock has noted, politicians may shift the boundary between the set of positive net claimants and negative net claimants. Persons in the second set will, of course, support an open policy of default on all claims. To the extent that this group of potential net gainers from default increases in size so as to approach that of the group of potential net losers from default, the whole structure is likely to develop into essentially a zero-sum political struggle; see Gordon Tullock, *Economics of Income Redistribution* (Boston and The Hague: Kluwer-Nijhoff, 1983). My approach in this chapter is based on the presupposition that such a struggle is not desirable, that even those persons who now are legally net debtors to the system might prefer the sort of changes suggested to open default of claims of legal creditors.

continuation of an admittedly misconceived and worsening structure on the one hand and massive default on the set of implicit contracts that the structure embodies on the other. Political economists fulfil their proper role when they can show politicians that there do exist ways to close down the excesses of the welfare state *without* involving default on the contracts that this state has obligated itself to.[4] This approach to reform not only meets ordinary precepts of fairness; it also facilitates the political leader's task of organizing the consensus necessary to allow any institutional changes to be made at all.

X. Conclusions

Should the welfare state be dismantled? If so, how should the process be implemented?

My response to these questions posed at the outset may be simply summarized. The welfare state should be dismantled if those who gain from the change can pay off those who have positive claims and still have some surplus left over. The process can be implemented politically if the payoffs are actually made, but not otherwise. I do not suggest that reforms based on this Wicksellian approach will be easy to accomplish. The detailed working out of the set of compensations required will indeed be complex and tedious. And as I have already noted, there should be no illusion about the apparent cost that the reforms would make explicit. The political and ideological errors of more than a half century cannot be erased as if they had not happened. In the larger sense, however, the cost of continuing the existing welfare state structure without substantial change looms much larger than that of taking the decisive action that I have suggested. The fundamental question is whether or not the political decision structures of modern Western nations are capable of taking the decisive reforms that are clearly within the realm of the politically attainable.

---

4. For an early discussion of this role for the political economist, see James M. Buchanan, "Positive Economics, Welfare Economics, and Political Economy," *Journal of Law and Economics*, 2 (1959), 124–38.

Name Index

Subject Index

agreement: compensation required to
secure, 116–17; in constitutional choice
made under ideal conditions (Rawls),
160; in constitutional economics, xii;
contractarian interpretation of, 28–29,
159–60, 165–71; discourse, or dialogue,
notion, 155–56, 165–71; emergence and
enforcement, 91–93; on Pareto-relevant
reform, 374–75; in politics, 155–71; role
in exchange, 247–48; in social contract
theories, 155–56, 159–60; truth tested
by, 175–76; with uncertainty about
rules, 162

agreement, constitutional: in
contractarian framework, 165–71; in
discourse, or dialogue framework,
155–56, 165–71; with ignorance of rules
furthering interests, 189; interest-based
obstacles, 128

anarchist: boundaries to individual rights,
23–25; criticisms of libertarian, 21–23;
differences from and similarities to
contractarian, 18–21, 27

anarchy: of constitutionalist-
contractarian, 27; Lockean variants
of, 26

arrangement, constitutional: compliance
and renegotiation problems, 163;
stability and fairness of, 162–63

authoritarianism: as alternative to
constitutional order, 180; paradigm of,
17–18

authority: logic of, 16–19; rational
deference to well-informed, 190–91

bargaining: behind veil of ignorance,
300–301; model predicting
sustainability of institutions, 296–304;
model to produce Rawls's maximin
solution, 291–96

budget: balanced budget amendment,
proposed, 58–59, 310; Constitutional
Economics applied to, 13–14

Budget Reform Act (1974), 57n. 5, 310

bureaucracy: coordination role in political
pricing, 257–58; difficulty in
dismantling, 350–52; economic
approach to, 107; growth of federal,
348–50; inability to control American,
104–5; opposition to modification of
institutions, 359; shift of public attitude
toward, 348–50. *See also* discretion,
bureaucratic

catallactic perspective: for economic
interaction, 60; on politics and political
order, 62–63; revival of, 240

central planning: Hayek's critique, 140

choice: constraints on behavior to make,
156–57; contractarian interpretation of
voluntariness of, 165–66; of experts in
markets and in democracy, 135–39;
implied choices with scarcity, 239;
interest- and theory-components in,

462

This book is set in Minion, a typeface designed by Robert Slimbach specifically for digital typesetting. Released by Adobe in 1989, it is a versatile neohumanist face that shows the influence of Slimbach's own calligraphy.

This book is printed on paper that is acid-free and meets the requirements of the American National Standard for Permanence of Paper for Printed Library Materials, z39.48-1992. ♾

Book design by Louise OFarrell, Gainesville, Fla.
Typography by Impressions Book and Journal Services, Inc., Madison, Wisc.
Printed and bound by Sheridan Books, Inc., Chelsea, Mich.